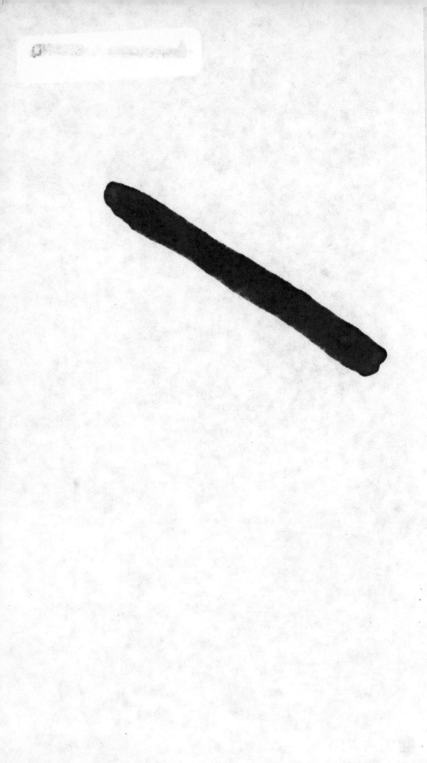

ADULT EDUCATION:

The Open Door
to
Lifelong Learning

Dr. Roger Axford
Arizona State University
Tempe, AR   85281

The A. G. Halldin Publishing Company

Indiana, PA   15701

i

"Writing is an act of community . . . it is an expression of love
and concern for each other."

Dorothy Day . . .

ISBN 0-935648-01-1

Copyright © , 1980

To Geri, Naida, Scott, and Vickie,
who we hope will enjoy lifelong learning.

IN PRAISE OF LEARNING

Learn the simplest things.
For you whose time has already come
it is never too late!
Learn your A B C's, it is not enough,
but learn them!
Don't let it discourage you, begin!
You must know everything!
You must take over the leadership!

Learn, man in the asylum!
Learn, man in prison!
Learn, wife in the kitchen!
Learn, man of sixty!
Seek out the school, you who are homeless!
Sharpen your wits, you who shiver
Hungry man, reach for the book: it is a weapon.
You must take over the leadership.

Don't be afraid of asking, brother!
Don't be won over,
see for yourself!
What you don't know yourself,
you don't know.
add up the reckoning.
It's you who must pay it.
Put your finger on each item,
ask: how did this get here?
You must take over the leadership.
Bertolt Brecht
From my Finnish Friends and Adult Educators

FORWARD

All of us who are interested in adult education feel a new sense of urgency these days, and it is for this reason that we welcome books such as this.

Why the sense of urgency? First, because life moves much faster these days than it has in the past. The trained citizen may be well prepared for the problems of today, but the problems of tomorrow will be different because of the onward movement of science, technology, and world events. So training can never end; it must be continued. As present specialties disappear, human beings need to be ready for new specialties. As new problems appear, citizens must be ready to meet them. So we must keep learning, all of our lives, at every educational level, and we must train teachers of adults while we are training teachers of the young.

Second, this nation finds itself in a great crisis, a crisis of our cities, a crisis of race and poverty. We are rethinking our attitudes. We are seriously trying to wrestle with the great issues of our time. Young people can be prepared to grapple with these problems. But that is not enough. Those who have graduated or who have left school must be prepared, too. Some can be trained or retrained so that they can move out of the poverty levels. Others can be trained to move further up the economic scale or to help the less fortunate with the improvement of their condition. And all adults need understanding - understanding of the difficulties of our urban culture as well as political, social, and cultural understanding. Even in the leisure arts (an important aspect of adult education) we often touch on the basic problems of today. Adult education aimed at self-improvement and enjoyment may ·lead one into conservation, appreciation of the arts of minority groups, the American role in the world, and so on.

Yes, there is much to do. Adult education is a lively, vigorous field, building on a long and interesting past and getting ready for an important future. Curiously, however, the area has had relatively little attention from scholars. These were a few books of interest published here and in Great Britain before the 1920's. The Carnegie Corporation financed a significant series of studies in the years before World War II, and in the last decades many special studies have appeared. Along with this we have the rise of graduate and undergraduate courses in higher education and the development of a research and teaching specialty in adult education.

This volume fits into this trend. It brings together much of the scholarly work of recent years, and it points to much that can be done in the future. So it is a summary and an introduction - a sort of welcome to a field of growing significance.

Dr. Fred Harvey Harrington
President
The University of Wisconsin

LIFE LONG LEARNING:

"Lifelong Learning" as a concept has come into focus on the American education scene. The Council is concerned that **lifelong learning** as a concept and the possible first priority for American education has not been fully examined by the total education community." President's National Advisory Council on Adult Education, 1977 Report p. 17.

"America is . . . on the verge of becoming truly a 'learning society' . . . . Adult education in many forms--public and private, formal and informal, for pleasure and for profit--nowadays touches the lives of nearly half the adult population at one time or another . . . . Universal education is far closer of achievement than it has ever been, anywhere in the world . . . . It has made a major contribution--perhaps the major contribution--to keeping our democratic principles and institutions strong and vibrant."

> Stanley Elam, "Toward 'A Learning Society', in **A Nation of Learners**, Leroy V. Goodman (ed.) p. 196

ACKNOWLEDGMENTS

Every author is indebted to many persons for the insights and inspiration provided in his education. I am grateful to my professors at the University of Chicago, and in particular to Cyril O. Houle.

I am appreciative of the many hours spent discussing world issues, and topics of adult education with my friend and colleague, Mark Rossman, Department of Higher and Adult Education, Arizona State University. Many graduate students have raised questions and provided program ideas and insights for which I am eternally grateful.

My colleagues at the University of Wisconsin, Florida State University, Indiana University of Pennsylvania, University of Maine, Northern Illinois University, and University of Southern California have all made my teaching in adult education a rich experience. Association with colleagues at Inter-American University in San German, Puerto Rico, the University of Puerto Rico and the University of Alaska, have made me aware of the adult education possibilities in developing areas. Work with Dr. Felix Adam and the Seminars at Universidad Nacional Experimental Simon Rodriquez Caracas, Venezuela have made me conscious of our responsibility for a new Good Neighbor policy, and for closer ties with our Latin American neighbors. I am grateful to Karen Moller and Paul Kjaer of the International

People's College at Elsinore, Denmark, as well as Dr. Peter Mannicke for the opportunities to see the Danish folk schools in action, and to learn of the importance of informal learning, and the joy of lifelong learning, so well exemplified in the Scandinavian folk schools.

I want to thank Callistus Milan, Marian Axford, and Susan Paddock for suggestions regarding the revision of the manuscript. The author is grateful to his wife Geri for her patience and support during the preparation of this new edition.

For the many persons who have granted permission for use of the materials I want to say thanks.

I would like to thank typists Eve Mantel and Dorla Nelson, the librarians and the supportive staff of the Department of Higher and Adult Education, Arizona State University for their loyal support.

Roger W. Axford

PREFACE

The goal of this book is to acquaint the reader with the most rapidly growing sector of American education -- **adult education**. Adult education is carried on under the umbrella of continuing education, lifelong learning, education permanente, and community service. The field is a broad one, encompassing numerous agencies, institutions, and media of communication. This book attempts to give an overview, useful for one who is working in the field, or is new to the field. The book does not attempt to describe the scores of agencies in any detail, since they are covered in other publications. This book is written for persons who want to know more about this expanding field, as well as for teachers of adults, and administrators of adult programs and agencies, volunteer adult workers, social workers, community education workers, and students who are considering adult education as a profession. The author has found such satisfaction in organizing programs for adults, teaching adults, and graduate students in adult education that I wish to share some of the insights, philosophy, research, and program ideas with the reader.

The first chapter gives a number of definitions of adult education, some with a narrow focus, and some with a world perspective. The next chapters gives an overview of the "Why of Adult Education" and then explores areas in which adult education is making an impact: coping with social change, self improvement, women's continuing education, literacy education, older learners and aging, community education, training and retraining and the involvement of business and industry in adult education.

The "Why's of Adult Education" grew out of seminars with graduate students, from national conferences, visits with adult education administrators, and from classes of adult learners. The many purposes of adult education are examined as they apply to our accelerating technology. Consideration is given to whether the primary purpose of educating adults should be that of fulfilling the needs of the individual, or that of society. I try to address the question as to whether both can be adequately fulfilled at the same time, and by the same institution.

Adult educators need to know their historical roots. Therefore, a chapter on the "Background of the Adult Education Movement" sketches some of the contributions made by both British and American adult education institutions. "Adult Education Pioneers" gives a limited number of biographical outlines of pioneers in the field who emblazoned their imprint upon special institutions of adult education, many of which are still thriving, some of which have waned. Since the "institution is the shadow of a person", these individuals are important for the reader's fuller understanding of the subject. There are so many significant pioneers, the author found it difficult to choose more than a few, realizing that some powerful adult education leaders have been excluded.[1] The ideas and methods of continuing education of these early pioneers were given institutional expression through imaginative and charismatic leadership which still benefits many adults to this day. It is the author's hope that other researchers will document the contributions of other pioneers in the area of lifelong learning.

Every educator of adults must have a sound philosophical foundation. "A Philosophy for Adult Education" treats the differing points of view within the field and suggests sources for pursuing the study in more depth. In the jargon of the market place, this is "where the rubber hits the road." A section is devoted to philosophy because teachers and administrators of adult programs, students in adult classes, and professionals in many areas of adult learning have expressed a desire for a clearer understanding of different philosophical positions as a necessary prelude to developing their own philosophies of adult education.

"Understanding the Adult Learner" describes a national survey conducted to identify the characteristics of adult learners in the United States and presents some of their reasons for seeking learning activities in various forms.

"Who Is an Adult Educator?" identifies some of the qualities which the author feels are imperative in the effective educator of adults. This topic is given high priority because of the increasing and immediate need for qualified persons to enter the profession as a lifetime career. Too many persons with inadequate training or limited philosophical undergirding have made only marginal contributions. They may have used their position as a stepping stone to larger administrative responsibilities.

"What Is An Ideal Adult Education Teacher?" is examined for this person is the key to effective learning among adults. What are the qualities required for teaching those with extensive experience, mature minds, and intellectual curiosity? Why do teachers of adults so frequently find their classes challenging and stimulating? Why can some teachers relate to youth, but less effectively to adults? These are the questions asked in illustrating a model for the ideal teacher of adults.

In a new chapter, the outreach function of educational institutions is discussed as a way of carrying knowledge to the people. Media of many types are developing to fulfill this function, and adults are making new demands for community service. "Programming in Adult Education" is what curriculum construction is to schooling for youth. Effective program planning makes possible the conditions for learning. To program "with" or to program "for" the adult is a major consideration. Discussion of how educational objectives are determined is a central consideration.

For every good adult course that has succeeded perhaps an equally excellent course has failed. "Promoting the Adult Education Program" goes to the root of the problem. Recognizing that a multitude of good courses and programs do not materialize for lack of effective promotion and publicity, I devoted a chapter to some current methods and communication techniques for letting people know the opportunities that exist for adult learning. The practitioner must know promotional methods and skills. Therefore illustrations are given of proven techniques, with testimonies from directors of adult education. The author found administrators most anxious to share ideas for promotion.

"Counseling Adult Learners" deals with ways of viewing counseling and the need to help adults suffering from vocational wanderlusts and confusion as to their life goals. Various sources for testing and guidance are suggested, and illustrations are provided for councils where adult educators work together to coordinate educational opportunities, make referrals, and raise the efficiency peak of the community's continuing education engine.

The subject matter of "Evaluating Programs of Adult Education" is a must if we are to know that our adults are really learning. How do we determine whether we are attaining our objectives in teaching? What are the reactions of adults to being tested and then informed of their progress or failure to meet certain goals? These are the topics which this chapter analyzes to help us better determine our mark and then measure how close we have come to hitting it. Evaluative techniques are discussed as means for motivating adults to continue to learn. Samples of a limited number of instruments are given as illustrations.

Admittedly our knowledge about adult learning, adult needs, and adult interests is still inadequate. Why do adults drop out? Why do some adults continue to learn through various media throughout their lifetime? These and other topics are considered in "Research, and Research Needs in Adult Education," the concluding chapter. Areas needing further investigation should stimulate the reader to do research or to seek out the literature on what has been discovered to date. With departments of adult education or continuing education being added each year in our colleges and universities, many students would do well to concern themselves with various aspects of adult education in disciplines such as sociology, psychology, anthropology, and social work. More research is needed on how adults can and do learn. The adult educator with an inquiring mind will naturally be a researcher.

At the end of each chapter is a list of questions which the author hopes will prove provocative. The questions are built upon the material provided in the chapter, and can be used for discussion, and for developing some research questions. Perhaps the questions raised by the chapter may be as, if not more important, than the data provided with each subject.

This edition has provided extensive bibliographies, including some films, and other media suggestions. The bibliographies may assist educators who wish to pursue a topic in depth. This work is written by a practitioner with many years of experience in university extension, in teaching graduate classes in adult education, and in participating in adult education administration, community organization, and volunteer work. Each year brings new insights. I recognize that I have encompassed only a fraction of what is to be known about adult education, but I hope the book will inspire people with inquiring minds to enter the field and assist in the liberation of the human spirit. In adult education the lamp of learning is our symbol, and the "glory of the lighted mind" is our objective. Adult education may be the open door to self-realization, to the abundant life, to lifelong learning.

Roger W. Axford
Arizona State University,
Tempe, Arizona

Chapter I:

SOME DEFINITIONS OF
ADULT EDUCATION

Because of the many approaches to adult education it is difficult to find any one universal definition in the field. As the definitions presented below indicate, slightly different emphases are given adult education by the agency or individual defining it. I have been trying to find and refine a useful definition which will be inclusive enough to be useful to the individual and to the many agencies operating programs under the umbrella of "adult education" but precise enough to be definitive.

The most limited definition is UNESCO's, which views adult education as **"education provided for the benefit and adapted to the needs of persons in the regular school and university system and generally fifteen and older."** [1]

A broader definition, but one which still focuses on organized, formal activities is Richard Greenough's: "Adult education today is regarded as a process whereby persons who no longer attend school on a regular or full-time basis can pursue organized studies and activities to develop their knowledge, aptitudes and skills that will equip them to perform roles in society in a more or less creative or critical fashion to be of use and profit to themselves, their families and the community at large."

An emphasis upon the range of providers of adult education is found in Coolie Verner's definition of adult education:

Adult education is any planned and organized activity provided by an individual, an institution, or any other instrumentality that is intended specifically to assist an adult to learn and which is under the immediate and continuing supervision of an instructional agent who manages the conditions for learning in such a way as to facilitate the successful achievement of the learning objectives. [2]

In contrast to the foregoing definitions, which emphasize the **structure** of adult education, other authors have concentrated on the **process** of adult education.

Liveright offered this definition: "Adult education is a process through which persons no longer attending school on a regular, full-time basis undertake activities with the conscious intention of bringing about changes in information, knowledge, understanding, skills, appreciation, and attitudes" [3]   Cyril O.

Houle defines adult education as "the process by which men and women (alone and in groups) attempt to improve themselves by increasing their skills or knowledge, developing their insights or appreciations or changing their attitudes; or the process by which individuals or agencies attempt to change men and women in these ways" [4] A more global definition is that of Paul Bergevin, for many years head of the Department of Adult Education at University of Indiana, and a student of Gruntvig's philosophy: "Adult education is any kind of learning that alters the way we think about something, changes the way we behave, or adds to our supply of information and knowledge." [5]

Finally, Edward C. Lindeman, an adult education-sociologist defined adult education in a way that is both concise and universal. "Adult education is the process through which learners become aware of significant experience."

In reviewing these definitions, and in reflecting on experience, this author has developed a definition of adult education which, it is hoped, reflects the major concerns and programs of adult education.

My definition of ADULT EDUCATION is "Planned and organized learning activities chosen on either a formal or informal basis with the conscious intention of self-fulfillment, including information seeking, understanding, skill acquisition, and identifying and solving personal and community problems . . ." This author also defines adult education as "the process of bringing about intelligent change in mature individuals, and in our community or society, through programs and agencies for continuing education."

A CLASSIFICATION FOR LIFE-LONG EDUCATIONAL ACTIVITIES [6]

One way to define adult education more precisely is to categorize its myriad activities. Many scholars have been struggling with a workable classification of adult education. The classification scheme developed by Dr. Seth Spaulding, formerly of the United Nations (UNESCO) is a particularly good working model for such classification. (see Table I) Spaulding moves from **Type I**, the highly structured and rigid educational programs with a highly prescriptive content, to **Type VI** -- Services which provide a broad range of informational and educational media, such as television, radio, magazines, newspapers, libraries, bookstores, newsstands, and information centers. Learning activities also move from highly formal to informal.

Because Spaulding's approach is a continuum, from the

2

TABLE I

LIFE-LONG EDUCATIONAL SERVICES AND ACTIVITIES

Dr. Seth Spaulding

Open, Non-Competitive, Non-Selective (or self-selective) activities and services, depending solely on interest of participants for choice of what will be done, listened to, read, or studied; little formal structure in course format; little or no certification of achievement; immediate satisfaction from participation and/or immediate perception of usefulness of content.

TYPE VI: Services which provide a broad range of informational and educational media from which people select according to their interests; although there may be structured services linked to other educational programs, most cater to serving a broad spectrum of individual interests.
EXAMPLES: Television, radio, magazines, newspapers, libraries, bookstores, news stands, information centers, etc.

TYPE V: Participant-governed groups in which people elect to join in activities with others of similar interests: programs often include seminars, courses, and speakers, but such formal activities are secondary to the basic goals of the group.
EXAMPLES: Youth organizations, political clubs and organizations, social groups and clubs, service clubs and organizations (Rotary, etc.), labor organizations, cooperative organizations, religious groups and institutions.

TYPE IV: Loosely structured educational services which seek to find and influence people with a fairly prescriptive message and content; people can elect to listen or participate if they wish; often seek to encourage groups in TYPE V to assist in spreading the message.
EXAMPLES: Agricultural extension services; health education services; land-reform education programs; community-development education ("social education" in India); on-the-job training schemes; "animation" (French); population education; environmental education.

2a

TYPE III: Moderately structured educational activities and institutions usually consisting of formal courses and seminars directed toward prescriptive learning goals.
EXAMPLES: Community centers; self-learning centers; work-study schemes; correspondence education; "university- without-walls" (USA); open university (UK and elsewhere); teachers' centers (especially UK); armed forced training schemes; career education (USA); farmer training; adult basic education (USA); functional literacy (UNESCO).

TYPE II: Highly structured and prescriptive educational activities with long-term goals, but involving a degree of flexibility in structure and program.
EXAMPLES: Alternative schools (UK and USA); multi-unit schools; individually prescribed instruction schools; comprehensive schools, etc.

TYPE I: Highly structured and rigid educational programs and structures with a highly prescriptive content.
EXAMPLES: Traditionally structured elementary, secondary, technical, and higher education institutions.

Closed, selective, competitive services, depending primarily on standards set by the authority as to who should (or be allowed to) study or do what at what ages; usually structured in the form of courses, with recognized certification of attainment; little immediately; perceived usefulness of content, deferred satisfaction and acceptance of long-term goals.

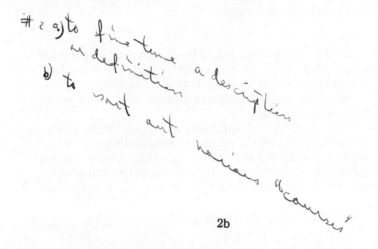

2b

least structured to the most structured educational program, the classification can prove useful to those working domestically and internationally, in both developed and developing countries.

1 A distinction is made in the manual between formal and nonformal adult education according to whether participants are enrolled/registered or not. This quotation is from UNESCO ADULT EDUCATION information notes, No. 3/1975, p. 4. The manual referred to is "Manual for the collection of adult education Statistics" (CSR/E/15, available in English, French, Russian and Spanish languages. Its worthy goal is greater accuracy, honesty, comparability and availability in statistics regarding adult education.

2 Verner, Collie, "Fundamental Concepts in Adult Education." in Internationales Jahrbuch fur Erwachsenenbildung 1975, ed. Joachim H. Knoll. Berlin: Bertelsmann Universitatsverlag, p. 181.

3 Liveright, A. A., A Study of Adult Education in the United States, Center for the Study of Liberal Education for Adults, 1968.

4 Class notes, University of Chicago, 1960.

5 Bergevin, Paul, A Philosophy for Adult Education, N.Y. Seabury, Press, p. 51.

6 Lecture notes, 1974, University of Pittsburgh. Classification developed by Dr. Seth Spaulding, UNESCO and International Education Dept. University of Pittsburgh.

Summary

In defining adult education some persons place an emphasis upon the **individual** and the benefits to be derived by the individual from continuing education, while others place the emphasis upon the improvement of **society**. Adult education **can** help solve social problems in our communities. In fact, during times of social stress, agencies are called upon to try to remediate where the elementary and secondary schools and the home have failed. For example, the adult basic education programs, our learning centers, and our general education development tests (G.E.D.) are attempts to make up for deficiencies in youth learning. On the other hand, we must not lose sight of the importance of the individual in adult education and of adult education to the individual.

Scholarly thought needs to be given to a sharper definition of adult and continuing education. In the final analysis each of us as adult educators must develop our own definition with which we feel comfortable for program planning and execution. This author finds his definition taking on broader meanings as his experience deepens with teachers of adults, adult learners, and administrators of adult programs. It will be remembered, for some persons society will be changed through the impact of

3

individual adult education, while others emphasize in their definition the institution, the need to use adult education to change society. As we approach the year 2,000 with our new leisure time, with an aging population, and an expanded technology, our definitions may be far more inclusive. The question is, will our definitions be adequate to the challenge?

QUESTIONS: Definitions and Classifications

1. What do you feel should be the focus of adult education? How is this reflected in the definition you like best?
2. To what use might you put the classification suggested by Seth Spaulding, developed at UNESCO?
3. What future developments might influence your definition of adult and continuing education?
4. Where might you look for additional definitions of adult education?

Bibliography (Definitions and Classifications)

Dickerson, Gary, CONTRIBUTIONS TO A DISCIPLINE OF ADULT EDUCATION, A Review and Analysis of the Publications of Coolie Verner, Centre for Continuing Education, The University of British Columbia, Vancouver, Canada, V6T 1W5 Paper 18.

Gross, Ronald, THE LIFELONG LEARNER, Simon and Schuster, N.Y. 1977.

Jensen, Liveright, and Hallenbeck, **Adult Education: Outlines of an Emerging Field of University Study.**, Adult Education Association, U.S.A., Washington, D.C. 1964.

Knowles, Malcolm, **The Modern Practice of Adult Education**, Association Press, N.Y. 1975.

Smith, Aker, Kidd, HANDBOOK OF ADULT EDUCATION, MacMillan, N.Y. 1970.

Chapter II:

WHY ADULT EDUCATION?

When does education begin? From grammar school of course! When will it end? After graduation from a university. This is what ordinary people will answer; and from the standpoint of common sense, this answer seems to be correct. However, in Talent Education we say, "Education begins from one's birth and ends at one's death."

-Dr. Masaaki Honda, M.D.
Director, Talent Education, Tokyo, Japan
Statement sent to author

Some Purposes of Adult Education

Because our society is pluralistic in its system of values, the spectrum of adult and continuing education embraces numerous approaches to the improvement of the individual and the society of which he or she is a part. In our Western culture, unlike that of much of the Orient and parts of Latin America, we have made certain philosophical assumptions that are reflected in the multiplicity of programs for adults in universities, public schools, and voluntary agencies and by radio, television, and correspondence study--to name only a few.

We are imbued in our culture with the fundamental beliefs of the Judaeo-Christian tradition: the perfectability of humans, the equality of humans in pursuing equal opportunity, social mobility, and the right of people to improve themselves through questioning, enlightenment, organized political activity, and respect for human freedom.

Throughout history culture has been perpetuated through education. Education has taken the form of tribal initiation, training youth in the responsibilities of community life, and informal methods of impressing upon members of a clan or tribe the demands of citizenship in the community. Through the centuries such methods of education and training have developed a more organized approach, resulting in the establishment of institutions of learning to inculcate the mores of society and to improve the lives of the people. Because of the range of agencies and organizations which have arisen to facilitate the process of helping people to learn throughout their lifetimes, it is possible in this work to discuss only a limited number of agencies engaged in activities of adult education in the United States. We shall describe some of the major purposes of education for adults in contemporary society with the full realization that this is a dynamic condition with technological changes bringing about new forms of communication, new organizational structures, and new agencies--hence new methods for learning. We are a part of what Robert Blakely calls a homeodynamic society, in a state of flux, but with certain enduring values worthy of being perpetuated if our society is to survive in an atomic age.[1]

It is the author's purpose in the limited scope of this book to assist the adult educator to develop a personal philosophy of adult education upon which to build a program through whatever institutional form or media is appropriate.

Some Levels of Development

We are a people, who have a high level of educational and economic development. The late Harold Benjamin, an authority on the education of developing countries, has reminded us that the kind of education which a country needs and can use is very closely related to the course and level of the social and economic development of the country. This relates to the spectrum of education and to higher education in particular. Our country, the United States of America, is described as being on the highest plane of development, as free from hunger, disease, and oppression as science and political skill can make it. Our economy is vigorous and has a maximum of flexibility. It has a vast number of highly trained personnel, employed by both governmental agencies and private associations. We have attained a high level of industrialization. Our commerce and currency are now carefully regulated, and we are expanding in our technological research and development.[2] We enjoy the greatest opportunities for adult learning in the world.

Agencies abound for adult education in this country. They are as varied as they are numerous. In addition, these agencies and institutions responsible for the education of adults approach that responsibility in a variety of ways--some have adult education as a **primary** function, while others have it as a coordinate or as a subordinate function. For example, the Cooperative Extension Service of the U. S. Department of Agriculture serves thousands of adults as a primary function. This agency has a highly trained staff with personnel located in almost every county in the United States. The high stage of development of this adult education agency has been so effective that underdeveloped countries throughout the world are calling upon Cooperative Extension personnel who serve as change agents, to assist in developing training programs to eradicate disease and pests on farms, and to increase crop production through the adoption of sound agricultural practices. Universities have as one of their functions the continuing education of adults, but often as a **coordinate** function. Public schools, which account for the training of millions of adults in evening programs, also often recognize the activity only as a marginal function because they see the primary responsibility of schools is to educate youth. Labor unions and industry consider the education of the adult as a **subordinate function**. More and more frequently, however, the continuing education of the worker is given a high priority, both in staying abreast of the times and in retraining to salvage talents of workers being displaced by automation.

Some Goals and Aims of Adult Education

When we look at the diversity and disunion of adult education as observed through history we come to the conclusion that the field lacks any master plan or design. Adult education programs and agencies for continuing education have responded to specific needs [5] and, as a result, have tended to be episodic. The lyceum of Josiah Holbrook (1826) is an example of the lack of ongoing institutionalization of an adult education form which arose, met a need, and waned. Blakely has shown concern for a sharper definition of the aims of adult education and a clearer statement of a philosophy for the field.

Hardly another topic takes up more time among adult educators than the discussion of the aims of adult education. Many note the emphasis given to education outside our formal system. Says John W. Gardner, of Common Cause, former Secretary of Health, Education, and Welfare:

If we really believe in individual fulfillment, our concern for education will reach far beyond the formal system. We shall expect people to continue to learn and grow in and out of school, in every possible circumstance, and at every stage of their lives."

Some Goals and Aims of Adult Education

The person seeking continuing or adult education comes with specific needs. These needs often relate to the integration of mind, body and spirit. In this society, where the media bombards the individual, it is difficult to keep the necessary balance in our lives to live productively and happily, to address needs in all

7

three corners of the "triangle of life." Institutions that seek to serve people not as compartmentalized organisms but as integrated individuals will attract a growing clientele. Thus, the goals of adult education today - and tomorrow - must address the needs of holistic humans.

We need to develop programs to help persons find their fullest life, which might include topics as varied as jogging, journal writing, meditation, library skills, or tips on how to approach special projects.

Some educators are troubled by this lack of unity and growing diversity in purposes of adult education. Others see this as a strength and believe that the diversity, profusion, and variety of programs is characteristic of the **pluralism** in our society. Special needs are met through unique tailor-made programs built around particular institutions. The libraries, for example, have embraced the Great Books discussion groups, while state departments of education have chosen to administer adult basic education.

One aim of adult education is institutional collaboration. Public institutions may become so identified with particular programs that their energies and resources, both in terms of funds and personnel, are swallowed up in single efforts--to the neglect of other important tasks. An alternative to concentrating adult education in the kindergarten-through-twelfth grade public school program is to support many and diversified programs and to provide a wide range of services, some sponsored by the schools themselves, some in collaboration with other agencies, and some housed in schools but operated by other agencies.[4] This collaboration becomes essential when one realizes that adult education is a field which at the same time has "no aim" and is "well aimed". As Broady notes:

Education, being purposive, has aims, and it is proper to inquire into their nature; but any inquiry into the aims of adult education comes up with some paradoxes. In one sense, adult education seems to have no aim at all. Profusion and variety rather than unity and order characterize its programs, and the more successful these programs become, the more apt this characterization becomes. In another sense, no educational program is so well "aimed" as the adult one . . . it is supplied by the purposes of the learner.[7]

A survey of adult educators by the author substantiates Broady's belief, for the respondents identified the following reasons or purposes for adult education:

Remedial or literacy education
Cultural education
Retraining
Vocational Education
Development of recreational or leisure time skills
Cultivation of philosophy of maturity and tranquility in change
Development of human relations skills
Training in how to learn through techniques such as reading improvement
Family life education
Consumer education
Preservation and perpetuation of the cultural heritage
Healthy and safety education
Techniques of information retrieval
Knowledge of the history of mankind
Discovery of new knowledge and integration of this knowledge with life's needs
Creation of change, develop methods of adaptability, and learn how people change
Self understanding
Citizenship education
A liberal education, mental stimulation, and self-expression

Idea exchange--an opportunity to examine ideas of past and
   present
Degree completion
Women's education

Most adults know the familiar story of the blind men of Hindustan.
When asked what the elephant is like, each blind man described the
elephant by what he felt. Like the blind men, the adult learner reacts
to and describes his experiences with adult education by how he feels.
He usually responds to the adult learning activity by the totality of his
impressions. If the adult learning experience is positive, useful, interesting and inviting, he will be inclined to continue his education.
If the experience is negative, unpleasant, or uninteresting, the learner
becomes a potential educational dropout.

Some Seek An Intellectual Adventure

Adult education is for those who have a deep and abiding
faith in the possibilities of an intellectual adventure. If we believe in human beings and their infinite potential for growth,
we look upon their potential for self-improvement. William H.
Lighty, one of the university extension workers in the early
twentieth century, devoted his life to helping adults realize
their intellectual potential through self-culture halls, correspondence study, radio, and university extension classes. He stated
as his credo:
   The great adventure of adult life in infinitely more
   baffling, more implicated with the possibilities of pleasure
   and pain, of success and failure, than any world cruise.

You may not be captain of the social craft in which you journey, but you can be captain of your own inner life, and of the expression you give to it.

This great adventure, and the relation of adult education to it, takes on new meaning when one recognizes that as we move through the passages of our lives we have new learning needs and tasks.

Through adult education, we can develop and master an adaptability to change. In education, as in transportation, we need to be continually repairing the old roads (remedial education), to be building new roads (degree completion programs), and to be experimenting with new and better ways of travel (research, professional updating and in-service programs). To catch up, keep up, and to forge ahead are the goals of adult education.

We will examine more closely some additional purposes and directions of adult education in the next chapters.

The reasons for "Why Adult Education?" are not static; educators of adults who are alive to the needs of the times will continue to revise their lists in keeping with changing societal and community needs.

Summary

We have found that in our pluralistic society there are many purposes for adult education. Some have as their purpose the improvement of the individual and some the improvement of society. One philosopher points out the paradox of "no aim" for adult education, but no educational program so well "aimed" as the adult one, for it is supplied by the purposes of the learner.

The multitude of purposes for adult education were described when a group of adult educators were asked, "Why Adult Education?" with twenty-two reasons listed. The purposes are as varied as the reactions of the blind men in the fable who examined the elephant.

Some of the purposes next described in some detail are self-improvement, literacy education, training and retraining for adults, the preparation of senior citizens, and the reclaiming of women's talents through educational programs.

Some of the aims and goals of those who undertake adult education are summed up by Cyril O. Houle:
1. To make up for the deficiencies of incomplete earlier schooling. Here the goal is usually stated in terms of the accomplishment of some formal certificate such as a diploma or a degree.
2. To extend and develop further an interest which is already held.

11

3. To meet personally felt needs:
   (a) A better, broader, and more integrated viewpoint.
   (b) Greater understanding of civic affairs.
   (c) Better personal adjustment to increasing age.
   (d) Better health.
   (e) More effective adjustments in home life and family relationships.
   (f) More refined cultural and appreciational abilities.
   (g) Greater social effectiveness.
   (h) More effective discharge of social responsibilities.
   (i) Vocational advancement.
   (j) Higher social prestige.
4. To fulfill a compulsory requirement set upon the individual from outside.
5. To follow a conscious pattern of maintaining breadth of view.
6. To carry on a habit.

It is suggested that every agency working in the field of adult education periodically examine its aims and objectives to see if the actual needs of the adult clientele are being served. Since adult education is a part of the society in which it finds itself, the educator of adults must continually update his reasons for "Why Adult Education?" in order to stay abreast of the changing times and his community needs, whether local, national, or international.

Bibliography

Adolfson, Lorentz H. "The University's Role in Adult Education," Adult Education, Vol. 5, No. 4(Summer 1955), pp. 231-232.
Axford, Roger W. "Never Too Old to Learn," Tallahassee: Florida Institute for Continuing University Studies, 1965.
——————— "The Stage of the Empty Nest," Continuous Education, Vol. 6, No. 5 (September-October 1967)
Blakely, Robert J. Adult Education in a Free Society. Toronto: Guardian Bird Publications, 1958.
Caliver, Ambrose. "The National Concern for Adult Education," Social Life, Vol. 59, No. 5 (May 1957), pp. 9-12.
Clark, Burton R. Adult Education in Transition: A Study of Institutional Insecurity. Berkeley: U. of California Press, 1956.
Crabtree, Arthur. "Purposeful Education for Adults," National Education Association Journal, Vol. 50 (October 1961), pp. 27-28.
Crimi, James E. "Adult Education in the Liberal Arts Colleges," Notes and Essays on Education for Adults, Number 17. Chicago: Center for Study of Liberal Education for Adults, 1957.
Goals for Americans. The Report of the President's Commission on National Goals. Englewood Cliffs, N.J.: Prentice-Hall, 1960.

Grattan, C. Hartley. **American Ideas About Adult Education,** 1710-1951. New York: Columbia U.P., 1959.

Harrington, Fred, **The Future of Adult Education,** Jossey-Bass, San Francisco, 1977.

Houle, Cyril O. **The Inquiring Mind.** Madison: U. of Wisconsin Press, 1961.

Jensen, Gale and others. **Adult Education, Outlines of an Emerging Field of Study.** Washington, D.C.: Adult Education Association, 1964.

Lindeman, Edward C. **The Meaning of Adult Education.** Montreal: Harvest House, 1961.

Peers, Robert. **Adult Education, A Comparative Study.** London: Kegan, Paul, 1958.

Shannon, Theodore. "The Study of Objectives for Selected Areas of University Extension." Unpublished Ph.D. dissertation, Yale University, June 1958.

————, and Clarence Schoenfeld. University Extension, the Library of Education. New York: Center for Applied Research in Education, 1965.

Stensland, Per G. "What is Adult Education?" Adult Education, Vol. 5, No. 3 (Spring 1955), pp. 136-138.

Thatcher, John (ed.). **Public School Adult Education: A Guide for Administrators.** Washington, D.C.: National Association of Public School Adult Educators, 1963.

QUESTIONS:

1. What are some of the religious-philosophical considerations in answering the question: "Why Adult Education?"
2. What are some primary purposes of adult education?
3. How would you help people keep a balance of spirit, mind, and body? How would you program for these needs?
4. What would you describe as the "intellectual adventure"?
5. How do you deal with differing perceptions of adult learners
   a. in a class?   b. in counseling?   c. in program planning?
   (Example: the blind people of Hindustan).

FILMS:

"A Day In The Life Of Bonnie Consolo", A woman without arms copes positively with life. - 20 minutes

"Everybody Rides The Carousel", An illustration of Erik H. Erickson's theory of personality development from birth to death color - 72 minutes

"The Other Way", An exploration of the possiblities for more human, self-sustaining communities - color - 29 minutes

"You Can", A young man experiences the adult education process, a promotional film on adult education - color - 30 minutes

1 Robert Blakely. The Homodynamic Society. Center for the Study of Liberal Education for Adults, Boston University, 1966.

2 Harold R. W. Benjamin, Higher Education in the American Republics, McGraw-Hill, New York, 1965, pp. 3-10.

3 The author observed cooperative extension workers assisting in the training of personnel in the Dominican Republic and in Venezuela. Personnel from Texas A & M teach young men in horticulture, agronomy, and animal husbandry in the Agricultura' School at Santiago deCaballeros, Dominican Republic.

4 Classnotes - University of Chicago

5 Bernard J. James, "Can Needs Define Education Goals?" Adult Education, VII:1 (Autumn 1956), pp. 19-26.

6 Cyril O. Houle, "Back to New Francisco," address to the Adult Education Association, U.S.A., and the National Association of Public School Adult Educators, Chicago, November 15, 1966, Adult Leadership, February 1967, p. 261.

7 Harry S. Broady, Aims in Adult Education: A Realist View, Center for Study of Liberal Education for Adults, Boston, 1960, p. 1.

8 Roger W. Axford, "William H. Lighty -- Adult Education Pioneer," Ph.D. dissertation, University of Chicago, 1961, p. 70.

14

Chapter III:

WHY ADULT EDUCATION: SOCIAL CHANGE

I recall a member of the Labor Department predicting that his office would become the largest adult education agency by the year 2,000. With the proliferating programs in manpower training that prediction is rapidly approaching fulfillment. Social Security, through training programs in every state and territory, is now educating foster parents, nutrition aides, and aides for nursing homes, to name but a few. Community colleges and universities are being called on to "train the trainer", and Divisions of Continuing Education are finding a fertile field for community service in this area.

Adult education can help solve some of the social problems of our society, but it cannot become a "cure-all". Modern societies, and in particular the North American society, have achieved an unprecedented high level of productivity and affluence. However, such rapid growth has created a gap between the "haves" and the "have-nots". With a world shrinking, with multinational corporations using natural and human resources throughout the world, any gap in resources or in knowledge is not only undesirable, but dangerous. Those who do not possess knowledge, skills, and current information may be unable to cope with an alien society, and conditions may become economically, socially and culturally unbearable.

CHANGE AS A WAY OF LIFE

In a consideration of the quality of life in the United States author/historian James A. Michener puts change as the first consideration for our future quality of life. He feels that practically everything we know today will change. He says,

"points of reference will fluctuate; values will alter; capacities will be modified and opportunities will be so magnified as to terrify the cautious and delight the adventurous. It is obvious that science stands at the threshold of fantastic accomplishments, each of which will require new mental adjustments; but almost all other aspects of life also stand at the edge of change." [2]

Writing as a futurist and a world citizen rather than as a corporation executive, C. E. Meyer, Jr. the President of Trans-World Airlines writes in an issue of his company's magazine which was devoted entirely to change:

"After submitting my own response to the question, What is the most significant change of the past decade in your respective field?, . . . I reflected that it may well be that the most important change of the past 10 years had little to do with scientific progress or technological advancement-- the customary yardsticks by which our era seems to measure change.

The most important change of all, affecting every field and indeed every aspect of our national life, may be the virtual revolution that has occurred during the past decade in our COLLECTIVE SOCIAL AWARENESS" (emphasis mine.⁴

Like Michener, Meyer puts emphasis on the qualitative change in our collective national attitude that has occurred. Meyer lists as our social priorities on the national agenda:

- preservation of our environment,
- conservation of Earth's finite resources,
- greater job security for our work force,
- new dignity for the handicapped,
- an enhanced sense of purpose for the aged, and
- a higher regard for the consumer--instead of a cavalier "let the buyer beware."

Meyer suggests that "all these former subjects of heated contention have become accepted, at least in principle, as rightful items of our society's unfinished business; all are being addressed with some earnestness."⁴

Both historian and airline president have outlined an agenda for our adult education programs for at least the next decade, possibly for the twenty-first century. What the list suggests is a re-arrangement of our **priorities,** an examination of our value system, a re-examination of what we as a people think is important. Meyer might have added the impact of nuclear energy and its threat to human life, and the potential of the computer technology on our mode of living. It is significant that no less a scientist than Albert Einstein, reminded us of our need for **changing** our way of looking at the world when he said, "The splitting of the atom has changed everything save our modes of thinking, and thus we drift towards unparalleled catastrophe."

EDUCATING FOR CHANGE-HANDLING STRESS

I am convinced after many years of working with professional adult educators that the major competency we need to develop is the ability to cope with change. "Stress Seminars", and "Coping Skills"⁵ courses are evidence of the recognition that our

16

clientele can benefit from such training.

Dealing with change and the stress that accompanies it has fostered an entire industry to cater to these needs. The individual who learns to handle stress most easily is the person who learns to be in balance, "someone who avoids excesses that make it difficult to function." This person searches for holistic health and sees the value of continuing education activities such as assertiveness training; behavior therapy; gestalt, rational living, pragmatism or other forms of psychiatric services; Zen; meditation; yoga; biofeedback; hypnosis; mind control; relaxation response training; even mountain-climbing, or river-rafting; not to mention all the "standard" courses we normally think of as continuing education.

Evidence of the need to deal with change before it occurs is the emergence of such groups as Robert Theobald's Future Frontiers Project, headquartered in Wickenburg, Arizona, and the think tank of the Rio Salado College, a college without walls, which has a Futures Studies Program through a grant from the National Foundation on the Humanities. [6]

Change is illustrated by the chart below which shows more jobholders, more working wives, more early retirements, more divorces, more one parent homes, and more childless families. Each of these changes gives opportunities for program planners in adult education. We will deal with literacy and citizenship, training, and retraining, aging and early retirement, and women's continuing education in following discussions. Adult education administrators and teachers should look on these as opportunities rather than problems, for we can provide the content for the enlightened mind, and the educated heart. [7]

More at Work [8] More Jobholders	Changing Family Patterns Divorces
Employed persons age 20 and older 1970..........72.5 mil. ....58% of adults 1977..........82.9 mil. ....59% of adults	1970..................708,000 1977................1,097,000
More Working Wives	One-Parent Homes
1970..........18.4 mil. ....41% of married women 1977..........22.4 mil. ....47% of married women	1970................6,830,000 1977................9,213,000
More Early Retirement	Childless Families
Workers retiring before 65 under Social Security 1970..........745,000.......56% of all retirees 1977........1,064,000.......67% of all retirees	Share of women without children among those who have been married at least once-- 1970..................16.4% 1977..................19.2%

This opportunity can be seen in a view of 1985 by Harold L. Hodgkinson, Executive Director of the Professional Institute of the American Management Association.

"We have discovered that although we have declined in our numbers of 18-year olds the number of adults in this country who genuinely wish to and are capable of taking part in a program of life-long learning has made the ultimate size of the post secondary operation enormous in the United States. There is no reason to believe that there will be any cutback in the size of the operation although 18- to 21-year olds will diminish consistently but predictably. For their loss however, we can postulate a 15 percent gain in the number of adults who take courses in various locations for various kinds of credit as they move toward using education to become more literate, more concerned, more humane and happy in their work at home."[9]

Summary

Adult education can be looked on as a potential solution to social problems. Our priorities in society need to be examined as well as what we think is important, of value, and worth paying for. We need to educate for change, and for handling the stress of change. In this chapter we also took a look into the future, and tried to ask what adult educators can do to influence the future in our society. How can adult educators be effective "change agents" for a better world was discussed with some suggested readings.

Bibliography

Bowman, Jim; Kierstand, Fred; Dede, Chris; and Pulliam, John. **The Far Side of the Future: Social Problems and Educational Reconstruction.** World Future Society, 1978.
Brameld, Theodore. **The Teacher as World Citizen: A Scenario of the 21st Century.** ETC Publications. 1976.
Dreifus, Kurt. **The Other Side of the Universe,** Twayne Publishers, N.Y. 1961. (Delightful science fiction)
Frymier, Jack R. **A School for Tomorrow.** McCutchan, 1973.
Glines, Doc C. (compiler). **Educational Futures I, II, and III.** Anvil Press. 1978.
Gross, Ronald. **The Life Long Learner.** Simon and Schuster. 1977.
Henley, Stephen P. and Yates, James R. **Futurism in Education: Methodologies.** McCutchan. 1974.
Hodgkinson, Harold L. "What Will Education Look Like in 1985: A Future History", A.A.C.J.C. Annual Report, 1977.
Hostrop, Richard W. (ed.) **Education Beyond Tomorrow.** Etc. Publications. 1975.

Kauffman, Draper L. **Futurism and Future Studies: Developments in Classroom Instruction.** National Education Association. 1976.

Rubin, Louis. **Educational Reform for a Changing Society.** Allyn and Bacon. 1978.

Rubin, Louis (ed.) **The Future of Education: Perspectives on Tomorrow's Schooling.** Allyn and Bacon. 1975.

Shane, Harold G. **Curriculum Change Toward the 21st Century.** National Education Association. 1977.

Shane, Harold G. **The Education Significance of the Future.** Phi Delta Kappa Educational Foundation. 1973.

Sullivan, Edward A. **The Future: Human Ecology and Education.** Etc. Publications. 1975.

Theobald, Robert. **Futures Conditonal.** The Bobbs-Merrill Co., Inc. Indianapolis, 1972 (Wickenburg, Az. 85358).

Toffler, Alvin. **Learning for Tomorrow: The Role of the Future in Education.** Vantage. 1974.

World Future Society. **Cataglo: Books, Magazines, Newsletters, Learning Materials, Audio Tapes, Games and Films.** A free copy may be obtained through a request of the World Future Society, 49196 St. Elmo Avenue (Bethesda) Washington, D.C. 20014.

Yearbook of Adult and Continuing Education, 1978-79. Contents: (1) Adult education (general); (2) Adult career education; (3) Cooperative education; (4) Community education; (5) Adult basic education; (6) Alternatives and innovations; (7) Indexes: Subject/Geographic. Approx. 650 pages; Pub. Sep. 1978. LC No. 75-13804; ISBN O-9380-3104-5; $37.50 H.B.

"Every Man takes the limits of his own field of vision for the limits of the world." Arthur Schopenhauer

FILMS

"Future Shock" - Toffler film, narrated by Orsen Wells.

"Fast Forward" - Series of TV films produced by Canadian Film Board. Deals with the impact of modern technology on our society. Ontario Educational Communications Authority, Canada Square, 2180 Yonge St. Toronto, Ontario, Canada M4S 2C1

QUESTIONS:

1. Why does the level of development of a country make so much difference in the kind of adult education that country organizes?
2. In what ways can adult education help solve social problems?
3. How can we help people deal with rapid technological change in our society?
4. How would you rearrange our national priorities to effect

a peaceful world?
5. How would you help people handle stress? How can we program for this need?
6. How do you attempt to be a futurist? Should adult educators think of themselves as futurists? In what ways?
7. What implications do major social changes have for adult education programming?
8. How would you utilize changing family patterns to build relevant adult education programs?
9. Do you think the "world citizen" can be realized in this decade? What are the implications? Do you think space-ship earth can bear the growing population? What has adult education to offer?
10. How would you build programs around Michener's ideas of the "quality of life"?
11. What do you think the "futurists" have to offer adult educators?

1 See **Multinational Monitor** published by Ralph Nader, which provides a critical focus on the work of world-wide corporations. The purpose of the publication is to offer a citizen perspective. (c) Corporate Accountability Research Group, P.O. Box 19312, Washington, D.C. 20036.

2 Michener, James, A. **The Quality of Life**. New York: Girard Company, 1970; p. 8.

3 **Ambassador Magazine**. Vol. 11, No. 7, p. 12.

4 Ibid, p. 2.

5 Searles, John E. **Coping Skills**, Continuing Education, College of Education, The Pennsylvania State University, 1974, Described as "Being a Paper Designed to Provoke Discussion among Teachers, Students, and Other People who by their Living Together Cause much Joy and Sorrow, One to Another". 47 pp. (Mimeo)

6 For Information on FUTURE STUDIES PROGRAM, contact Director, Rio Salado, A Maricopa Community College, 2300 No. Central Ave., Phoenix, AZ 85004.

7 A bibliography is provided at the end of this chapter for those who wish to explore the literature and to program in the area of futurism.

8 U.S. News & World Report, Aug. 21, 1978, p. 57.

9 Hoekinson, Harold L. "What Will Education Look Like in 1985: A Future History", American Assoc. of Community and Junior Colleges Annual Report, Washington, D.C. 1978, p. 12.

Chapter IV:

WHY ADULT EDUCATION: SELF IMPROVEMENT

> IF ADULT EDUCATION IS EVERYONE'S CONCERN, THEN WE SHOULD ALL BE INTERESTED IN DOING SOMETHING ABOUT IT!
> Paul Bergevin, A Philosophy for Adult Education

If this century were to be named, I think it would be appropriate to term it the century of SELF-IMPROVEMENT. In the last decade numerous books have flooded the market dealing with self-help, self-fulfillment, successful living, and understanding oneself. When I served as Dean of a University Extension Division we could count on a filled class if we called the course "UNDER-STANDING HUMAN PERSONALITY" and had it taught by one of the professors from the Psychology department.

This trend is also seen in **Passages,** a best seller which describes the predictable crises and patterns in adult life -- patterns of adult development which, when recognized, can be managed. Gail Sheehy set three objectives in writing **Passages**: 1) to locate the personality changes common to each stage of life; 2) to compare the developmental rhythms of men and women -- which she found strikingly unsynchronized; and 3) in light of this, to examine anticipated crises.

Similarly, Dr. Daniel J. Levinson in **THE SEASONS OF A MAN'S LIFE** [1] developed the patterns of life cycles. Levinson and his fellow researchers identified three adult stages: Early Adult Transition (ages 17 to 22); Mid-Life Transition (40 to 45) and Age Fifty Transition (50 to 55), (see figure).

One adult education response comes from churches, which have begun programming for self-improvement. Short courses like "Who Am I Now That I Am Alone" have attracted singles and divorced persons on large numbers. Growth groups have given persons an opportunity to "get in touch with their emotions". Some groups take a particular book for intensive study while others use structured exercises. Marriage Encounter and follow-

THE SEASONS OF A MAN'S LIFE

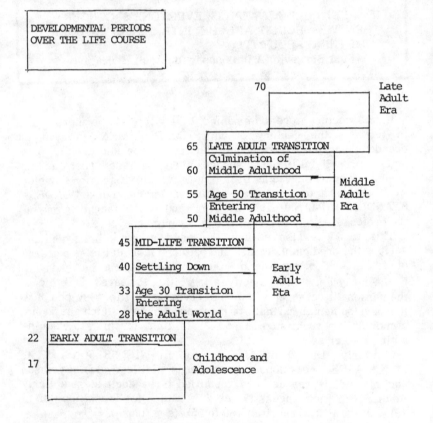

DEVELOPMENTAL PERIODS
OVER THE LIFE COURSE

70 — Late Adult Era

65 — LATE ADULT TRANSITION
Culmination of
60 — Middle Adulthood
Middle
55 — Age 50 Transition   Adult
Entering   Era
50 — Middle Adulthood

45 — MID-LIFE TRANSITION
40 — Settling Down   Early
Adult
33 — Age 30 Transition   Eta
Entering
28 — the Adult World

22 — EARLY ADULT TRANSITION
17 — Childhood and Adolescence

up study groups have given support to couples who are finding new ways to dialogue. In a period when in some areas of the United States the number of divorces is equaling the number of marriages, these programs move toward self-improvement through heightened self-awareness and the development of communication skills. Many persons are tying in their new self-awareness with career changes. Examining one's talents, and where they can be best used is one of the purposes of Richard Bolles thoughtful book, **WHAT COLOR IS YOUR PARACHUTE?** [2] I have had a number of persons re-direct their lives after reading the book which helps persons examine their purposes in life, their skills, ambitions, and their cultivated talents. Another helpful handbook is Richard Irish's book **GO HIRE YOURSELF AN EMPLOYER.** [3] Anyone who is bent on self-improvement will find the pointers of this executive headhunter useful, if sometimes brutally frank.

Also to be found are other types of study-discussion groups. The groups represent communities and meet regularly. Initially they may receive help from their local library, which provided reading materials for discussion. Every month each person is responsible for reading the assigned materials. Then each individual is expected to discuss the topic or chapter. Two persons act as discussion leaders and delve more intensively into the subject of the month. The group meets for two or three hours on the designated afternoon.

In the five years one group has met, a variety of topics have been read and discussed. "All feel more secure with published study materials," one of the committee commented. Topics discussed from readings include: Great Issues in American Politics; Study of Foreign Policy; Modern Art, followed by visits to an art center. Exploration of the Universe, supplemented by television programs; and now they are starting Ways and Mankind, a study of how cultures mold man into the kind of creature he becomes. Religions of the World is the next major topic which interests the largest number in the group.

Many church groups also have reading programs which carry the adult student into current events, problems of missions, or discussions of the problems of family life. Some groups study one topic for an entire year, such as "Problems of Africa." Local librarians can be a rich source of information for such groups and can provide provocative study materials. The Layman's Academy (P.   ) is an illustration of adults continuing to learn through religious organizations.

Democracy and civilization are dependent upon study and public discussion. We must encourage and cultivate enclaves of continuing learners. Louis Pasteur said it so well, "Chance favors the prepared mind." And cultural enrichment no less than vocational

23

improvement, is a worthy purpose of adult education.

SUMMARY

As Socrates said, the "unexamined life is hardly worth living." Each of us want to continue our education. The more systematic we can make it, the more productive should be the outcome. For many persons self improvement is the means of improving society. We find that many programs are built around this idea. Numerous books such as **Passages**, and **The Season's of a Man's Life** are helping persons face the developmental tasks we face in going through life.

Churches, fraternal organizations and university extension divisions are programming around the self-improvement approach. Caring groups, marriage encounters, and self-awareness discussion groups are enrolling thousands of adults. Role changes bring new vocational groups, and we find adults changing careers, some re-careering after retirement.

Finally, understanding ourselves better is considered through discussion groups. Outlined are some do's and don'ts for facilitators and leaders of discussion groups. An informed electorate is dependent upon persons seeking better understanding of themselves, and the crises we meet in life, and how to face up to them. Following Louis Pasteur's dictum that "Chance favors the prepared mind' we are encouraged to find many methods for self-instruction, and for life-fulfillment.

GAINING SELF-UNDERSTANDING THROUGH DISCUSSION GROUPS

"To gain respect for and understanding of the great literature of the world through the Socratic method of discusssion" is the stated purpose of the Great Books Discussion Program carried on in many of the libraries, schools, social centers, and recreation departments throughout the United States. Often cosponsored by a local library, the program tends to attract adults interested in serious reading of the great works of the past. Leadership training courses are given to discussion leaders on an annual basis. Persons from an entire region are brought together for intensive training. Leaders are volunteers, but the Great Books Foundations in Chicago lends a hand in keeping the program going. Eight training sessions make the discussion leader familiar with techniques of drawing people into intellectual dialogue. "Learn the art of questioning" is the phrase used to attract potential leaders (see "Some Do's and Don'ts for Leaders.")
Figure-: SOME DO'S AND DON'T FOR FACILITATORS -

24

DISCUSSION LEADERS

Use questions only; don't make statements or answer questions.

Don't ask too many questions and keep them short.

Ask questions to get the author's ideas expressed (Level 1), examined (Level 2), and evaluated (Level 3).

Be a gadfly by probing cautiously the ideas of the author and participants for clarification, defense, consequences, and consistency.

Get the author's ideas applied to imaginary situations or current events.

Use provocative questions that divide the group into camps of pro's and con's.

Don't let the discussion wander from the point.

Stop splinter discussions.

Redirect the question from the monopolizer and the non-reader.

Ask the participant who says, "It's all through the book" for a specific example.

Don't let the group bring in outside information about the author's time and place.

Don't let the group attack the character of the author but only his ideas.

Don't let the group cite outside authorities.

Don't dispute facts; either disregard them or assume they are true and try to find out what they imply about the reading.

Get the definitions of important words out of the text, not from the dictionary.

Get the group to keep one foot in the text, but not two.

Don't introduce or sum up a discussion.

Avoid saying, "I'll tell you where it is."

Adjust to your coleader by listening carefully to where he is going with his questioning.

Don't take things for granted.

Don't cling too closely to an outline; relax and let the discussion go if it is relevant to the text.

Encourage everyone to question one another.

Get the group to remember and compare the authors.

Keep an open mind; entertain any notion as possible and probe it impartially.

Get the group to avoid strong emotions like anger and/or impatience.

Show patience and use humor; be leisurely in attitude.

Don't fear small silences.

Don't take a vote to determine an issue.

Ask questions not only about what the author says, but how he says it -- his style.

Don't reduce the plot of a play to an issue.

Get the group to examine closely passages from works of fiction for effect and overtones.

Don't stop with an agreement, go on to find out why.

Don't try to cover the whole book; cover about four issues, but get the group to look for a while at the books as a whole. Get everyone into the discussion early.

QUESTIONS:
1. How would you utilize books like **Passages** and **The Season's of a Man's Life** in program development?
2. How would you program effectively for singles?
3. Where would you look for resources for adults who are seeking career changes?
4. How can you most effectively use published materials for discussion groups? Illustrate.
5. How would you try to stimulate interest in public affairs?
6. How would you utilize the do's and don'ts for discussion leaders?

Bibliography

Frankl, Victor. Man's Search for Meaning: An Introduction Logotherapy. New York: Washington Square Press, 1963. (Also paperback) Story of Frankl's struggle in a concentration camp, WW II, and his ways of finding meaning in tragedy-powerful).

Greenwald, Gerry. Be the Person You Were Meant to Be. (antidotes to Toxic Living.) A Dell Book, 1974.

Harris, Obadiah. The New Consciousness (Next State in Human Development) Pendell Publications, Midland, Mich. 1977.

Harris, Obadiah. Self Knowledge and Social Action. Pendell Publications, Midland, Mich. 1974.

Hiemstra, Roger. Lifelong Learning. Lincoln, Nebraska. Professional Educators Publications, Inc. Library of Congress No. 76-7114, 1978.

Knowles, Malcolm. Self-Directed Learning. (A procedure for contract learning). Association Press, 1975.

Kubler-Ross, Elizabeth. On Death and Dying, N.Y. Macmillan, 1970.

Levinson, Daniel. The Season's Of A Man's Life. Alfred Knopf, New York, 1978. (40 case studies of men, their life development).

Olson, Kenneth. How To Hang Loose In An Uptight World. O'Sullivan-Woodside Co., Phoenix, Az. 1975. (Discusses stress and how to deal with it).

Overstreet, Harry A. The Mature Mind. Franklin Watts, Inc., and W. W. Norton Co., New York. 1959. (Discusses wholeness of life, and how to move toward it).

Powell, John. Why Am I Afraid To Tell You Who I Am? Niles III: Argus Communications, 1969 (Deals with fears in being open with persons)

Selye, Hans. The Stress of Life. N. Y. McGraw-Hill and Co., 1956 (Approaches to handling stress in our lives).

Sheehy, Gail. Passages. E. P. Dutton Co., Inc., N.Y. 1976. (Discussion of developmental passages through which women pass).

Staton, Thomas. How To Study. P.O. Box 6133, Montgomery, Ala. 36106. (Psychological factors influencing learning, tools, tips that will improve studying, class discussion, and taking tests).

1 Levinson, N. Darrow, B. Klein, and Alfred A. Knopf, THE SEASONS OF A MAN'S LIFE. N.Y. 1978.

2 Bolles Richard, What Color is Your Parachute, Ten Speed Press, (Revised, 1978) Berkley, Cal.

3 Irish, Richard, Go Hire Yourself an Employer, Anchor Books, (Doubleday & Co.) Garden City, N.Y. 1978.

Chapter V:

WHY ADULT EDUCATION: CITIZENSHIP AND LITERACY

"THE ABILITY TO USE SKILLS AND KNOWLEDGE WITH THE FUNCTIONAL COMPETENCE NEEDED FOR MEETING THE REQUIREMENTS OF ADULT LIVING IS OFTEN CALLED "FUNCTIONAL LITERACY," "SURVIVAL LITERACY," OR OCCASIONALLY "COPING SKILLS.""

Final Report: The Adult Performance Level Study
University of Texas, 1979

ADULT EDUCATION AS LITERACY EDUCATION

As noted earlier, UNESCO has provided a narrow but workable definition of adult education which focuses on literacy. A literate person is defined by UNESCO as "one who can, with understanding, both read and write a short, simple statement on his everyday life." [1]

Similarly, the United States Bureau of the Census defines literacy as the "ability to read and write a simple message in any language." The U. S. Bureau of the Census uses the number of years of schooling as the criterion for "literacy" in data collection, and persons who have completed five years of schooling are automatically considered literate. [2]

Literacy education becomes a concern of adult education through Adult Basic Education General Equivalency Diploma, and English as a Second Language Programs.

Adult Basic Education (A.B.E.) is learning to speak, read, and write the English language, master basic arithmetic or improve these skills up to their potential. It is a continuing education for adults who lack sufficient training to enable them to function effectively in our modern society and may also include training for citizenship and for family and civic responsibilities.

General Educational Development (GED) is training to prepare adults to pass examinations leading to a GED (high school equivalency) Certificate.

Over the years in which the Adult Education Act has been in effect, there have been gains in enrollment numbers as well as gains in adult education generally. (See Charts 1 & 2). For instance, the number of illiterate adults reported in the 1960 census has been significantly reduced during this past decade. The median years of school completed is now over 12 years and the success ratio of adult education is twice that of elementary and secondary. And adult education is the fastest growing branch of the educational system in the U.S. with 32 million enrollees each year.

CHART I
LITERACY IN THE STATES-1970

State (NAPCAE Members)	Total Population Age 25 and Over	No. Functional Illiterates (4th Grade or Less)	% Functional Illiterates
Alabama 34	1,808,798	193,964	10.7
Alaska 10	134,948	7,960	5.9
Arizona 12	915,737	55,643	6.1
Arkansas 18	1,057,512	110,831	10.5
California 69	10,875,983	471,945	4.3
Colorado 14	1,141,138	35,760	3.2
Connecticut 36	1,685,598	72,011	4.3
Delaware 13	287,395	10,686	3.8
District of Columbia 42	423,051	22,533	5.3
Florida 65	3,967,881	234,871	5.9
Georgia 22	2,355,810	261,237	11.1
Hawaii 10	384,843	32,080	8.3
Idaho 0	368,912	8,530	2.3
Illinois 139	6,089,328	249,397	4.1
Indiana 49	2,746,414	88,140	3.2
Iowa 52	1,540,588	28,619	1.9
Kansas 42			
Kentucky 23	1,713,298	160,289	9.4
Louisiana 24	1,809,914	237,349	13.1
Maine 32	537,823	15,200	2.8
Maryland 54	2,082,549	93,920	4.6
Massachusetts 60	3,142,463	129,461	4.2
Michigan 120	4,594,461	173,234	3.9
Minnesota 36	1,990,367	47,049	2.4
Missouri 29	2,602,279	112,527	4.3
Mississippi 24	1,111,789	137,800	12.4
Montana 2	364,508	10,002	2.8
Nebraska 19	804,623	19,437	2.4
Nevada 1	265,089	5,477	2.1
New Hampshire 35	397,681	9,420	2.3
New Jersey 67	4,056,606	192,543	4.7
New Mexico 10	489,623	43,564	8.9
New York 157			
North Carolina 19	2,646,272	264,531	10.0
North Dakota 10	318,339	13,048	4.1
Ohio 52	5,700,317	197,250	3.5
Oklahoma 15	1,422,569	79,531	5.6
Oregon 22	1,156,024	26,948	2.3
Pennsylvania 58	6,689,938	278,354	4.2
Rhode Island 13	524,082	28,315	5.4
South Carolina 52	1,283,837	155,762	12.1
South Dakota 5	349,497	9,309	2.7
Tennessee 37	2,127,946	202,564	9.5
Texas 60	5,817,155	540,743	9.3
Utah 8	492,337	9,988	2.0
Vermont 3			
Virginia 41	2,446,082	187,415	7.6
Washington 27	1,825,888	40,032	2.2
West Virginia 17	969,436	71,046	7.4
Wisconsin 18	2,329,796	74,887	3.2
Wyoming 6	175,649	4,646	2.6
Canada 49			

Taken from the U.S. Census of Population, 1970

CHART 2

Federal Adult Basic Education Enrollments, 1965-1974

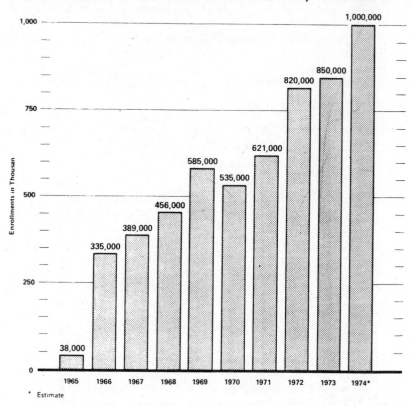

* Estimate

*A TARGET POPULATION IN ADULT EDUCATION, Report of
the National Advisory Council on Adult Education,
November, 1974

Despite obvious gains, problems ramain; the task is unfinished.
The 1970 census found 54.3 million adults 16 years and older
who were not required to be enrolled in school and who had
not completed their high school education. Of these 54.3 million
Americans, only 24 million were gainfully employed (20.7 million
full-time). Twelve and one-half million adults earned less than
$5,000 per year.

The Adult Performance Level (APL) Study, sponsored by the Office of Education's Adult Education Division, found that in 1976 one out of five American adults lacked the skills and knowledge needed to function effectively, and another 33.9 percent are but marginally competent. Further, according to the study, less than half of all Americans function with any degree of real competence.[3]

Reading Expert Worries About Illiteracy

Dr. Janet M. Abbott
battling illiteracy.

The director of Concerned Citizens for Early Reading, based in Athens, W. Va., says, "I believe functional illiteracy poses an honest-to-goodness threat to the survival of our national culture. Everyone who helps a person learn to read is helping society."

Dr. Abbott reports 20 percent of the U.S. adult population is unable to handle the most basic requirements of a literate society, and 15 percent of our 17-year-olds are unable to read well enough to pursue any activity which requires even a minimum of reading.

On a larger scale she notes, "Of the illiterate one-third of this world's population, **60 percent are women**. This means the dilemma will be passed on to the next generation because these mothers cannot exert proper learning influence at home."

A faculty member at Concord College, in Athens, Dr. Abbott is an expert in reading and writing. As a result, parents frequently contact her with questions on how to help with reading difficulties.

As an outgrowth of this need, Dr. Abbott developed WINGS, a reading newsletter. The newsletter's title is derived from Dr. Abbott's belief that books free the intellect to take wing.[4]

The military has long been aware of the seriousness of the literacy problem. In World War I, it was estimated that between 12% and 25% of the recruits read below a 4th grade level, which is still the military criterion for literacy. During World War II, Korea, and Vietnam, there were similar indications that the literacy problem was more severe than census figures had indicated. In 1966, the Army began Project 100,000 by which it admitted recruits who would not previously have met the minimum academic requirements for induction. At that time, they found that 30% of these "New Standard Men" fell below a 4th grade level, another 10% below a 6th grade level. The average

31

score of the "New Standards Men" who had completed high school was 4.4 years below grade level. Even the regular recruits were at least one year below grade level. [5]

The Adult Performance Level Study

The Adult Performance Level Study (known as APL) is a new approach to curriculum development in adult education. In September, 1971, the United States Office of Education funded the Adult Performance Level Project, a study directed by personnel from the University of Texas. This project focused on two major activities: first, to determine the meaning of literacy in terms of specific competencies needed to function in everyday life; and second, to develop the means to measure these competencies.

A survey of a representative sample of the U.S. population showed surprisingly large numbers of adults functioning with difficulty in completing everyday competencies such as correctly addressing an envelope. Seventeen percent, or approximately 20.1 million adults, could not determine how much money was deducted from their paycheck. Twenty six percent, or approximately 30.7 million adults, could not determine the best buy among three boxes of cereal.

According to criteria subsequently developed by the project, nearly 20 percent of the population over 18 years of age could not function successfully with minimum survival and life coping skills. These individuals were classified as APL Level I. In addition, 33.9 percent of the nation's adult population were functional but could not proficiently perform everyday life tasks. These people were classified as APL Level II. Less than half (46.3%) of the adult population over 18 years of age were deemed able to function successfully in our society. (APL Level III).

In determining the APL theory of functional competency, staff members conducted many conferences concerning adult needs, surveyed state and federal agencies, conducted extensive interviews and received related literature and research to determine the factors which distinguished successful adults from those who are not. From those findings were developed the general knowledge areas of Consumer Economics, Occupational Knowledge, Health, Government & Law, and Community Resources. Next, the skill areas were determined. They were Communication, Computation, Problem-solving, and Interpersonal Skills. Competencies to be mastered were thus identified.

The competencies are behaviorally measurable so that they serve as objectives, and also as predictors of success in life. Instructional materials were also developed to fit the APL matrix. [6]

As the data above and the chart below indicate, the goal of universal literacy is yet to be realized. This is a serious task for **adult education.**

Relationship of Populations

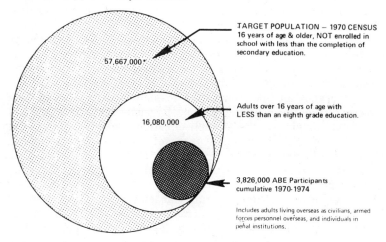

TARGET POPULATION – 1970 CENSUS
16 years of age & older, NOT enrolled in school with less than the completion of secondary education.

57,667,000*

Adults over 16 years of age with LESS than an eighth grade education.

16,080,000

3,826,000 ABE Participants cumulative 1970-1974

Includes adults living overseas as civilians, armed forces personnel overseas, and individuals in penal institutions.

Source: A TARGET POPULATION IN ADULT EDUCATION, Report of the National Advisory Council on Adult Education, Nov. 1974 U.S. Gov. Printing Office, Washington, D.C. #5203-00047.

Adult Education for Citizenship

A democracy is dependent upon citizens who are committed to acquiring fundamental knowledge and a broad understanding of human problems and community awareness. Jefferson reminded us that "a nation that expects to remain free and ignorant in a state of civilization, expects what never was and never can be."

Adults make public policy, and therefore, public affairs education must be a continuous process, not limited to education of youth. There is a question whether youth has had time to get the experience to benefit from such education. If we are to perpetuate a democratic society, we must see that citizenship education obtains a high priority. As long as the adult has the power to vote, it is of utmost importance that the agencies of adult education help the individual to make the most intelligent choices.

Citizenship programs in the form of Americanization courses resulted from the need for assimilating millions of immigrants between 1903 and 1914. Congressional legislation in 1917 added the necessity for literacy in order to become naturalized and brought about expanded programs in public schools. Congress authorized the Federal Immigration and Naturalization Service to work with public schools in providing such educational programs. Citizenship textbooks and teaching materials were provided to schools without cost, and toward the end of World War II one of the leading activities of public evening schools was conducting educational programs for foreign-born. Even today, one of the largest programs of the Chicago Board of Education is the Americanization program.

Many bureaus of adult education in state departments of education and adult education divisions in numerous public schools trace their origin to the Americanization classes which began around World War I. In many large cities Americanization and citizenship classes became the predominant program, and even today some persons think adult education is primarily the naturalization programs for new citizens.

With the advent of the atomic and electronic age, the world has become smaller and its problems more complex. This creates the necessity for every citizen to learn as much as possible about world affairs because today world citizenship is at our very doorstep.

No longer is the study of foreign affairs a frill or a marginal program activity. It is a primary **necessity**. Johnstone noted that less than 3 percent of the population participates in public affairs education. [7] Houle and Nelson have reduced the need for education in international relations to a series of propositions:

1. Democracy is the best form of government.
2. In a democracy, decisions about policy are ultimately made by the people.
3. The quality of these decisions depends upon the degree of enlightenment of the people.
4. The increase of enlightenment can only be achieved by education.
5. Among the decisions which must be made in every democracy are those which have to do with foreign affairs.
6. Therefore, education in foreign affairs is essential for the wise conduct of foreign affairs in a democracy.[8]

The propositions could hardly be more clearly stated for a discussion of "Why Adult Education?" The cogency of the need became most evident when a colleague of mine at a great university asked a teacher from Latin America participating in a training project on the campus, "Where is Venezuela?"

We found that the Latin American teachers knew much more of

34

our affairs than did we of theirs. Our very future as a civilization depends upon our becoming an enlightened people in both domestic and foreign affairs.

SUMMARY

In this chapter the UNESCO definition of literacy was presented along with the definition used by the United States Bureau of the Census, and the usual criterion used for adult basic education. "What is Literacy?" was discussed, along with some of the data from the National Advisory Council on Adult Education (See annual reports). A chart illustrating the relationship of populations and the number of persons being reached by Adult Basic Education is graphically presented. Federal Adult Basic Education enrollments are presented with figures on the growth of the program. Literacy figures for the states gives each adult educator a chance to see his/her target population.

Next presented is a new approach to curriculum development known as the ADULT PERFORMANCE LEVEL study made by the faculty of the University of Texas, and underwritten by the U.S. Office of Education. Skills needed for coping in our society, even at a low level of literacy are: communication, computational skills, problem solving, and interpersonal skills. Many ABE programs today are building their curriculum around these skills. Literacy is still a major concern in the U.S. and public and private education will have to deal with the problem in the years ahead.

We examined the seriousness of illiteracy in the armed forces. Each of the wars of recent years has made us more aware of the problem. The army started Project 100,000 in 1966 as a way to give recruits a minimum foundation of literacy so that they could handle academic pursuits. They found that 30% of those "New Standard Men" fell below the 4th grade level, while another 10% fell below the 6th grade level.

Literacy remains a block to employment for many persons. It is one of the key targets for adult educators.

Finally, this chapter discussed the importance of adult education for citizenship education. Citizenship education is becoming increasingly important in our electronic-atomic world.

QUESTIONS:

1. What are the implications of a high illiteracy rate in a democracy?
2. How would you try to motivate persons who are illiterate, and to what agencies would you refer them?
3. What is the Adult Performance Level study? How would you try to prepare people for the four skill areas?
4. What are some of the qualities needed to deal with adults coming

to adult basic education classes?

5. What is meant by the G.E.D.? How do you think the General Educational Development tests compare with the high school diploma?

6. How would you best prepare a teacher to work with adults who can neither read nor write?

7. What are some resources you can use to teach literacy?

Bibliography

Adult Functional Competency Final Report, U. S. Office of Education, H.E.W., August, 1977.

Bormuth, J. R., Reading Literacy: Its Definition and Assessment, 1975. In J. B. Carroll and J. S. Chall (eds.) **Toward a Literacy Society.** N.Y.; McGraw-Hill 1975.

Corder, Reginald, **The Information Base for Reading**: A Critical Review of the Information Base for Current Assumptions Regarding the Status of Instruction and Achievement in Reading in the U. S. Educational Testing Service, Berkeley, CA 1974. Sponsored by National Center for Educational Research & Development. ED 054-922.

Cassidy, Jack. High School Graduation: Exit Competencies? **Journal of Reading,** (February,1978) pp. 398-402.

Cavlor, J. S., et al. **Methods in Determining Reading Requirements of Military Occupational Specialities.** March,1973. Hum-RRO, Alexandria, Va Ed 0 74 343.

Charnley, A. H. and Jones, H. A. **The Concept Of Success In Adult Literacy**, 1979, Huntington publishers Limited, Sussex House, Hobson Street, Cambridge CB1-INJ (England).

Dauzat, Sam V., & Dauzat, Joann. Literacy: In Quest of a Definition. **Convergence.** 10.1 37-41. 1977.

DeCrow, R.E. **Adult Reading Ability: Definitions and Measures.** 1973. ed 068 810

Educations Crock or Panacea: Implications of APL Project. **Adult Literacy and Basic Education.** Vol. 1, No. 2, pp. 45-50, Summer, 1977.

Gray, W. S. **The Teaching of Reading.** Switzerland: UNESCO, 1969.

Griffith, W. S. and Cervero, R. M.,The APL Program: A Serious and Deliberate Examination. **Adult Education,** 27, 209-224, 1977.

Harris, L. (et al) **The 1971 National Reading Difficulty Index: A Study of Functional Reading Ability in the United States,** Harris & Associates, Inc. New York, National Reading Center Foundation, Washington, D.C., August,1971. ED 057 312.

Hensler, Vicki, **A New Option in Adult Basic Education: The APL High School Diploma.** 1976. Ed 128 770.

James, Wayne B., What APL is -- and is not. **Adult Literacy and Basic Education.** Vol. 1, No. 1, pp. 13-20 Spring,1977.

Nafziger, D. H. et al. **Tests of Functional Adult Literacy: An Evaluation of Currently Available Instruments.** Portland, Ore., N.W. Regional Educational Lab. 1975.

National Center for Health Statistics **Literacy Among Youths 12-17 years.** Baltimore, Maryland: HEW Publications and (HRA) 74 - 1613, 1973.

Northcutt, N. et al. **Adult Functional Competency: A Summary.** Texas University, Austin. Division of Extension, March, 1975. ED 114 609.

Sharon, A. T. **Reading Activities of American Adults,** Princeton, ETS., December,1972.

Shelton, Elaine, **The Adult Performance Level Competency— Based High School Diploma Program** - 4th ed. University of Texas, Austin. 1978.

Smith, A.D.W. **Generic Skills for Occupational Training** Prince Albert, Saskatchewan Training Research & Development sl., 1973.

Weber, Rose-Marie. Adult Illiteracy in the United States, in Carroll, J. and Chall, J. **Toward A Literate Society.** N.Y. McGraw-Hill Book Co., 1975.

1 UNESCO, 1970 Report

2 Hillerich, R. L. Toward an Assessable Definition of Literacy, **English Journal,** Vol. 65, No. 2, pp. 50-55, February, 1971.

3 National Advisory Council on Adult Education Report, May, 1977, p. 2.

4 Arizona Statesman - Spring 1979 p. 29 Arizona State University, Tempe, AZ

5 Corder, Reginald. **The Information Base for Reading:** A Critical Review of the Information Base for Current Assumptions Regarding the Status of Instruction and Achievement in Reading in the U.S. Education Testing Service, Berkeley, CA 1971. Sponsored by National Center for Educational Research & Development, ED 054-922.

6 Further information regarding APL, c/o The American College Testing Program, P.O. Box 168, Iowa City, Iowa 52240. Phone (319) 356-3943.

* 7 W. C. Johnstone and Ramon J. Rivera, **Volunteers for Learning,** John Aldine, Chicago, 1965, p. 51.

8 Cyril O. Houle and Charles A. Nelson, **The University, the Citizen, and World Affairs.** American Council on Education. Washington, D.C. 1956, p. 9.

Chapter VI:

WHY ADULT EDUCATION: CONTINUING EDUCATION FOR WOMEN

"WOMEN HAVE BEEN GOING BACK TO SCHOOL IN UNPRECEDENTED NUMBERS DURING THE LAST SEV-ERAL YEARS. THIS TREND CONSTITUTES ONE OF THE MOST SIGNIFICANT MOVEMENTS IN HIGHER AND ADULT EDUCATION IN THE PAST DECADE"
Jack Mezirow & Amy D. Rose - - Evaluation Guide for College Women's Re-entry Programs.

WOMEN - NOW THE MAJORITY IN THE U.S. LABOR FORCE
The Occupational Handbook is a goldmine of information in analyzing the potentials of the future. The handbook for 1978-79 describes a dramatic increase in the number of women in the labor force, as illustrated in the chart below.

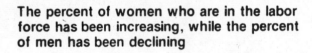

The percent of women who are in the labor force has been increasing, while the percent of men has been declining

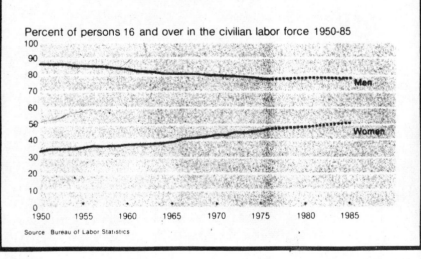

Percent of persons 16 and over in the civilian labor force 1950-85

Source Bureau of Labor Statistics

Some Facts On Women Workers

Source: The following facts are taken from data prepared by the Women's Bureau, Office of the Secretary, U.S. Department of Labor.

1. A majority of women work because of economic need. Nearly two-thirds of all women in the labor force in 1977 were single, widowed, divorced, or separated, or had husbands whose earnings were less than $10,000 (in 1976).

2. About 40 million women were in the labor force in 1977; they constituted more than two-fifths of all workers.

3. Fifty-seven percent of all women 18 to 64 - the usual working ages - were workers in 1977, compared with 88 percent of men. More than 48 percent of all women 16 and over were workers. Labor force participation was highest among women 20 to 24.

4. Fifty-one percent of all women of minority races were in the labor force in 1977 (5.3 million); they accounted for nearly half of all minority workers.

5. Women accounted for nearly three-fifths of the increase in the civilian labor force in the last decade - 12 million women compared with 8 million men.

6. The average worklife expectancy of women has increased by more than one-half over the two decades since 1950. In 1970 the average woman could expect to spend 22.9 years of her life in the work force.

7. The more education a woman has, the greater the likelihood she will seek paid employment. Among women with four or more years of college about three out of five were in the labor force in 1977.

8. The unemployment rate was lowest for white adult men (20 and over) and highest for minority young women (16 to 19) in 1977:

	Percent
White adult men	4.6
White adult women	6.2
Minority adult men	10.0
Minority adult women	11.7
White teenage men	15.0
White teenage women	15.9
Minority teenage men	37.0
Minority teenage women	39.9

9. Women workers are concentrated in low-paying, dead-end jobs. As a result, the average woman worker earns only about three-fifths of what man does, even when both work full-time, year-round.

10. Fully employed women high school graduates (with no college) had less income on the average than full employed men who had not completed elementary school - $8,377 and $8,991 respectively, in 1976.

11. Among all families, nearly one out of seven was headed by a woman in 1977 compared with one out of 10 in 1967; 37 percent of black families were headed by women. Of all women workers, about one out of five minority women workers was a family head.

12. Among all poor families, nearly half (48 percent) were headed by women in 1977, about two out of three poor black families were headed by women. In 1967 about two-fifths (43 percent of all poor families were headed by women and 57 percent of poor minority families had female heads.)

Women are finding more places for themselves in the business and professional world. Each year more women enter the labor force - and now a majority in our work force. The greatest growth will be in the professional and technical jobs. Science and technology are attracting women to these fields. Universities are now beginning to see their responsibilities. With women surviving men on the average of 16 to 17 years, women must continue their education.

"Women of today are seeking knowledge related to self, family, local, national, and international citizenship," reports Professor Dorothy Miniace, Coordinator for Women's Continuing Education at The University of Wisconsin. "Their contribution to society can be greatly enhanced by further education and we want to assist them in every possible way."

Universities can help with testing, counseling, scholarships, placement, and innumerable educational services.

WOMEN'S STUDIES, CENTERS FOR WOMEN'S CONTINUING EDUCATION, CONFERENCES

The 1970's have seen a growth of Women's Studies programs. Some colleges and universities are assigning a faculty person to organize and publicize the credit and non-credit offerings. Some examples of such programs are given on the following pages. Many popular magazines such as NEW WOMAN, MS. and writings targeted at the new returnee to college, the office, or to management are well received by the woman seeking a new role in our society. And some fine films such as WOMEN IN MANAGEMENT are helpful for discussion groups.

Among the earliest continuing ed. programs for women were: (1) The Minnesota Plan (1960) which was a comprehensive program in a large university with individualized counseling, financial aid, child care facilities, and job placement services;

(2) The Radcliffe Institute of Independent Studies which was established in 1960 to support independent projects of highly qualified women; and (3) The Center for Continuing Education of Women at Sarah Lawrence College opened in 1962 with the primary purpose of allowing women who dropped out of college to continue their undergraduate study on a part-time basis.

An important point is that most of those programs focused on middle - class, educated women, while there were few CEW programs aimed at the less educated and low-income women. Furthermore, although continuing education programs have helped mature women to develop their intellectual and vocational skills and talent, the same women find that the job placement services attached to these programs are inadequate or non-existent. [1]

In a review of the research and literature pertaining to women's continuing education, Gaillard points out that the dimensions of each program tend to reflect the convictions of the institution's administration and source of funding. In discussing the background of continuing education programs for women, Gaillard points out that the official beginning of the thrust spans the years 1960-66, which paralleled the national concern about the under utilization of talented women. She praises the National Commission on the Status of Women and the Women's Bureau of the U.S. Department of Labor in their role of urging educational institutions to make available for women an education suitable for their time, talents, and special needs. A highlight Gaillard points out is the establishment of the Continuing Education of Women Section of the Adult Education Association, U.S.A. [2]

What kind of motivation has brought these women back to the colleges? Not so many years ago women's place was in the home, and educational opportunities were very limited. Today, however, women have many years remaining for a career after the last child has left home or married. According to the national average, a woman has her third and last child at age 27. Dr. Mirra Komarovsky, Professor of Sociology, Columbia University, says we have a new social phenomenon: "A new stage has been added to the family cycle - the stage of the empty nest."

A questionnaire filled out by mature women seeking guidance and advice at the university revealed the motivations of those returning to the campuses:

"Since my children are now at school, I feel I should use my education and intelligence to help more than my immediate family, who are needing less and less service from me."

"I have always had curiosity and a great need to learn. After working in several types of office work, I found none of it rewarding to me and realized that higher education is required to qualify for any type of more demanding vocation.''

"Death of my husband, desire, and necessity to go back to work.''

"Want to travel. Growing children. Desire to keep my mind alive.'' [2]

Typical is the response of a city mother of two with whom I talked. A college graduate with a major in speech, she said, "The need is not for a specialized curriculum for women, but for a time schedule which will accommodate women. This refers to both time and residence requirements for completing degrees. The need is for more flexible daily scheduling.''

Interviews with counselors show that many mature women lack the confidence to return to school and need only the reassurance that they are capable of competing with younger teachers.

"The mature adults are some of the best students in our classes,'' say some of the professors. Studies show that older adults are more serious and know why they are there.

One of the major points in the arguments for special programs is that women's intellectual talents are not being used for the good of our society or for the benefit of the woman herself. Three reasons given by the Center for the Study of Liberal Education of Adults for women continuing their education are:

"I want something that will broaden my horizons, deepen my cultural background, and get me away from the children!"

42

1. Recognition of the obvious fact that a role outside the home is necessary for most women - if at no other time during life, certainly at the even longer end of it, when children are grown.
2. Acceptance of the fact that intellectual pursuits by women are not "unnatural."
3. The willingness of society to give help to women who wish to assume roles outside the home.

A great reservoir of talent is awaiting those agencies of adult education which will provide counseling services, guidance tests, and training opportunities for women.

"No, I want auto mechanics. He gets the needlepoint!"

WOMEN'S CONTINUING EDUCATION:
Some Case Studies

SANDY BLACK -- "ANY WOMAN CAN" Philosophy

Sandy Black, Assistant Coordinator of Financial Aids at Arizona Western College, was named by the College's faculty and staff as AWC's recipient in the 1979 Arizona State Community College Board - Arizona Copper Mining Industries Outstanding Alumni Award.

A graduate of Noblesville Senior High School in Indiana, Sandy attended Anderson College and holds an Indiana Real Estate License. She previously worked as office manager for Psychiatric Clincis of Indiana, and served as Personnel Assistant for a 340-patient general hospital.

Married for 21 years, Sandy and her husband Norman have five children, aged 20 to 14. Mrs. Black earned her Associate of Arts degree at the College in December, 1977, with a 3.6 grade point and was named to the Dean's List. She is a member of Phi Theta Kappa, honorary society for community college students, the National Secretaries Association, (Yuma President 1977-78), Beta Sigma Phi Sorority, and Order of the Eastern Star. She now has her sights set on a bachelor's degree.

Speaking about her decision to return to school after many years' absence, Mrs. Black says she has an "Any Woman Can" philosophy, referring to a series of programs at AWC to help women enter and continue in higher education. At 37, while working as Secretary to the Coordinator of Financial Aids, she continued her education at night, and participated in several of the women's workshops. "It is a wonderful world we live in that we can at any age achieve our goals." She continues, "Not too many years ago a woman returning to college and setting new goals at 40 would have been looked down upon or laughed at. Even with those changing roles, I proudly say that my family gave me full support and this made reaching those goals easier. I'm happy that we now can not only reach our goals but are recognized for it."

As Assistant Coordinator of Financial Aids, Mrs. Black works closely with all types of students of all ages, most of whom comment on her good relations with her financial aid clients. "I do feel very student-oriented and dedicated to serving them well. I enjoy the humanistic work and if I do have to say no, I like to be known as having said it with a smile on my face."

Dr. Kenneth Borland, President of AWC, comments, "Sandy is totally dedicated to people, her clients and the whole college, and she seems to bring out the best in others. She really cares."

THE TWO CAREER FAMILY

The man and wife both working is a growing phenomenon in our society. Take Linda and Mike Campbell, for instance.

He just asked her why she wanted a degree at her age!

For Linda, returning to college at Boston College after a hiatus of many years was a tonic, just as she hoped it would be. It gave her the opportunity to make new friends, provided a stimulating environment, and afforded her a new outlook on life.

Twenty-nine years of age, married, with two small children, Linda had completed three semesters of college nearly a decade before. In the interval, she had been principally a housewife but had also worked in community service and volunteer capacities.

Once the children were enrolled in grade school and her husband began progressing in his career, Linda began to feel restless and increasingly unsatisfied. "Frankly, I felt rather left behind," she said, "and didn't like the feeling that I was somehow stagnating and that life was passing me by."

"I decided to take the chance and return to college, and although my previous marks hadn't been as good as they might have been - I was dating Mike at the time - I knew I could do better."

Even though Linda and her husband discussed her taking courses, and Mike was particularly supportive of her plans, once Linda's new academic interests began to grow, some unexpected problems arose. Increasingly, Linda felt the need to address those issues so that she could derive maximum benefit from all her efforts.

Time, for example, was a problem. Having adopted new responsibilities, she nevertheless felt obliged to continue with the full agenda of old ones. Understandably, she found herself constantly running out of time.

Caught between the demands of the classroom, the need to read and reflect upon assigned materials, to prepare papers and review for examinations, and to meet the demands of her family, Linda occasionally found herself subject to anxiety and irritation. "I was always coming or going," she recalls.

In time she came to see herself with this dilemma: What was, in fact, her primary responsibility? Was it her own development and the college career which she did not wish to postpone any longer? Or was it her family and her husband to whom she was totally committed but felt she was shortchanging?

These feelings created guilt for Linda and occasional hostility toward the family. She often felt they did not understnad the situation, and therefore were not being as helpful as they might.

"The way things are going, by the time we're grown,
there'll be no barriers left for us to break."

Having defined the problem in such a confrontational fashion, however, Linda was beginning to feel she had to make a choice between college and family. Not surprisingly, she did not wish to do so.

It was at this point that she decided to discuss the increasingly uneasy situation so she might be able to define the real issues and make some realistic decisions. She therefore made an appointment to talk to the Evening College counselor.

In speaking with the counselor, Linda came to see that the most destructive course of action was that which forced her to choose between college and home. What was necessary was the creation of some situation which would enable her to integrate academic interests with her other obligations.

It appeared that this integration could be achieved by somehow mitigating Linda's tensions and guilt feelings while simultaneously allowing her to derive the maximum advantage and self-satisfaction from her newborn academic career.

For Linda, the situation began in the family, with the help of her husband and children.

While Mike, Linda's husband, had been initially supportive of her college plans, he had been unaware of the degree of commitment demanded by even a part-time program. He found himself steadily more unhappy about the changes in the household routine which Linda's college program necessarily entailed. His initial support seemed to soften considerably as meal times were changed or delayed, as laundry wasn't done quite as often as before, and as he found himself forced to cope with two small children in new and unexpected ways.

Nevertheless, Mike was as committed to Linda's plans as she was. They decided, therefore, to undertake a more equitable division of household tasks and similar obligations. This division would implicitly recognize the co-equal value of Mike's job and Linda's academic career, which was no longer to be regarded as a luxury grudgingly allowed her, threatening to the regular and established modes of family life. Their children, too, were brought into the decision-making process and agreed to undertake a greater share in running their home.

Secondly, and equally important, Linda reevaluated her academic commitments.

Impatient to achieve and to accomplish her goal as quickly as possible, she came to the conclusion that she had overextended herself by signing up for more courses than she could reasonably handle. To reduce her obligations and thus be able to approach them with greater equanimity, she decided to lessen her class load, cut it back, but still to enroll and therefore make continued progress towards her ultimate goal, a baccalaureate degree. "Alternating my course schedule has really made a difference." said Linda. "One of my classes is on Monday evenings and the other is on Saturday, which means Mike is available to take care of the youngsters. When this solution is no longer the most convenient, I plan to enroll in a day course which I can do through the Evening College program. This really will make sense for me because the children will be in school. Even though it seems a bit more expensive to do it this way, the extra cost may be worth having a less frazzled husband around the house."

As a result of this rethinking process, the situation between Mike and Linda is better today than it was six months ago.

"Mike feels better about my going back to school, and not just because I'm taking fewer classes, either, though admittedly this has helped."

"It's more than that: we have now worked out a more complete partnership in our marriage. He's more involved in the home, the youngsters see more of him, and I feel freer and more satisfied."[3]

Summary

Realizing that women are now a majority of the workers in the labor force, we examined the dramatic increase and considered the implications   for adult education. Some facts on Women Workers were presented with some of the socio-economic percentages, such as 43% of all poor families are headed by women, and 57% of poor minority families have female heads.

We then examined some of the developments by universities in establishing programs and departments to serve the interests of women returning to the classrooms. Some of the reasons for women returning are given from interviews, revealing the motives of mature women seeking more education.

Two case studies give us models for women thinking about returning to higher education, one a woman who combined raising a family with improving her skills as a financial aids officer. The other is from a two career family, a more common present day phenomonon in urban centers, telling the story of a woman who returned to an Eastern university to improve herself, and enter the job market. Many women can identify with Linda Campbell's feelings as she became freer and more satisfied with her expanding life.

QUESTIONS:

1. How do you feel that women's continuing education can contribute to "the quality of life"?

"Dear — cold cuts and salad in the refrigerator. Don't wait up for me. I'm going to law school. See you in three years."

2. Do you think there should be separate continuing education for women (Women's Studies), and why?
3. What are some of the key issues in human liberation, including the liberation of women? How can you program for this?
4. What are some of the values for men, in women being liberated?
5. How can we prepare men for the dual-career family? How would you program for this new relationship?
6. What are the benefits of assertiveness training? Some of the potential pitfalls?
7. How can you build study groups around the interest groups described in the CONTINUING EDUCATION FOR WOMEN CONFERENCE described?
8. How can adult educators assist women in understanding the concept of "systems", such as the informal organization, and the unwritten rules of institutions?

Bibliography

Agin, A. A. and J. P. Prather. "Emerging Women: Implications for the Community College and the Business-Industrial Community." **Adult Leadership.** June 1977 (pages 299-300).

Anderson, G. Lester. **Trends in Education for the Professions.** ERIC/Higher Education Research Report No. 7. Washington, D.C.: American Association for Higher Education, 1973.

Astin, Helen S. **Some Action of Her Own.** Massachusetts: Lexington Books, 1976.

Axford, Roger W. **Adult Education: The Open Door.** Indiana, Pennsylvania: A. G. Halldin Publishing Company, 1969.

Bart, Pauline B. "Why Women See the Future Differently From Men." In **Learning for Tomorrow - The Role of the Future of Education.** New York: Random House, 1974 (pages 33-55).

Berry, Jane and Rosalind K. Loring. "Continuing Education For Women." In **Handbook of Adult Education,** edited by Robert M. Smith and others. New York: MacMillan Publishing Co., Inc., 1970 (pages 499-511).

Boston Women's Health Book Collective. Our Bodies, Ourselves: **A Book By and For Women,** 2nd edition. New York: Simon and Schuster, 1976.

Brownmiller, Susan. **Against Our Will: Men, Women and Rape.** New York: Simon and Schuster, 1975.

Brandenburg, Judith Berman. "The Needs of Women Returning to School," **Personnel and Guidance Journal,** Vol. 53, No. 1, 1974, 11-18.

Campbell, J. W. "Women Drop Back In; Educational Innovation in the Sixties", in **Academic Women on the Move,** ed. by A.S. Rossi and A. Calderwood. New York: Russell Sage Foundation, 1973.

Chesler, Phyllis. **Women & Madness.** New York: Avon Books, 1972.

Chesler, Phyllis and Emily Jane Goodman. **Women, Money & Power.** New York: William Morrow and Company, Inc., 1976.

Continuing Education for Women: Current Development. Women's Bureau, Employment Standards Administration, U.S. Department of Labor, 1974.

Durcholz, Pat and Janet O'Connor. "Research: Why Women Go Back to College", **Change,** Vol. 5, No. 10, 1973, 52 and 62.

Elshof, Annette Ten and Carol Konek. "Providing a Re-entry Bridge for Women: A Need-Centered Continuing Education Program," **Adult Leadership** (April 1977): 239-241.

Eyde, Lorraine. "Eliminating Barriers to Career Development of Women", **Personnel and Guidance Journal,** Vol. 49, No.1, 1970, 24 and 28.

Feldman, Saul D. **Escape from the Doll's House: Women in Graduate and Professional School Education.** New York: Mc-Graw-Hill, 1974.

Fitzpatrick, Blanche. **Women's Inferior Education - An Economic Analysis.** New York: Praeger Publishers, 1976.

Freeman, Jo, ed. **Women: A Feminist Perspective.** Palo Alto, California: Mayfield Publishing Company, 1975.

Friedan, Betty. **The Feminine Mystique.** New York: W. W. Norton & Company, Inc., 1963.

Gaillard, Claudia R. "CEW Programs on College Campuses, A Review of Research and Literature," **Lifelong Learning: The Adult Years.** January 1979, pp. 8-9

Goldman, Freda H. **A Turning to Take Next: Alternative Goals in the Education of Women.** Massachusetts: Center for the Study of Liberal Education for Adults, 1970.

Gornick, Vivian and Barbara K. Morgan, eds. **Woman in Sexist Society: Studies in Power and Powerlessness.** New York: Basic Books, Inc., 1971.

Greer, Germaine. **The Female Eunuch.** New York: McGraw-Hill, 1970.

Grimstad, Kirsten and Susan Rennie, eds. **The New Woman's Survival Sourcebook.** New York: Alfred A. Knopf, 1975.

Hansot, Elisabeth. "A 'second-chance' Program for Women", **Change,** Vol. 5. no. 2, 1973, 49 and 51.

Homemaker News. University of Arizona: Cooperative Extension, March, 1977.

Kahne, Hilda. "The Women in Professional Occupations: New

Complexities for Chosen Roles", **Journal of NAWDAC** (Summer 1976): (179-185).

Knowles, Malcolm S. The Modern Practice of Adult Education New York, Association Press, 1970.

Kreps, Juanita and R. John Leaper. "The Future of Working Women", **MS**. (March 1977): 56-57.

London, Jack. "The Continuing Education of Women: A Challenge for Our Society", **Adult Leadership**, Vol. 14, No. 10, 1966, 326-328 and 338-340.

Loring, Rosalind K., and others. Section on "Continuing Education for Women", **Adult Leadership**, Vol. 18, No. 1, 1969, 5-36.

Manis, Laura and Jane Mochizuki. "In the Field", **Personnel and Guidance Journal**, Vol. 50. No. 7, 1972, 594-599.

Millett, Kate. **Sexual Politics**. New York: Doubleday & Company, Inc., 1970.

Mitchell, Beverly A. **An Investigation Into Personality Factors of Administrators of Women's Centers**. Ph.D. Dissertation, (unpublished) Arizona State University, 1976.

Morgan, Robin, ed. **Sisterhood is Powerful: An Anthology of Writings from the Women's Liberation Movement**. New York: Random House, 1972.

Mulligan, Kathryn C. **A Question of Opportunity: Women and Continuing Education**. The National Advisory Council of Extension and Continuing Education. Washington, D.C.: U.S. Government Printing Office, 1973.

Oltman, R.M. **Campus 1970: Where Do Women Stand?** Washington D.C.: American Association of University Women, 1970.

Oppenheimer, Valerie K. **The Female Labor Force in the United States**. Berkeley: University of California, 1970.

Opportunities for Women in Higher Education: Their Current Participation, Prospects for the Future, and Recommendations for Action. The Carnegie Commission of Higher Education. New York: McGraw-Hill, 1973.

Osborn, Ruth Helm. "Developing New Horizons for Women", **Adult Leadership**, Vol. 19, No. 10, 1971, 326-328 and 350-351 and 360.

Robinson, Lora H. **Women's Studies: Courses and Programs for Higher Education**. ERIC/Higher Education, Research Report No. 1. Washington, D.C.: U.S. Government Printing Office, 1973.

Roehl, Janet E. **Women's Continuing Education**. (unpublished paper) Tempe, Arizona: Arizona State University, 1977.

Ross, Susan R. **The Rights of Women**. New York: Avon Books, 1973.

Stacey, Judith and others, eds. **And Jill Came Tumbling After: Sexism in American Education**. Dell Publishing Co., Inc.,

1974.

Tripp, Maggie, ed. **Woman in the Year 2000.** New York: Dell Publishing Co., Inc., 1974.

U.S. Department of Labor, Women's Bureau. **Continuing Education Programs and Services for Women.** Washington D.C.: Government Printing Office, 1971.

U.S. Department of Labor, Women's Bureau. **Continuing Education for Women: Current Developments.** Washington D.C.: Government Printing Office, 1974.

U.S. Department of Labor, Women's Bureau. **1975 Handbook on Women Workers.** Washington, D.C.. Government Printing Office, 1975.

Warren, Constance. **A New Design for Women's Education.** New York: Frederick A. Stokes Company, 1940.

Wilson, Thomasyne Lightfoote. **Toward Viable Directions in Postsecondary Education: Nontraditional/Unconventional Education Through A "Community-Family Context".** San Francisco, California: Sapphire Publishing Company, Inc., 1976.

Women's Centers: Where Are They? The Project on the Status and Education of Women. Association of American Colleges, 1975.

The Dual Career Family -- Bibliography*

Bailyn, Lotte. "Career and Family Orientations of Husbands and Wives in Relation to Marital Happiness." **Human Relations,** Vol. 23, No. 2.

Baldrige, Letitia. **Juggling: The Art of Balancing Marriage, Motherhood and Career.** New York, NY, The Viking Press, 1976.

Berger, Michael. **Dual-Career Couples: Job Seeking Strategies and Family Structure.** (Paper presented at the American Psychological Association Symposium, September 1975).

Bralove, Mary. "Working Partners: For Married Couples Two Careers Can Be Exercise in Frustration." **The Wall Street Journal,** May 13, 1975.

Bryson, Jeff et al. **Professional Pairs: Relative Career Values of Wives and Husbands.** (Paper presented at the meeting of the American Psychological Association, Chicago, IL, 1975).

Bryson, Rebecca, et al. **Professional Pairs: A Survey of Husband-Wife Psychologists.** (Paper presented at the meeting of the American Psychological Association, Chicago, IL, 1975).

"Can Dual Careers Work?" **New Directions for Women,** Autumn 1977.

Committee on the Status of Women in the Professions. **Careers and Couples: An Academic Question.** New York, NY, Modern Language Association, 1976.

"Company Couples' Flourish." **Business Week,** August 2, 1976.

Dexter, Ed. "Creative Living: Marriage Without Proximity." **Marriage, Divorce and Family Newsletter,** April 1977.

Douvan, Elizabeth. "Two Careers and One Family: Potential Pitfalls and Certain Complexity." **Papers in Women's Studies,** University of Michigan, October 1974.

Dual Careers: A Longitudinal Study of Labor Market Experience of Women. Manpower Research Monograph #2, Washington, DC, U.S. Department of Labor, 1970.

DuBrin, Andrew J. **The New Husbands and How to Become One.** Chicago, IL: Nelson - Hall, 1976.

Dullea, Georgia. "So They Moved, Because of Wife's Job." **New York Times,** April 2, 1977.

Epstein, Cynthia Fuchs. "Law Partners and Marital Partners: Strains and Solutions in the Dual-Career Family Enterprise." **Human Relations,** December 1971.

Feinberg, Samuel. "The Two-Career Couple -- Curbing Conflicts, Crises." **Women's Wear Daily,** March 4, 1977.

Fogarty, Michael P. and Rapoport, Rhona and Robert. **Sex, Career and Family.** Berkeley, CA, Sage Publications, 1971.

Gallese, Liz Roman. "Woman Managers Say Job Transfers Present a Growers Dilemma." **The Wall Street Journal,** May 4, 1978.

Hall, Francine S. and Douglas T. "Dual Careers: How Do Couples and Companies Cope With The Problems?" **Organizational Dynamics,** Spring, 1978.

Holmstrom, L. L. **The Two-Career Family.** Cambridge, MA, Schenkman, 1972.

Johnson, Colleen L. and Frank A. "Attitudes Toward Parenting in Dual-Career Families." **American Journal of Psychiatry.** April, 1977.

Kramer, Sydelle, Editor. **The Balancing Act: A Career and A Baby.** Chicago, IL. Chicago Press/Swallow Press, 1976.

Kron, Joan. "The Dual-Career Dilemma." **New York,** October 25, 1976.

Mortimer, Jeylan et al. **Husbands' Occupational Attributes as Constraints on Wives' Employment.** (Paper presented at the annual meeting of the American Sociological Association, 1976).

Otten, Alan L. "Two-Career Couples." **Harvard Business School Bulletin,** January/February 1977.

——————. "Two - Career Couples." **The Wall Street Journal,** July 29, 1976.

Papanek, H. "Men, Women, and Work: Reflections on the Two-Person Career." **American Journal of Sociology,** January 1973.

Poloma, Margaret M. and Garland, T. Neal. **The Dual Profession Family: Summary of Research.** Washington, DC, Business and Professional Women's Foundation, 1971.

Rapoport, Rhona and Robert. **Dual-Career Families.** Baltimore,

MD, Penguin Books, 1971.

Rosen, Benson et al. "Dual-Career Marital Adjustment: Potential Effects of Discriminatory Managerial Attitudes." **Journal Marriage and the Family,** August 1975.

Schoen, Elin. "Sevin Two-Career Couples." **New York,** October 25, 1976.

"Sensitivity Essential for 2-Career Marriage." **Guidepost,** October 6, 1977.

Wallston, Barbara et al. **I Will Follow Him: Myth, Reality or Forced Choice - Career Decision Making by the Dual Career Couple.** (Paper presented at the American Psychological Association Symposium, Chicago, IL, 1975).

—————————. **Dual Career Couples: Job Seeking Strategies and Family Structure.** (Paper presented at the American Psychological Association Symposium, Chicago, IL, 1975).

Wellbank, Harry L. et al. "Planning Job Progression for Effective Career Development and Human Resources Management." **Personnel.** March-April, 1978.

"When Couples Want Careers--and Children". Lucie Mouat, Christian Science Monitor, Apr. 2, 1979.

"When Career Couples Have Conflicts of Interest." **Business Week.** December 13, 1976.

*Thanks to Drs. Mark and Maxine Rossman, Center for Higher and Adult Education for this bibliography

1 Gaillard, Claudia R , "CEW Programs on College Campuses, A Review of the Research and Literature," **Lifelong Learning: The Adult Years.** January 1979, pp. 8-9.

2 Ibid

3 Survey of Women's Continuing Education, University of Wisconsin-Milwaukee.

Chapter VII:

WHY ADULT EDUCATION: TRAINING AND RE-TRAINING

Training through business and industry has been a part of adult education since the days of Benjamin Franklin. Billions of dollars are spent on helping workers, foremen, middle management, and executives to keep up-to-date with modern technology. With the knowledge explosion, plus changing jobs three or four times during a lifetime, re-training has become big business. Even corporations have bought up publishing companies and now are in the continuing education business. Hardly a major conglomerate does not have its "education division".

Many companies are now doing their own training and have established Centers, such as the General Motors Training Centers found throughout the United States. Some corporations have residential centers to update, and to train new staff, such as the IBM Residential Center, and the 3-M Training Center in Minneapolis, Minnesota. Even labor has its own training center, the George Meany Center for Labor Studies in Silver Spring, Maryland which offers programs in:

Advanced Labor Studies, Arbitration, Building Trades Business Agents, Civil Rights, Collective Bargaining, Critical Issues in State Government, Health and Safety, How to Improve Leadership Skills, International Affairs, Labor Law, New Staff Programs, Organizing, Public Relations, Psychology for Union Leaders, Washington Workshop, Women in the Labor Force, and Testing.[1]

One corporation describes its training services as providing for "maximum use of human resources." They will provide training "in-plant" and on the job. The variety of training skills offered includes:

Psychological Consulting to Management - to solve problems concerning staffing, productivity, morale, teamwork, turnover, interpersonal relations, managerial effectiveness, skill development, and communications. Our expert consultants can serve your organization's immediate and long-term needs.

Career Assessment and Development - to identify and cultivate personnel with leadership potential, as well as to pinpoint problems and provide needed insights and solutions. Our Individual Evaluations, Career Counseling, and Career Development Review Systems help you discover and handle the varied capabilities of your company's work force.

Interviewer Training - to prepare interviewers for recruitment, screening, selection, placement and supervision. The Selection, Campus, and Exit Interview Workshops can be tailored to the specific needs of any organization. Public workshops are offered throughout the U.S. and Canada each year. Client-sponsored on-site workshops are also available for coordination with your organization's own training procedures.

Skills Development - to help individuals cope with the ever-changing demands of the work world. Career Effectiveness and Retirement Planning Programs offer counseling services to help persons deal with the many new situations that they must continually face - both professionally and personally.

The American Society for Training and Development is one of the largest membership organizations working in the field of human resource development. In describing what ASTD is they state:

ASTD is a national professional society of some 12,000 persons responsible for the training and development of today's work force. These individuals design and administer training and management development programs in all types of business, industrial, educational, government and service organizations. ASTD members represent more than 4,000 different organizations. The mission of ASTD, as a non-profit organization operating within the business, governmental, educational and community service sectors of society, is to benefit the professional growth, competence and effectiveness of its members. This mission will be accomplished by providing educational programs and services, disseminating information and knowledge and encouraging research and the free exchange of ideas that are related and pertinent to the optimum utilization and development of human resources.

ASTD was organized in 1944 and is recognized for its contributions to the advancement of the profession for the past quarter of a century. ASTD has grown steadily, and is recognized internationally.[2]

See Chart A

Training may be found in large federal, state, and municipal organizations too. The function may be found under many different terms: human resource development, manpower training, personnel training, and manpower resource development, to name but a few. The purpose of the training, often called continuing education, is to make the worker more productive, effective, and satisfied on the job.

CHART A

MONIES SPENT FOR ADULT AND CONTINUING EDUCATION
BY BUSINESS AND INDUSTRY

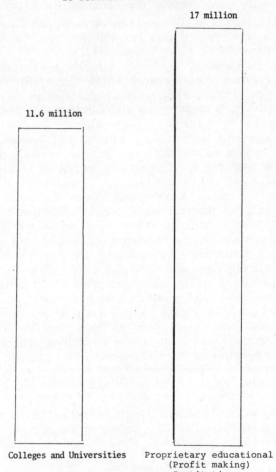

17 million

11.6 million

Colleges and Universities   Proprietary educational
                             (Profit making)
                             Institutions

4 Billion spent by Business for Training,

Source: Training Magazine (A.S.T.D.), February 1979, p. 8

In 1929-30, total expenditures for education were $3.2
billion, and by 1970 $77.60 billion was spent. (Digest of
Educational Statistics, 1971, National Center for Educational
Statistics, Table 25, p. 21.)

JOB OPTIONS EXPAND AND CHANGE

The reason for all this interest in training is that, in addition to an increasing number of workers, the job options for workers today are expanding and changing.

In addition, there are thousands of occupations - the newest **Dictionary of Occupational Titles** lists 20,000 separate titles - and a variety of education and training programs from which to choose.

In 1985, approximately 104.3 million persons will be in the civilian labor force. This is a 19-percent increase over the 1976 level of 87.5 million. (See chart below)[3]

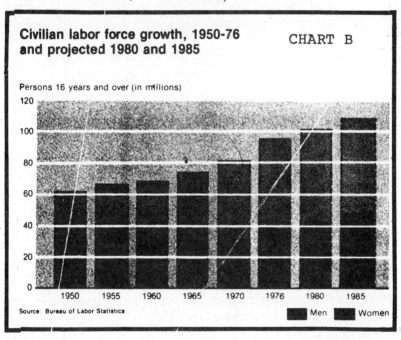

Civilian labor force growth, 1950-76 and projected 1980 and 1985   CHART B

Persons 16 years and over (in millions)

Source: Bureau of Labor Statistics   ■ Men ■ Women

Based on national employment statistics and trends, we are confident that the jobs are and will be available for trainees and graduates. The U.S. Department of Labor released statistics in 1978 which show that the amount of technical and vocational jobs in the United States will increase significantly - in some fields, double - by 1985. According to the statistics, many more occupational jobs will be available than the amount of workers who will be trained to fill them. See Chart C

CHART C

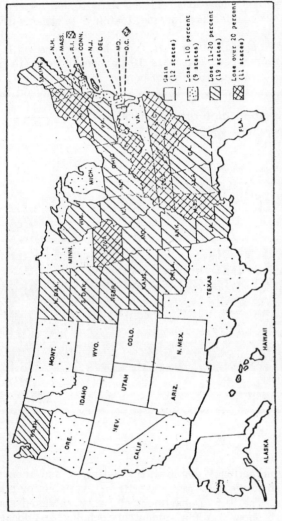

PROJECTED CHANGES IN THE 18-YEAR-OLD POPULATION: 1975-85

Gain (12 states)

Lose 1-10 percent (9 states)

Lose 11-20 percent (19 states)

Lose over 20 percent (11 states)

Note: These are projected changes in the number of 18-year-olds in the 1985 population compared with the 1975 figure. At the national level, there are expected to be 12 percent fewer 18-year-olds in 1985 than in 1975.

Source: Policy Analysis Service, American Council on Education based on U.S. Bureau of the Census, Current Population Reports, P-25 Series.

60

Jobs. Population growth necessitates growth in services, in industry, and in jobs. Homes must be built; automobiles and industrial vehicles must be maintained; we'll need cooks and chefs for our restaurants and nurses and medical technicians for our hospitals. The list is endless. See Charts D and E

Jobs . . .   CHART D

Nation-wide jobs in 10 special career areas* are expected to double by 1985.

CAREERS	JOB INCREASES
Air conditioning, refrigeration, heating mechanics	87,500
Computer service technicians	25,000
Dental hygenists	13,500
Emergency medical technicians	143,500
Health service administrators	80,000
Marketing researchers	12,500
Sewer plant operators	50,000

*Career programs not offered but rated in the top 10 include industrial-machinery mechanics, insulation construction, and occupational therapy.

Figures quoted from 1978 U. S. Department of Labor job statistics.

. . . And more jobs .

Job openings in 25 career areas* are expected to reach new national peaks by 1985.

CAREERS	CHART F	JOBS by 1985
Secretaries, stenographers		875,000
Truckdrivers		400,000
Cooks and chefs		266,250
Registered nurses		240,000
Machinists		171,900
Welders		165,000
Teachers' aides		160,000
Carpenters		151,500
Heavy equipment operators		150,000
Engineers		146,250
Retail sales workers		135,000
Police officers		125,000
Real estate agents		112,500
Construction workers		107,250
Auto mechanics		105,000
Bookkeepers		85,000
Computer operators		84,750
Drafters		80,000

*Career programs not offered but rated among the top 25 include accounting, law, labor-relations administration, social work, cosmetology, bank management, and insurance brokerage.

Figures quoted from 1978 U. S. Department of Labor job statistics.

It is important for adult educators to know the directions of the job market, so that we can program to help people become qualified for jobs. To know "Where People Work" can be of use in. planning. In analyzing the industrial profile, it is customary to divide our economy into nine industrial categories as illustrated in the accompanying chart.

See Chart F

The number of persons in each of the occupational groups are described in millions in the following chart provided by the U.S. Bureau of Labor Statistics.

See Chart G

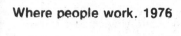

Where people work. 1976

CHART F

Wage and salary workers except agriculture, which includes self-employed and unpaid family workers

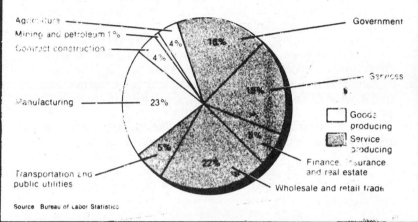

- Agriculture
- Mining and petroleum 1%
- Contract construction
- Government
- Services

Manufacturing — 23%

4% 4% 16%

Transportation and public utilities — 5%

22%

Finance, insurance and real estate

Wholesale and retail trade

Goods producing

Service producing

Source Bureau of Labor Statistics

Employment in major occupational groups

CHART G

Workers, 1976 (in millions)

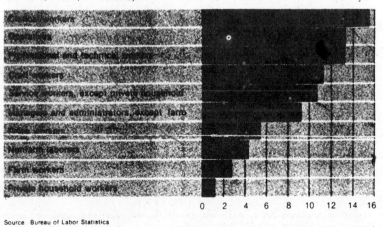

- Clerical workers
- Operatives
- Professional and technical workers
- Craft workers
- Service workers, except private household
- Managers and administrators, except farm
- Sales workers
- Nonfarm laborers
- Farm workers
- Private household workers

0 2 4 6 8 10 12 14 16

Source Bureau of Labor Statistics

63

Service-producing industries have expanded rapidly since the World War II period. Migration from rural to urban areas plus the expanded need for more local and state government workers, plus the increased living standard and income of the U.S. population have increased demands for additional health and educational services.

A decrease in jobs will be at the levels requiring little education; the increase in jobs in the United States will be in the scientific and engineering fields, space technology, chemicals, and communications. Mobility of population increases the need for more adequate vocational training, since persons tend to go where there are jobs, or opportunities to train for jobs. The trend to urbanization brings large populations of unskilled and unemployed persons to cities in need of a chance to learn new skills and trades.

It is significant that the white-collar workers have steadily grown in importance, until they now represent more than half of the total in the work force. The white-collar workers are those in the managerial, professional, technical, clerical, and sales jobs. Blue-collar workers are included in the craft, laborer, and operative jobs.

The trend toward more white-collar workers making up the labor is seen as continuing through 1985, and possibly beyond.

The number of professional and technical workers, which demands a high degree of training and skill, will continue to grow. Scientists, engineers, teachers, medical practitioners, entertainers, pilots, and accountants are included in this category. The Bureau of Labor Statistics predicts that this group will expand by about 18 percent from 13.3 million to 15.8 million workers, between 1976 and 1985, important for educational planning. Competition will be high among teachers, airline pilots, oceanographers, and artists and entertainers. The number of self-employed managers will decline, as business is increasingly swallowed up by large corporations and multinational companies. Salaried managers will still have a high demand for their services as quick service groceries and fast-food restaurants grow.

This decline in agricultural workers and rise in the number in our country working in service industries is shown in the accompanying charts, provided by the Bureau of Labor Statistics.

See Charts H and I

Every year new occupational groups are being added. Our vocational and adult schools will have to gear up for the change.

See Chart J

Some occupations will be phased out, or reduced, while new ones are being added. Who could have predicted that the computer

64

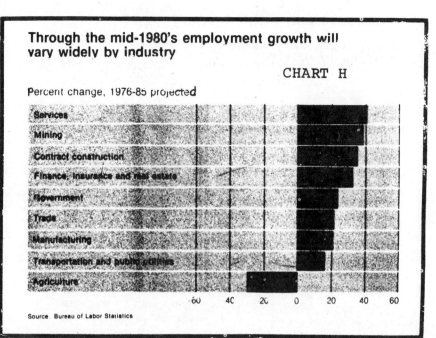

Through the mid-1980's employment growth will vary widely by industry

CHART H

Percent change, 1976-85 projected

Services
Mining
Contract construction
Finance, insurance and real estate
Government
Trade
Manufacturing
Transportation and public utilities
Agriculture

-60   40   20   0   20   40   60

Source: Bureau of Labor Statistics

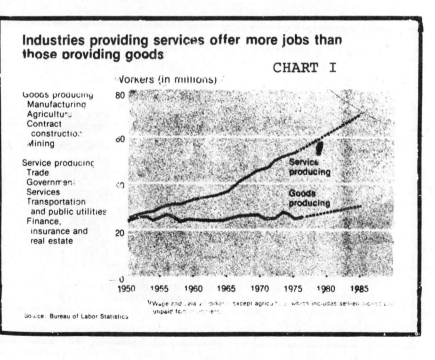

Industries providing services offer more jobs than those providing goods

CHART I

Workers (in millions)

Goods producing
Manufacturing
Agriculture
Contract
 construction
Mining

Service producing
Trade
Government
Services
Transportation
 and public utilities
Finance,
 insurance and
 real estate

Service
producing

Goods
producing

80
60
40
20
0
1950   1955   1960   1965   1970   1975   1980   1985

Wage and salary workers except agriculture which includes self-employed and unpaid family workers.

Source: Bureau of Labor Statistics

65

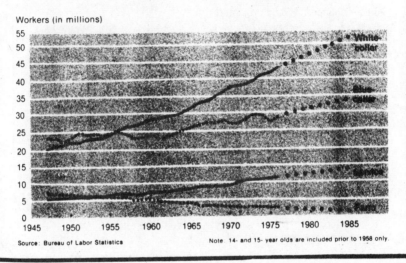

The shift toward white-collar occupations will continue through 1985

CHART J

Workers (in millions)

White-collar

Blue-collar

Service

Farm

1945 1950 1955 1960 1965 1970 1975 1980 1985

Source: Bureau of Labor Statistics

Note: 14- and 15- year olds are included prior to 1958 only.

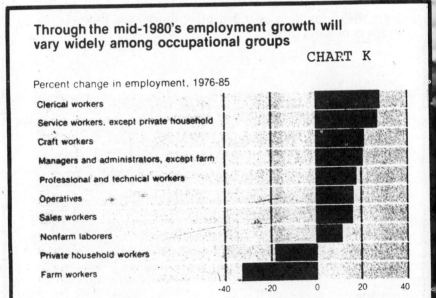

Through the mid-1980's employment growth will vary widely among occupational groups

CHART K

Percent change in employment, 1976-85

Clerical workers

Service workers, except private household

Craft workers

Managers and administrators, except farm

Professional and technical workers

Operatives

Sales workers

Nonfarm laborers

Private household workers

Farm workers

-40   -20   0   20   40

Source: Bureau of Labor Statistics

66

industry would become one of the largest in the world? Who could have predicted that the energy crunch would produce new jobs, and new technology? See Chart K

Adult Education can provide vocational training and retraining as the number of millions of workers shift from industries providing goods to those providing services.

THE COMPREHENSIVE EMPLOYMENT AND TRAINING ACT: CETA

Our technologically unemployed demand retraining. A recognition of the need for retraining of persons displaced by automation and resulting technological unemployment is reflected in the Area Redevelopment Act of 1961 and the Manpower Development and Training Act of 1962 which continues with amendments. ARA retraining is restricted to areas of chronic labor surplus. Sixteen weeks is the maximum period stipulated for courses. However, the MDTA (Manpower Development and Training Act) can extend courses up to 52 weeks. There has been a determined effort to train and retrain welfare recipients.

Reports show between 70 and 75 percent of the trainees in the programs have been placed in jobs following such courses, most in occupations related to their training. However, it was found that, taken as a whole, trainees in the federal programs are better educated than the unemployed workers in the labor force.

The CETA program is operated through Skill Centers, and often the County Board of Supervisors has the funding power. The author has observed many CETA training programs including welding, secretarial skills, adult basic education, meat cutting, hospitality skills, and nursing aide programs. Some CETA programs are tied to alternatives to incarceration, working with ex-offenders from prisons.

In observing some of the CETA programs the author found the short-term training program relieving unemployment, and making productive workers out of men and women with no saleable skills. The community colleges also have had a major role in implementing the services of the CETA program, and no doubt will play an even larger role in the future, as seen in the following announcement from the national office of the American Association of Community and Junior Colleges.

TRAINING OF THE HANDICAPPED

Although Vocational Rehabilitation has been working on a one-to-one basis with handicapped for many years, it was not until 1976, through the leadership of William Langner, a member of

Federal Report

THE 1978 CETA ACT - A GREAT OPPORTUNITY

Near the end of the 95th Congress new CETA legislation was enacted. This legislation makes CETA a permanent $10 billion per year program for the next four years. It has great potential and opportunity for our institutions to give service to their communities.

In early January, I sent a 54-page booklet we had put together on the new CETA law to each of our institutional representatives. In it we covered the following:

1 - An introduction to CETA.
2 - Critical excerpts from the legislation.
3 - A six-page digest of the bill.
4 - A list of 22 possible services under CETA.
5 - Steps in applying for CETA funds.
6 - A checklist for a Prime Sponsor - Education Agreement.
7 - The contracting process and a model contract.
8 - The allocation of funds, for each prime sponsor, for Titles II and VI.

(We have a few extra copies of this booklet. If you could use it at your college, drop me a note.)

I would like to point out a few very important items for all community colleges.

1 - Community and junior colleges and technical institutes are included in ALL parts of the law as directly eligible, except in subpart 3, of Part A, of Title IV.

2 - There are funds for education and training spread throughout the bill and not merely in the Youth Programs.

3 - Title II, Part D, for example, calls for a $3 billion appropriation for this year. The bill requires that 10 percent of this (or $300 million) must be used for training! It raises this to 15 percent in FY'80, 20 percent in FY'81 and 22 percent in FY'82. Thus, if the appropriation remained at three billion in FY'82, $660 million would be mandated for training - from this one part of the bill.

During the debate on the bill we monitored the development step by step in the House and Senate. One night it was pointed out in the House debate that only five percent of the people from CETA public service jobs moved to unsubsidized jobs in the private sector, while 50 percent moved from training to unsubsidized jobs in the private sector. It was moved, and passed, to transfer $500 million from Public Service Employment to training in the bill!

With the "crunch" on local, state, and, to some extent, federal funds, here is a very substantial program for possible use in your institution. The decisions are made in your area, either by the prime sponsor or in the Governor's office. Our member institutions that have been active in working one or both of these sources, in some cases, have received millions of dollars (in some small colleges) to assist in this important national effort to reduce structural and countercyclical unemployment. •

John E. Tirrell

Community and Junior College Journal
March, 1979
1 DuPont Circle, Washington, D.C.
(20036)

the Board of the National Advisory Council on Adult Education and a handicapped person himself, did the Council go on record with the following resolution:

A review of census data indicates that **handicapped** adults in the United States have not achieved the educational competencies needed for economic success in today's society.

Therefore, the Council recommends that increased awareness and attention by the Congress and the Executive Branch be given to the educational needs of the **handicapped** adult to ensure opportunities for greater self-sufficiency and productivity.

At the time of the civil rights movement and the declaration of the Supreme Court on equal rights for education, handicapping conditions came into focus. Approximately ten years later, in 1963, with the onset of Title I, National Defense Education Act, laws and appropriations were made by Congress. Through the Adult Education Act ABE and GED are ongoing educational support programs serving the needs of the handicapped. At least 20% of appropriations set aside for adult education are specifically designated for institutionalized handicapped.

TRAINING AND RETRAINING
SUMMARY

We learned that **Dictionary of Occupational Titles** lists more than 20,000 separate titles giving the worker today a variety of options for new jobs, retraining, or upgrading a worker's position. More women are entering the labor force, with a majority of jobs now held by women in our country. By 1985 it is expected the nation will have 12% **fewer** 18 year olds than in 1975, with profound implications for adult education.

Business and industry is spending billions of dollars for training and retraining. The training function appears under ·many names, such as human resource development, manpower training, personnel training, and foreman training. Both large corporations, and labor unions are in the training function, and examples are given of each. Proprietary educational institutions are more prominent in continuing education for business and industry than are colleges and universities. The American Society for Training and Development, working in the human resource development field is described, representing members from hundreds of organizations.

Approximately $4 Billion is spent by business for training and retraining.

It was noted that service-producing industries are surpassing good-producing industries in terms of the number of workers utilized, and that the gap appears widening. Agriculture is projected to lose workers while Health and educational services are growing in demand, with an expanded need for trained local and state government workers. The increased living standard plus the improved income of workers has brought these demands.

The impact of the Comprehensive Employment and Training Act was discussed, with a realization that the Labor Department is becoming one of the largest purveyors of adult education programs in our national life. The benefits of CETA programs for ex-offenders health aides, metal and secretarial skilled workers can not be overestimated. The question is whether there will be enough jobs to go around.

The training of the handicapped will take on a major emphasis in the years ahead due to current legislation, with ABE mandated to set aside 20% of appropriations designated for the institutional handicapped. Vocational Rehabilitation will continue to serve on a one to one basis.

Predictions are that training and retraining will continue to grow, and be one of the growth areas of adult education.

QUESTIONS:

1. What are some of the major agencies involved in training and retraining? What are their clientele?
2. What is the future for the unskilled worker? The semi-skilled worker? For the farm worker? For the technically trained?
3. What are some of the kind of training programs provided for management?
4. What provisions are being made for educating the handicapped adult? Name some specific programs.
5. What implications are there in training and retraining for agencies of adult education?
6. Do you make a distinction between training and education? In what ways do you feel there is a difference?
7. What are some practical ways that the adult can avoid intellectual and job obsolescence?
8. What are some of the implications of shifts from blue-collar workers to white-collar workers, for adult education?
9. What federal government agencies would you turn to for information on occupational shifts, and current information regarding the labor force? How would you use this information in programming?

Bibliography

Adult Training as an Instrument of Active Manpower Policy
(Paris: OECD, 1972).

Becker, Gary Human Capital (New York: Columbia University
Press, 1964)

Cross, Patricia Beyond the Open Door (San Francisco: Jossey-
Bass, 1971), p. 164.

Day Care Services: Industry's Involvement (U.S. Department of
Labor, Employment Standards Administration. Women's Bureau,
March 1974).

Eckaus, Richard's "Economic Criteria for Education and Training," Review of Economics and Statistics, May 1964. For a
more complex treatment of the data coming from the Employment Services Dictionary of Occupational Titles, see Ivar Berg's
Education and Jobs, The Great Training Robbery (New York:
Praeger, 1970).

Elbing, A.O. Gadon, Herman and Gordon, John "Flexible Working
Hours; Its about time," Harvard Business Review, January -
February 1974; Wheeler, Kenneth E. "The Four-Day Week,"
AMA Research Report (New York: 1972): Allenspach H. "Work-
ing Hours Per Week and Day-Flexible Working Time" (Paris:
OECD, 1973): Hedges, Janice "New Patterns for Working Time,"
Monthly Labor Review, February 1973: Martin, Neil "Can the
Four-Day Week Work?" Dun's Presidents' Panel. Dun's July
1971.

Goldstein, Harold and Delaney, William "The Need for Job Related Training Throughout Adult Life." The National Manpower
Institute, 1974.

Job Satisfaction: Is There A Trend? (U.S. Department of Labor,
Manpower Research Monograph No. 30, 1974), p. 6.

Levitan, Sar A. Johnston, William B. And Taggart, Robert Still
A Dream: The Changing Status of Blacks Since 1960 (Cambridge,
Mass.; Harvard University Press, 1975), p. v.

Levintan, Sar A. And Taggart, Robert "Employment and Earning
Inadequacy: A Measure of Worker Welfare," Monthly Labor
Review, October 1973, p. 19.

Major Collective Bargaining Agreements: Training and Retraining Provisions (Bureau of Labor Statistics, Bullitin No. 1425-7,
1969), p. 8.

Work In America: Report of a Special Task Force to the Secretary
of the Health, Education, and Welfare, prepared under the Auspices
of the W. E. Upjohn Institute for Employment Research (Cambridge, Mass.: The MIT press, 1973). The Task Force was
Chaired by James O'Toole. For more detail, see the recent book
"Work and the Quality of Life. Resource Papers for Work in
America", edited by James O'Toole.

Neary, James H. "The BLS Pilot Survey of Training in Industry," Monthly Labor Review, February 1974, p. 26.

Recurrent Education: A Strategy for Lifelong Learning (Paris: Centre for Educational Research and Innovation (CERI) of the Organization for Economic Co-operation and Development, 1973), p. 18. Recurrent education experience in Europe see: Herbert Striner, Continuing Education as a National Capital Investment (The W. E. Upjohn Institution for Employment Research, March 1972): Rudolph, et al., Recurrent Education in the Federal Republic of Germany (Paris: CERI of OECD: Re-training of Adults (1969), draft reports for OECD: Retraining of Adults in Sweden, 1968; Labour and Automation-Manpower Adjustment Programmers; I-France.

Sheppard, Harold L. and Herrick, Neal Q. **Where Have All the Robots Gone?** Prepared under the auspices of the Upjohn Institute for Employment Research (New York; The Free Press, 1972).

Shimberg, Benjamin Esser, Barbara and Kruger, Daniel H. **Occupational Licensing: Practices and Policies,** A Report of the Educational Testing Service (Washington, D.C.: Public Affairs Press, 1972).

U.S. Civil Service Commission, **Employee Training in Federal Service**, FY 1971 (Washington D.C.: U.S. Government Printing Office, 1972), p. 2

Why Women Work (U.S. Department of Labor, Employment Standard Administration, Women's Bureau, Bulletin 296).

Wirtz, Willard, **The Boundless Resource,** (A Prospectus for an Education/Work Policy) New Republic Book Co., Washington, D.C. 1975.

WOW/Careers for Peers (Washington D.C.; Washington Opportunities for Women).

1 George Meany Center for Labor Studies, Inc. 10000 New Hampshire Ave. Silver Spring, Maryland, (20903)

2 Who's Who in Training and Development, 1977, p. 12. American Society for Training and Development, Inc. P.O. Box 5307, 6414 Odana Road, Madison, Wis. 53705.

3 OCCUPATIONAL OUTLOOK HANDBOOK, EIC, 1978-79 Edition, U.S. Dept. of Labor Bureau of Labor Statistics, Bulletin 1955, "Tomorrow's Jobs" pp. 19-27.

Chapter VIII:

AGING

Grow old along with me!
The best is yet to be,
The last of life, for which the first was made;
Our times are in His hand
Who saith, "A whole I planned,
Youth shows but half; Trust God, see all,
nor be afraid."

Robert Browning

AN AGING POPULATION

It is projected that in the year 2030, 17% of our population, 6% more than the present, will be 65 years of age or older. In one day, says Dr. George Maddox, one of the nation's experts on Aging and Director of the Center for the Study of Aging and Human Development at Duke University, 4,000 people reach age 65, while 3,000 people over age 65 die.[1] Therefore, we are getting 1,000 older people a day. We are becoming a nation of older people, as shown in the chart below.

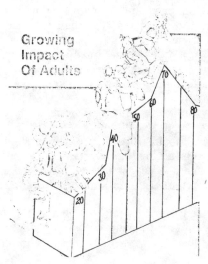

Growing
Impact
Of Adults

More of Them

As children and youths increase little in numbers

		People under age 21
1970	80.8 mil.	40% of population
1978	76.9 mil.	35% of population
1990 (est.)	78.6 mil.	32% of population

Adults will make up a bigger share of U.S. people—

Young Adults		21 to 39 years
1970	50 mil.	24% of population
1978	63.1 mil.	28% of population
1990 (est.)	74.5 mil.	30% of population

The Middle Aged		40 to 64 years
1970	54 mil.	26% of population
1978	55 mil.	25% of population
1990 (est.)	63 mil.	26% of population

The Elderly		65 years and over
1970	20.1 mil.	10% of population
1978	23.7 mil.	11% of population
1990 (est.)	28.9 mil.	12% of population

Source: U.S. Dept. of Commerce

Dr. James Birren, Director of the Andrus Gerontology Center, University of Southern California, reminds us that, of all the technically developed countries in the world, the United States has the largest sex gap in life expectancy. America is relatively favorable to life expectancy of women and very unfavorable to men, showing nearly eight years' life difference at birth between males and females. This is in comparison to some countries where it is as small as one and one-half to two years. [2]

We are told that **one-sixth** of the population that is old is in poverty. By 1980 a million persons over 65 will be in nursing homes, at a cost of more than $8 billion. In addition to the 5% of the population in nursing homes at least another 5% will be immobilized at home.'' [3]

WILL WE LIVE LONGER??
RESEARCH ON AGING

Thursday, April 26, 1979 State Press Page 11
Scientists explore ways of extending life span

TUCSON (AP) - Some of the projects sound like science fiction, but scientists working on the human aging process say they are seeking ways to lengthen life expectancy and prevent the maladies of old age.

The **Tucson Citizen** reported Wednesday that among the projects disclosed at a meeting here last week of scientists and insurance company officials from around the country were:

- A system to stifle the aging process by finding and manipulating what apparently is a control center in the brain that eventually allows the body's cells and immune system to wear out.

- A **"smart pill"** that can help increase a person's short-term memory capabilities.

- An artificial heart weighing less than two pounds and powered by batteries strapped around the waist.

- An after dinner drink that would keep the body from absorbing the harmbul ingredients of rich and fatty foods.

The meeting was sponsored by the Institute for Higher Studies and Dr. Alex Comfort, a specialist on aging, was among the participants. Comfort said science eventually will go beyond the idea of an aging process and get to the point of controlling life span.

Another scientist, Dr. Leonard Hayflick of the Bruce Lyon Memorial Research Laboratory in San Francisco, said he thinks science eventually will leave people with little or no choice in the cause of death.

Hayflick, a cell biologist known for discovering the life span of cells, said he is working to find out what limits there are on the life span of cells. He said he thinks the answer is in genetics and the nucleus of cells.

There is a kind of clock mechanism in cells with a genetic message for aging that has a limited amount of information and eventually it wears out, Hayflick said. Ironically, he said, the answer may lie with cancer cells, which do not die but continue multiplying.

Some of the other anti-aging projects in the works are being handled through the Glenn Foundation, a research organization headed by Paul Glenn of Scottsdale.

Glenn said his foundation is improving the concept of an artificial or mechanical heart to replace the human heart when it wears out or will not work any longer.

"If your marbles are beginning to fade, choline can help for short-term memory loss," said Glenn, who added that he takes a gram of choline each day.

Myths About Senior Citizens

Most people who think about a senior citizen think about a myth.

Fred Lengfeld, Chairperson of the University of Wisconsin's Extension Program on Aging, reports that studies he did turned up repeated popular myths about old people. For instance, younger people tend to think their lives and interests will change in later life--he found they don't.

Lengfeld is himself in the sixties, and likes to ask people if they believe persons over sixty-five: (true or false?)

1) often feel physically miserable?
2) have more auto accidents?
3) are often bored, isolated and lonely?
4) are more religious?

Lengfeld found that answers to all of the questions are false.

Here listed are some of Lengfeld's examples of Myths and realities, which explode commonly-held myths about the nation's more than 22 million persons aged 65 or older:

--Besides vision and hearing, touch is the other of the five senses which most often diminishes as a person ages.

--Only 15 percent of the elderly live below federal poverty levels.

--Physical strength often declines in old age, but many authorities believe that stems primarily from reduced exercise.

--Only four and eight-tenths percent of the nation's aged live in long-stay institutions such as nursing homes.

--Older people may take longer to learn something new, but given adequate time they learn it at least as well as the young.

--Twelve percent of the elderly hold paying jobs. Nineteen percent are involved in volunteer work.

--Older workers are more dependable and have fewer accidents.

Lengfeld relates a favorite story about attending a recent senior citizens' group dance where an elderly woman dropped dead of a heart attack in the midst of a vigorous polka.

Instead of widespread horror, he says, most of the elderly dancers simply nodded to each other, saying, "Wasn't that a nice way for her to go?" The anecdote, Lengfeld says, sums up a lot of what it means to be old. As he puts it: "Death is very common and it's just part of the performance. It's indicative, again, of how tough old people really are."

In another study Lengfeld found that undergraduates' favorite activities are things like horseback riding, sailing or basketball. But, when listing what leisure activities they actually pursued most often, they recorded napping, walking, eating, conversation, in that order. In a similar survey among the elderly, Lengfeld found the senior citizens' most common leisure activities were napping, walking, eating, and conversation, in that order.[4]

The stereotype of the older adult is also exploded by the Power Riders of Sun City, Arizona. The club has been in existence for more than 15 years and is a group of 38 "retirees" who ride motorcycles - not mopeds. Members of the Power Riders range from 55 to 79 years in age and have been riding anywhere from six to 64 years. The club is not restricted to men either. A number of the women ride along with their husbands, although none of them ride their own bikes. That was not always the case. Mrs. Herzog points out that when the club was organized, the first president was a woman, Celeste Spurlock, who "rode her own machine."[5]

The Power Riders have a sense of humor, too. Their insignia, which is emblazoned on shoulder patches, shows a man doing wheelies on a motorcycle with his long white beard flowing behind him in the breeze.

The aging person has much to teach us, both in the process of maturing, and in developing a philosophy for lifelong learning.

HOW TO STAY YOUNG

"Youth is not a time of life. It is a state of mind. Nobody grows old by merely living a number of years. People grow old by deserting their ideals. Years wrinkle the skin, but to give

76

up enthusiasm wrinkles the soul. Worry, doubt, self-distrust, fear and despair - these are the long, long years that bow the head and turn the growing spirit back to dust. Whether seventy or sixteen, there is, in every being's heart the love of wonder, the sweet amazement at the stars and the starlike things and thoughts, the unfailing childlike appetite for what is next, and the joy and the game of life. You are as young as your faith, as old as your doubt; as young as your self-confidence, as old as your fear; as young as your hope, as old as your despair." [6]

AGING AND IMPLICATIONS FOR ADULT EDUCATION

The impact of the growing aging population in our country is only beginning to be felt. Senior Citizen Centers, Nutrition Centers for the Elderly, programs in the Community Colleges and special programs conducted for professionals and para-professionals by Area Commissions on Aging are growing yearly.

In many colleges and universities a program has been initiated where persons carrying "retiree" cards are admitted to classes without fee. Through the "Sixty-Plus" operation provided by the community colleges, senior citizens identify with their local educational institutions, instead of fighting the tax levied for the college. They feel they are a part of it, that it is "their college". As Representative Claude Pepper of Florida, Chairman of the House Special Committee on Aging, has noted: "In terms of formal schooling, older people are the most poorly educated segment of the population. Studies reveal, however, that older persons are capable of an educational response far greater than that currently achieved by existing opportunities." [7]

With a tax-conscious public, it may be wise for colleges and universities to consider the utilization of the consortium, the cooperative efforts of a number of institutions working together for a common goal. A pattern for the wise utilization of human and financial resources has been established by the three universities in Arizona. This Consortium on Aging sponsors an Elderhostel program and research activities along with the development of curricula in geriatrics and subsequent teaching. The purpose is the cross-fertilization of ideas, with some circuit riding faculty members, serving a number of the universities, instead of only one. There is an opportunity for students to move from one university to another to enrich their program in learning to work effectively with the elderly. The consortium could have a constructive impact on the health and health maintenance of the older adult in the state. More information on the Consortium is provided in the goals and history described below.

A SAMPLE LIST OF ONE UNIVERSITY'S

MULTIDISCIPLINARY OFFERINGS IN GERONTOLOGY FOR FALL, 1979

Course Pfx No.	Course Title	Sem Hrs.	Meeting Time	Days	Bldg & Room	Instructor
CED691	S:Counseling Problems in Adult Development		1:40-4:30	M	EDB407	Dr. Robert A. Heimann
AED525	Characteristics of Adults as Learners (NOTE: One unit of this course will deal with aging.)	3↓	6:40-9:30	M	Farmer 308	Morris Okun
FON449	Geriatric Nutrition	3	6:40-9:30	Th	HEC224	Kathy Lewis
REC540	Recreation Services for the Aged	3	4:40-7:30	Th	PE East Rm 121	new staff
SOG591	Cross Cultural Aspects of Aging	2	5:30-7:40	M	TBA	G. Hall
SWG591	Social Work with the Aging	3	TBA	TBA	TBA	B. Albert
SOC498	PS:Overview of Aging	3	6:40-9:30	W	TBA	D.A. Sullivan
NUR494	Multidisciplinary Overview on Aging	3	6:40-9:30	W	TBA	B. Albert
SW 498	Multidisciplinary Overview on Aging	3	6:40-9:30	W	TBA	B. Albert
COM479	Communication and Aging	3	6:40-	W	STA315	B. Arnold
COM494	Communication and Aging	3	Correspondence Course			B.Arnold

Mr. Haid of Registrar's Office has been very helpful in getting these courses
listed as a special group toward the front of the Fall   class schedule.
(He also said he got the best response from our Interdisciplinary group!)

EDUCATION - UNIVERSITY CONSORTIUM ON AGING
Short-term Goals (two years)
1. Inventory and document current activities in age-related teaching, research and public service, learning where there might be either duplications or gaps in services.
2. Facilitate opportunities for students and faculty members to move from one to another of the three state universities for teaching and research activity.
3. Organize training programs for professionals and para-professionals in Area Agencies on Aging, hospitals, nursing homes, etc., to facilitate their increased ability to serve the aging population.
4. Encourage public service activities among faculty, and strengthen collaborative relationships between faculty and others concerned with programs for the aging.

5. Strengthen geriatric faculty and training in the University of Arizona College of Medicine.

Long-range Goals (four years)

1. Develop such a strong Department of Geriatrics in the University of Arizona College of Medicine that it will merit national prestige.
2. Develop undergraduate and graduate curricula in gerontology which will include units in all three state-supported universities, each school having its own areas of special expertise.
3. Open the doors of all three universities to senior citizens, without fee, on a space-available basis.
4. Provide, through the Cooperative Extension Service of the University of Arizona, programs in all fourteen counties designed to serve the state's elderly population on a par with services offered currently to the state's youth, homemakers, farmers, and ranchers.
5. Inventory information about needs and problems of Arizona's elderly and plan research and public service programs to meet those needs.
6. Bring national leaders in gerontology and geriatrics to Arizona's campuses for seminars and conferences, or in conjunction with other gatherings.

Establishment of the Consortium

The primary recommendation of the Governor's Task Force on Retirement and Aging in 1976 for the field of education was the development of a consortium in gerontology by the three state universities, the University of Arizona, Northern Arizona University and Arizona State University. The establishment of the Arizona Consortium on Aging was made possible in the fall of 1977 by the diversion of $40,000 of Title IV-A training funds under the Older Americans Act from the state's Area Agencies on Aging. The consortium was formally accepted by the State Board of Regents in January 1978.[8]

RETIREMENT AND AGING

"I am convinced that health actually improves after retirement in the majority of cases," stated Dr. Linda K. George, a senior Fellow in the Center for the Study of Aging and Human Development at the Duke University Medical Center. The years past 60 are divided into not one, but "two generations" claims Dr. George. She says you would never consider lumping together a 15 year and a 30-year-old. "Yet we tend to generalize that everyone over age 60 is the same." [9] This is just not true. We become more "individual" after age 60 this author finds.

Says Linda George . . . "I'm not sure that there is a very

79

attractive term for the division of the ages. But some authorities label those from 65 to 75 as the young-old, and those 76 and older, the old-old." She says that one way to categorize is by the physical and personal circumstances. The old-old are usually in poor health, they are predominently widowed and they are pretty straight-forward in identifying themselves. Says Dr. George, "People at the age of 80 start thinking of themselves as old; they may even exaggerate their age."[10]

There is some evidence that women have a more difficult time with retirement because, for the most part, they begin working in their later years. This means they may be more dependent on the income. And they have put in a relatively shorter period of work. They have not reached the saturation point with work as has a man who's been on the job 20 to 30 years. Apparently, more men than women experience severe stress with the loss of a mate, though men more frequently remarry.

Senior citizen centers are growing in number throughout the country. Nursing homes and retirement centers are springing up and requiring trained personnel. Industry and unions are recognizing a responsibility to the older person who has done his share in production. Progressive companies put special emphasis on preretirement planning and welfare funds for their employees.

The author helped organize a pilot project cosponsored by the University of Wisconsin and Racine's Western Printing and Johnson Wax companies. Specialists discussed such topics as "Where shall we live after retirement?" "What community resources are available to the retiree?" and "What should I know about budgeting and investments?" The program was well attended, and a similar class was opened later to the public. Marquette University has had a program on preparing for retirement. Fordham University has a training program for preparing leaders to initiate discussion groups on planning for retirement. Discussion programs have been held by YMCAs on preretirement planning. The University of Chicago's Industrial Relations Institute serves thirteen colleges and universities in programs of preretirement planning.

Most agencies of adult education have now resolved the dilemma, "Shall we set up a special program for the older adult?"

Interviews with many senior citizens reveal that they would rather take part in the regular classes or activities of a center, library, university, or vocational adult school than to be separated out. In one of the programs the author worked with an adult student who began oil painting at age 78 - and is mastering the skills of the art. Let us not forget that some of the world's leading scientists and philosophers did their greatest work after 70. If the mind has been kept active, it is never too late to learn!

Research proves this true.

One forward-looking city the author visited turned the basement of the city auditorium into a drop-in center for senior citizens. Cards, shuffleboard, discussion programs, and other activities were provided, as were periodic trips to historic sights throughout the state. The Recreation Department of the city staffed the center with people who understood the older adult and his special needs. Furniture was provided by a local union, and the center was strategically located close to the public library. Other towns can emulate this idea of a center for senior citizens.

The **library** has a very special opportunity to provide reading, discussion groups, and special programs for the senior citizen. Many libraries do. Rose Vainstein, Public Library Specialist for the U.S. Office of Education, states that "in its work with the aging and the aged, the library actually performs many roles and serves many publics. These should all be kept clearly in mind so that the full library potential can be realized." [11] She feels also that the library should help the middle-aged adult prepare for retirement. Traditionally, the library has provided information, inspiration, recreation, and culture. These have special relevance for the older adult who has more time, more experience, and more needs. I recall the inscription on the wall of the library: "The Public Library is the Poor Man's University." Yet a man need not be poor to enjoy the library as a fountain of knowledge. Books, records, flms, magazines - all these enrich life. Librarians should take a special interest in the needs of the aged; most of them are eager to help.

Nearly every state now has an area agency on aging which provides ideas and guidance to communities for meeting needs of older adults. Federal funds are available for experimental projects on aging. Some cities have a committee which works with the welfare council or agencies of adult education and recreation to provide more opportunities for the aging to use their creative skills. Some agencies train volunteers: Gray Ladies help in Red Cross, hospital work, interviewing, and driving. Area Agencies on Aging hold hearings throughout the states to learn of the interest and needs of older adults. Vocational and adult schools, university centers, and social agencies all can use this information to build programs interesting and attractive to retirees and to those approaching retirement.

With more and more retirement communities developing in Florida, California, Arizona and the Western states, and with the declining enrollment of the post high school graduates, our adult education institutions can well afford to become involved in programs like the Elderhostels,[12] which provide short courses in summer schools throughout the nation, filling the campus dormitories with people over sixty-five in courses like "Understanding the Amish" in Pennsylvania and "Native-American Folklore". In 1979 there will be more than 18,000 senior adults in Elderhostel programs going to the campuses for culture, much like the Chautauqua of earlier years. The Retirement College of Yavapai Community College, Prescott, Arizona reminds one of the opportunities provided to "pensioners" in the Scandinavian folk high schools. (see listing of schools in Appendix)

PROGRAM DESCRIPTION

ELDERHOSTEL, a national program for persons over 60, combines the best traditions of education and hosteling. Inspired by the youth hostels and folk schools of Europe and guided by the needs of older citizens for intellectual stimulation and physical adventure, ELDERHOSTEL is for elder citizens on the move -- not just in terms of physical movement and travel -- but in the sense of reaching out to new experience. It is based on the belief that retirement does not mean withdrawal. Indeed, retirement should be viewed as an opportunity to enter and enjoy new life experiences.

ELDERHOSTEL consists of a network of over 200 colleges and universities in 30 states which offer special low-cost, one-week residential academic programs for older citizens during the summer months. Each week-long program is limited to 30-40 elders. Programs begin Sunday evening and end Saturday evening. Participants use the network for an educational hosteling experience, moving from campus to campus, taking the courses which appeal to them and exploring the interesting cultural and environmental resources of the local area. ELDERHOSTEL provides an informal and human atmosphere where the individual is important and making new friends is easy.

EDUCATION

Elderhostel

Learning Vacations

Newsweek, August 21, 1978

Ira Wyman

Summer students on Amherst campus (above) and working with Cousteau:
Some toy with the hobo's life, others read 'Beowulf' and the Bible

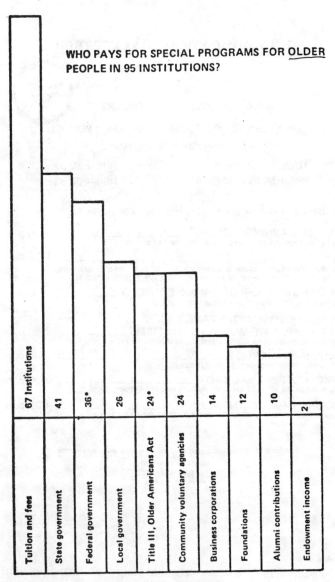

WHO PAYS FOR SPECIAL PROGRAMS FOR <u>OLDER</u> PEOPLE IN 95 INSTITUTIONS?

Tuition and fees	67 Institutions
State government	41
Federal government	36*
Local government	26
Title III, Older Americans Act	24*
Community voluntary agencies	24
Business corporations	14
Foundations	12
Alumni contributions	10
Endowment income	2

*Some overlap exists between these two categories.
 Source: AED Survey 1974

The educational backgrounds of the some 22 million elderly of our nation vary from individual to individual. With that background comes years of experience and knowledge.

ADULT EDUCATION FILM FESTIVAL

A.B.E. COMMISSION CONFERENCE

DEL WEBB'S TOWNEHOUSE   PIZARRO ROOM D
PHOENIX, ARIZONA

TUESDAY, APRIL 5,	—	1:00-4:30 p.m.
WEDNESDAY, APRIL 6,	—	1:00-4:30 p.m.

FILMS WILL RUN CONSECUTIVELY IN THE FOLLOWING ORDER:

1. **ADULT LEARNING CENTERS** _____ 1:00 p.m.
   A PICTORIAL DESCRIPTION OF THREE CENTERS AND HOW THEY OPERATE.

*2. **PEEGE** _____ 1:30 p.m.
   A YOUNG MAN BREAKS THROUGH COMMUNICATION BARRIERS TO REACH HIS GRANDMOTHER
   WHO HAS BECOME ISOLATED BY AGE AND FAILING MENTAL AND PHYSICAL CAPACITIES.

3. **A DAY IN THE LIFE OF BONNIE CONSOLO** _____ 2:00 p.m.
   A WOMAN WITHOUT ARMS COPES POSITIVELY WITH LIFE.

4. **ALCOHOLISM AND THE FAMILY —**
   THE SUMMER WE MOVED TO ELM STREET _____ 2:30 p.m.
   FOLLOWS THE FAMILY OF AN ALCOHOLIC THROUGH DAILY ACTIVITIES AND ANXIETIES.

5. **WHY MAN CREATES** _____ 3:00 p.m.
   DEMONSTRATES THE IMPORTANCE OF CREATIVE VISION.

*6. **THE SHOPPING BAG LADY** _____ 3:30 p.m.
   HOW UNTHINKING ATTITUDES CAN INFLICT NEEDLESS CRUELTY ON OTHERS.

7. **SOUND OF MY OWN NAME** _____ 4:00 p.m.
   ADULTS FROM DIFFERENT BACKGROUNDS RETURN TO SCHOOL FOR A BASIC EDUCATION.

COORDINATED BY THE FOLLOWING MEMBERS OF THE CENTER FOR HIGHER AND ADULT EDUCATION

ARIZONA STATE UNIVERSITY
DR. ROGER W. AXFORD
MS. LINDA B. KNOBLOCK

SUMMARY

We have learned that we are becoming an aging population,
that by 1990 it is estimated the elderly will consist of 28.9 million
in our U.S. population, (12%), as compared with 20.1 million in
1970 (10%). This has major implications for our programming
in adult education. Senior Centers, Gray Panthers, American
Association for Retired Persons, all have social and political
impact, and we must program with these groups if our institutions

84

are to remain relevant to the times.

Dr. George Maddox, warns us that by 1980 a million persons over 65 will be in nursing homes, costing more than $8 billion per year. Dr. Linda George makes a category of "two generations", labeling the 65-70 as "young-old," and the 76 and older the "old-old". Dr. George warns that the women have a more difficult time with retirement, the evidence shows, because most started working in their later years. The Center for the Study of Aging and Human Development at Duke University, and the Andrus Gerontology Center at the University of Southern California are examples of research centers aiding adult educators to look realistically at the aging population, and to see the "life-long-learning" possibilities.

Some stereotypes of senior citizens are examined as well as some myths about senior citizens. Fred Lengfeld's studies at Wisconsin show that leisure activities of senior citizens is not too different from those of youth. He notes that older people may take longer to learn something new, but given adequate time they learn it at least as well as the young. Older workers were found to be more dependable and have fewer accidents. Twelve percent of the elderly have paying jobs, and 19% are involved in volunteer work. Unfortunately 15% of the elderly live below federal poverty levels.

Special programs in colleges and universities have "60 plus" and retiree cards for senior citizens, allowing entrance without tuition. The consortium on aging is pointed out as a way of schools cooperating for a better use of talent and resources. Short term and long term goals are suggested. The Elderhostel program, which offers "learning vacations" is another model worth emulating and expanding to hundreds of higher education institutions.

QUESTIONS:
1. What are the implications of a growing population of senior citizens for adult and continuing education?
2. What are some agencies dealing with the problems of the aging citizen?
3. What do you think we can do to improve the life expectancy of men? How can we help women learn to live with widowhood?
4. What do you consider old? How do you think one can cope with aging? What does this have to say to agencies of adult education?
5. What are some stereotypes regarding the senior citizen? How can we change these stereotypes?
6. Who pays for special programs for older adults?
7. What can we do to help young people learn to cope with the aging parent?

8. Do you think there is a "youth cult" in the United States? How do you think we can overcome this in our culture, and help people be proud of their "maturity"?
9. What are you doing to prepare for retirement?
10. What learning resources can you bring to bear on the subject of aging?

1 "Understanding the Elderly," Program 1 of Colloquies in Gerontology, Roerig, Pfizer Pharameuticals, N.Y., N.Y. 1976. (Tape)

2 Op. cit.,

3 Op. cit.

4 Associate Press Education Special Report, Nov. 15, 1978.

5 Liggett, Fran, "That Motorcycle 'Gang' you just passed is make up of men over 60." **Phoenix Living,** March 1979 pp. 50-51. (Fran Libbett is a writer working in Aging at Arizona State University)

6 Written by the late Samuel Ullman, Birmingham, Alabama

7 Congressional Record, No. 32, Vol. 2124, Washington, D.C. March 8, 1978.

8 **The Elderly Arizonan, Update, 1978** Report to the Governor, Council on Aging, p. 11.

9 Lecture, Gerontology Conference, Dept. of Higher and Adult Education, Arizona State University, Dec. 7, 1978

10 **Ibid**

11 Rose Vainstein, "The Public Library and the Older Adult," **North Country Libraries,** March-April 1960. (A bimonthly publication of the Maine, New Hampshire, and Vermont State Libraries.)

12 See "Learning Vacations" **Newsweek,** August 21, 1978 p. 47. For details on Elderhostel programs, write ELDERHOSTEL, 55 Chapel St., Newton, Mass. (02160) 617-964-6920.

Bibliography

Arnold, William E. **The Credibility of the Old: Sage or Senile.** Unpublished manuscript. Arizona State University, 1977, 39 pp.

Becker, Howard. **Personal Change in Adult Life.** in B.L. Neugarten (ed.), **Middle Age and Aging,** University of Chicago Press, Chicago, 1968, pp. 148-156.

Berger, Peter L. **Invitation to Sociology.** Doubleday, Garden City, 1963.

Bernier, John, and Wright, Alice. **Serving Elders Through Independence Enhancing Relationships.** New England Gerontology Center, 1977, 18 pp.

Boas, Ernest P. M.D. and Norman F. M.D. **Add Life to Your Years.** American Medical Association called it the best medical thinking on old age.

Butler, Robert. **Why Survive? Being Old in America.** New York: Harper Row, 1975.

Carlin, J. **Nutrition Education for the Older American.** New England Gerontology Center, 1977.
The book includes sections on:
1. Nurtrition Education for Older Americans
2. Creating the Right Environment for Nutrition Education
3. Some Ways to Approach Nutrition Education
4. Shopping Assistance for the Older American
It is a good source book for providing a curriculum and program for adult education nutrition programs.

Carmichael, Carl W. **Communication and Gerontology: Interfacing Disciplines.** Western Speech Communication Vol. XL (Spring, 1976), pp. 121-129.

Chinoy, Ely. **Automobile Workers and the American Dream.** Beacon Press, Boston, 1955.

Cooley, Leland F. and Cooley, Lee M. **How to Avoid the Retirement Trap.** (See Also the Retirement Trap), Nash Publishing Co., 9255 Sunset Blvd. Los Angeles, California 90069, 265 pp.
Deals with the three stages of retirement, active-sendentary-terminal. The great leisure lie, investments, living in a foreign country, heredity and aging, recreation, and the advantages of living in the West. Explains why to plan retirement, beginning with the middle years.

Downs, Hugh, **Thirty Dirty Lies About Old.** Argus Communications, 744 Natchez Avenue, Niles, Illinois 60648.

Major theme: that aging is a positive developmental process with unique joys as well as challenges.

Drake University Retirement Planning Center, (Manpower Project, U.S. Department of Labor). **Annual Report.** DesMoines, Iowa, August, 1969.

Goffman, Erving. **On Cooling the Mark Out: Some Aspects of Adaptation to Failure.** Psychiatry: Journal for the Study of Interpersonal Relations, November 15, 1952, pp. 451-463.

Hunter, Woodrow W. **Preparation for Retirement.** University of Michigan, Ann Arbor, 1968.

Kaighn, Raymond P. **How to Retire and Like it.** Association Press, 1965.
A small book with many things in it you wonder about.

Kasschau, Patricia L. **Reevaluating the Need for Retirement Preparation Programs.** Industrial Gerontology, Winter, 1974, pp. 42-59.

Knight, Josephine, et al. **Six Dimensions for People Over Sixty.** Report Consortium of Six Community Colleges in Arizona, Title I, Higher Education Act 1975-77, Phoenix, Arizona.

Knox, Alan B. **Adult Development and Learning.** Jossey-Bass, San Francisco, California, 1977.

A handbook on individual growth and competence in the adult years for education and the helping professions. Synthesizes findings from more than 1,000 studies in adult development and learning.

Koch, Roy S. **Zestful Living for Older Adults.** Herman Press, 1963.

A small pamphlet, giving advice on living long without aging.

Lowenthal, M.F., Paul Berkman and Associates. **Aging and Mental Disorder in San Francisco.** Jossey-Bass, San Francisco, 1967.

Lowenthal M.F. and Associates. **Four Stages of Life.** Jossey-Bass, San Francisco, 1975.

Marr, Henry S. and Joseph A. Kuypers. **From Thirty to Seventy.** Jossey-Bass, San Francisco, 1974.

Mow, Dr. Anna B. **So Who's Afraid of Birthdays?** (pocketbook) Pillar Books, Harcourt Brace, Jovanovich, N.Y., 1969.

Author Mow was many years a missionary in India, and taught for many years at Bethany Seminary in Chicago. She deals humorously, but effectively with security, flexibility, religion, views of the church, leisure, continuing education, death as friend or foe, dying to the self at sixty, plus some recommended reading.

Neugarten, B.L., Joan Moore and John Lowe. **Age Norms, Age Constraints, and Adult Socialization.** American Journal of Sociology, May 1965, pp. 719-717.

Otten, J. and Shelley, F. **When Your Parents Grow Old.** Funk and Wagnalls, 1976. 298 pp.

The book attempts to answer questions related to parent-offspring relations as the parent grows old. Issues include: nursing home care, living with parents, financial needs, and financial opportunities. The book can be a valuable source for retirement, human relations programs in adult education.

Oyer, Herbert & Oyer, E. Jane. **Aging and Communication.** Baltimore: University Park Press, 1976.

Peck, Joseph H. M.D. **Let's Rejoin the Human Race.** Prentice-Hall, 1963.

Rosencranz, Howard A. **Pre-Retirement Education: A Manual for Conference Leaders.** Program in Gerontology, University of Connecticut, Storrs, Connecticut, 1975.

Gives:
1. Organization and description of pre-retirement programs.
2. Retirement decision-making processes.
3. Information and resource materials. Gives an excellent listing of fifty films dealing with aging and pre-retirement, with description. A goldmine for program planners.

Roth, Julius A. **Timetables.** The Bobbs-Merrill Company, Indiana-polis, 1963.

Special Committee on Aging Developments in Aging: 1974 and January - April 1975. Washington, D.C. Government Printing Office, 1975.

Spence, D.L. **The Meaning of Engagement.** Aging and Human Development, October 6, 1975.

Spence, D.L. and Thomas Lonner. **"The Empty Nest: A Transition in Motherhood."** The Family Coordinator, October 20, 1971, pp. 369-375.

Spence, D.L. and Thomas Lonner. **Career Set: A Resource Through Transitions and Crises.** Aging and Human Development, forth-coming.

Stauffer, John. **A Description of a National Volunteer Literacy Program.** A Presentation to the Adult Education Research Con-ference, 1974.

Steltzer, Mildred, et al., ed. **Gerontology in Higher Education: Perspectives and Issues.** Belmont: Wadsworth Publishing, 1978.

Strauss, Anslem. **Mirrors and Masks: The Search for Identity.** The Sociology Press, San Francisco, 1969.

Subcommittee on Aging, Post White House Conference on Aging Reports. Washington, D.C. Government Printing Office, 1974.

Wermel, M. and G. Biedeman. **Retirement Preparations Programs, A Study of Company Responsibilities.** California Institute of Tech-nology, Los Angeles, April, 1961.

AGING - **Alternatives for Later Life and Learning,** American Assoc. of State Colleges and Universities, Dec. 1974 (Programs designed for older adults)

Education for Older People

Aker, George F. **Learning and the Older Adult.** In A Manual on Planning Educational Programs For Older Adults, Andrew Hendrickson, ed. Tallahassee: Florida State University, 1973.

Outlines some of the factors which inhibit learning per-formance in the aged. Lists ten guidelines for arranging, designing, and developing "meaningful and reality-centered learning experiences for older adults."

Andrews, Elizabeth. **A Survey of Educational and Informational Needs of Older People Living in the Schoolcraft College District.** Ann Arbor, Michigan: Institute of Gerontology, University of Michigan, September 1972.

Reports a survey of the cultural, informational, and edu-cational interests of older people in the Schoolcraft College district. Found that interest was expressed most frequently in retirement subject matter, such as medical care and services, social security benefits, making the most of retirement income, legal information, and good health during retirement.

Ash, Philip. **Pre-Retirement Counseling.** Reprinted from The Gerontologist, Vol. 6, No. 2, June 1966, pp. 97-99.

Describes a pre-retirement counseling program which seeks to encourage individuals to plan ahead for retirement. The program is carried out in five stages. Counseling is made available to employees at age 55, at age 60, and at 65, just prior to retirement date. After retirement, contact is maintained with retiree through special letters and visits.

Birren, James E. and Diana S. Woodruff. **A Life-Span Perspective For Education.** NYU Eudcation Quarterly, Vol. 4, No. 4, Summer 1973, pp. 25-31.

Emphasizes the need for education throughout the life-span to enable people to adapt to accelerated changes in society. Identifies factors which may contribute to an increased participation by future generations of older people in educational activities. Outlines developmental tasks concepts and the value of using developmental tasks associated with each life stage as a basis for planning educational programs.

Charles, Don C. **Evaluation of the Drake University Pre-Retirement Planning Program.** Ames, Iowa: Iowa State University, undated.

Reports findings of a study which evaluates the seven-week Drake University Pre-Retirement Planning Program. The study compares the concerns, involvements and self-attitudes of participants before and after the course.

Eklund, Lowell. **Aging and the Field of Education.** Chapter 11 in Aging and Society, Volume 2: Aging and the Professions. Matilda W. Riley, John W. Riley, Jr. and Marilyn Johnson, eds. New York: Russell Sage Foundation, 1969.

Examines the psychological, biological and physiological aspects of aging related to education for older people. Argues that many of the handicaps of the aged can be remedied through appropriately designed educational programs. Emphasizes the need for an educational system which encouraged motivation to continue learning past the years of formal schooling. A major redirection of our educational system is called for even though for the present remedial programs may be necessary for such groups as the elderly.

Geist, Harold. **The Psychological Aspects of the Aging Process.** St. Louis: Warren H. Green, Inc., 1968.

Outlines psychological changes associated with aging. Draws on findings of experimental studies of learning and aging and recommends appropriate methods for facilitating learning in older people: clear presentation of material so that essentials can be perceived; pace should be decreased to enhance comprehension as learning progresses; learning by activity is superior to memorizing; training should be spaced with pauses to decrease fatigue; ambiguities should be reduced to a minimum.

Grabowski, Stanley, and Mason, W. Dean. **Learning for Aging.** Adult Education Association, ERIC "Living with a Purpose", 1973.

Good overview, excellent bibliography, Introductory.

Granick, Samuel and Alfred Friedman. **Educational Experience and the Maintenance of Intellectual Functioning by the Aged: An Overview.** In Intellectual Functioning in Adults, Jarvik, L.' Eisdorfer, C.; and Blum, J., eds. New York: Springer Publishing Co., Inc., 1973.

Reviews research on the intellectual functioning of the aged. Concludes that older people have the ability to learn and can benefit from educational programs. Emphasizes the value of intellectual stimulation through educational programs for maintaining intellectual functioning.

Green, Mark. **Pre-Retirement Counseling, Retirement Adjustment and the Older Employee.** Eugene, Oregon: Bureau of Business Research, University of Oregon, October 1969.

Reports findings of a study which examined the effects of pre-retirement counseling programs conducted at four firms on the adjustment of retirees and on employees. Found a positive impact on adjustment, morale and job-related attitudes.

Hand, Samuel. **What It Means to Teach Older Adults.** In A Manual on Planning Educational Programs for Older Adults. Andrew Hendrickson, ed. Tallahassee: Florida State University, 1973.

Outlines some of the physiological and psychological changes which occur with the normal aging process, the ways in which these changes influence learning abilities, habits and attitudes, and the implications of these changes for the way older people should be taught.

Havighurst, Robert J. **Changing Status and Roles During the Adult Life Cycle: Significance for Adult Education.** In Sociological Backgrounds of Adult Education. Hobert W. Burns, ed. Syracuse, N.Y.: Syracuse University, March 1970.

Outlines a series of dominant concerns which characterize eight age periods and recommends use of this type of developmental psychology framework as a basis for planning adult education programs.

Heimstra, Roger P. **Continuing Education for the Aged: A Survey of Needs and Interests of Older People.** Adult Education, Vol. XXII, No. 2, 1972, pp. 100-109.

Reports findings of a study of educational preferences of older people living in retirement apartments and members of a senior center in Nebraska. Found that the older people sampled preferred instrumental over expressive educational activities. Emphasizes the need for instrumental educational activities for older people.

Hendrickson, Andrew, ed. **A Manual On Planning Educational Programs For Older Adults.** Tallahassee: Florida State University, 1973.

A comprehensive guide to counseling and teaching older adults, and planning educational programs for them. Presents background material on the physiological, pschological and social aspects of aging. Outlines elements of program planning: determining needs, ordering priorities among needs, discovering resources, developing the programs, promoting the program, operating the program, evaluating the program, and re-planning.

Hunter, Woodrow W. **A Longitudinal Study of Pre-Retirement Education.** Ann Arbor : Institute of Gerontology, University of Michigan, 1968.

Reports findings of an evaluation study of a pre-retirement education program. Results showed that the program reduced retirement dissatisfaction and health worries and encouraged participation in activities with family and friends.

Hunter, Woodrow W. **Preparation For Retirement.** Ann Arbor, Michigan: Institute of Gerontology, The University of Michigan - Wayne State University, 1973.

A Handbook containing guides and resource material for a group method program for pre-retirement education.

Jacobs, H. Lee, W. Dean Mason and Earl Kauffman. **Education for Aging: A Review of Recent Literature.** Washington, D.C.: Adult Education Associaton, 1970.

A detailed comprehensive review of the literature on education for older people. Covers the topics of learning characteristics and abilities of older adults; opportunities and needs for programs in the educational system; job retraining and informal educational programs; and preparation for retirement.

Johnstone, John W.C. and Rivera, Ramon J. **Volunteers for Learning.** Chicago: Aldine Publishing Company, 1965. Out of print.

Reports the findings of a national sample survey of participation in educational activities.

Knox, Alan B. and Richard Videbeck. **Adult Education and Adult Life Cycle.** Adult Education, Winter 1963, pp. 102-121.

Research on adult education and social participation is reviewed. Findings of a survey of adults in a midwestern state regarding the relationship between participation in educational activities and various status characteristics. Found that participation in adult education was associated with age and socio-economic status but not community size or sex.

Kuhlen, Raymond G., ed. **Psychological Backgrounds of Adult Education.** Notes and Essays no. 40, Syracuse, N.Y.: Center for the Study of Liberal Education for Adults, Syracuse University, March 1970.

A collection of papers which summarizes research on adult learning abilities, personality development during the adult years, motivational changes in adulthood, and the relation of psychological characteristics to instructional methods in adult education.

McClusky, Howard Y. **Education: Background Paper for 1971 White House Conference on Aging.** Washington, D.C.: Administration on Aging, 1971.

Presents a hierarchical view of the educational needs of older people based on a theory of the margin. Argues that education for meeting coping needs should be given even higher priority than education for meeting expressive, contributive and influence needs. Reviews the knowledge available regarding levels of formal education, participation in adult education and ability to learn of older people. Describes the role of the formal and informal response systems in providing educational programs for older people, pre-retirement programs and problems and approaches to recruiting older people for educational activities.

Monk, Abraham. **A Social Policy Framework for Pre-retirement Planning.** Industrial Gerontology, Vol. 15, Fall 1972.

Identifies two categories of company pre-retirement programs: limited and comprehensive. Advocates the sponsorship of pre-retirement programs through a social service agency network, with a Federal agency advising employers and employees of available services and providing assistance to those developing programs.

NEVER TOO OLD TO LEARN--Academy for Educational Development, Inc. 680 Fifth Ave. N.Y. June 1974 Guidelines for Educational Programs, Characteristics of Programs for Older Adults. (Useful)

Sarvis, Robert E. **Educational Needs of the Elderly: Their Relationships to Educational Institutions.** Lynnwood, Washington: Edmonds Community College, March 1973.

Twente, Esther E. **Never Too Old.** Jossey Bass, San Francisco, 1970. Deals with alienation of our older people from society. Useful in helping professions, holistic approach to work, mental health, and dealing with hostility.

Reports a study of educational interests of older people and educational opportunities available to them through community colleges in Washington State. Found that the older people surveyed were most interested in constructive crafts, consumer protection, foreign languages, and the senior power movement. The survey of the community colleges revealed that senior citizens most often enroll in basic education courses followed by communications (writing, speaking, reading, listening) and creative arts.

Verner, Coolie and John S. Newberry, Jr. **The Nature of Adult Participation.** In Participants in Adult Education. Coolie Verner and Thurman White, eds. Washington, D.C.: Adult Education Association of the U.S.A., April 1965.

Reviews correlates of social participation in general (socio-economic status, age, sex, rural-urban differences, religious and ethnic groups) and of participation in adult education specifically (formal schooling, age, and occupational status). Advocates a change in the present system of adult education which seems to attract the minority ''who need it least'' toward involving the majority who currently do not utilize educational resources.

Weg, Ruth B. **Reality and Potential of Roles and Education For The Aged: A Necessity for Change.** Los Angeles, California: Andrus Gerontology Center, University of Southern California, 1973.

Discusses the educational needs of older people as one aspect of the need of society for life education.

Wientge, King M. **A Model for the Analysis of Continuing Education for Adults.** Adult Education, Summer 1966, pp. 246-251.

Describes a model for analyzing continuing education for adults that incorporates ''decade of development'' as one of its three dimensions. The other two dimensions are types of activity (lecture, group participation with leader, and leaderless group discussion) and degree of literacy (illiterate, functionally literate, literate, highly literate).

U.S. Department of Health, Education, and Welfare, Social and Rehabilitation Service. **A Trainer's Guide to Andragogy: Its Concepts, Experience and Application.** Washington, D.C.: U.S. Government Printing Office, Revised Edition, May 1973.

Traces the development of andragogy. Provides guidelines for staff training specialists for planning, conducting and evaluating learning experiences for adults.

One of the useful resources dealing with aging is a filmstrip and tape produced by the College of Nursing, Arizona State University, Bernita Steffl & Jeff Stanton, entitled the MEANING OF TOUCH (30 minutes), 1379 N. 44th St. Phoenix, Az. 85008,

($75.00) Illustrates the language and meaning of touch in working with elderly adults. Designed to be used as a teaching-learning tool to sensitize students, professionals, and paraprofessionals to sensory needs of the aged. Slides and music illustrate many kinds of touch.

Selected Audio-Visuals For PRE-RETIREMENT*

Availability, financial cost and relevance to PRE for leadership training and sessions were the main criteria used for selection. All resources listed are available for educational use throughout the State of Connecticut. The complete names and addresses of distributors are listed at the end of this section. Recognizing the financial constraints of most programs, the selected films are available at no or minimal cost. Thus, the often used phrase "short term loan" means that a particular film or tape may be borrowed for temporary use at no cost, or at most, for the cost of one-way shipping charges. Relevance was considered critical - is the subject matter, content and presentation germane to the retirement process? Recommendations for audience suitability are given in the annotation of each film.

This compilation should not be considered a complete listing of films and tapes on aging. Some material was deliberately omitted because of poor technical quality, outdated information, or the content was deemed less appropriate. For example, cross-cultural films were excluded. Not all topics, however, were deliberately omitted. 'Love, Sex and Marriage' represent topics of film scarcity. There is also a paucity of films which give attention to regional, cultural and ethnic differences.

In fact, positive realistic profiles on aging of the 'average' citizen are hard to come by on film.

To facilitate selection, the films have also been categorized by themes in Section II. These are topical classifications, not rigid categories since many films include secondary themes. The alphabetical listing of each film in Section I provides both technical and content information. Since all films are 16mm sound films, this information is not repeated, whereas size is indicated for filmstrips and video tapes. Films are of average technical quality unless otherwise noted. Titles followed by an asterisk* represent commentaries or documentaries (usually critical), whereas those not marked are factual or narrative in presentation. The annotations also vary. Emotionally neutral, informative or narrative films are generally accompanied by a brief descriptive summary of content, whereas critical and evaluative comments generally accompany the more emotionally charged documentaries or narratives.

Films can enhance training of PRE participatory sessions, as well as serve the function of recruitment. A film can be informative or provide the stimulant for increased awareness, sensitivity or discussion of a particular issue or topic. However, the particular objective and selection of a film is the user's responsibility and **previewing** is recommended at all times.

(M.K.)

I. FILMS
AFTER AUTUMN
10 minutes, Color, 1971

'Portrait' of an 82 year old farmer, Howard Drury, living alone, coping and expressing his philosophy on living, being poor and dying. Produced by HEW for the 1971 White House Conference on Aging.

Short term loan (DOA)

AFTER THE APPLESAUCE
29 minutes, Color, 1970

Social Security, retirement and disability benefits are discussed in a circus setting. A mini tour of the Baltimore Central Office is also included. This film cannot be considered a substitute for a Social Security Administration field representative. The circus story is often distracting. Produced by Social Security Administration. Available handout: **Your Social Security** (SSA) 75-10035.

Short term loan (SS)

AGED*
17 minutes, Color, 1973

The problem of aged and disabled parents as it devastates a recently returned young Vietnam veteran. Attempting to provide for his parents, he is bankrupted by a nursing home, loses his job and his wife, and is given the run around by various social agencies until he contacts the Geriatric Project at Bellevue Hospital in New York City. Produced by WNET/Channel 13; Carousel Films.

Rent $8.00 (UC)

ANTONIO
28 minutes, B & W

A warm and human portrayal of an Italian immigrant widower who lives with his 'God', Dante and memories. He reminisces about the good and bad times, family, work and friends. Antonio waits many days for that important invitation from his son. Disappointed, he visits with a compatriot in the hospital to reminisce about their boisterous wine-making escapades. Though lonely and sad at times, Antonio chooses to live independently in the city. Produced by Film Board of Canada.

Short term loan (DOA) (MH)

ATTENTION MUST BE PAID

28 minutes, B & W or Color, 1973

An enlightening and joyous statement about the power of love and friendship among senior citizens, who share a residence in Florida. Mr. Cahn, a retired professor, is dying of cancer (a fact not known by the other residents) Rather it is Mr. Cahn's optimism, 'joie de vivre' and love that helps the residents develop a sense of joy and community. Only wealthy, snobbish, unpopular Mr. Weber resists. Cahn sees a lonely man through this facade, but Mr. Weber only comes around after he experiences financial disaster. Somewhat moralistic and preachy in Hollywood fashion, but the message, "It's who your are that's important", is worthwhile. Cast includes George Tobias, Ned Glan and Amzie Strickland. Produced by Paulist Productions.

Rent $18.95 Color; $12.95 B & W (ASF)

THE AUTOBIOGRAPHY OF MISS JANE PITTMAN

116 minutes, Color, 1974

Fortunately, this award winning T.V. performance by Cecily Tyson, of a black woman from early adulthood through advanced old age, is now available on film. Aging modifies her physical features and slows her gait but in no measure alters her strength of character or indomitable will. Produced by Learning Corporation of America.

Contact: (LPL)

BY CHANCE OR BY CHOICE

26 minutes, Color, 1962

This film deals with the process of selecting a nursing home matched to the particular individual needs (medical and social) of the patient. In a low key, criteria for evaluation and selection are presented. With today's perspective, one questions whether that many choices are realistically available. Produced by Colorado State Department of Health.

Short term loan (PHE)

DON'T STOP THE MUSIC*

18 minutes, Color

Diversity is stressed. These different tempos, themes, life styles and satisfactions are not magically discarded as one turns 60 or 65. Older Americans, such as Maggie Kuhn, speak for themselves and against 'ageism'. But not all older people are in 'political action' movements and involved. Understanding and improved community services for the elderly are advocated to promote an active and productive older American citizenry. Produced by AOA, HEW.

Short term loan (DOA)

FINANCIAL PLANNING FOR THE LATER YEARS

4 minutes, B & W

One of the vignettes on pre-retirement produced by the University of Michigan. Joe, the recurring character of this series, expresses dismay to his wife about the cost of groceries, and gifts for the grandchildren. Designed to stimulate discussion on financial planning.

Short term loan (DOA) (CC)

GOLDEN AGE

28 minutes, B & W

Three different men, three different approaches and solutions to the 'golden years' and compulsory retirement at age 65. Using a case history technique, second careers, new goals, developing additional interests, etc., are examined. The need for careful planning is stressed. A good recruitment or introductory PRE film. Produced by the National Film Board of Canada.

Short term loan (MH)

HAPPY BIRTHDAY MARVIN

28 minutes, Color, 1973

Humor is an effective foil in this probing look at middle age crises and the broader implications of aging. Marvin believes he will die at age forty. Upon his wife Gert's urging, he consults his family doctor. Can Marvin "take it straight" that he is "all right" and just doesn't want to be forty and grow older? Following several comic anecdotes Marvin is able to face his fears, and realize that each age has its problems, but also its satisfaction. A happy ending. (Bob Newhart and Anne Francis are starred). Produced by Paulist Productions.

Short term loan (MH)

HEALTH DURING THE RETIREMENT YEARS

4 minutes, B & W

Joe, a retired man, feels dizzy, has pains in his legs and despite his wife's urging will not call a doctor. Through his wife's efforts he does get to see a doctor and finds that he does not have a serious health problem. One of a series of vignettes designed to promote pre-retirement discussion on the dangers of self-diagnosis, self-treatment and the importance of regular medical checkups. Produced by the University of Michigan.

Short term loan (DOA) (CC)

THE LAST DAY ON THE JOB

4 minutes, B & W

Scene is set in the locker room of a plant. The clothes may be somewhat outdated, but the phrases "good luck, come back and visit, how I envy you" are alive and well. What happens on that last day on the job? How does Joe really feel? How do the other employees respond? One of the series of vignettes on pre-retirement education produced by the University of Michigan. Short term loan (DOA) (CC)

MATTER OF INDIFFERENCE*

45 minutes, B & W, 1974

A hard hitting commentary on "ageism" as "something we've just begun to identify in our society, just as we've faced up to racism and sexism" by Maggie Kuhn, organizer of the Grey Panthers. Though other older Americans speak such as Max Mannes (Chairman for Adequate Social Security), it is primarily Ms. Kuhn who critiques such topics as identity, loss of work, youth culture, nuclear family, retirement villages and social action. For some audiences the length, slow pace, and strong message may be counter productive but certainly relevant for those working with and for the elderly. Produced by John M. Hanick. Rent $50.00 per day (PF)

MEDICARE: HOW IT HELPS YOU

29 minutes, Color

A case history approach with voice-over narration explaining some of the services provided by Medicare. Covered benefits include: in-hospital care, extended facilities care and home health care. In addition, explanation of Part B of the medical insurance plan is provided. As with any such film one must be on the alert for legislative changes, nor does this substitute for direct contact with a Social Security officer or medical service representative. Produced by Social Security Administration. Accompanying material: Your Medicare Handbook (SSA-74-10060) August 1974. Short term loan (SS)

NEVER TRUST ANYONE UNDER 60*

60 minutes, Color, 1971

A rather lengthy, dramatic conglomeration of short films loosely tied togehter by the theme of "aging". Included are the complete short films "After Autumn" and "Step Aside/Step Down", which are available separately. Other film sequences are: "The American Dream" (youth orientation); "Throw-Away Culture", and "Falling Through the Cracks". An advocate for community programs, this film offers examples of 'how it can be done'. Produced by the White House Conference on Aging. Short term loan (DOA)

NO MAN IS AN ISLAND

29 minutes, Color

A documentary on the several services and programs offered by the Salvation Army. A brief film sequence (approximately 3 minutes) is devoted entirely to programs for the elderly. Produced for the Salvation Army.

Short term loan (SA)

OLDER WORKER AND PRESSURES ON THE JOB

4 minutes, B & W

Joe, the older worker, is being hassled by an aggressive, ambitious, younger worker to 'speed-up' and change his work production methods. Designed to elicit discussion, this is one of the pre-retirement series films produced by the University of Michigan.

Short term loan (DOA) (CC)

A PLACE TO LIVE*

26 minutes, B & W

An obviously older film, dated by technique and dress. It is, however, not outdated, for the ideas are very contemporary and relevant. In fact, the film's age emphasizes the lack of progress in dealing with the problems of the elderly. Special attention is placed on developing standards for Homes of the Aged. Still existing are the fine models as well as the poor and problematic conditions spoken of by Mother Bernadette, former Connecticut State Commissioner on Aging. Produced by Dynamic Films.

Short term loan (MH)

PEEGE

28 minutes, Color, 1974

A feeling of worth, knowing someone cares are shown to be important needs at any stage of life. A family visits a dying grandmother in a nursing home. She is blind and has lost some of her mental faculties. The visit is awkward and when the family leaves the young grandson stays with her for a few minutes. He whispers in her ear, touches her and is successful in triggering a response. The communication barrier has been broken and when he leaves she is again alone but knowing someone cares. Produced by David Knapp and Leonard Berman.

Rent $40.00 (PF)

PREPARATION FOR REITREMENT FILMS

(annotated alphabetically)

4 minutes each, B & W

A series of seven vignettes designed to stimulate discussion, by depicting Joe, an elderly man, and sometimes his wife, in various situations. These are not documentaris of aging, nor are solutions given to problem areas.

Titles of individual films:

The Sixty-Fourth Birthday
Financial Planning For the Later Years
Health During The Retirement Years
Retired and Home All Day
Retired and Living With One's Children

Older Worker and Pressures on the Job
Last Day on the Job
Produced by the University of Michigan under the direction of Woodrow Hunter.
Short term loan (DOA) (CC)

PROUD YEARS
28 minutes, B & W, 1956
"To live means to move and to be active". Following the recovery and rehabilitation of stroke victims, this film shows how disabilities can be minimized. Given the services, many elderly patients do recover to lead active, satisfying and self sufficient lives. In addition, the importance of the will to live is stressed as the most important factor in recovery. Produced for Pfizer Labs under the supervision of New York State Department of Health.
Short term loan (MH) (PHE)

REST OF YOUR LIFE
28 minutes, Color
A recruitment film designed to stimulate thinking and planning for pre-retirement. A "20 year award" serves as the catalyst for a round robin discussion among a group of workers in a shop regarding their retirement plans. Questions pertaining to finances, time use, living arrangements, when to start planning and the like are raised. Sharing and discussing with one's spouse (wife) is stressed. The cast (all male workers) and setting (plant) combined with the length of time, may well serve as an audience limitation. Produced in collaboration with Mayor's Commission for Senior Citizens - City of Chicago. Accompanying material: **Rest of Your Life** (pamphlet for self-administration).
Short term loan (DOA), Pamphlet from DOA

RETIRED AND LIVING WITH ONE'S CHILDREN
4 minutes, B & W
Another one of the pre-retirement vignettes produced by Michigan University. Joe, now widowed, goes to live with his children in a different part of the country. Designed to elicit discussion on feelings, conflict and situations which can occur in the three generation household.
Short term loan (DOA) (CC)

RIGHTS OF AGE*
28 minutes, B & W, 1967
For Mrs. Vicary, an elderly frail widow, her home is her castle. For the viewer (some elderly people might find this too painful), her home is a self-imposed prison of isolation. Her independence is shattered by a bad fall, involving her with community health and welfare agencies. Following her recovery, a social worker persuades the frightened and reluctant Mrs.

Vicary to try moving to public rental housing for the elderly. Not only does this film make a pitch for services for the elderly, but it also raises questions regarding how well-suited these services are to the individual as a total human being. Produced as an Affiliated Film Production, written and directed by Irving Jacoby.

Short term loan (DOA)

SEASONS*

16 minutes, Color, 1971

A touch of humor is interspersed among the serious questions: What is the normal aging process, how good are our best nursing homes, what facilities and services are available? While some questions are merely raised, others are answered pictorially by fine examples of geriatric care and rehabilitation. This film was produced for the White House Conference on Aging and it certainly emphasizes that in terms of numbers served our records are not impressive.

Short term loan (DOA)

SIXTY-FOURTH BIRTHDAY

4 minutes, B & W

One of a series, designed to stimulate pre-retirement planning. As Joe blows out the candle on his birthday cake, he and his wife express their feelings about his future retirement. Joe's 'wait and see' attitude is contrasted by his wife's attitude it's better to 'plan ahead'. Though different personality facets are expressed, the introductory situation seems somewhat contrived. Produced by the University of Michigan. Available supplementary material.

Short term loan (DOA) (CC)

SPEAKING FOR THE CONSUMER: CONSUMER PROTECTION FOR SENIOR CITIZENS*

15 minutes, B & W, 1969

Interview with Sholom Bloom, Executive Director of the Department on Aging, on kinds of consumer protection services available for senior citizens. One of a series conducted by Dr. Elsie Fetterman, Family Economics and Management Specialists. The wallet size consumer guide published by DOA and referred to in the film is no longer available. Produced by the University of Connecticut.

Rental $3.50 (UC)

SPEAKING FOR THE CONSUMER: ESTATE PLANNING

15 minutes, B & W, 1972

George Ecker, economist, is interviewed by Dr. Elsie Fetterman, both faculty members of the University of Connecticut. The discussion of wills, trusts, estates and inheritance taxes brings forth the complexity of the legal structure as well as the need for a personal plan. As stated, the public is advised that this is not a 'do it yourself project' but suggests consulting with one or more of the following: attorney, accountant, insurance agent and/or trust department of a bank. Unfortunately, the sound track is mediocre. Produced by the University of Connecticut. Available supplementary material: **Estate Planning** (75-1).

Rental $3.50 (UC) Pamphlet from UCE $.25

SPEAKING FOR THE CONSUMER: PROBLEMS OF THE ELDERLY*

15 minutes, B & W, 1971

An interview with Mother Bernadette de Lourdes, o.c., former Connecticut State Commissioner on Aging. The special problems and needs of the elderly citizen are discussed as well as some of the programs developed to meet these needs. Probably most useful to planners, community action groups, or those working in the service fields. For up to date information on programs and centers, contact the Connecticut State Department on Aging (address listed in film index). Produced by the University of Connecticut.

Rental $3.50 (UC)

STEP ASIDE - STEP DOWN*

20 minutes, Color, 1971

First depressing, a collage of problems. Then cynical, "If a program has failed with everyone else then it's time to try it on the aged". The major portion is enlightening and optimistic. Model programs, both private and governmental, in the areas of housing, transportation, nutrition, senior centers, etc., are shown. Underscored is the diversity of people, from different Indian tribes, Chinatown (San Francisco), to the Mid-West. An awareness and understanding of different ethnic backgrounds will hopefully lead to more successful community solutions to the problems of the elderly. A good training or community action film. Produced for the White House Conference on Aging.

Short term loan (DOA)

STEPS OF AGE

25 minutes, B & W, 1950

A poignant dramatization of the effects of retirement upon a couple. Mr. Potter, unprepared, views retirement as a problem. He cannot cope, develops a severe depression and dies. Mrs. Potter, without financial resources, loses her home, and is further frustrated in her unsuccessful attempt to seek employment. Consequently she moves in with her married daughter. The steep steps are symbolic of the difficulty of her adjustment. Unfortunately, the film print is also weary (poor sound and dated). Otherwise this would be a touching and effective film emphasizing the importance of individual preparation for both sexes in facing the realities of retirement. Produced by Helen Levitt.

Short term loan (MH)

STICKY MY FINGERS, FLEET MY FEET

23 minutes, Color, 1970

A group of professional and executive type middle-aged men are united in their addiction to Sunday afternoon orgies of touch football in New York City's Central Park. Dreams of physical prowess, virility and winning super teams are dissolved in mud puddles when a 15-year-old boy joins their game. Thus wit, humor and sympathy are combined to lay bare the flimsy thread between fantasies of youth and glory and the realities of aging. Except for the 'rahs', dialogue is sparse. Relevant for physical fitness and attitude sessions. Produced by The American Film Institute.

Contact (LPL)

STRING BEAN

17 minutes, Combination Color and B & W

A poetic, silent film. Set in France, the story depicts an elderly seamstress and her love and care of a potted string bean plant. Thriving with an abundance of TLC, the plant outgrows its indoor quarters, and is transplanted in a formal public garden. Daily, from a nearby park bench, the elderly woman keeps a vigilant watch. The ultimate fate of the plant and its owner's reaction is an optimistic and profound statement on life at any age. Produced by Cladon Productions.

Rent $7.35 (CF)

SUN CITY, ARIZONA

23 minutes, Color

"Get out of the big central cities, the harsh climates" . . . and come live in a "dream world". That's the promotional pitch of this film tour of this self-contained leisure, retirement community. It shows 5 different housing options, 8 different recreational facilities, shopping malls (275 stores), churches, libraries, medical facilities and more, all reached by bus, bicycle or private golf cart. A relevant, housing alternative for the affluent. A vacation special is offered to families, with one member over 50 years of age. Produced by Del E. Webb Development Company.

14 day loan (DWC)

THAT THE LAST BE THE BEST*

28 minutes, Color, 1971

Using an identical format, and identical abbreviated clips, this film is a shorter version of **Never Trust Anyone Under Sixty**. Accordingly, it's not advisable to use both for the same group of viewers. Recent events cast shadows of credulity and irony as former President Nixon addresses the final session of the White House Conference on Aging with "let the last days be the best". More appropriate for training of leaders or social service personnel rather than PRE participants. Produced for HEW by Eli Productions.

Short term loan (DOA)

A TIME FOR LIVING

10 minutes, Color, 1975

A delightful and technically excellent film designed to stimulate preparation for retirement. The themes of time and change are interwoven, creating a subtle yet meaningful counterpoint. Moving from the past to present to the future, the effects of time and change are interwoven, creating a subtle yet meaningful counterpoint. Moving from the past to present to the future, the effects of time and change on the individual are poetically explored. Sometimes change can cause anxiety and pain and often the anticipation of change is worse than the change itself. But, change can also be a challenge and provide a **Time for Living,** if one is prepared to shape the change. Positive and upbeat this should be an effective recruitment film with wide audience appeal. Ray Bolger enhances this film with his warm and empathetic narration. Perhaps his final whimsical comment captures the essence of that "retirement" feeling. Produced by the Media Center and Program of Gerontology at the University of Connecticut.

Rental $3.50 (UC) Short term loan (DOA)

TRIGGER FILM SERIES

14 minutes (Total), Color, 1971

A series of five brief and affective dramatizations of situations common to older people (all on one reel, but could be used selectively). The combination of silent, major characters (except for Mrs. P.), low key music, and general quality of understatement delivers a powerful emotional wallop.

1. **To Market, To Market** - 2.04 minutes - An elderly lady shopping carefully in a supermarket. The only verbal note is the cashier yelling across the store, "What do we do with food stamps?"

2. **Mrs. P.** - 4.05 minutes - An elderly, black woman with poor mobility, "loves children and older people" and just wants "to work". This combination of attributes and desires creates a 'problem'.

3. **The Center** - 1.22 minutes - Is shared by teenagers and the elderly, eliciting a powerful interplay of gapes and gawks across the generational fence.

4. **Dinner Time** - 4.10 minutes - Modern appliances, elegant furnishings, an opulent crystal chandelier and a catchy tune serve as counterpoints to an elderly lady's lonely dinner of tea, toast and cottage cheese.

5. **Tagged** - 1.53 - Are all the furnishings including the swaying rocker occupied by one small old lady. The moving men grouse, shouting to each other through the house, "everything tagged goes". The woman clutches the rocking chair tag just a little tighter.

All or anyone of these (if not too painful for the group) should provide enough stimulant for a good discussion. Produced for AOA by Alfred Sloate.

Short term loan (DOA)

WE'VE COME OF AGE*

12 minutes, Color

Clips from W.W.I. parades, technological feats, national dignitaries such as Eleanor Roosevelt, Hemmingway and other memorabilia are shown to emphasize the achievements of this nation's 'present elders'. Yet these very 'elders' are in need of "jobs, better Medicare benefits, better housing . . . and have the right to a dignified life". The solution presented is one of involvement and organization of the elderly to achieve strong, national Senior Power. Narrated by Walter Abel. Supplementary Material. Produced by SCAD Productions for the National Council of Senior Citizens.

Short term loan (UAW)

WHAT PRICE HEALTH*

52 minutes, Color, 1972

Peripheral to, and not recommended for, pre- or post-retiree sessions, but a pertinent documentary for those actively involved and concerned with national health insurance legislation. Lack of availability, quality and cost of medical care are problems, particularly for rural areas, urban ghettos, the elderly and chronically ill. This crisis in the health care delivery system exists in spite of rich medical institutions, research, and various government and private health care plans. Gory (emergency-room clips), depressing (case histories personally narrated), and political (supports the proposed Kennedy-Griffith Health Bill) but excellent if appropriate. Produced by NBC shown on T.V., narrated by Edwin Newman.

Short term loan (UAW)

WHAT YOU DO SPEAKS SO LOUD

15 minutes, Color

A large number of older people shown working as volunteers in a variety of different activities in the Retired Senior Volunteer Program (R.S.V.P.) The virtue and satisfaction of each volunteer activity is expounded by one or more of the participants. The sense of 'usefulness' and value expressed is indeed praiseworthy. It's just 'too much of a good thing' in the given footage. This stress on moral rectitude and the glory of work may be counter productive for recruitment purposes. This film, however, should be useful for individuals and groups beginning to get organized in volunteer programs. Produced for R.S.V.P.

Short term loan (DOA)

WHEN PARENTS GROW OLD

16 minutes, Color

Edited from the fine feature film, **"I Never Sang For My Father"** with Melvyn Douglas as the widowed, ailing father and Gene Hackman as a young man about to marry. What is it like to be a proud, self-made 80 year old man, who should not for health reasons be left alone in his house? What are alternatives that he can accept? What does a son do when torn between a desire to marry and a feeling of responsibility for his father? The conflict is left unresolved and thus should provide excellent discussion for 'living arrangements' and 'family relationship' sessions. The gamut of emotions from anger to compassion portrayed by both characters is at times painful, but never maudlin. Produced by Learning Corporation of America.

Short term loan (MH) (PLC)

WILD GOOSE

18 minutes, B & W, 1973

John, puckish, rebellious and lovable, is a resident of a straight laced nursing home in New England. Though confined to a wheel chair, he successfully badgers and harasses the other residents and two gargantuan staff nurses. Birthday parties, cartoon shows, poetry readings and somber meals provide ideal targets for John's mischievous antics. Following some spills, smiles and waves, John manages his escape (wheel chair and all) amid a rising chorus of 'Hallelujah'. The satirical, slapstick comedy of this film softens, but also accentuates, the depressing, stifling and impersonalizing atmosphere of old age homes. John, perhaps epitomizes the 'human spirit and will' that battles to survive, in spite of the obstacles. An entertaining film for those working, and perhaps living, in these institutions. Would also add a light note to discussions of this serious and sometimes depressing topic. Produced and written by Bruce Cronin.

Rental $16.00 (FI) Purchase $175.00

WHITE HOUSE CONFERENCE ON AGING FILMS*

Color, 1971

A series of films which were part of the multi-media presentation at the White House Conference on Aging. Annotated by title, these films are:

After Autumn - 10 minutes

Let the Last Be the Best - 28 minutes

Never Trust Anyone Under Sixty (also includes portions of the White House Conference) - 60 minutes

Seasons - 16 minutes
Step Aside - Step Down - 20 minutes
Short term loan (DOA)

WHO CARES?
13 minutes, Color, 1969

An aging grandfather moves in with his daughter, her husband and two teenagers. Conflict between the generations centers on T.V. programs, noise, meals, respect and responsibility for chores. Mother is the unsuccessful arbitrator. As the problems continue to intensify, grandfather says he'll "move somewhere else . . . for when it comes to an old grandfather, who cares?" Produced by Noreland Latcher - part of Family Living Program.

Short term loan (MH)

WOO WHO? MAY WILSON
33 minutes, Color, 1970

Deserted at age 60 by her husband, 'traditional wife' (mother, housekeeper, cook), May Wilson, with considerable trauma tries to establish an independent life. Art, once a hobby activity in rural Maryland, now becomes central as a means of livelihood and a Bohemian lifestyle in New York City. The road to eventual 'artistic success' is laced not only by heartache and pain but a good deal of wit and humor as well. Obviously a relevant and enjoyable film for middle-aged women and older. Produced for Anamoly Films.

Rent $37.00 (AF)

YOU'LL GET YOURS WHEN YOU'RE SIXTY FIVE*
40 minutes, B & W, 1973

A scathing documentary (previously shown on T.V.), on Social Security and Medicare; showing 'care' and 'security' to be myths. Older Americans, dependent on these plans are seen and interviewed. Coverage is shown to be inadequate, unequitable (especially for females), abundant with loopholes and clearly inferior to that of several other nations. The conclusion is clear; sole dependence on our national plans makes a poor and meager retirement nest egg. Should certainly stimulate questions, financial planning and possible lobbying among pre-retirees. It's enlightening but depressing. Produced by CBS Carousel Films.

Rental $8.00 (UC)

II. FILM THEME CLASSIFICATION

ATTITUDES TOWARD AGING - PERSONAL
After Autumn
Antonio
Attention Must Be Paid

Golden Age
Happy Birthday Marvin
Rights of Age*
Sixty-Fourth Birthday
Steps of Age
Sticky My Fingers & Fleet My Feet
String Bean
Trigger Film Series
When Parents Grow Old
Wild Goose
Who Cares?
Woo Who? May Wilson

ATTITUDES TOWARD AGING - SOCIETAL

Aged*
Attention Must Be Paid
Don't Stop the Music*
Matter of Indifference*
Never Trust Anyone Under Sixty*
Older Worker and Pressures on the Job
A Place to Live*
Proud Years
Rights of Age
Seasons*
Speaking For the Consumer: Problems of the Elderly*
Step Aside-Step Down*
That The Last Be The Best*
Time for Living
We've Come of Age*
You'll Get Yours When You're Sixty-Five*

EMPLOYMENT

Golden Age
Last Day on The Job
Matter of Indifference
Older Worker and Pressures on the Job

FEDERAL PROGRAMS

After the Applesauce
Matter of Indifference*
Medicare: How It Helps You
Never Trust Anyone Under Sixty*
We've Come of Age*
What Price Health*
You'll Get Yours When You're Sixty-Five*

FINANCES AND FINANCIAL PLANNING

Financial Planning for the Later Years
Rest of Your Life
Rights of Age

110

Steps of Age
String Bean
Sun City, Arizona
When Parents Grow Old
Wild Goose
Who Cares?
Woo Who? May Wilson

RECRUITMENT FOR PRE SESSIONS
Golden Age
Rest of Your Life
Sixty-Fourth Birthday
Steps of Age
A Time for Living
Woo Who? May Wilson

SENIOR POWER AND POLITICAL ADVOCACY COMMENTARIES
Don't Stop the Music*
Matter of Indifference*
Never Trust Anyone Under Sixty*
A Place to Live*
Rights of Age*
Seasons*
Speaking for the Consumer: Consumer Protection for Senior Citizens*
Speaking for the Consumer: Problems of the Elderly*
Step Aside - Step Down*
That The Last Be The Best*
We've Come of Age*
What Price Health?*
You'll Get Yours When You're Sixty-Five*

TIME AND ITS USE
Don't Stop the Music*
Golden Age
Rest of Your Life
Retired and Home All Day
Sixty-Fourth Birthday
Step Aside - Step Down*
Time For Living
What You Do Speaks So Loud
When Parents Grow Old

WOMEN'S ROLE (Particularly relevant for or about)
Matter of Indifference*
Retired and Home All Day
Rights of Age*
Steps of Age
String Bean
Trigger Film Series

Woo Who? May Wilson
III. FILM STRIPS AND VIDEO TAPES

PRE-RETIREMENT EDUCATIONAL SERIES (Aetna)
35 mm, Film Strip with sound or record*, Color

Three filmstrips, each approximately 10 minutes, intended to be shown in the following sequence:

1. **The Best Is Yet To Be** - Introduction to planning for retirement in an attempted humorous manner. Clips of silent screen greats such as Charlie Chaplin are used. An emphasis on considering topics such as finances, housing, etc., to know what one 'will retire to'.

2. **Far Side Of The Moon** - Entirely devoted to financial planning; income versus expenses related to life style during the retirement years.

3. **The Time Of Your Life** - Differential time use in retirement; 200 extra hours a month.

A somewhat preachy and patronizing tone in all three segments, which could be modified by a good discussion leader. Available material: Discussion Guide with suggested questions and format. Also includes instructions for use of equipment.

Loan: (ALC)

READY OR NOT SERIES
3/4'' U-video cassette, 30 min. (each), Color, 1974

A pre-retirement educational T.V. series of ten programs 30 minutes each was originally aired on Connecticut Public Television. This series provides an alternative to the lecture-discussion model offered in small group PRE sessions. The entire series or segments are available for distribution, however, requiring special equipment for video tapes. (For information on loan arrangements and instructions contact AEV).

Overall, this series provides rather broad audience appeal and projects an optimistic approach. Retirement is viewed as an enjoyable and productive experience if it is well planned far in advance. Several combinations of formats are used throughout the series to enhance the value of long-term preparation. A broad spectrum of pre- and post-retirees are viewed and interviewed in the different subject programs. Authoritative support is conveyed by the commentaries and mini-lectures of doctors, lawyers, judges, educators, etc. Geographical scope is achieved by using footage from many of the films previously cited. However, the mix and blend of these different approaches is not always smooth. More often than not the jump between blackboard and lecture technique to case histories and testimonials makes for confusion. Though the subject matter at times seems poorly organized, Bob Earl, the narrator, supplies a friendly, professional tone to the series.

Each program accents the human and individual element of decision making, recognizing that choices must be made based on personal needs and life style. Commendable is the emphasis on including spouse and children in this planning process. Though many alternatives are viewed, discussed, and 'individual choice' is stressed, these all are presented within the framework of the virtues of 'physical activity, social participation and contribution, planning and record keeping, and the work ethic'. If the viewer agrees, then this is a rewarding fare.

The series consists of the following programs, 30 minutes each:

1. **Introduction** - A general overview of aging and areas in which adjustments have to be made in the retirement process. Aspects of the 'work ethic', income, leisure time, health, attitudes and personal philosophy, are covered. The importance of planning well in advance of retirement is stressed.

2. **Financial Planning - Part I** - Financial readiness, projecting income and expenditures, and the listing of assets are all part of the budgeting process. Social Security, pensions, annuities, investments and mortgages are examined. Suggestions for sources of further assistance are given.

3. **Financial Planning - Part II** - Definitions and explanations of 'gross estates', the importance of a will and keeping it up to date, federal estate taxes, and effect on spouse, are coherently and well presented. The advantages of 'estate planning' and accurate records are emphasized.

4. **Consumer Education** - Topics covered include food, clothing, insurance, houses, car purchases and maintenance, as well as appropriate channels for complaints. Getting the most for the money.

5. **Health** - A list of 'do's and don'ts' regarding exercise, diet and mental attitude and the relationship to good health. Unlikely that this approach would attract any converts, just reinforcements for believers. A very positive contribution is the information on "patients' rights" for an elderly population vis-a-vis the medical establishment.

6. **Housing and Living Relationship** - A listing of reasons for staying, reasons for moving and the major alternatives available upon retirement. The complexity of making a choice is stressed by several authorities.

7. **Employment - Part I** - A well taken approach recommending early planning for successful 'second career' choices. Some of the myths regarding older workers are debunked. The underlying assumption of this segment is that older people want to work and are better off doing so. Consequently tips on seeking employ-

ment successfully are given. Present economic conditions and socio-political national policy warrant doubt regarding the realization of this assumption.

8. **Employment - Part II** - Again, a reinforcement of 'work' as an important factor of well-being. A focus on part-time jobs, either hourly or seasonal. Self-employment is another option, presented with a cautionary note - statistics on small business failures are cited.

9. **Leisure Time - Part I** - According to George Bernard Shaw, "A perpetual holiday is a good working definition of hell", and it also is the axiom adhered to in this program. Examples of 'meaningful' activities include: education, volunteerism, cultural pursuits, senior citizens centers, travel, and crafts. In addition, guidelines for planning, participating and need assessment are provided, as well as scenes of 'involved' retirees. Essentially this segment provides further confirmation of the 'work ethic'.

10. **Leisure Time - Part II** - The importance of an 'active interest and participation' is again emphasized, both visually and verbally. Community service is commended not only for its contribution to others but also for the job-related satisfactions it provides for the retirees. The concluding message, "It's your retirement, it's up to you . . . are you ready or not?"

Director: John Hershberger, produced by Manpower Education Institute.

Loan: (Contact AEV)

Supplementary Material: **Ready or Not: A Study Manual for Retirement.** Single Copy $2.50. Bulk: 100 or more copies, 20% off (MEI)

NEG SERIES

video tapes, (varying lengths), 1974

The New England Gerontology Center has produced a number of tapes covering subjects such as nutrition, housing and other community services for the elderly. Special equipment, such as either a Panasonic or Sony playback recorder and a television monitor with a video-tape recorder input connection, is needed for viewing. These tapes may be previewed free of charge and purchased for approximately $25.00 each. Contact NEG.

IV. KEY TO ABBREVIATIONS OF DISTRIBUTORS

AEV   Adult Education Unit - Audio Visual Resources
        Connecticut State Department of Education
        P. O. Box 2219
        Hartford, CT 06115

AF   Anomaly Films
        267 West 25 Street

New York, New York 10001
ALC Film Librarian, Audio Visual Resources
Public Relations & Advertising Department
Aetna Life & Casualty
151 Farmington Avenue
Hartford, CT 06115
ASF Association Sterling Films
410 Great Road
Littleton, Mass. 01460
CC Community Colleges
CF Contemporary Films - McGraw Hill
1221 Avenue of the Americas
New York, New York 10020
DOA Film Librarian, Audio Visual Resources
Connecticut State Department on Aging
90 Washington Street
Hartford, CT 06115
DWC Advertising Department
Del E. Webb Development Company
P. O. Box 666
Sun City, Arizona 85351
FI Films Incorporated
440 Park Avenue
New York, New York 10016
PF Phoenix Films Inc.
470 Park Avenue South
New York, New York 10016
PHE Public Health Education Section, Room 122
Connecticut State Department of Health
79 Elm Street
Hartford, CT 06115
LPL Local Public Library or
Film Service Connecticut State Library
90 Washington Street
Hartford, CT 06115
MEI Manpower Education Institute
127 East 35 Street
New York, New York 10016
MH Film Library, Room 222
Department of Mental Health
90 Washington Street
Hartford, CT 06115
NEG Media Specialist, Gerontology Center
New England Center for Continuing Education
15 Garrison Avenue
Durham, N.H. 03824

SA   Local Salvation Army or
The Salvation Army
Territorial Development Department
Attention: Brigadeer Paul D. Seiler
120 West, 14 Street
New York, New York 10011

SS   Local Social Security Administration Office
or Social Security Administration
Division of Training and Career Development
6401 Security Boulevard
Baltimore, MD 21235

UAW   Film Library, CAP Director
U.A.W.
8 Ellsworth Road
West Hartford, CT 06107

UC   Center for Instructional Media & Technology
University of Connecticut
Storrs, CT 06268

UCE   Cooperative Extension Service - U-35
College of Agriculture and Natural Resources
University of Connecticut
Storrs, CT 06268

* Appreciation for use of this list from Dr. Howard A. Rosencranz, Program in Gerontology, University of Connecticut, Storrs, Conn.

1 "Understanding the Elderly," Program 1 of Colloquies in Gerontology, Roerig, Pfizer Pharameuticals, N.Y., N.Y. 1976. (Tape)

2 Op. cit.,

3 Op. cit.

4 Associate Press Education Special Report, Nov. 15, 1978.

5 Liggett, Fran, "That Motorcycle 'Gang' you just passed is make up of men over 60." Phoenix Living, March 1979 pp. 50-51. (Fran Libbett is a writer working in Aging at Arizona State University)

6 Written by the late Samuel Ullman, Birmingham, Alabama

7 Congressional Record, No. 32, Vol. 2124, Washington, D.C. March 8, 1978.

8 The Elderly Arizonan, Update, 1978 Report to the Governor, Council on Aging, p. 11.

9 Lecture, Gerontology Conference, Dept. of Higher and Adult Education, Arizona State University, Dec. 7, 1978

10 Ibid

11 Rose Vainstein, "The Public Library and the Older Adult," North Country Libraries, March-April 1960. (A bimonthly publication of the Maine, New Hampshire, and Vermont State Libraries.)

12 See "Learning Vacations" Newsweek, August 21, 1978 p. 47. For details on Elderhostel programs, write ELDERHOSTEL, 55 Chapel St., Newton, Mass. (02160) 617-964-6920.

Chapter IX:

WHY ADULT EDUCATION: COMMUNITY EDUCATION

One of the leaders in the theory behind community education is Jack D. Minzey, for many years head of the Center for Community Education, Eastern Michigan University. He points out that there is considerable disagreement regarding the defining and meaning of community education. "In general", he says, "they emphasize the fact that there is a great difference between the philosophical claims of community education and the actual programs which are in operation." [1]

The confusion arose because of the historical development of community education. It is an idea which evolved over the years. During its developmental stages, community education was at various times synonymous with extra-curricular activities for children, adult education, and the recreation programs. Minzey points out that community education oriented schools have addressed themselves to community concerns and the better utilization of services and resources in order to improve community life.

Minzey proports that while there are specifics of Community Education which will vary from one community to the next, depending upon the characteristics of that community, there are certain components necessary for all effective programs:

THE INGREDIENTS IN COMMUNITY EDUCATION

Component I   Community Involvement
Component II   Delivery and Coordination of Community Services
Component III   Activities for Adults
Component IV   Activities for School-Age Children and Youth
Component V   Use of Facilities
Component VI   Kindergarten through grade 12

Minzey further explains that Components III - VI deal mainly with programs with little community involvement. In contrast, Components I and II deal with 'process', the true essence. The Community Education Community School advisory councils representative of a cross section of the community is the vehicle that provides community input (process) in programming and community development.

COMMUNITY EDUCATION--MORE THAN FOR THE POOR

John E. Walker, in a discussion of the philosophy of community education, points out that the public must understand that programs and activities follow community educational class lines. He says:

> Another misunderstanding about community education is the idea that it is a program for the poor . . . the belief that certain segments of our society need such a program because it can help them move into the mainstream of American life. The inference is that the rich do not need it for they already have the good life. But unfortunately societal and personal problems affect rich and poor alike. The community school is there to help all members of the community.[2]

It should be apparent that ADULT EDUCATION is only one aspect of the community school concept. However, I would advise that if you want to sell your school board or community on the idea of opening our schools to adults and to the community, there is no more effective way than to take your board members, faculty, community representatives to Flint, Michigan and participate in one of their COMMUNITY SCHOOLS SEMINARS. I took 18 superintendents, school board members, and faculty from Pennsylvania for one look-and-see, and it proved productive in seeing the adult schools in action. Seeing is believing, and from the experience we made a tape filmstrip, TURN ON THE SCHOOLS, which was used throughout Pennsylvania. [3] Community education has model community school programs in most states which could be recommended by the Coordinator of Community Education in the State Department of Education.

Community education is described as "PEOPLE HELPING PEOPLE". An effective community school does the following:
- Extends its services around-the-clock throughout the year

- Includes all people of all ages within the community as members of the student body

- Is for the whole family; it builds individual and family strength

- Sets the environment for the community to get to know itself and its difficulties

- Furnishes supervised recreational, educational, social and vocational opportunities

- Promotes democratic thinking and action

- Initiates programs of usefulness for persons of all backgrounds, classes, and creeds

- Provides leadership in planning and carrying out constructive community projects

COMMUNITY EDUCATION ENCOURAGES AND PROMOTES:

- Maximum use of school facilities and resources

- Community involvement

- Cooperation and coordination among agencies serving people

- Advisory council development

- Enriching the regular school program

- Developing a concern for meeting human needs

- Utilizing existing and potential community resources

- Study and assistance in the solution of community problems

- Community leadership in the educational process

- Strengthening the family unit through shared activities

- A sense of community

Leadership is a key to the successful implementation of community education. Usually a Community School Director is hired by the district to coordinate and develop a community educational program. The Community School Director, like the adult educator, is the catalyst for assessing community needs and turning them into programs. The tasks of the community school director are:

Acquaints himself/herself with children, families, business people, and agencies in the attendance area.

Becomes aware of the needs and wants of people in the area and serves as a catalyst in developing programs to meet those needs and wants.

Identifies human and physical resources available within the community.

119

Coordinates the various social, educational, cultural, and recreational activities.

Becomes involved with juvenile delinquency, **adult education**, recreation, enrichment programs, senior citizen activities, and preschool programs.

Works under the supervision of the building principal and with the faculty.

Provides a forum for the discussion of social problems.

The Mott Foundation has put millions of dollars into training programs for Community School Directors, and has set up regional centers for dissemination of information regarding the community school concept. In 1978-79 the Charles R. Mott Foundation expended over $2.5 million in supporting Centers for Community Education Development. I observed one center in Pennsylvania administering a statewide Elderhostel program with 14 colleges and universities.

THE COMMUNITY SCHOOL--ADULT EDUCATIONAL PROGRAM

It is the philosophy of the community schools that the changing social and technological climate of our society has mandated a higher level of understanding and technical skills for many of the people in our community. Since educational experiences which are meaningful in our regular secondary school program are not always suited to the needs of adults, the local Community School shall instigate the development of the Adult Evening Education Program to better facilitate the educational needs of this segment of our community. The program shall operate according to the following:

Objectives

A. To help the learner achieve a degree of happiness and meaning in life.
B. To help the learner understand himself, his talents, limitations, and his relationships with other persons.
C. To help adults recognize and understand the need for lifelong learning.
D. To provide conditions and opportunities to help the adult advance in the maturation process spiritually, culturally, physically, politically, and vocationally.

E. To provide, when needed, education for survival, in literacy, vocational skills, and health measures.[4]

Special Programs

1. Adult Basic Education Program - The curriculum of this program will consist of basic courses in reading, writing, arithmetic, social studies, sciences and foreign languages.
   a. Communication skills (reading, English as a second language, writing and speaking, and arithmetic)
   b. Social studies, sciences and foreign languages.

The program is specifically designed to help the unemployed, the underemployed, and the individual with low vocational potential due to educational handicaps.

The individual who could be considered for this program must be over 16 years of age and has not completed eighth grade, or over 18 years of age and functions in reading, writing and arithmetic below the eighth grade level. This, of course, will include those who can neither read nor write.[5]

The Community Education Adult Education program emphasizes seven major areas as a general rule:

1. Adult High School Equivalency Program - The curriculum of this program will be designed to appeal to two types of adults.
   a. The individual who takes a course or courses just because he or she is very interested in the academic subject.
   b. The individual who takes a course or courses for credit which could lead to a high school equivalency certificate
2. Home and Family - These courses are designed primarily to provide an opportunity for adults to discuss relationships within the home and family. It is intended that participants will share experiences in an attempt to better understand the various roles and responsibilities of the family members.
3. Adult Vocational Education (Trades and Occupations) - This program is designed for two types of adults.
   a. Those who wish to take a vocational course purely out of interest.
   b. Those who wish to take a course because they feel that it will enhance their potential in a present vocation, or that it will enable them to go into a different vocation.
4. Business and Office Related Training -- This series of courses is presented to provide extended opportunities for office personnel to improve their competencies. Other courses or seminars will be developed which allow an opportunity for businessmen to discuss common problems.
5. Arts-Crafts and Hobbies -- This area of the adult education program is designed to provide opportunities for adults to

receive training which allows them to pursue leisure activities with increased satisfaction.

6. Leadership Development -- This area is designed to provide adults increased learning skills, experience in decision-making and leadership, and an enlarged awareness of community and societal problems.

7. A process whereby people can improve the quality of life in their community by identifying problems and through an assessment of community resources, human and material, come up with a plan of action that will help remedy the existing need. It is an opportunity for democratic participation in the decision-making process not only at the community level but also at state, national and international level.

A model resolution is one passed by the Phoenix, Arizona Elementary School District where an imaginative and assertive community school director, Mary Lou Immer proposed!

"The Board of Trustees for the Phoenix Elementary #1 School District will continue to encourage and support the cooperation of this school system with other local education, governmental, social and cultural institutions in developing community school programs that will prove beneficial to the total community.

These centers have helped school districts and other agencies in about 1,400 communities to instill a better sense of community through community education. Some centers work out of universities, some out of state, city or county education agencies. A few are national service centers for such special groups as community colleges and the hearing-impaired. Most, in the spirit of community, are jointly sponsored.

COMMUNITY EDUCATION PROCESS MODEL

DEFINITION → ORIENTATION → LEADERSHIP → PROCESS → PROCESS ACTIVITY & ORGANIZATION → PROCESS PRODUCTS → COMMUNITY PRODUCTS

Community Education

A cooperative community involvement process, including but not limited to the identification, development and utilization of all applicable human, financial, and physical resources to meet people's identified academic, recreational, cultural, and social needs.

Awareness

To explain the concept of community education to community residents and interested agencies and organizations.

- Conceptual clarification
- Rationale clarified
- Motivation
- Internalization
- Commitment

Leadership

An individual or group takes the initiative to help the community use available resources to solve problems held in common.

CITIZEN INVOLVEMENT

To provide a mechanism wherein the greatest possible citizen involvement in the decision making process is realized.

- Community Council
- Steering Committee
- 'Super' Council
- Citizen Input in decision making
- Block Councils

TRAINING

To provide technical assistance which assists the community develop its greatest potential.

- Conflict resolution
- Group processes
- Needs/resource identification

ASSESSMENT

To determine the needs/interests/concerns of community residents and to inventory available community resources.

- Demographic study
- All people's needs identified
- Available resources identified

COORDINATION

To avoid costly duplication of services and develop interagency cooperation in identified areas.

- Facility use maximized
- Cooperative agreements
- Combined budgeting
- Clearinghouse

PROGRAMMING

To assist in the development of programs to meet identified community needs.

- Programs developed to meet identified needs utilizing existing resources
- Resources developed
- Academic, recreational, cultural and social offerings

- Evaluation processes which insure renewal in the face of changing situations.
- Coordination, planning, involvement, and comprehensive educational and service activities for all people of a community.

Horyna, Dick, A Process Model for
Community Education Development, Free
from Nevada Center for Community Educ.
Nevada Dept. of Educ. 400 W. King St.
Carson City, Nevada, 89710

QUESTIONS:

1. How would you describe the concept of community education? What part does adult education play as a part of community education? What foundation has given major support to training of community school directors?
2. What are some of the program emphases of the community education adult education programs?
3. Where would you turn for resources dealing with community school materials and audio-visual presentations?
4. How can Community School and Adult Education Directors do a better job of providing lifelong economics to the residents in their community?
5. Write an essay on "How can community colleges, universities and community schools cooperate in their efforts to serve people?"

Some of the resources available on Community Education are the following:

Regional centers - technical assistance
National centers -
State Department of Education
State and National Community Education Organizations

FILMS

"Pioneers in Community Education," available from the Foundation.

"A Sense of Community," available on free loan from Modern Talking Pictures Service, 2323 New Hyde Park Road, New Hyde Park, New York 11040.

"To Touch a Child," the story of how community schools started in Flint, Michigan. Available for free loan from any of the centers for community education and from the Conferences and Visitations Department of the Flint Community Schools, 923 East Kearsley Street, Flint, Michigan 48503. The film can be purchased from Centron Corporation, 1621 West Ninth Street, Post Office Box 687, Lawrence, Kansas 16044.

"Community Education Processes: How They Work," a multimedia teacher-training program. Includes films, filmstrips and workbooks on how to start a community education program, role of community school coordinator and community council, and cooperative agency relationships. Available from centers.

PERIODICALS, MONOGRAPHS AND PAPERS

Community Education Journal, scheduled to be published as
a quarterly by the National Community Education Association.

COMMUNITY EDUCATION BIBLIOGRAPHY

Asimov, Isaac. **"Change", The American Way.** (in Flight magazine
of American Airlines), 1975.
Bruscemi, John N. **Community Education Principles: An Analysis
of Related Ideas from Selected Writings of John Dewey.** An
unpublished doctoral dissertation, Arizona State University;
Tempe, Arizona, 1975.
Clapp, Elsie R. **Community Schools in Action.** New York: Viking
Press, 1939.
Clark, Phillip A., and Edward G. Olson. **Life-Centering Educa-
tion.** Midland, Michigan: Pendell Publishing Company, 1977.
Ciavorella, Michael A. **Community Education Funding Guide.**
Shippensburg, Pennsylvania: Shippensburg State College, 1977.
Cropley, A. J. **Lifelong Education: A Psychological Analysis.**
Pergamon Press, 1977, 196pp.
Dave, R. H. **Lifelong Education and School Curriculum.** Mono.
No. 1, UNESCO Institute for Education, Hamburg, Germany,
1973.
Dave, R. H., and N. Stiemerling. **Lifelong Education and the
School.** Mono. No. 2, UNESCO Institute for Education, Ham-
burg, Germany, 1973.
Dewey, John. **Democracy in Education: An Introduction to the
Philosophy of Education.** Textbook Series in Education, ed.
Paul Monroe. New York: Macmillan Co., 1916 (32nd print-
ing, 1960).
Dewey, John & Evelyn Dewey. **Schools of Tomorrow.** New York:
E. D. Dutton and Co., 1915.
Everett, Samuel. **The Community School.** New York, D. Appleton-
Century Company, 1938.
Faure, Edgar, et al. **Learning To Be: The World of Education
. Today and Tomorrow.** UNESCO, Paris, 1972.
Ford, George A., and Gordon L. Lippitt. **A Life Planning Work-
book for Guidance in Planning and Personal Goal Setting.**
NTL Learning Resources Corporation, Fairfax, Virginia, 1972.
**Goulette, George, et al. The Conference Coordinator: A Compil-
ation of Articles and Presentations on His Role.** University
of Colorado, 1973, 66pp.
Gross, Ronald. **New Paths to Learning: College Education for
Adults.** Public Affairs Comm., 1977, 128 pp.
Hart, Joseph K. **The Discovery of Intelligence.** New York: The

Century Company, 1924.

Hesburgh, T. M., P.A. Miller, and C. R. Wharton, Jr. **Patterns for Lifelong Learning**. San Francisco: Jossey-Bass, Inc., 1973.

Hickey, Howard W. and Curtis Van Voorhees, et al. **The Role of the School in Community Education**. Midland, Michigan: Pendell Publishers, 1969.

Houle, Cyril O. **Continuing Your Education**. McGraw-Hill Book Co., Inc., New York, 1964.

Jessup, F. W., ed. Lifelong Learning: **A Symposium on Continuing Education**. New York: Pergamon Press, 1969.

Kerensky, Vasil M. and Ernest Oscar Melby. **Education II: The Social Imperative**. Midland Michigan: Pendell Publishing Co., 1971.

Knowles, Malcolm S. **Self-Directed Learning, A Guide for Learners and Teachers**. Associated Press, 1975, 135pp.

Lengrand, Paul. **An Introduction to Lifelong Education**. UNESCO, Paris, 1970.

LeTarte, Clyde E. and Jack D. Minzey. **Community Education: From Program to Process**. Midland, Michigan: Pendell Publishing Co., 1972.

Lifelong Learning During Adulthood. The Advisory Panel on Research Needs in Lifelong Learning During Adulthood. CEEB, 1978.

Lifelong Learning. Journal of Research and Development in Education, Vol. VII, No. 4. College of Education, University of Georgia, Athens, 1974.

Ohliger, John, and Colleen McCarthy. **Lifelong Learning or Lifelong Schooling?** Syracuse University Press, Syracuse, New York, 1971.

Pendell, Richard. "In Memorium." **Community Education Journal**. Vol. 2:5, November, 1972.

Schmuck, R. A., and Matthew B. Miles. **Organization Development in Schools**. Palo Alto, California: National Press Books, 1972.

Seay, Maurice F., et al. **Community Education: A Developing Concept**. Midland, Michigan: Pendell Publishing Co., 1974.

Shaw, Nathan. **Administration of Continuing Education**. National Association for Public and Continuing Education, Washington, D.C., 1969.

Torsten, Husen. **The Learning Society**. New York: Harper and Row, 1974.

Totten, W. Fred. **The Power of Community Education**. Midland, Michigan: Pendell Publishing Company, 1970.

Vermilye, Dychman W., ed. **Lifelong Learners -- A New Clientele for Higher Education**. San Francisco: Jossey-Bass, Inc., 1974.

Chapter X:

THE BACKGROUND OF THE ADULT EDUCATION MOVEMENT

> A third meaning combines all the processes and activities of adult education into the idea of a **movement or field**. In this sense "adult education" brings together into a definable social system all the individuals, institutions, and associations concerned with the education of adults and portrays them as working toward such common goals as the improvement of the methods and materials of adult learning, the extension of opportunities for adults to learn, and the advancement of the general level of our culture.
>
> -Malcolm Knowles, **The Adult Education Movement in the United States,** Holt, New York, 1962, Preface, p. vi.

The fact that throughout most of the nineteenth century constant efforts were made to build up a system of higher education suited to the needs of adult men and women suggests that such needs are not the outcome of a merely evanescent interest or fashion but are founded on permanent needs which, when frustrated in one direction, seek satisfaction in another. Adult education is not a new concept. Since the beginning of recorded history we have evidence of persons who have learned throughout their individual lifetime and have used numerous informal methods to perpetuate culture. But formal institutional adult education on any large scale is relatively modern. The development of programs has been marked by diversity because of the changing interests and the variety of needs of adults. Adult education has been identified with the institutional organizations which have been created within society to provide meaningful learning experiences for individuals and groups. These institutions and agencies of education for adults have usually been organized so that persons at the same stage of development or having similar interests may receive instruction efficiently and effectively.[1]

There is a similarity in the programs of different countries since the basic needs of adults are similar in all countries at specific stages in human development. In their particulars, however, the adult educational agencies and institutions of each country tend to reflect the distinctive culture of the country in which they have developed. At times, for example, adult programs in various countries have been so dominant that persons have identified adult education with some particular institution, as in the case of the Danish folk high schools.[2]

Examination of a few of the highlights of the institutions of adult education in England and America will provide a background for understanding the movement.

ENGLISH HERITAGE IN ADULT EDUCATION

Although educational opportunities progressed slowly through the centuries, the industrial revolution in Britain made people realize that education was a privilege for more than the elite. British historian Robert Peers contends that the movement for adult education was part of the revolution which transformed a country of small-scale craftsmen and farmers into a great industrial democracy.[3] He further ties this economic trend to the religious awakening of the mid-eighteenth century, and both of these movements to the dissolution of the old social order in England and the drift of population to the towns.

Mechanics' Institutes

Dr. George Birkbeck, founder of the Mechanics' Institute movement, was Professor of Natural Philosophy at Anderson's College in Glasgow in 1799. He had become aware of the unsatisfied desire for knowledge of the workers while supervising mechanics in the production of apparatus required for his demonstrations. Birkbeck was so taken with the interest shown by the workmen that he proposed the establishment of a Mechanics' Class. It was an immediate success. In 1804 Birchbeck moved to London, but the work was carried on by his successor, Dr. Andrew Ure.

People's Colleges

In 1842, an independent minister, the Rev. R. S. Bayley, criticized the shortcomings of the Mechanics' Institutes in meeting the needs of working men for higher education. Bayley recognized that many workingmen were not ready for higher studies, and that provision needed to be made for more elementary subjects. He succeeded in establishing a People's College in Sheffield to provide general education of a humane character. The number of students at this College rose rapidly until in 1849-50 there were 630 enrolled. The London Working Men's College was founded by a group of Christian Socialists in England in 1854. This institution was a practical experiment in social reform undertaken by Frederick Denison Maurice and his colleagues.

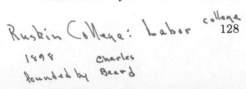

Ruskin College: Labor college

1898   Charles
founded by Beard

University Extension

Frederick Maurice intended that the Working Men's College should work closely with existing institutions such as the universities. He even hoped that the universities would accept persons coming from the Working Men's Colleges, as they would from any other, and that they would grant students their degrees, through examinations, once the work was completed. Maurice felt confident that no fee would stand in the way of working men's obtaining the same advantages as their countrymen possessed. [4] Unfortunately, Maurice's hopes for adult students' going from the London College to Oxford and Cambridge did not come to realization.

Two rather distinct approaches to the conception of university extension emerged in England. One has been that mainly associated with Cambridge, which was primarily concerned with the promotion of serious, systematic study. The other, characterized mostly by the Oxford movement in university extension, has been the idea of the stimulation of intellectual life at numerous levels of adult development. University extension lectures tended to accomplish the second objective more successfully than they did the first. Later developments of colleges and centers grew out of a desire for more continuous and systematic study than was offered by university extension lectures. One of the leading examples of an expression of the Oxford point of view in university extension was the work of Canon Samuel A. Barnett at Toynbee Hall.

Toynebee Hall

Toynbee Hall was founded in 1883, and emphasized a new recognition among the universities of their responsibilities to the underpriviledged. Canon Barnett brought many men from the Colleges of Oxford to Toynbee Hall, where they worked in the heart of the London slums in both social settlement house and educational endeavors. Later movements in adult education in England and America took inspiration from the efforts of these idealistic young scholars. The very idea of tutorial classes grew out of the experience of Canon Barnett in his extension lectures at Toynbee Hall.

ADULT EDUCATION IN THE UNITED STATES

The definitive study of the origins of university extension in this country was published by Herbert B. Adams in 1900. [5] In it he pointed out the interrelationship of democratic traditions of education between England and the United States. England, perhaps, received impulses in the direction of democratic education from the American and French revolutions, but in later stages the role of leadership was reversed. The rise of educational democracy was an outgrowth of the pioneer influence of the English leaders of social enlightenment and was closely tied in with the reform movements in British politics, particularly with the extension of suffrage.

Organized adult education in the United States began in colonial days. It was a fruit of the Protestant revolt of the sixteenth century and the general awakening of Europe taking place at that time. [6] An early form was the proprietary school, which taught vocational subjects in classes which usually met in the evening. Arithmetic and language were staple parts of the curriculum.

With the continued influx of early settlers from Europe, the need developed for a culture that would bring cohesiveness to this new land. The founders of the new nation realized that political independence was not sufficient, and that in addition there must be an informed electorate. Thus ensued during the early part of the nineteenth century in the United States a number of loosely organized efforts in adult education, many of them unrelated to each other.

Lyceums

One of the most important of these individual group efforts was the lyceum. Farmers, mechanics, and other groups with some formal education organized small local associations for self-improvement. They were concerned not only with their own improved learning but with the development of a public school system. Josiah Holbrook was a leader in the establishment of lyceums in New England, the first of them being held at Millbury, Massachusetts, in 1826. [7]

The lyceum concentrated on self-culture, instruction in speech, debate, and discussion of common public interests. These town lyceums grew rapidly, and by 1839 some three thousand existed throughout the country. Through the years they became potent influences in promoting public education. Many participants assumed educational leadership. These groups included in their ranks some of the leading intellectual figures of the time-Henry Ward Beecher, Wendell Phillips, Ralph Waldo Emerson, Oliver Wendell Holmes, Bayard Taylor, Horace Greeley, Frederick Douglass, and George William Curtis. The most famous was Abraham Lincoln. [8]

But like so many ventures of adult educator, which tend to be episodic, [9] the lyceum waned just before the beginning of the twentieth century. During the period that the lyceums were gaining strength, other agencies of adult education were developing. Some of these grew out of the interests of those active in the lyceums-museums, libraries, lecture series, mechanics' institutes, and publicly supported evening schools. All of these bred more intellectual curiosity. While the lyceums began their decline, many other institutions tended to become permanent For example, 1833 saw the first tax-supported library in Peterborough, New Hampshire.

The Chautauqua Institution

Lyceums had given Bishop John H. Vincent an example of what could be done in adult education. In 1874 Bishop Vincent and his colleagues embarked on an expansion of a Sunday school association and established the Chautauqua Institution. The name "Chautauqua" can be considered both as a place and as an idea. Bishop Vincent chose, as the place, Lake Chautauqua in southern New York. The idea was that annually, during the summer months, thousands of persons would go there to hear lectures and music, and to attend courses of instruction especially developed for Sunday school teachers. Bishop Vincent held that all learning is sacred and that the secular life should be pervaded by the religious spirit. This spirit he meant to achieve through the Chautauqua Institution. He early emphasis was on training Sunday school teachers, but he soon added to the usual Biblical study in the curriculum a variety of additional subjects: literature, languages (ancient and modern), history, art, science, music, elocution, and physical culture.

Chautauqua offered one of the earliest correspondence study programs in America. The early program was carried on through the Chautauqua Literary and Scientific Circle (known as CLSC), founded in 1878.[10] Then an now, CLSC provided a number of "reading courses" available by mail. In 1883 a program leading to a diploma through correspondence study was also added to Chautauqua, so that a student could continue his study through the mails.[11] This set a pattern later adopted by university extension when William Rainey Harper founded the University of Chicago in 1892.

UNIVERSITY EXTENSION

University extension is another expression of the desire of adults in America for increased enlightenment.[12] History records that university extension was first publicly presented in the United States at sessions of the American Library Association at Thousand Islands, New York, in September 1887. This essentially English system, adapted to local needs in America, was taken up by many public-spirited librarians in America in

Chicago, St. Louis, and New York.[13]

In January 1888 Melvil Dewey, Chief Librarian of Columbia University, laid before the regents of the University of the State of New York a plan for university extension in connection with public libraries. On May 1, 1891, $10,000 was appropriated for the state organization of university extension. The bill stipulated that no part of the grant should be spent on lectures, but that the entire sum should be used "for purposes of organization, supervision, and printing."[14]

Following the lead of the University of the State of New York, another major educational extension effort in the United States was undertaken by the American Society for the Extension of University Teaching. This Society was organized in Philadelphia in 1890. Public-minded institutions cooperated with able and well-trained lecturers (many invited from England), extending their service to the cause of popular education in America. The American Society was supported by subscription; a periodical, **The Citizen and the University Extension**, was published to unite and promote the extension movement.

For a decade the Society flourished. The University of the State of New York reported in June 1899 that the American Society for the Extension of University Teaching gave lecture courses in fourteen places in Philadelphia and in twenty-nine towns throughout Pennsylvania and in states nearby.[15] The activities of of this Society, however, began to wane after the turn of the century.

OTHER EXTENSION VENTURES

During the period of 1880-1900 many efforts were made to transplant to the United States the forms of university extension which had proved successful in England. In 1892, at a national congress held for those interested in the extension movement, it was reported that in the past four years twenty-eight states had organized extension programs. The University of Wisconsin listed a group of extension lecturers as early as 1890-91 and offered them to groups off the resident campus.[16]

Morton reports that by the turn of the century, however, university extension ventures had diminished almost to the vanishing point.[17] Some of the reasons listed for the decline in extension efforts during this period were inadequate financing, unavailability of suitable lecturers, inability of university staffs to understand the interests and capacities of adults, and the great increase of university campus enrollments. By the early 1900's the enrollment bulge of undergraduate day students taxed university facilities and the energies of the faculty. Consequently most faculty members were unwilling to lecture off campus.

A PROTOTYPE: THE UNIVERSITY OF WISCONSIN AND UNIVERSITY EXTENSION

The University of Wisconsin pioneered in the development of a general educational outreach in this country and over the years has been a leader in dynamic programs of adult education and public services. With the appointment of Charles R. Van Hise as its president in 1903, Wisconsin led among public institutions of higher learning in taking the stored-up knowledge of the university to the people beyond the immediate campus. James Creese in his book **The Extension of University Teaching** has stated that "in the entire history of university extension, no event had more critical importance than the reestablishment of the Extension Division of the University of Wisconsin by President Charles R. Van Hise and Dean Louis E. Reber in 1906-07. The revival at Wisconsin led to restoration of partly abandoned extension divisions in universities all over the country, at privately endowed institutions as well as at state universities."[18]

Wisconsin had provided education for its adults not only through the University of Wisconsin but also through other institutuions. A system of Vocational and Adult Schools was founded through the imaginative leadership of Charles McCarthy in 1911 and is unique to Wisconsin in its statewide pattern. The Free Library Commission, through the vision of Frank A. Hutchins, has enriched the enlightenment of adults by more than a half-century of services to the people of the state. And the Cooperative Extension Service has carried on a broad program of public service through joint support by U.S. Department of Agriculture, the state, and county governments. Cooperative Extension, General Extension, radio, and television are now all combined in the University of Wisconsin Extension Division.

THE NATIONAL UNIVERSITY EXTENSION ASSOCIATION

One of the vital organizations for taking knowledge to the people through universities is the National University Extension Association, made up of more than 150 universities throughout the United States.

Founded in 1915 by a group of extensionists headed by William H. Lighty and Louis E. Reber of The University of Wisconsin, the organization was launched with twenty-two institutions as charter members. The NUEA is an organization of member educational institutions, which describes itself as "An official and authorized organization through which colleges and universities engaged in university extension, adult education, and other public services may confer for development of best ideals, methods, and standards of accomplishing their programs."[19]

The organization now has more than sixty-two universities offering correspondence study and annually publishes a cooperative "Guide to Correspondence Study in Colleges and Universities,"[20] which lists all the courses offered by the various universities.

NUEA "is an association of institutions of higher learning in the United States dedicated to the idea of continuing education and improved public services. Members make their university resources available beyond college walls - to youths and adults, to individuals and groups, to voluntary organizations, and to governmental units. They link living and learning by drawing people and the university together in attempts to make education both attractive and necessary and easily available to all. Their purpose is to enrich the lives of individuals through the utmost self-development and to improve the bases of popular decision and action in our citizens."[21]

THE ADULT EDUCATION ASSOCIATION U.S.A.

In a discussion of the strivings for a national organization for adult education, Malcolm Knowles describes the struggle for national unity of adult education during the period 1924-61. Credit for unifying the field is given to Frederick P. Keppel and the Carnegie Corporation of New York. In the 1920's they gathered and published extensive information about adult education. They were concerned about the fact that "though many national bodies deal with different parts of the field, there is no agency that concerns itself with the problem of adult education as a whole."[22] The American Association for Adult Education was created in 1926 and stimulated and coordinated activities in the field through 1951. In Columbus, Ohio, on May 13-15, 1951, two hundred elected delegates founded the Adult Education Association, U.S.A., with the executive boards of the AAAE and the National Education Association Department of Adult Education simultaneously agreeing to dissolve their organizations to form the new organization.

A year after the founding of the AEA in February, 1952, organizational representatives formed the Council of National Organizations of the AEA to exchange information by means of a clearing house and to discover possible areas of cooperation among participating organizations in developing and maintaining new program services. The organization has reached as high as 125 affiliates and includes the major professional associations.

The AEA publishes a **Handbook of Adult Education** which is used by practitioners and students of adult education. The book is published every ten years and covers a wide range of history, teaching techniques, and organizational information. **Adult Education** and **Lifelong Learning** are its professional journals for workers in the field.

ADULT EDUCATION ASSOCIATION

Sections of the A.E.A.

 1. ADULT BASIC EDUCATION

 9. LIBERAL ADULT EDUCATION

 2. ARMED FORCES EDUCATION AND TRAINING

 10. MASS MEDIA IN ADULT EDUCATION

 3. COMMUNITY DEVELOPMENT

 11. PUBLIC AFFAIRS EDUCATION

 4. EDUCATION FOR AGING

 12. RELIGIOUS ADULT EDUCATION

 5. EDUCATION AND INDUSTRY

 13. RESIDENTIAL ADULT EDUCATION

 6. HOME AND FAMILY LIFE EDUCATION

 14. RURAL ADULT EDUCATION

 7. INTERNATIONAL AFFAIRS

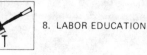 8. LABOR EDUCATION

 15. TRAINING AND PROFESSIONAL DEVELOPMENT

THE NATIONAL ASSOCIATION FOR PUBLIC CONTINUING ADULT EDUCATION

The membership in NAPCAE, as the organization in now known, is limited to persons employed by public schools or state departments of education. The organization has a series of publications useful to teachers in adult education and holds annual conferences. The stated purposes of the group are to increase public understanding of public school adult education and to support state and federal legislation in support of public school adult education. The president of NAPCAE is an ex officio member of the AEA Executive Committee. A policy of holding periodic joint meetings of the two associations has been adopted.

THE ASSOCIATION OF UNIVERSITY EVENING COLLEGES

In 1939, the AUEC emerged as an offshoot of the Association of Urban Universities, which was organized the same year as the NUEA, 1915. One hundred twenty-eight institutions had affiliated by 1959, and now the group exceeds 150 institutional members. Committees are organized to conduct studies and furnish data for improvement of instruction, teacher selection and training, curriculum building, services to the community, and promotion of the evening college idea. One of the major achievements of the AUEC was the founding of the Center for the Study of Liberal Education for Adults (CSLEA) in 1951 with financing from the Fund for Adult Education. CSLEA publications and reports are valuable to professionals in the field of adult education.

FOUNDATION SUPPORT OF ADULT EDUCATION

Knowles reports that the field of adult education has benefited from contributions amounting to over $76,250,000 from at least three major foundations. The Ford Foundation provided a total of $47,400,000 to the Fund for Adult Education, which initiated programs and sponsored scholarships and fellowships for leaders in the mass media. Between 1951 and 1957 the Fund for Adult Education awarded grants totaling $11,666,291 to underwrite the establishment of educational radio and television facilities and to stimulate development of programs. The Mott Foundation of Flint, Michigan, is providing money to adult education programs. The Kellogg Foundation has put millions into supporting the establishment of Centers for Continuing Education such as those at Michigan State University, the University of Chicago, and the University of Georgia.

Risk capital is needed to support experimental programs and allow the field to strengthen its leadership, expand its research and literature, and encourage closer unity and cooperation between the agencies of adult and continuing education.

The Historical Development of Adult Education is shown in the following chart.

ENGLAND--
EARLY VENTURES IN ADULT EDUCATION

Date	Event	Person(s)	Purpose	Implications
1730	Circulating Schools of Wales	Religious leaders founded	Teach reading skills so that Bible could be read	Originally intended for working women. Supported by voluntary effort. Declined in mid 19th century but revived in late 19th & 20th centuries.
1789	Birmingham Sunday Society	Sunday School teachers (Mark Jones)	Moral instruction plus lecture courses on secular topics	
1798	Adult School (Nottingham)	Religious leaders	Desire to reduce literacy & promote Bible reading. Also taught writing & arithmetic	
1799	Mechanics' Institute (Glasgow)	Dr. George Birkbeck	Satisfy artisans desire to understand industrial conditions & resulting social reforms	Birkbeck later took concept to London where he gained the support of both gentry and working class.
1842	People's College (Sheffield)	Rev. R.S. Bayley	Provide general education of humane nature to working men	
1854	London Working Men's College	Frederick Maurice	Practical experiment in social reform	Day-school for infants. Evening school to teach boys & men. Added support of academicians. Upward movement to Oxford & Cambridge never occurred.
1873	Syndicate for Extension Lectures	James Stuart	Provide lecture courses throughout country	Beginnings of university extension movement. Student costs lead to decline. Gave rise to establishment of more colleges.
1883	Toynbee (Prototype of Steelement House)	Canon Barnett	Lectures by Oxford educators given in heart of London slums	New recognition by universities of their responsibilities to the underprivileged.

Ulich, Mary Ewen. Patterns of Adult Education. Pageant Press Inc., 1965.

Thanks to Phyllis Estock for assistance in this Chart.

"Adult Education," Encyclopaedia Britannica. Vol. 1, 1969.

Date	Event	Person(s)	Purpose	Implications
1607	Jamestown landing of the settlers		Survival in a strange land	Apprenticeship to learn trades in New World was main educational instrument.
1636	Founding of Harvard College	Josiah Quincy, pres.	Sponsored by religious sects to prepare ministers but did prepare lawyers and physicians also	By 1769 a total of nine colleges had been established in the colonies.
1642	Massachusetts law		Held parents and masters responsible for teaching young to read and write	Parents looked to others more competent to teach. Church was single most universal instrument for intellectual activity.
	Establishment of private schools		For vocational education, language and arithmetic	Need to survive and to create new satisfactory life. Latin grammar schools, English schools and academies developed.
⅄ 1727	Junto	Benjamin Franklin	For discussion of morals, politics and natural philosophy	Through his writings and life example Franklin was major influence in development of Am. compulsion for self-improvement.
1731	Subscription library	Benjamin Franklin	Increase numbers of books available to members	Cost was high which limited use to the wealthy. Franklin Institute established in 1824.
1776 to 1781	American Revolution	Thomas Jefferson		University of Virginia
	Post-war upsurge			Period of nationalism and the creation of a new nation.
1820	Mechanics' Apprentices Library in Boston N.Y.Mercantile Library		Directed toward technical needs of young artisans and mercantile workers.	Fees much lower than subscription library. Provided lecture series, scientific collections and periodicals.
1824	American Sunday School Union		Focus on religious education of children	Resulted from transplantation of of Sunday School movement in England which began in 1785.
⅄ 1826	Lyceum	Josiah Holbrook	Advancement of education and general diffusion of knowledge	Most spectular offspring of hunger for knowledge of this period. Demonstrated feasibility of integrated organization for purposed of A.E. Developed education technique--lecture forum. Published "scientific tracts" for home study. Suggested ida of national popular movement for advancement of A.E.
1825-1850	Battle for public education		Tax support for education of children	Was essentially an adult educational process.
1830	Origin of lecture circuit in New Haven, Conn. (Yale)	Benjamin Silliman	Emerged from desire of the people to hear of new discoveries in natural science being made in Europe	Forerunner of the university extension idea.
1836	Lowell Institute (Boston)	John Lowell,Jr.	Religious motivation. Had broader base than earlier libraries	Expression of American belief in the efficacy of lectures as a means of moral and intellectual improvement. Still in existence. Cooper Union founded by Peter Cooper in New York in 1859 was of similar nature.
1842	Free town library Peterborough,N.H.		Supported by municipal tax	Followed by passage of first state enabling law in New Hampshire in 1849.
1852	Boston Public Library			Public library concept as we know it today. First large donations began with Astor gift of half a million dollars. Andrew Carnegie contributions between 1881 and 1917 in major urban areas.

Date	Event	Person(s)	Purpose	Implication
1851 1852 1855	Y.M.C.A. U.S.Agric.Society Y.W.C.A.			Emergence of voluntary associations
1857	National Teachers' Association		Organization to represent teachers nationwide	Became National Education Association in 1870.
1861 to 1865	Civil War			
* 1862	Morrill Act		Provided land endowment for establishing colleges to teach agriculture, mechanics, home economics and military science	Need to produce military leaders to fight Civil War and farmers to produce food for armies.
1865 to 1914	Post-war surge			Proliferation of voluntary associations. Expansion of museum movement. Immigration movement.
* 1874	Chautauqua	Dr. John Vincent & Lewis Miller	Summer education for Sunday school teachers	Expanded to include secular education. Series of summer courses including language, liberal arts, music, library training, etc. Early director was William Rainey Harper. Next came correspondence courses during winter months.
1878	Chautauqua Literary & Scientific Circle		Four year program in history and literature	First integrated core program of adult education.
1887	Hatch Act		Provided each state with a federal appropriation for agric. experimental station	Grange Farmers Union
1891	N.Y.university extension appropriation	Melvil Dewey	First state organized university extension	
1892	Univ.of Chicago Correspondence Division	Wm. Rainey Harper	Education by mail	
1904	Farmers' cooperative demonstrations	Seaman Knapp	Persuaded farmers to change methods by actual demonstration of new techniques	
1906	Wisconsin Idea	Louis E. Reber	Revival of university extension concept	Broaden role of university to serve the full scope of life problems--economic,political, cultural & moral. National Univ. Ext. Assoc. founded 1915.
1910	University summer school		Six weeks session usually attended by teachers	Started at Harvard in 1869. Common in universities throughout country by 1910.
1914	Smith-Lever Act		Established Cooperative Extension Service	Largest single adult education organization ever created. Most highly organized,highly pervasive instrument of A.E.in U.S.
1914 to 1918	World War I			Necessity to feed nation and allies. County agent idea implemented. State support for evening schools.
1918 to 1930	Post-war surge			Labor interest shown by permanent educ. dept. being organized by two unions.
1918	Compulsory school attendance			Began prior to Civil War in Mass. and N.Y. but not extended to all states until 1918.
1926	Am. Assoc. for A.A.C. founded	Morse A. Cartwright		
1928	Adult Learning published (Book)	Edward L. Thorndike	Highlighted growing interest of social scientists in adult learning process	Proved ability of adults to learn declined very little with age.
1930 to 1940	Work relief programs	Franklin D. Roosevelt		Use of professional & skilled workers as teachers for adult classes.
1940 to 1945	World War II		Training civilians and military personnel in highly specialized technological warfare	

Date	Event	Person(s)	Purpose	Implication
1945 to 1955	Post-war surge G. I. Bill			Returning veterans and government subsidized education. Rise of foundations with financial support.
1951	A.E. Assoc. of U.S.A. formed		Provide unified focus for all working in field of A.E.	Ford, Kellogg & Mott
1957	Sputnik launch			Marked beginning of space exploration. Emphasis and funds concentrated.
1959	Assoc. of Univ. Evening Colleges	Dr. George Parkinson		
1965	Adult Education Act.		Literacy Education	Adult Basic Education

*Thanks to Phyllis Estock for assistance with this chart.

SUMMARY

Although adult education is not a new concept, we find many institutional forms have developed in recent history. We found that formal institutional adult education on a large scale is relatively new. Because of the diversity of the programs and institutions serving adults, we have examined some of the historical roots of the movement.

First we examined the English heritage in adult education, because of the close ties between Great Britain and the adult education movement in the United States. Examined are the mechanics institutes, the people's colleges, the movement for university extension, and the development of Toynbee Hall and the extension lectures in the settlement houses in England.

The growth of the adult education movement in the United States is traced to the colonial days. Historians attribute the development of adult education to the Protestant revolt of the sixteenth century and the general awakening of Europe taking place at that time. An informed electorate became an objective of the founding fathers, realizing that political independence was not sufficient.

The lyceum movement was an important institutional form for self-culture, debate, and discussion. Josiah Holbrook led the organization to more than 3,000 lyceums by 1839. The Chautauqua Institution under Bishop Vincent and Dr. William Rainey Harper trained Sunday school teachers both in residence and by correspondence study. The universities were important in bringing culture to adults and the Philadelphia Society for the Extension of University Teaching promoted the idea of lectures and classes. Described are some of University Extension efforts, including a prototype, the University of Wisconsin and its Extension Division founded in 1906.

National organizations promoting adult education developed such as the National University Extension Association founded in 1915, the Adult Education Association, U.S.A. in 1951, the National Association for Public School Adult Education, an affiliate of the National Education Association, and the Association of University Evening Colleges with 128 affiliated institutions by 1959.

Foundation support is important to the growth of adult education in the United States - Ford, Kellogg, and Mott being major contributors.

BACKGROUND OF THE ADULT EDUCATION MOVEMENT

QUESTIONS

1. What are some of the British models for adult education?
2. Who were some of the leaders in the adult education movement in Great Britian?
3. What were some of the purposes of the young scholars working in such settlement houses as Toynbee Hall?
4. What are some of the social reforms that gave an impetus to extension programs in the United States?
5. What were some of the purposes of the lyceum movement?
6. Who were some of the leaders in the Chautauqua Institution, and what were their objectives?
7. Describe one of the prototypes for University Extension.
8. What are some of the sections of the ADULT EDUCATION ASSOCIATION, U.S.A.? What are some of the publications?
9. Name some of the other national associations concentrating in adult and continuing education?
10. What foundations have given support to adult education, and in what ways?
11. Name some of the key historical developments in the field of adult education, and the leading name associated with the development.

BIBLIOGRAPHY

Adams, James Truslow, Frontiers of American Culture. N.Y.: Charles Scribner's Sons, 1944.

Alford, Harold, CONTINUING EDUCATION IN ACTION, Residential Centers for Lifelong Learning. John Wiley & Sons, N.Y. 1968

Axford, Roger W. "William Henry Lighty - Adult Education Pioneer." Ph.D. dissertation, University of Chicago, 1961.

————. **College-Community Consultation**. DeKalb, Ill.: Enlightenment Press, 1967.

Bittner and Mallory, UNIVERSITY TEACHING BY MAIL, Macmillan, (A Survey of Correspondence Instruction conducted by American Universities), Macmillan N.Y., 1933.

Cartwright, Morse A. **Ten Years of Adult Education**. New York: Macmillan, 1935.

Grattan, C. Hartley. **In Quest of Knowledge**. New York: Association Press, 1955.

————. **American Ideas About Adult Education**, 1710-1951. New York: Columbia U.P., 1959.

Houle, Cyril O. **Universities in Adult Education**. Paris: UNESCO, 1952.

Knowles, Malcolm. **Handbook of Adult Education**. Washington, D.C.: Adult Education Association U.S.A. 1960.

————. **The Adult Education Movement in the United States**. New York: Holt, 1962.

Morton, John R. **University Extension in the United States**. Birmingham: U. of Alabama Press, 1953 (study of National University Extension Association).

National University Extension Association, in Stanley J. Drazek (ed.), **Expanding Horizons, Continuing Education**. Washington, D.C.: North Washington Press, 1965.

Rosentreter, Frederick M. **The Boundaries of the Campus**. Madison: U. of Wisconsin Press, 1957.

Smith, Aker, and Kidd, HANDBOOK OF ADULT EDUCATION, Macmillan Co., N.Y., 1970.

Tarbell, Robert W. **A History of the Milwaukee Vocational and Adult Schools**. Milwaukee, Wis. M.V.A.S. Press, 1958.

Vance, Maurice M. **Charles R. Van Hise**, Madison: State Historical Society of Wisconsin, 1960. (Story of a Scientist-Progressive and father of "The Wisconsin Idea.")

1 See Adult Education Committee of the British Ministry of Reconstruction, **A Design for Democracy**, 1919, p. 161.

2 Cyril O. Houle, "Adult Education," **Encyclopaedia Britannica**, Vol. 1 (1957), p. 184.

3 Robert Peers, **Adult Education: A Comparative Study**, 2nd ed. New York: Humanities Press, 1959, pp. 3-30.

4 **A Design for Democracy**, The Adult Education Committee of the British Ministry of Reconstruction commonly called the "1919 Report." (New York Association Press, p. 188.) Quoted from the "Original Cicular of the Working Men's College," issued in 1854.

5 Herbert B. Adams, **University Extension in the United States**, Government Printing Office, Washington, D.C., 1900, p. 275.

6 Ellwood P. Cubberley, **Public Education in the United States**, Houghton, Boston, 1947.

7 Homer Kempfer, **Adult Education**, McGraw-Hill, New York, 1955, p. 4.

8 Adams, **op. cit.**, p. 298. See also **American Journal of Education**, Vol. 14 (October 1826), p. 535, and Carl Bode, **The American Lyceum**, Oxford U.P., New York, 1956, pp. 19-26.

9 Cyril O. Houle, **op cit.**, p. 185.

10 Ronald Brandt, "Culture by Correspondence: The Chautauqua Literary and Scientific Circle," unpublished paper, July 1960 (author's files), Research based on W. R. Harper's letters, Harper Library, University of Chicago.

11 W. S. Bittner and H. F. Mallory, **University Teaching by Mail**, Macmillan, New York, 1933, p. 17.

12 Mr. M. E. Sadler, Secretary of the Oxford Delegacy, is quoted as saying that "the phrase 'University Extension' seems to have become current in the discussions on University reform during the years immediately preceding 1850." George Henderson, Report upon the University Extension Movement in England. Published by order of the Philadelphia Society for the Extension of University Teaching, 1600 Chestnut Street, Philadelphia (n. d., ca. 1890), p. 3.

13 J. N. Larned, "An Experiment in University Extension," **Library Journal** (March-April 1888), p. 75.

14 Adams, **op. cit.**, p. 303.

15 **Ibid.**, p. 307.

16 Copy in author's files.

17 John R. Morton, **University Extension in the United States**, U. of Alabama Press, Birmingham, 1953, p. 5.

18 James Creese, **The Extension of University Teaching**, American Association for Adult Education, New York, 1941, p. 98.

19 "Adult Education," in Christian E. Burchel (ed.), **The College Blue Book**, 9th ed., Universal Lithographers, Inc., Baltimore, 1959, p. 218.

20 National University Extension Association, Washington, D.C.

21 Phillip E. Frandson, Chairman, Joint AUEC-NUEA Committee on Minimum Data and Definitions, 1961.

22 Malcolm Knowles, **The Adult Education Movement in the United States**, Holt, New York, 1962, p. 190.

143

Chapter XI:

SOME ADULT EDUCATION PIONEERS

> There are a few characters which have stood the closest scrutiny and the severest tests, which have been tried in the furnace and have proved pure, which have been weighed in the balance and have not been found wanting, which have been declared sterling by the general consent of mankind.
> -Thomas Babington Macaulay,
> **Critical and Historical Essays**

Youth need models of excellence; no less do new and inexperienced workers in a field such as adult education. Look at the heroes of a culture and you can tell a great deal about the value system of that people.

Although we know that institutions arise to meet the sociological and technological needs of a society, the influence of persons of ideas is not to be depreciated nor diminished. Had it not been for the tenacity, imagination, and forbearance of Thomas Edison, the Wright brothers, and other men of science like them, we might still be using kerosene for illuminating our homes instead of powering supersonic jet airplanes with it. So also with the field of continuing education. Men and women of innovation, program ideas, and organizational ability have emerged to lead the way for developing institutional patterns which will benefit society and provide individuals with the vehicle for individual learning and improvement.

To paraphrase Victor Hugo, nothing is truer than the power of an idea when its time has come - but that idea must be borne by a person with the vision, leadership and moral fortitude to recognize the validity of the idea and institutionalize the values.

Even today, when bureaucracies are stifling the creativity and initiative of many potential intellectual and moral leaders, it was never more true that an institution is the shadow of a person. We shall examine in a cursory and abbreviated form some biographical sketches of pioneers in adult education, hoping that the serious student of the field will pursue the more detailed biographies for further inspiration and enlightenment.

We have chosen a few of those individuals who innovated institutional patterns or developed media or agencies for disseminating knowledge. Undoubtedly some of the great leaders

144

of the field have been omitted, but we have tried to include representative ones with the hope that a more definitive publication of the pioneers of adult education may be taken up by other historians and scholars in the field of adult education.

HEROES OF ADULT EDUCATION

Indian Squanto (? - 1622):
First "County Agricultural Agent"

Living in the area where Plymouth, Massachusetts, was founded was Tisquantum, better known as Squanto, an Indian of the Pawtuxet tribe in the federated Wamponoag tribes. Enticed aboard an English ship, he was taken to Spain and sold into slavery but escaped to England. There he was befriended by John Slaney, a merchant in London. Squanto returned to America with Captain Thomas Dermer in 1620.

In the spring of 1621, three months after the Pilgrims landed on Plymouth Rock, Squanto and a friend came upon the starving settlement and arranged a meeting with Massasoit. This resulted in the now famous treaty with the Indians.

Squanto instructed the Pilgrim colony in the arts of fishing and agriculture. He acted as interpreter to the few Indians still living nearby. He showed the early colonists the many uses of the edible plants and how to hunt animals and wildlife, and acquainted them with uses of shellfish and other seafood.

The lives of many Pilgrims were saved by Squanto, who showed them how to prepare maize. Perhaps all of the early settlers would have starved had they not learned the arts of the primitive life from this Indian.

Again it was Squanto who demonstrated to the colonists how to plant corn (maize) correctly when spring came. He illustrated how to place three fish with the heads pointing in and the tails out, like the spokes of a wheel. The seed was to be planted in the center. The first great harvest was celebrated by the Pilgrims because they followed Squnto's demonstrations and instructions. It was celebrated with great King Massasoit and his tribe.

So far as research can determine, this was the first use of the demonstration-method technique in agricultural history in the United States and the first agricultural extension work recorded in American history. Perhaps we can say Squanto was our first U.S. agricultural county agent.[1]

145

Benjamin Franklin (1706-1790):
Patron Saint of Adult Education

Sometimes called the patron saint of adult education, Benjamin Franklin was a founder of more than one agency of adult education. Born in Boston on January 17, 1706, he had founded the first Junto by the time he was twenty-one. It was organized in Philadelphia in 1727 to debate ideas about morals, politics and natural philosophy. The Junto has been hailed as the prototype of Rotary International. The Philadelphia Junto was revived in 1941 as an independent agency of adult education with the motto "Fun in Learning", with a somewhat different clientele than the Leather Apron Club, as the original group was sometimes called.

The earliest American subscription library was a brainchild of Franklin. The need for easier access to books by members of the Junto led to the founding of the Library Company of Philadelphia in 1731. Wages of the first "professional" librarian in America, Louis Timothee, were paid by the Junto. The Junto and the library linked Franklin to the lower middle classes, while the Masonic Lodge linked him to the upper classes.

It was Franklin's "Proposals Relating to the Educating of Youth in Pennsylvania" in 1749 which was instrumental in organizing the Academy of Philadelphia in 1751. This grew into the University of Pennsylvania. Franklin was a great believer in study and self-cultivation. He was a founder of the American Philosophical Society. In 1730, Franklin became the public printer for Pennsylvania, a position that brought him political power and intellectual leadership. Most people know him best for his humorous **Poor Richard's Almanack**, which he wrote and published from 1732 to 1757, making a fortune from it. He organized the first volunteer fire department in the United States and, through the Franklin Institute, founded the Philadelphia Mutual Fire Insurance Company. Perhaps as much as any American hero in adult education, he has influenced favorably attitudes toward continuing education.

A man of curiosity and self-discipline, Franklin was a statesman of unusual ability, a book printer, a newspaperman, an author of distinction, a soapmaker, an agriculturalist, a writer on the rise of tides, an historian, the inventor of the Franklin stove and bifocal glasses, and a leader in the study of electricity. He was a model for adult education and a "patron saint" of the field.

Grundtvig

Nicolaj Frederik Severin Gruntvig (1783-1872):
Denmark's Folk School Adult Educator

The Danish Lutheran Bishop Nicolaj Frederick Severin Gruntvig is called the father of the Danish folk school and is responsible for reawakening national pride during a period when Denmark had suffered defeats in the Napolenic Wars and loss of land following Bismarck's rise to power in Germany. Grundtvig shifted the direction of the people's interest from external affairs to the rich cultural heritage of the country's long and colorful history.

He established schools of adult education, known as the Danish folk schools, revitalizing the young farmers who had grown pessimistic and lethargic in their suffering. A student of Latin, Greek, and theology, he studied Fichte, Schelling, Goethe, and Shakespeare, and became himself a poet. In 1810, he suffered a brief mental breakdown but returned to his childhood faith and became a reformer. It was his calling to encourage the fellowship of Christians and lead the Danish people to a new pride in their history and culture. He did research in Anglo-Saxon history in England and translated **Beowulf** into Danish. In England, he observed how the British tested theories by demonstrating how they worked in life rather than by research from dusty tomes.

During the period 1830-40 he authored three books of sermons, hymns, and a three-volume history, and developed his ideas about a new concept, the Folkehjskolen, or Danish Folk High School. He came to the conclusion that only the adult is mature enough to truly understand life. He became convinced the farmers and artisans should all take part actively in Danish legislation. To do so they must know their history and heritage he reasoned.

This remarkable man felt that the folk high school should give the Danish citizens a thorough knowledge of social institutions and a history of their country. Efficient management of farms was another subject to be taught through living and demonstration. By traveling, Grundtvig intended the Dane to become acquainted with the animals, birds, and human beings of the many small islands. Singing and the merry joke were to be emphasized, and the "living word" and inspired speech were to prevail.

Christian Flor and Christian Kold helped construct the specific schools. Grundtvig raised money for the construction of a school at Ryslinge in 1850. "It is to the adults, not the children, that we must look for a better future . . . education for life, not book study." Since 1844, 177 folk high schools have been started, though some have not survived. [2]

William Rainey Harper (1856-1906):
Chicago's Correspondence Study Pioneer

The father of the university press, the university extension program in the United States, and the four-quarter system was a Latin and Greek scholar born of Scotch-Irish ancestry. William Rainey Harper had earned his B.A., from Muskingum College by age 14 and his Ph.D. at 18, writing his dissertation on "A Comparative Study of the Prepositions in Latin, Greek, Sanskrit, and Gothic." While teaching Semitic languages at the Baptist Union Theological Seminary in Chicago he developed a correspondence course and became enamored of the efficacy of the method. He claimed he could teach students as well by correspondence as he could face-to-face. He resisted a number of offers for college presidencies until John D. Rockefeller urged him in 1890 to join in the project of establishing the University of Chicago. This he could not resist.

During his tenure as principal of the Chautauqua College of Liberal Arts from 1885 to 1891 Harper experimented with varying adult education methods. He helped establish a correspondence study program at Chautauqua which is still in operation today, and the Chautauqua Literary and Scientific Circle, which sends out books and study guides.

Harper, indeed, pioneered the idea of a university summer school. He attracted leading scholars from all over the world:

John Coulter, pioneer plant ecologist; Albert A. Michelson, who was honored by being the first American to win the Nobel prize in physics; Paul Shorey, classical scholar; and F. R. Moulton, the astronomer who formulated the planetesimal theory of the origin of the solar system.

Harper also proved that correspondence study should be an integral part of any great university. He would not agree to Rockefeller's offer to come to found the University of Chicago in 1891 until it was stipulated that the Extension Division would be a basic part of the organizational structure of the university in order to take knowledge to the people through whatever means possible - lectures, correspondence study, and the university press.

Many pioneers in adult education got either their inspiration or training from Harper. As early as 1885 Harper had founded the American Institute of Sacred Literature to teach Hebrew by mail. Charles R. Van Hise, father of the "Wisconsin Idea," taught for Harper at the University of Chicago before being called to the presidency of the University of Wisconsin. William H. Lighty went to Chicago to study in the summer of 1897 and was inspired by this great scholar. Many institutions owe their inspiration for extending higher education to Harper, university extension pioneer.

William Henry Lighty (1863-1959):
Radio and Extension Pioneer

William H. Lighty ✗

Many adult education agencies trace their origin to William H. Lighty. Trained at Cornell University, Lighty was for years a leader of the St. Louis Ethical Society, heading an adult education agency, the Self-Culture Halls. Called to head the new correspondence study department of the University of Wisconsin in 1906, he was one of the founders of the new famous University of Wisconsin Extension Division, best known for the "Wisconsin Idea." He founded the National University Extension Association, now representing more than 200 colleges and universities, which first met in Madison, Wisconsin, in 1915. He was its first program chairman and wrote the constitution. Lighty was also a founder of WHA, Madison, Wisconsin, the university's educational station and one of the oldest radio stations in the nation. He was also its first program director. He worked with scientists Earle M. Terry and Malcolm Parker, pioneers of radio. In 1911, Lighty was a moving force in the establishment of the Institute of Charities and Corrections in Wisconsin, now the Wisconsin Welfare Council. In 1913, he organized a Correspondence Bureau for the American Ethical Union. Through the NUEA he helped organize the National Association of Educational Broadcasters.

He first engaged Prof. Edgar Gordon of the University of Wisconsin music department in what is now the "Wisconsin School of the Air," blanketing classrooms throughout the state. He informed the members of the NUEA through his surveys of university radio stations. He was elected president of the NUEA in 1927. Until his death he held the distinction of being the only person not a dean or director of extension to serve in this national capacity.

A friend of historical societies, he was an honorary member of the Minnesota Historical Society, addressed the Missouri Historical society in 1901, and was a member of the State Historical Society of Wisconsin, which he described in his speeches as "a model." He served as secretary of the Saturday Lunch Club, made up of more than two hundred influential persons from the university and government in Wisconsin, many of whom were LaFollette progressives.

Through the National University Extension Association, Lighty influenced the utilization of correspondence study as a respected method of academic instruction. His visitors at the University of Wisconsin from Australia, Russia, Germany, and other countries studied methods of correspondence study as developed by Lighty and his staff.

Charles R. Van Hise (1857-1918):
University Extensionist, Father of the Wisconsin Idea

"It is the duty of the staff of the state university to be at the service of the state along all lines in which their expert knowledge will be helpful; it is their duty to assist in carrying knowledge to the people" said Charles R. Van Hise, the scientist-progressive and president of the University of Wisconsin from 1903 to 1918.

As far back as 1890, Wisconsin had held mechanics' institutes and general institutes patterned along the line of the Chautauqua lecture courses. But under Van Hise's administration enough faculty, regent, and state support was secured to establish a permanent general extension program. It was Van Hise who fathered the "Wisconsin Idea" that the **boundaries of the campus should be the boundaries of the state**, a principle which other nations and states are still trying to emulate and are in some cases surpassing.

President W. R. Harper had considerable influence on Van Hise, for Harper's goals and working habits were carefully observed at the University of Chicago where Van Hise served as a visiting lecturer in geology. As Maurice M. Vance points out in his biography of Van Hise, "the two men within a year of the same age, had a number of similarities of character and personality, and it was not surprising that Van Hise should profit by his acquaintance with his professional senior."[3]

Van Hise remembered that Harper had said that the motto of the universities of modern times should be service to humanity. As a president of a land-grant university, Van Hise hoped to build a university "as broad as human endeavor."[4] He argued that the idea of culture was (and to a large extent still is) the central ideal of the colleges of liberal arts, whether a part of a university or an independent college. Van Hise held that the idea of service may be said to be the ultimate purpose of the ideas of culture, vocation, and research.[5] He stated that the service here under special consideration is that directed to the people of the state and nation and known as University Extension. For knowledge to be useful, it must be put where people can apply it, and Van Hise gave the organizational vehicle for universities to do that task.

Seaman A. Knapp (1833-1911):
Father of Agricultural Demonstration System

Born to a family of seven generation farmers, it is perhaps natural that Seaman Knapp should have developed into a hard-

151

working farmer by the age of sixteen. In his youth, the Knapp family had moved to a farm at Schroon Lake, N.Y., near Lake Champlain.

Even though the family had limited finances, Seaman had a burning desire to attend college. He became a student at Union College, Schenectady, N.Y., in 1853. This was one of the first colleges to raise the sciences to the level of the classics.

Following the Civil War, Knapp and two other gentlemen formed the Ripley Female Seminary, one of the first schools to issue degrees rather than diplomas to women. His wife was also a teacher, and they had both taught at Fort Edward Collegiate Institute before the war.

As a result of a knee injury incurred while playing baseball, Knapp had developed poor health. The doctor recommended outdoor life. The family moved to a farm near Vinton, Iowa, in 1866, where he became a minister for the Methodist Episcopal Church, moving about in a wheel chair. Knapp was a chronic organizer and very early organized a local YMCA. He then taught in the state school for the blind for a period of five years.

With health returning, Knapp continued his study of scientific farming and beginning in 1875 wrote numerous articles on farming and farming methods. Soon he began to fight for an agricultural experiment station and encouraged the use of high-quality livestock for breeding. He was elected professor of agriculture and later appointed president of Iowa State College at Ames. The college became nationally known under his leadership.

An opportunity arose in 1886 when he was put in charge of a plan to colonize a million acres of marsh and prairie land in Louisiana.

Knapp formed the Rice Growers Association and persuaded farmers from the Midwest to move into the area and raise rice and cotton. He established the **Rice Journal** and the **Gulf Coast Farmer** in 1897. Rice varieties were introduced from China, Mexico, Japan, and Puerto Rico. The attack on the cotton boll weevil made Knapp famous. Not until his ideas were demonstrated on a farm at Terrell, Texas, were his scientific methods in the cultivation of cotton accepted. Forty thousand dollars was earmarked for demonstration work.

He proved that the "demonstration agent" in each country could diffuse knowledge, for seeing was believing. Knapp was past 70 when he established the county demonstration system in 1904. Today the program is known as the Cooperative Agriculture Extension Service and reaches into every county in the United States, Puerto Rico, Hawaii, and Alaska. He was the father of Agricultural Extension, now copied the world over.

152

Lillian Wald (1867-1940):
Public Health Pioneer

Lillian Wald was born in Cincinnati, Ohio, of wealthy Polish-German-Jewish parents. She spent her youth in Rochester, New York, but at sixteen entered Vassar. Once she visited her older sister who was expecting a baby and talked to her sister's nurse, a graduate of Bellevue Hospital in New York. She was fascinated by nursing and determined to become a part of this new world.

Miss Wald entered Nurses' Training School in a New York hospital in the summer of 1889. She learned to submit to the discipline of the hospital, which was a world of rules and regulations. After eighteen months she was graduated, but desiring more knowledge, entered the Women's Medical College of New York. During those years she was asked to teach an adult education class, a group of immigrant women at the College Settlement. On New York's Lower East Side she learned of poverty and squalor. This determined her life work. She and a friend, Mary Brewster, founded the Nurses' Settlement in 1893, later called Henry Street Settlement House. This was just eighteen years after Toynbee Hall was started in East London, beginning the settlement-house movement.

Lillian Wald is credited with coining the term "public-health nursing." She and her helpers distributed sputum cups and disinfectant to the pioneer tuberculosis nurses. Public school nursing in America was started by her in 1902. She investigated unemployment, cases of dispossessed tenants, midwives in New York, physical defects of children, child-labor problems, construction camps throughout the state of New York, and working girls' conditions in factories, canneries, and sweatshops. She initiated visiting nursing to industrial policy holders of the Metropolitan Life Insurance Company in 1909. She served on the State Immigration Committee and in 1912 was instrumental in helping establish the Federal Children's Bureau. She established the Rural Nursing Service of the American Red Cross and was first president of the National Organization for Public Health Nursing. She used the settlement houses to teach parents health education, instructing immigrants in nursing care, hygiene, cooking, and English. She brought musicians, actors, speakers, dancers, and educators to the settlement houses. Thousands of immigrants mourned her death, but she had shown the way to public health.

Robert L. Cooley (1869-1944):
Vocational Adult Educator

A farmer by birth, Robert L. Cooley worked as a boy loading gravel but determined to go to school and get an education. Throughout his life he carried with him the practical philosophy of his farm youth, which is often reflected in his now famous epigrams known as "Cooleygrams." [6]

Cooley progressed from teacher of a country school to assistant principal of a Wisconsin high school, then principal and finally superintendent. In Milwaukee, Cooley was the first director of what is today the largest Vocational and Adult School in the world, five institutions under one roof with two TV stations. In 1912 he accepted the position as the founder and first director of the Milwaukee Vocational School. Cooley soon became a national figure in vocational education. Believing deeply in both extended training and the ability to do practical work, Cooley is credited with saying, "An untrained man is like a farmer going to market with an empty wagon box." Our milions of dollars for retraining and vocational education were reflected in his visionary statement: "Vocational education is in the swaddling-clothes age."

Cooley was a man of the people and moved among them. "The needs of the students shall determine the curriculum," reflected his educational philosophy. He was continually on the lookout for able and flexible teachers who understood vocational education. He surrounded himself with young and talented vocational educators, many of whom became leaders throughout the nation in programs of vocational and adult education. He knew that now all could have the opportunity to learn, but warned, "You cannot have horses without raising colts." Continually trying to raise the level of education, he reflected, "I'd rather raise the general level an eighth of an inch than build up a few mole hills."

The educational world beat a path to the door of the Milwaukee Vocational and Adult Schools to study innovations and observe programs of this imaginative adult educator. For three summers Cooley conducted courses at Columbia University. In 1927 he was elected president of the Wisconsin Teachers Association and the same year was president of the powerful American Vocational Association. Stout Institute in Wisconsin (now a state university) conferred upon him the degree of "doctor of science."

His objective was to save humanity from the junk heap. His Cooleygrams expressed this aim - "The county spent millions to provide an impressive environment to send people to jail, so why not spend a small amount to make keeping them out of jail impressive?" and "Human junk is so expensive we must quit making it."

Frank Avery Hutchins (1851-1908):
A Father of Libraries

Over seven hundred libraries of the state of Wisconsin owe their origin to the influence of a quiet-spoken and dedicated educator of adults, Frank A. Hutchins. Often spoken of as the "Father of the Wisconsin library system," Hutchins was born in 1851 in Norwalk, Ohio. When he was three his family moved to the Wayland Academy in 1857 and then to Beloit College in 1871. He was an editor of the Beaver Dam Argus for a period and organized the Beaver Dam Free Library Association. This library claims to be the second library in the United States to open its shelves to the public, for Hutchins believed that browsing stimulates curiosity and encourages learning. Hutchins published a select list of books for school libraries after visiting numerous rural school libraries. Hutchins' list set standards and sugguested a method for establishing more effective school libraries. In 1891 he organized the Wisconsin Library Association, a now powerful group for promoting libraries. He served as its president from 1894 to 1897.

It was Hutchins, along with Charles McCarthy and Henry E. Legler (later of the Chicago Public Library), all of the Wisconsin Free Library Commission, who urged president Charles R. Van Hise to establish firmly the University Extension Division in order to diffuse knowledge throughout the state. Hutchins was instrumental in innovating a method of spreading knowledge, known as the traveling library system. The Free Library Commission would send reading materials to communities throughout the state on a topic requested. He kept in touch with more than seven hundred communities reached through the traveling library. This was perhaps his greatest achievement. He helped write the bill creating the Free Library Commission of Wisconsin and served as chairman from 1895-97. He also helped establish the Legislative Reference Library, which assists legislators in drafting bills. Later the idea was adopted by the federal government, and numerous other states emulated the Wisconsin Legislative Reference Library.

Hutchins believed that "a knowledge of good books, with a good librarian, would do more than any other agency toward beating the devil."[7] He was instrumental in creating a Wisconsin summer school of library science. Between 1906 and 1907 he was a field organizer for the then new University of Wisconsin Extension Division. He made materials available for study between lectures offered by the University. He organized and was the first director of the Department of Debating and Public Discussion, which sent clippings, pamphlets, and other discussion materials to study groups throughout the state. He helped plan and inspired the Christmas Seal campaign for the Wisconsin Anti-Tuberculosis Association and was responsible for passage of a law creating a state park commission.

Charles McCarthy (1873-1921):
Vocational Educator - Friend of the Dropout

Charles McCarthy was fond of athletics and books. In his youth he held a variety of jobs: dock worker, common laborer, factory worker, seaman on vessels, and finally a scene shifter in a theater. This son of a poor Irish shoemaker developed an interest in history which stimulated an omnivorous appetite for reading.

A star of the football team at Brockton High School, Massachusetts, he made poor marks in mathematics but did excellently in history. He entered Brown University in the fall of 1892 and made a fine record, which led him to the University of Wisconsin, where he studied with the famous historian, Frederick Jackson Turner. He received his Ph.D. from Wisconsin in 1901 and an honorary degree of Doctor of Letters in 1913 from Brown University. He was a scholar in American History in 1899-1900 and a fellow the next year.

Turner found difficulty in placing McCarthy, although he was a brilliant scholar. He was rough and outspoken. McCarthy worked as a document clerk with Frank A. Hutchins in the state Free Library Commission and they became fast friends, later to fight through and win the University Extension battle in 1906, resulting in the University of Wisconsin Extension Division. A bill creating the Legislative Reference Library was passed in 1901, and by 1907 McCarthy was chief of the Library. He exerted a monumental influence on legislators, for he was often consulted on the wording of bills for the state legislature.

In 1910 the opportunity of a lifetime presented itself. McCarthy traveled to Europe and investigated the system of education in Germany. He was so impressed with its vocational education system that he returned to write a report which resulted in the passage of the bill creating vocational and adult schools throughout Wisconsin. The bill provided that each city with 5,000 population or more could have its own separate tax base for a board of vocational education. The city superintendent became an ex officio member of the board, but both labor and industry had to be represented on the vocational school board.

Schools for artisans sprang up throughout the state after 1911, for Wisconsin was the only state in the union with this unique system providing for sound financing of vocational and adult education. The schools provided that dropouts under age 16 must attend school at least one day a week and must be released from work by the employers for their education. As a result, Wisconsin has one of the lowest dropout rates of any state in the union. McCarthy was a friend of history and libraries, but above all he will be remembered as the father of the vocational and adult schools.

Paul Ansley McGhee (1900-1964):
New York's "Mr. Adult Education"

"His devotion to scholarship and to continuous learning was as inspiration to us," commented David Boyd Chase who, for twenty-three years, heard Paul McGhee open New York University's Institute on Federal Taxation. This institute, just one of many at New York University, runs for nine days and enrolls more than eight hundred business executives, accountants, and lawyers from fifty states studying and working together to keep abreast of the times. Said Chase, "I never saw Paul turn from a student, or from an associate, or an acquaintance who might need counsel or advice."

Paul Ansley McGhee was a guest in a sminar held at the University of Chicago in 1955. As chairman of the seminar, the author had the privilege of introducing him to the group of graduate students in adult education, some just beginning their careers. McGhee was an inspiring advocate of continuing education and an administrator par excellence. Robert L. Leslie, who worked with McGhee in organizing the Center for Publishing and the Graphic Industies in McGhee's Division of General Education, said at McGhee's memorial held in New York that even when Leslie reached seventy-five Paul still believed that Leslie could learn that no one is too old to learn.

McGhee was educated at the University of Rochester, (A.B.), Princeton University, (M.A.), and received honorary degrees from the University of Miami (1954) and New School for Social Research (1960). He served as instructor in English, first director and then dean of the Division of General Education, and professor of General Education at New York University. He drew around him bright young men like Dr. Milton R. Stern, author of **People, Programs, and Persuasion,** and McGhee thought it important to be training University Extension personnel with a vision to the future.

As Abbott Kaplan points out, "For three decades Paul McGhee occupied a unique position nationally and internationally in the field of adult education." Kaplan attributes McGhee's leadership to his extraordinary educational program developed at New York University, and the ideas and insights he contributed to the field. He exemplified and embodied the qualities of a great educator and human being. McGhee demonstrated in an urban university a noncredit program of richness and intellectual depth and excitement.

He contributed to the adults' intellectual and cultural development by creating the kind of atmosphere conducive to maximum adult learning. In the essay "Higher and Adult Education" he said, "The fact is that too often we talk continuing education and practice terminal education." A School for Optimists, published by the Center for the Study of Liberal Education for Adults, is one of McGhee's best works.

Helen Graham Lynch (1895-   ):
Americanization Educator

The National Association for Public School Adult Education, 5,000 strong, was meeting in Chicago in 1966. The banquet was held to honor a lady who over a period of twenty years had personally influenced at least a quarter of a million immigrants in the Chicago area. The author began his adult education career in Chicago and taught for Mr. Vernon Bowyer and Mrs. Helen G. Lynch in an Americanization class on the seamy side of Chicago. In 1948 our class met in an orthodox synagogue on the West Side. I shall never forget how much I learned teaching those immigrants English and the songs we made up to learn to pronounce the words correctly. I was one of hundreds of teachers who came under the influence of Helen G. Lynch.

The award to Mrs. Lynch, described as the "grand lady of adult education," reads, "Here is a woman in Chicago who has taken the inscription on the statue of liberty, GIVE ME YOUR TIRED, YOUR POOR, YOUR HUDDLED MASSES YEARNING TO BREATHE FREE, to heart. During the past two decades she has personally influenced at least a quarter of a million immigrants who came to make their home in the Chicagoland area." She was presented the award from the Citizens of Greater Chicago for her work with adults in the Americanization and Adult Education program, and two years before received the Immigrant Service Leaque Award of the year as a native-born citizen who "made the greatest contribution working with new citizens." The NAPCAE award stated that each adult education program in Northern Illinois owed some of its success to Mrs. Lynch. Mrs. Lynch also founded the Citizenship Council of Metropolitan Chicago in 1956, dedicated to helping new Americans become responsible citizens. This is done through welcoming receptions each week. To help the immigrant understand voting procedure, Voter Education Workshops are held throughout the year.

CITIZENSHIP COUNCIL of METROPOLITAN CHICAGO
AN ILLINOIS CORPORATION NOT-FOR-PROFIT

Dedicated to helping new Americans become responsible citizens

7 SOUTH DEARBORN STREET • CHICAGO, ILLINOIS 60603
TELEPHONE: 236-1199

OFFICERS
CHAIRMAN OF THE BOARD
JAMES J. O'CONNOR
PRESIDENT AND EXECUTIVE DIRECTOR
MRS. HELEN G. LYNCH
BUS. 236-1199
RES. 771-5815
VICE PRESIDENTS
H. HAYWARD HIRSCH
WILLIS A LEONHARDI
TREASURER
DONALD J. CROWDER
SECRETARY
DR. EDWARD M. MARTIN
CONSULTANTS
BURTON DUFFIE
HAROLD W. CALHOUN
BOARD OF DIRECTORS
MRS. THADDEUS V. ADESKO
L. RAYMOND BILLETT
RICHARD O. BOYD
MRS. CHARLES HENRY BROWN
MRS. GARDNER BROWN
HAROLD W. CALHOUN
THOMAS H. COULTER
DONALD J. CROWDER
BURTON DUFFIE
MRS. EARLE B. FOWLER
H. HAYWARD HIRSCH
JAMES H. HYNES
WILLIS A. LEONHARDI
MRS. JEAN FOX LEWIS
ERLING H. LUNDE
MRS. HELEN G. LYNCH
J. DE NAVARRE MACOMB, JR.
DR. EDWARD M. MARTIN
JAMES J. O'CONNOR
MRS. ROBERT GRAY PECK
MRS. EDWARD S. PRICE
MRS. DONALD SCHILLER
MRS. W. GLENN SUTHERS
JOHN M. WEINER

ADVISORY BOARD
JOHN A. BARR
ROSS J. BEATTY
HARRY O. BECHNER
A. ANDREW BOEMI
STANTON R. COOK
JACK H. CORNELIUS
DR. JOSEPH M. CRONIN
MILTON F. DARR, JR.
NEIL DARROUGH
JOHN A. DAWSON
MRS. EVERETT MCKINLEY DIRKSEN
ROBERT M. DREVS
MRS. ONE A. DU VAL
DANIEL J. EDELMAN
E. STANLEY ENLUND
LEWIS H. ERLICHT
DAVID FERGUSON
VICE ADMIRAL E. P. FORRESTEL (RET.)
DOUGLAS A. FULLER
NICHOLAS GALITZINE
LOUIS GOLDBLATT
MRS. WENDELL E. GREEN
MRS. PAUL W. GUENZEL
CHARLES HALL
CORWITH HAMILL
DR. CYRIL O. HOULE
JAMES H. INGERSOLL
WILLIAM INGRAM
HAROLD L. JOHNSON
RICHARD K. JOHNSON
EDMUND L. KELLY
MRS. LOUIS ELLSWORTH LAFLIN JR.
JEWEL LAFONTANT
REVEREND JAMES F. MAGUIRE S.J.
THOMAS W. MANN
HOWARD MAYER
WILLIAM F. MC CURDY
HENRY W. MC GEE
DAVID MELLON
MRS. C. PHILLIP MILLER
ROBERT W. MURPHY
WILLIAM F. MURRAY
RALPH S. NEWMAN
HON. RICHARD B. OGILVIE
MRS. DAVID L. OSTFELD
MARTIN PALTZER
DR. ROBERT BRUCE PIERCE
HERBERT W. PROCHNOW
DR. JOHN T. RATALLIATA
JOHN O. ROOT
A. ABBOTT ROSEN
RABBI IRVING J. ROSENBAUM
NORMAN ROSS
JOHN W. SHELDON
GEORGE F. SIELER
GERALD A. SIVAGE
HAROLD BYRON SMITH, JR.
LEN YOUNG SMITH
HAROLD R. SPURWAY
HON. WILLIAM G. STRATTON
MRS. L. L. STUART, JR.
ROBERT D. STUART, JR.
CARROLL H. SUDLER, JR.
RICHARD L. THOMAS
JOHN T. TRUTTER
MORRISON WAUD
BETTY ROSS WEST
CHARLES S. WINSTON, JR.

September 26, 1977

To: Directors, Advisory Board Members, and Friends
From: Helen G. Lynch, President
Subject: Citizenship Day and Constitution Week

On the evening of September 19, 1977, in the auditorium of the Prudential Building in Chicago, the Citizenship Council of Metropolitan Chicago observed their 22nd annual Citizenship Day and Constitution Week Program. The stage of the auditorium was again decorated with plants and floral pieces by the Chicago Park District. At the rear of the stage were the usual "Flags of American Liberty," sent by the Republic Company of Chicago. This was a fitting welcome for the representatives of our 10,000 New Citizens of the past year.

Since the Proclamation of President Eisenhower, each President has issued a Proclamation asking ALL Americans to pay tribute to the New Citizens of the past year and to the Constitution. The Citizenship Council of Metropolitan Chicago is pleased to carry out the President's Proclamation.

As the guests gathered, Cathryn Bennett, one of Chicago's leading musicians, Music Director for the Rotary Club of Chicago, and accompanist for the weekly Welcoming Receptions for our New Citizens, welcomed them with patriotic music.

At 7:30 p.m., the United States Army Color Guard, Fort Sheridan, Presented the Colors. Following this inspiring ceremony, Mr. David V. Vandersall, District Director, Immigration and Naturalization Service, opened the Naturalization Ceremony. Mr. Harold W. Calhoun, Assistant District Director for Citizenship, Immigration and Naturalization Service, made a Motion for Admission of four hundred Petitioners for Naturalization.

Ambrose Caliver (1894-1962):
Literacy Educator

On November 15, 1963, the National Commission for Adult Literacy of the Adult Education Association, U.S.A. honored the life of Dr. Ambrose Caliver for his work as a teacher, administrator, and pioneer in education of blacks.

Caliver, who began working in a coal mine at the age of eight, is remembered for his belief that the education of a person is incomplete if he has failed to learn to work with his hands. He studied at the University of Chicago, Tuskegee Institute, Harvard University, and the University of Wisconsin, from which he received his Master of Arts in 1920. A faculty Scholarship Department and finally as Dean of the University in 1927. He wrote widely and did research on topics such as student preparation for college, education and the manual arts, and curriculum and guidance.

Of Dr. Caliver a friend wrote, "A cultural pioneer must have courage, patience, perseverance, resilience, and vision. That Ambrose Caliver had these in adequate measure was evident, at least to those who worked with him, in his indomitable insistence upon achieving a goal or furthering a project that he felt important."[9] Caliver was responsible for organizing the National Advisory Committee on the Education of Negroes, the National Survey of the Higher Education of Negroes, conducted during 1930-41. He was appointed a Specialist in the Education of Negroes in the United States Office of Education in 1930 in the Department of the Interior. Eradicating illiteracy became one of his lifelong passions. He wrote:

Raising the nation's illiterate adults to functional knowledge standards will help alleviate existent group tensions. It is definitely a first and a must in the development of better intergroup relations. It will enable groups such as the Negro to become better and healthier citizens and better workers.[10]

In the Office of Education he served 78,000 Black undergraduate, graduate, and professional students enrolled in institutions of higher learning, plus 70,000 teachers and administrators in schools and colleges for Blacks. He developed criteria for simple reading material for adult literacy and distributed these criteria widely. In 1961 Dr. Caliver was elected president of the Adult Education Association, U.S.A.

SUMMARY

Believing that adult educators need models of excellence no less than the youth of our world, the author has chosen a few adult education pioneers who stand out as leaders in the movement. Believing that men of ideas can bring forth new institutions, we have examined some of the ideas and programs of some men and women with a vision. Leaders from various fields are chosen as examples.

Squanto, perhaps our first agricultural agent in the United States, instructed the Pilgrims in the arts of fishing and agriculture. Benjamin Franklin, sometimes called the patron saint of adult education, inaugrated the Junto and founded the earliest subscription library. "Fun in Learning" is the motto of the present revised Junto. This printer, writer, philosopher, and agriculturist warrants extensive study by educators of adults.

Nicolaj Frederik Severin Gruntvig established the prototype of the Danish Folk School, revitalizing young farmers who had grown pessimistic in their suffering. William Rainey Harper, Greek and Latin scholar, was founder of the University of Chicago with its university press, university extension program, and correspondence study.

William Henry Lighty, a product of the early settlement-house movement, was a founder of the University of Wisconsin Extension Division, a radio pioneer with WHA, one of America's oldest radio stations, and a founder of the National University Extension Association. Charles R. Van Hise, President of the University of Wisconsin, gave organizational leadership to "extending the university" and is the father of the Wisconsin Idea-"the boundaries of the campus shall be the boundaries of the state." Seaman A. Knapp is called the father of the agricultural demonstration system, and is remembered by the land-grant institutions as a leader in the education of adults, particularly farmers.

Paul Ansley McGee is described as New York's "Mr. Adult Education." Helen Graham Lynch is an Americanization educator, Ambrose Caliver a literacy educator, Lillian Wald a public health pioneer, and Robert L. Cooley a vocational educator. Frank Hutchins, a father of libraries, and Charles McCarthy, librarian and vocational educator, were contemporaries and pioneers as adult educators. These men and women have led the way for future educators of adults, and provide us with a vision.

QUESTIONS:

1. What is the value of knowing some of the intellectual and organizational pioneers in the field of adult education?
2. Who is your model of excellence as an adult educator, and why?
3. How can we use the experience of these pioneers?
4. How would you like to be remembered as a pioneer in adult education?

REFERENCES

Axford, Roger W., William Henry Lighty: Adult Education Pioneer. Unpublished Ph.D. dissertation, University of Chicago, 1961.

Baldwin, Stanley E., Charles Kingsley. Ithaca, N.Y.: Cornell U.P. 1934.

Bode, Carl. The American Lyceum, Town Meeting of the Mind. New York: Oxford U. P. 1956.

Chamberlin, Thomas C. Biographical Memoir Charles Richard Van Hise, 1857-1918. Washington, D. C.: National Academy of Sciences, Government Printing Office, 1924.

Daniel, Walter G., and John B. Holden. Ambrose Caliver. Washington, D.C.: Adult Education Association, U.S.A. 1966

Fitzpatrick, Edward. McCarthy of Wisconsin. New York: Columbia U.P., 1944.

Kelly, Thomas, George Birkbeck. Pioneer of Adult Education Liverpool U.P. 1957.

Knudsen, Johannes. Danish Rebel. A Study of N.F.S. Grundtvig Philadelphia: Muhlenberg Press, 1955.

Koch, Hal. Grundtvig. Translated from the Danish with introduction and notes by Llewellyn Jones, Yellow Springs, Ohio; Antioch Press, 1952.

Lindhardt, P. G. Grundtvig, S.P.C.K., London, 1961.

Lund, Ragner. Scandinavian Adult Education. Copenhagen: Det Danske Forlag, 1952.

Manniche, Peter. Denmark: A Social Laboratory. Pergamon Press, Oxford, 1969.

Martin, Robert Bernard. The Dust of Combat: A Life of Charles Kingsley. London: Farber, 1959.

Nordic Council of Ministers. Recurrent Education in the Nordic Countries. Secretariat for Nordic Cultural Cooperation, Copenhagen, 1977.

Nielsen, Ernest D. N.F.S. Grundtvig. An American Study. Rock Island, Ill: Augustana Press, 1955.

Okun, Morris A., and Pristo, L. J. "Prominent Contributors to the Field of Adult Education" Lifelong Learning: The Adult

Years, Jan. 1979, pp. 14-16.

Rordam, Thomas. The Danish Folk High Schools. Association of Folk High Schools and Agricultural Schools. Copenhagen, 1965.

Storr, Richard J. Harper's University. Chicago: U. of Chicago Press. 1966 (History of the University of Chicago).

The International People's College, 1921-1971, L. H. Andersens Fogtrykkeri Printers. Helsingor.

Thuringer, E. Kresent, The Development of Adult Education in Germany: Historical and Political Implications Prior to the Twentieth Century, an unpublished paper. April 1978. Arizona State University, Tempe, Arizona 85281.

Vance, Maurice M. "Charles Richard Van Hise, A Biography." Master's and Ph.D. Theses, University of Wisconsin, 1952.

Woerdehoff, Frank. Dr. Charles McCarthy: His Educational Views and Influence Upon Adult Education in Wisconsin. Ph.D. Thesis. University of Wisconsin. 1954.

1 Appreciation is expressed to L. C. Smith and P. G. Jaeger, Kenosha county agents, Kenosha, Wisconsin; also to **Bradford's History** by William Bradford, and to "Early Explorers of Plymouth Harbor" by Henry F. Howe.

2 "The Church Educating Adults," The Board of Parish Education, United Lutheran Publishing House, Philadelphia, Pa., n. d., p. 1.

3 M. M. Vance, **Charles Richard Van Hise**, State Historical Society of Wisconsin, Madison, 1960, p. 86.

4 **Ibid.**, p. 110.

5 Speech, First National University Extension Association, Madison, Wis., March 10, 1915.

6 See Roger W. Axford, "Dr. Robert L. Cooley, Adult Educator," **Historical Messenger**, Milwaukee Historical Society, September 1964, pp. 41-43.

7 Fred L. Holmes (ed.), **Wisconsin: Stability, Progress, Beauty**, Lewis Publishing Co., Chicago, 1946, vol. 2, p. 380.

8 The author is indebted for the material from **In Memoriam**, edited by Warren Bower, New York University, 1965.

9 Walter G. Daniel and John B. Holden, **Ambrose Caliver: Adult Education and Civil Servant**, Adult Education Association, U.S.A., Washington, D.C., 1966.

10 Ambrose Caliver, "Needed Another Crash Program," **Adult Leadership**, Vol. 7, No. 4 (October 1958).

Chapter XII:

WHO IS AN ADULT EDUCATOR?

> In America, a land of idealism, the profession of teaching
> has become one of the greatest of human employments.
> -George Herbert Palmer
> (Professor of Philosophy Emeritus
> Harvard University), **The Ideal Teacher**,
> Houghton Mifflin Company, Boston, 1910.

THE PROFESSION OF ADULT EDUCATION

The adult educator is called to one of the greatest professions
in our world.

Why is this a great profession? Because the person is teaching
mature adults who are not waiting fifteen or twenty years to become a part of the world's work but are now making decisions
and policies that are shaping hundreds and thousands of lives.
They, the adults in our society, are now determining whether
or not our children shall have expanded opportunities of all kinds.

It is time that adult education gained its rightful place among
the professions, especially within the profession of education.
Too long adult education has been peripheral, marginal, expend-
able; too long the education of adults has been the first to be
trimmed from the budget; too often the profession has been sold
short by administrators who did not clearly see that the learning
done by adults is multiplied and proliferated - for most adults
are parents and are the molders of young minds and attitudes.
As has been remarked, "Change a child and he may become
a leader; change a Churchill and you change the destiny of the
world."

Adult Education must be woven into the fabric of our institutional pattern of living. Continuing education must be made as
natural as brushing our teeth. And it must be made as readily
available as the water we use for brushing them. Learning opportunities for adults must also be made as economical as the
toothpaste we purchase. When this is true, adult education will
be as fundamental, if not more so, as literacy.

We wager that by the time you have read this chapter, you
will recognize an adult educator when you see one. The person
is a special breed of human being.

164

A HUMANE HUMAN BEING

Humaneness is the primary and indeed most important characteristic of an adult educator. The person possesses empathy, understanding, concern, warmth, and rapport with people. Many of us know people who call themselves educators but who are aloof, detached, distant, difficult, and unconcerned. They certainly are not adult educators. They could not be true adult educators since they lack the qualities to make good in our field. Besides, the adults they deal with, most of whom are involved in continuing their education on a voluntary basis, would soon outstrip them. Technical training alone does not replace the quality of being a humane human being. That quality of humaneness is the prerequisite to being an effective educator of adults.

A NOSE FOR NEEDS

A real adult educator has community consciousness, a nose for needs. He or she recognizes a need when seen and is continually on the lookout for it in the community. An adult educator is not afraid to bring people together who can do something about that community need. He or she believes in people and their ability to solve their own problems. I think of a Quaker friend who works among the village people of Puerto Rico. He trains his staff to have a nose for needs, but they must be recognized as needs by the people themselves. I wish I know better how this quality for community consciousness can be taught. Perhaps it must be caught. A man or woman with a nose for community needs is a natural for an extension agent, community development organizer, an evening-school director or dean, vocational school coordinator, community action worker, or a director of adult education. They are, in fact, agents of change.

AN ORGANIZER

A person who is an ersatz educator dislikes working with people But one can recognize the adult educators, for they are catalysts in bringing together specialized knowledge and expertise to use on social problems that need to be solved. They know the community and its power structure. Unless they choose their institution wisely, they will occasionally get into policy problems. Even if they have a good school board, they will continually have to educate the members, as well as their constituency. If fortunate enough to have a socially conscious board, chances are they will have occasional opposition to the ideas, philosophy, and program of adult education. In fact, the more effective the adult educator is as a community organizer and program planner the more chance there is he or she will get into some difficulty. As a change agent, the adult educator is bound to run up against the status-quoers who want things "the way they have always been."

Fortunate is the adult educator who, has a dean or president with enough fortitude to be willing to stand up for the staff, for what is best for the community, and for the adult education program.

FLEXIBILITY

The teacher of adults or administrators of adult education programs must be ready for the arrival of a visitor from Mars, and not even appear perplexed or shocked. Flexibility is the watchword of the person working in adult programming.

If your educator of adults gets rattled when the motion picture projector won't run, when the film does not arrive on time, or when the long-time secretary is about to leave the evening adult program, he or she is not fit to be called an "adult educator."

Once I was to give a television program, using transparencies and an overhead projector. Exactly one minute before the show was to begin there was a sputter when the producer pulled the TV camera back and blew a fuse, killing the current. Neither the camera nor the overhead projector would light up. But the lack of electric current did not kill the program. We found a blackboard as a substitute for the overhead projector and proceeded with the class. By being ready with more than enough material, the educator of adults can adjust to the interests and needs of the learners. That takes the indispensable quality of flexibility. This ability always shows up high in a rating scale for the effective adult educator.

A SHARER OF IDEAS

A true adult educator has ideas. He or she is a person who could have been with an advertising agency, but either is too dedicated to educating adults, or isn't smart enough to know there is considerably more money in advertising. An honest-to-goodness adult educator is ready, willing, and anxious to have ideas duplicated, emulated, replicated, or even stolen.

A fine example of this is a story told me by a member of the consultant staff of a State Department of Public Instruction. He wanted to be an adult educator. He went to a North Chicago community because he knew a master adult educator lived nearby.

166

The experienced administrator of adult programs gave him counsel, promotion advice and samples, encouragement in time of poor enrollments, and tips on school system politics. The new educator was ready, willing, and anxious to learn, and the experienced adult educator was willing to share ideas, programs, titles, and above all else, friendship.

These men are now a part of a professional group known as the Northern Illinois Adult Education Roundtable - men and women who meet as a seminar once a month to keep abreast of new developments in the field, initiate research on adult learning problems and organization, maintain liaison with the State Department of Public Instruction, and enjoy fraternity in the cause of educating more effectively the adults of Northern Illinois. They are a potent force with the state legislature, and you can tell which of them are adult educators.

A PHILOSOPHER

Don't let your friends tell you an educator of adults doesn't need or have a philosophy of adult education. He or she does! The subject of conflicting philosophies in educating adults will be dealt with more fully, but rest assured an educator who works with adults has some kind of philosophy of adult education.

Only a very few questions are needed to unveil the philosophical level on which our adult educator is operating. If you will but ask, "What is your criterion of success in your program?" and be told, "Well, I have twelve hundred cars in the parking lot on Monday nights," you already know considerable about his philosophy of adult education.

If you ask, "Have you tried any programs in foreign affairs?" and the answer is "Oh, people in this community aren't interested in things like that, and besides, it's too controversial," you know a lot more about your adult educator's philosophy than may be stated in his catalog.

If, however, you ask your adult educator, "Are you meeting the needs of your community adequately?" and are told, "We are starting to deal with people's problems, but we have only scratched the surface," you know enough now to be assured that this person is actually an adult educator, and not a substitute.

A PROMOTER

I know a director of adult education who makes friends for adult education wherever he goes. He talks with legislators about continuing education, he is chairperson of the state legislative committee for adult education, he is a regional represen-

167

tative for the Adult Education Association, U.S.A., he is on the board of the National Association of Public School Adult Educators, and he devotes much time to convincing local school board members, his superintendent, and the school teachers in his system that they should do more for educating adults. With no apologies for the term, I think of this man as a leading "promoter" of adult education, and he deserves a medal of honor no less than the men in the trenches. Incidentally, he has one of the best-developed evening adult programs in the public schools of any person in the Midwest. He even found time to conduct a study tour to Europe during the summer.

A TRAINED PROFESSIONAL

Although there are very effective adult educators who have become such by the hunt-and-peck method, I know more who have benefited from more formal training. Some excellent adult educators work with organizations such as labor unions and management training in industry without formal academic experience. However, chances are that more formal training in the field of adult education would be of considerable benefit to them. Such training gives a person more depth, broader understanding, techniques of research, deeper appreciation of programs and agencies, and insight into possibilities of the field for its future development. And the professional associations are not to be overlooked. Being just a practitioner limits one. To know how to read the findings of research and to be able to carry on research and interpret it in one's program area are fundamental tools any adult educator will want to have. I recall a mentor and professor friend I had at the University of Chicago, Kermit Eby, who said:

"I once thought all PhD.'s were definitely brilliant - intellectual luminaries in the dark skies of mental mediocrity. Now I think that the Ph.D. is more often than not a mark of persistence, not unrelated to the ability of students to give their professors what the professors want. Perhaps this is part of the vocationalism which makes the Ph.D. so necessary for those who aspire to college and university teaching. Therefore, recognizing this to be true, I sometimes encourage my students to earn their degrees as quickly and painlessly as possible, and then go about getting their education. In my more cynical moments I compare the Ph.D. to a card in Kenin's union (musicians) and remark, 'Membership doesn't mean greater ability to play the flute, only more opportunities!' " [1]

In 1962 fifteen universities in the United States had active programs leading to the master's and doctor's degrees in adult education.[2]

Today more than 83 colleges and universities now offer graduate courses in adult education in the United States and Canada. In a study of the doctorate in adult education from 1935 to 1965, Houle and Buskey found that thirty universities had awarded the doctorate in education.[3] Since 1955 there has been steady growth (except for 1962), and this rapid increase in the number of persons studying for advanced degrees in adult education has been spurred by grants to provide partial support for graduate study made available by the Fund for Adult Education, the Carnegie Corporation, the W. K. Kellogg Foundation, Eli Lilly Foundation, and scholarship funds from the federal government.

INVOLVEMENT

The alert adult educator will be involved in all of the above, will be a person broadly educated, socially concerned, and informed, and will be engaged in problems of bringing to bear knowledge upon areas such as health, housing, poverty, mental health, social welfare, social legislation, municipal reform, literary societies, library boards, historical societies, as well as state, national and international affairs.

Major universities such as the University of Wisconsin, and the University of Missouri have recognized the need for involvement and have combined general and cooperative extension. Of the New Extension, Donald McNeil says: "It means a direct and continuing involvement with people and their problems. This involvement ranges all the way from poverty to economic development, to the humanities, the fine arts, and the cultural side of society."[4]

A LEADER

Our adult educator will exemplify the qualities of educational leadership. He or she may even teach a course in leadership training, adult learning, or community organization. He or she will have that rare ability to bring together the expertise of the institution with the community which may not always desire knowledge. He or she will try to bring about solutions to some problems and allow the credit to go to those who may have had little to do with the success of the project or program. He or she will exemplify the qualities of leadership so effectively described by the Chinese sage Lao Tze hundreds of years ago, but never more pertinent than today:

A leader is best when people barely know he exists,
Not so good when people obey and acclaim him,
Worst when people despise him.
Fail to honor people, they fail to honor you,
But of a good leader who talks little,
When his work is done, his aim fulfilled,
They will all say, "We did it ourselves."

THE ADULT EDUCATOR AS CATALYST

ADULT NEEDS AND INTERESTS

Community needs
Adult interests
Agency training problems
Industry training needs
School in-service needs
Women's continuing education
Social welfare problems
Preretirement interests
Leisure time
Family problems
Retraining and automation
Financial planning

ADULT EDUCATION INSTITUTIONS

Library
University general extension
Liberal Arts College
Junior College
High School Public School
  Adult Education
Cooperative Extension
Museums
Social Agencies
YMCA-YWCA
Research Agencies
Government Bureaus

CATALYST

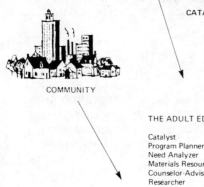

COMMUNITY

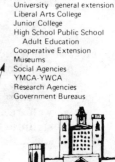

UNIVERSITY

THE ADULT EDUCATOR – Roles

Catalyst
Program Planner
Need Analyzer
Materials Resource
Counselor-Adviser
Researcher
Speaker
Consultant
Critic
Change Agent
Referral Source
Organizer

ADULT
EDUCATOR

PROGRAM PLANNER - CATALYST

The adult educator worthy of the name will have mastered many of the techniques of good program planning and will understand that literally millions of hours are wasted on meaningless or shallow programs of little social significance. By assisting community groups with speakers, programs, discussion leaders, and counsel, he or she can make the time of program chairman count for something meaningful. Pearl Buck said this about the influence of the program planner:

> The persons who have the greatest scope of influence today are the program planners. I wonder if they know this? I doubt they do. As I study the programs of many organizations and their content, I cannot believe that those who make them know their own potential usefulness.
>
> There is no time today for the trivial, the childish, immaterial program. Every hour that people are willing to give to come to a class or a meeting ought to be most carefully used and planned to give the utmost in accurate information presented in the most interesting way.
>
> We have no time to waste, as a nation. There is little time left in the world. It is true that our people as a whole do not realize the danger of being uninformed or misinformed, but it is the duty of the program planner to let them know. He has to combat not only ignorance but the reluctance of the average mind to be informed rather than amused.
>
> It is an old educational truth that nothing is taught where there is not the will to learn. The program planner must learn the skillful art of giving the people what they need to know and indeed must know, while he is giving them what they want. It takes a high integrity, a profound knowledge of people and where they are, as well as the techniques of popular education to be a good program planner. [5]

Groups with which Northern Illinois University works through its Department of Adult Education:
1. Belvidere Association of Commerce
2. Rockford Area Engineering Graduate Study Council
3. Illinois Valley Industrial Association, LaSalle, Ill.
4. Skokie Valley Industrial Association
5. Rock River Training and Development Council (Directors of Training)
6. Northern Illinois Adult Education Roundtable (Public School Directors of Adult Education)

7. Rochelle Association of Commerce (Personnel Managers)
8. Rochelle Industrial Committee (Safety Personnel)
9. Motorola, Inc. (Chicago, Ill.)
10. Argonne Laboratories, (Chicago, Ill.)
11. Sunstrand and Westclox, LaSalle, Ill.
12. The Bell Laboratories, Naperville, Ill.
13. The State of Illinois Personnel and Training Office, Springfield, Ill.
14. The Dixon State Schools (Staff Development)
15. DeKalb Supervisory Training Council (Personnel Managers, two-year certificates)
16. Fox Valley Art Association (Lecture Series), St. Charles, Ill.
17. Illinois Board of Higher Education, Community Service and Extension Committee
18. Illinois Adult Education Association (Affiliate of AEA, U.S.A.)
19. University Extension Committee, Illinois Public Universities (Coordination)
20. Illinois Chemical Society (Northern Illinois Chapter)
21. Department of Adult Education, Office of Superintendent of Public Instruction (Summer Institutes in Adult Basic Education for Administrators)
22. Illinois Junior College Board, Springfield, Ill.
23. U.S. Office of Education, Division of Adult Education, Washington, D.C.
24. Savannah Army Depot, Department of Education and Training
25. DeKalb Community Council, DeKalb, Ill.
26. University of Illinois, Division of University Extension, Champaign, Ill.

ONE WHO PRACTICES WHAT IS PREACHED

The true adult educator is a continuous learner, a lifelong learner. I admire most those administrators who sit in on one of their own institution's courses occasionally - for instance, an art or music course, or a discussion group in ethics or world affairs.

I know of nothing, quite as sad as a dean or director of a program who has ceased to learn, has given up systematic reading, is too busy to attend a lecture or concert series, or can't find time to sit in on in-service training sessions. An adult educator should fight off intellectual constipation or mental ossification. Administrative skills are no substitute for intellectual inquiry and academic enrichment. The faculty of an educational institution soon lose respect for the "educator" who is not a thinker, a reader, a writer, or an appreciator of the sciences, the arts, and the humanities.

We can identify a true adult educator who occasionally takes advantage of the rich programs he or she has helped develop. He or she gets a chance to evaluate teaching, acquire new knowledge, learn what adults are thinking, see flaws in program and promotion, and test some theories of how adults learn. He or she may do well to build some research into the observations. He or she may even want periodically to teach a course to keep alive in the field, and to keep close to the faculty of which he or she is a part. I know an adult educator who attended a series of illustrated lectures on the Scandinavian Arts and Crafts with his wife. It enriched their understanding of both the people and the crafts of Norway, Sweden, Denmark, and Finland. The couple obtained much information on the culture, and they now hope to visit the Scandinavian countries with their children. New tastes in furniture, glassware, and design were additional benefits, opening up new worlds of interest. The spouse is now enrolling in a weaving class as a follow-up. "We feel as if we know the Scandinavian people better," the adult educator voluntered, "and we won't be happy until we have seen the countries firsthand." He and his wife both are committed to continuous lifelong learning.

A THICK SKIN

Any person who has not experienced the agony of announcing a course, promoting it, registering it, and having to close the class and return fees for lack of enrollment, doesn't deserve the name of the high calling "adult educator." Such a painful experience is the boot camp of the administrator. Years ago, an experienced educator of adults advised me that if we do not have 10 percent of our classes experimental each semester, and have an occasional cropper, we are then insufficiently adventuresome, and are perhaps developing hardening of the program arteries.

The seasoned adult educator must be able to take criticism from the extreme right for putting on programs on foreign affairs and the United Nations, or from the extreme left for "middle class" programming of courses that benefit the individual through recreation, discussion, or skill development. The research bears out that it is the educated who seek more education, and we have to be continually experimenting with methods and techniques of involving more adults in learning from all classes of society, while we continue to serve those who already want to continue their education. A sound philosophy of adult education and a well-thought-out set of educational objectives for the institution can help prevent the novice adult educator from getting discouraged.

COMMITMENT

All of the above points add up to commitment. Without a commitment to the value of learning throughout life, a person cannot be an adult educator, and the educator of adults will become so discouraged that he or she will seek a more lucrative field. The field of adult education is marginal in some quarters and in many institutions, with a lack of clear visibility. Fortunately, however, salaries are improving for educators of adults, and millions of dollars are now being allocated for adult education in numerous programs from public school adult education to training programs, community action programs through colleges and universities, and workshops for teachers of adults. There is a crying need for well-trained educators of adults. Placement offices are getting frequent requests for persons with adult education skills.

The adult educator must know what he or she believes is worthwhile, what is worth learning, and what kind of society he or she wants for children and grandchildren, and what can prevent the world from being blown apart. Commitment to the learning process will be tested again and again by board members, colleagues, adult students, legislators, and teachers of adults who may not know why they are there. The creative adult educator must have the backbone to come up fighting for the rights of adults to learn in many forms, and must learn ways of achieving organizational goals while getting people to grow. He or she will follow that wise Canadian leader of the cooperative and adult education movement among the Antigonish who said: "The man who has ceased to learn ought not to be allowed to wander around loose in these dangerous days."[6]

We now know some of the characteristics of a real adult educator, a leader of the twentieth century. For it is the adults who vote, make public policy, and conduct wars. The challenge to the adult educator is the same as that given by Eby:

> But one thing is certain. If the American adult educator continues to be represented most generally by the symbol of a bought-and-paid for jellyfish, it is only too possible that some day the man who wants to "educate" will be lying side by side with the poor slob whom he tried in-

effectively to educate, in a common grave prepared by the men whose minds are too little in evidence to permit them to be at all openminded. [7]

The profession of adult education is developing, even though less rapidly than some of the other professions. We are developing a special language, and there is an increasing number of specialties in the field.[8] There is, thus, a need for more adult educators.

SUMMARY

Believing that the adult educator is called to one of the greatest professions in our contemporary world, we have examined some of the qualities most needed by teachers and administrators who call themselves "adult educators."

What are those qualities which are so imperative for success in working with adults? They are: a humane human being, a person with a nose for needs, an organizer, a person with flexibility, a sharer of ideas, a person with a sound philosophy of adult education, a promoter of adult education, a person with training, a person involved in the problems of society, an educational leader, a program planner, a person who practices what he preaches, a person with a thick skin, but above all a person with commitment to the value of learning throughout life.

Although it is recognized that each of us is in the process of becoming, the discussion of the qualities needed to make good as an adult educator will be useful for both those entering the field, and those now in the field. It is hoped each reader will add to the list and use the qualities enunciated as a basis for in-service programs and group discussion. Perhaps, as the profession matures, a model of the "ideal adult educator" can be pounded out against the anvil of time and experience.

Now that we know something about "Who is an adult educator," let us examine "Who is the adult learner?"

BIBLIOGRAPHY

Blakely, Robert J. **Adult Education in a Free Society**. Toronto: Guardian Bird Publications, 1958.

——————. **Toward A Homeo-Dynamic Society. Notes and Essays on Education for Adults**, No. 49, Center for Study of Liberal Education for Adults, Boston University, 1965.

Chamberlain, Martin, **The Professional Adult Educator**. Doctoral Dissertation University of Chicago, 1960.

Houle, Cyril O. "The Education of Adult Education Leaders," in Malcolm Knowles (ed.), **Handbook of Adult Education in** the **United States**. Adult Education Association, U.S.A. 1960, Chapter 10. See also . . . "The Educator of Adults" in 1970 Handbook of Adult Education, (Smith Aker & Kidd) p. 109

Kreitlow, Burton W. **Educating The Adult Educator, Part I - Concepts For The Curriculum**, Washington, D.C.: U. S. Department of Agriculture, Bulletin No. 573, 1965. (Endorsed by the Commission of Professors of Adult Education, the study prepared at the University of Wisconsin summarizes and relates the research contributions of various fields and disciplines toward a deeper understanding of selected concepts associated with continued learning.)

—————. **Educating The Adult Educator, Part II - The Taxonomy of Research**. Washington, D.C.: U.S. Office of Education, 1965. (The second part of U.S. Office of Education Research Project No. E-012, establishes a framework for research in adult education and identifies the areas needing attention.)

Lindeman, Edward C. **The Meaning of Adult Education**. Montreal: Harvest House, 1961.

Miller, Harry L. "What's Your Line? The Task of the Adult Educator," **Adult Leadership**, Vol. 6, No. 3 (September 1957), pp. 69ff.

"Professional Standards for Adult Education Administrators," **Bulletin of California State Department of Education**, Vol. XXIV, No. 16 (November 1955).

Public School Adult Education, A Guide for Administrators. Rev. ed. Washington, D.C.: National Association of Public School Adult Educators, 1963.

"Review of Educational Research." **National Education Association**, Vol. 23, No. 3 (June 1953).

Verner, Coolie. **Adult Education**. Washington, D.C.: Center for Applied Research in Education, Inc., 1964, Chapter 3, "The Adult Educator."

White, Thurman J. "Similarity of Training Interests Among Adult Educational Leaders," Ph.D. dissertation, University of Chicago, 1950.

1 Kermit Eby, **Protests of an Ex-Organization Man**, Beacon Press, Boston, 1961, p. 8.

2 Cyril O. Houle, "Emergence of Graduate Study in Adult Education," in Jessen, Liveright, and Hallenbeck, **Adult Education-Outlines of an Emerging Field of University Study**, Adult Education Association, U.S.A., Washington, D.C., 1964, pp. 69-84.

3 Cyril O. Houle and John H. Buskey, "The Doctorate in Adult Education, 1935-1965," **Adult Education**, Vol. 16, No. 3 (Spring 1966), pp. 131-168.

4 **The New Challenge in Life-Long Learning**, Resolutions and Proceedings of the Future Role of the University in Relation to Public Service, University of California, Los Angeles, p. 27. (No date)

5 Pearl S. Buck, **People**, East-West Association, Vol. 4, No. 8 (April 1945).

6 **Royal Bank of Canada Monthly Newsletter**, Vol. 44, No. 10 (October 1963).

7 Kermit Eby, "The Fraud in Adult Education" (mimeographed speech in author's file)

8 Lawrence Allen, Ph.D. Dissertation, University of Chicago, 1961, unpublished

Chapter XIII:

UNDERSTANDING
THE ADULT LEARNER

The **desire to learn,** like every other human characteristic, is not shared equally by everyone. To judge from
casual observation, most people possess it only fitfully
and in modest measure. But in a world which sometimes seems to stress the pleasures of ignorance, some
men and women seek the rewards of knowledge - and do
so to a marked degree . . . They approach life with an
air of openness and an inquiring mind.

-Cyril O. Houle, **The Inquiring Mind,**
University of Wisconsin Press, Madison, Wis.,
1961, p. 3

THE GROWING INTEREST IN ADULT
EDUCATION - A NATIONAL STUDY

"The man who stands still today is actually slipping back-
ward," chides a flyer from the University of Wisconsin, aimed
at attracting adults to the numerous programs offered throughout the state in continuing and adult education.

The United States is about to burst at the seams with programs
of adult education, according to a report by **Dr. John W. C.
Johnstone of the National Opinion Research Center at the University of Chicago.** [1] The report predicted that there will be
an adult education explosion, something like that experienced by
the secondary schools following the turn of the century.

Millions of adults continue their formal learning. The NORC
survey of educational pursuits of America's adults found that nearly
25 million adults (one in five) have been active in one or another
form of educational pursuit over the period of the previous year.
This figure, which surprised many educators, is about equivalent to the number of paid season tickets at the major baseball games.

"Educational activity" was broadly defined. The investigation
was concerned with all activities consciously and systematically
organized for purposes of acquiring new knowledge, information,
or skills. It included a somewhat wider range of behavior than
is often associated with the term "adult education."

PROFILE OF THE ADULT LEARNER

What would be a profile of the "typical" adult education student participating in programs of adult learning in the United States? Johnstone's study gives us a picture of that student:

The participant is just as often a woman as a man, is typically under forty, has completed high school or better, enjoys an above average income, works full-time and most often in a white-collar occupation, is typically white and Protestant, is married and a parent, lives in an urbanized area (more likely in the suburbs than in a large city), and is found in all parts of the country, but more frequently on the West Coast than would be expected by chance.[2]

To be an effective adult educator, we should understand the needs, aspirations, and desires of the learners we are to serve. Increasingly, more and more adults are becoming committed to life-long learning.

Tough, Arbeiter, and Knox have contributed to a better understanding of who the adult learner is, and some of the reasons participants' give for taking adult education in its many program forms.

Johnstone and Rivera did a monumental study in their **Volunteers for Learning**, and provided a model for understanding who participates in what kinds of learning activities. More recently, Solomon Arbeiter has assisted our understanding of the adult learner by utilizing findings from the National Center for Educational Statistics. Arbeiter[3] suggests that there are numerous definitions of "adult learners" and that some even define "adults" as individuals age 17 or older -- including, therefore, college students. In this way, studies which use such a broad definition derive much higher participating rates than do those which categorize adults as persons 25 years of age or older. Potential learners are sometimes confused with current learners, and even the definition of "learning", "continuing education", and "education" varies, depending on whether such programs as industrial training or military related courses are included or left out.

The total learning force varies significantly, e.g., two recent studies number adult learners, respectively, at 15.7 million and 32 million. It is important to remember that most studies are **national** in scope and are of little help to institutionally-based program administrators (such as dean's of continuing education) who are most interested in adult needs at the **local** level. State Departments of Education and local school boards are more helpful for figures at the state and local level.

Arbeiter has provided the practitioner seeking to "get a handle" on the major trends in adult learning with a special summary on adult learners and potential learners. It can help in understanding the adult learner.

First, we have reprinted information from the most recent national data on adult education developed by The National Center for Educational Statistics.

Second, we have consolidated trend data from several reports, eliminated gross numbers and, using six demographic variables (age, race, socioeconomic status, educational level, sex, and rural/urban), have displayed the trends among these adult populations. These rule-of-thumb guidelines can be applied to local populations and some foundation developed for more specific program planning. These data may be viewed as useful in stimulating thinking, but should be supplemented with local data and community input as a part of institutional program development.

In simplifying the data for easy review and use, we have undoubtedly caused some distortion in the substance of the original report. We offer two remedies: (1) An apology to the authors for any damage inflicted, and (2) a citation is given for **each** trend line and we invite the reader to refer to the original reports for more detailed analysis.

Participation in Adult Education, by Age and Race

| | 1969 |
| | 1972 |

Total Number of Adult Participants by Year

1969	13,042,000
1972	15,734,000
1975	17,059,000

Age 17 to 34

Number of participants in adult education

White	6,327,000
	7,920,000
Black	555,000
	629,000
Other	75,000
	95,000

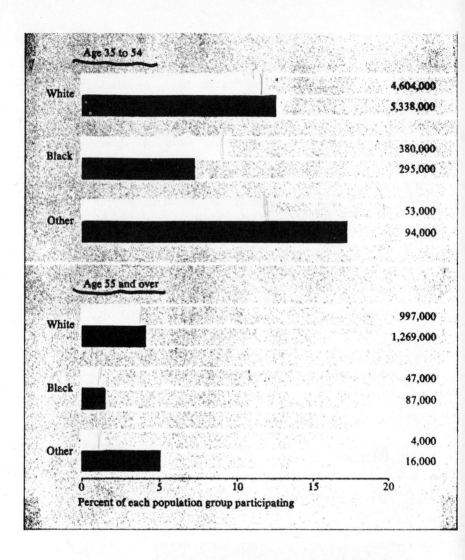

Age 35 to 54

White
4,604,000
5,338,000

Black
380,000
295,000

Other
53,000
94,000

Age 55 and over

White
997,000
1,269,000

Black
47,000
87,000

Other
4,000
16,000

0   5   10   15   20

Percent of each population group participating

Now that we have examined the adult student in America, let us look at some of the ways in which the adult learner differs from the youth and children in our society. Many scholarly studies have been made to help us better understand the problems of the child, and there has been a tendency to think that if we understand the child and his learning problems we can readily transfer this knowledge to the adult and his problems. Such is not the case.

180

THE ADULT LEARNER IS DIFFERENT

Few will question that the social roles of the adult and his responsibilities is society are quite different from those of the child or youth. Yet our whole system of education has given far too little consideration to the ways in which adults differ from children and ways in which we can accommodate the educational system to meet the learning needs of adults, what Havighurst speaks of as the developmental tasks.

For Roby Kidd, the factor of experience in the life of the adult learner is a principal consideration. We are reminded that the adult's sexual and social experiences and responsibilities are a kind that mark him off from the world of the child. To understand the adult learner we must continually be aware of three related points:

1. Adults have **more** experiences.
2. Adults have **different** kinds of experiences.
3. Adult experiences are **organized differently**. [4]

If we are to understand the adult who comes seeking knowledge, we must also be aware of the wide range of experiences which make up the adult life. An evening program for adults that is just a replica of the day curriculum for youth in a high school may prove quite inadequate for satisfying the needs of mature adults. For example, the discussion of citizenship and politics is a real and immediate problem, and active participation is probable and explicit. The adult wants answers that will relate directly to life. The adult will equate learning experiences to life experiences, will make qualitative judgments and will use life experiences to make new considerations. If the adult sees that relevant knowledge can be gained from activities in adult education, he or she will participate. If not, he or she will drop out. [5] The fact that the adult learner is different makes the understanding of what Havighurst calls the "**teachable moment**" so important. That moment comes when a person has need for a skill or knowledge which will help him solve a life problem.

CONDITIONS PRESENT IN OPTIMUM ADULT LEARNING

The psychologist Jacob Getzels at the University of Chicago examined the various learning situations in which adults find themselves. He found that the adult learns differently from the adolescent in a number of ways. He points out that most experiments on learning have been done with children or animals, and too often an attempt has been made to transfer the findings to adult learning situations. In his filmstrip "Learning Theory and Classroom Practice in Adult Education," Getzels show that adults learn best the things that are in keeping with their value systems and their personal biases. [6]

In a review of experiments in learning and learning theory, Getzels shows that adults learn best those things where they see relationships that are relevant. A summary of some of the conditions most often present in adult learning situations follows:

FOUR CONDITIONS USUALLY PRESENT IN ADULT LEARNING SITUATIONS

1. Most of the significant problems faced by the adult **do not** have correct answers in any **ultimately verifiable** sense. The important decisions are always made in the face of uncertainty. The laboratory animal is correct when he reaches the goal box; the child is correct when she gets 100% on a test. The adult can never know whether the time given voluntarily to studying library service might not be better used studying fingerpainting; or whether attendance at Great Book sessions is worth the loss of viewing the Wednesday night TV fight.

2. There **are stereotyped institutional solutions** that are correct because they are traditional rather than rational. The adult, more than the child, is bound by these stereotyped solutions and, although the solutions are modifiable, they are modifiable only in the face of severe internal and external pressures.

3. Any solution the **adult** makes to a problem is bound to have significant **effects upon other individuals.** He or she must predict not only his or her own reactions but the reactions of others. This is true for the educational problems in the classroom as well as for the personal problems of adult life.

4. The **solutions** to problems inevitably involve more than the assessment of objective facts. Perceptions and decisions may appear incorrect in the light of reality, but they are made because of emotional factors. By the time adults come to a learning problem, they are usually in one way or another deeply committed to a particular point of view regarding the significant matters at issue.

CAN THE ADULT STUDENT BE CLASSIFIED?

In an in-depth study of twenty-two cases of participants in adult

182

education activities, Cyril O. Houle of the University of Chicago investigated their purposes and objectives. He found that they fell into three broad categories: (1) the goal-oriented adult, (2) the activity-oriented adult, and (3) the learning-oriented adult. [7]

The present author has found the breakdown a useful framework in planning programs and valuable as a classification device for considering why adults attend programs. In numerous interviews we have found that adults interested in various programs anticipate the fulfillment in one or more of the three categories outlined by Houle.

I. THE GOAL-ORIENTED ADULT

The program planner will find numerous adults who have specific goals or a goal they contemplate achieving in an adult program. If they do not obtain that goal, they are frustrated, disappointed, and highly critical of the entire program. Professionals such as engineers may have as their primary objective the attainment of a grade for a course or the receipt of a certificate or a degree. Some may have as their goal the completion of a management course to help in their work.

The goal of the student may not always be that of the instructor. Often the educator of adults does not fully appreciate the specific goals of the student.

Charles Wedemeyer, for many years the head of Articulated Instructional Media and of Correspondence Study at the University of Wisconsin, and now William H. Lighty, Professor of Extension, found in studying correspondence students that those who dropped out often did not complete the total number of lessons because they already had attained what they wanted from the course. They had reached their objective from a particular part of the study guide and had no desire to go further with formal instruction by mail.

They were goal-oriented. Houle says the goal-oriented are the easiest to understand, chiefly because their views accord so well with the usual beliefs about education.

II. THE ACTIVITY-ORIENTED ADULT

Houle found that some adult students attend evening classes because they enjoy the social aspect of the experience. They find that they can experience fellowship, fraternity, and an intellectual climate to their liking. Houle learned that the activity-oriented person takes part in the learning experience primarily for reasons unrelated to the purposes or content of the activities in which he engages.

Who of us has not observed Great Books enthusiasts who have attended year after year, and when asked why they continue, they admit they find friends and fellowship within this group which keeps a continuing enclave? Although losing a few participants each year, the group often gains a few new members.

The square dance groups, the group-dynamics devotees, and the many groups in voluntary agencies are activity-oriented, and the learning aspect, if it does take place, is a secondary consideration.

III. THE LEARNING-ORIENTED ADULT

Houle found some adults who were learning for just the joy of learning. "Learning for learning's sake" seemed to be their objective. He found that for the learning-oriented, education seemed to be a constant rather than just a continuing activity. The desire to know is the continual objective of the learning-oriented adult.

"What they do has a continuity, a flow, and a spread which establish the basic nature of their participation in continuing education,"[8] says Houle.

Learning-oriented adults make a habit of frequenting the libraries, attending classes, and reading on their own. Even though they may be looked on as "oddballs" at the office, they continue to be curious and inquisitive and strive to satisfy their unsatiated intellectual hunger. They are the scholarly type, even though they may not be formally associated with an educational enterprise.

The husband or wife who is supportive of education seems to act as an encouragement to the spouse to continue education. One of the observations made by Houle in his study of adult learners is that no matter how intensely an individual may desire to learn, he or she usually does not do so actively if the marriage partner has an objection to the learning activity.[9] This finding has important implications for program planning, marriage counseling, and parent education. Program planners should offer opportunities for couples to learn together. At the University of Wisconsin, a successful program of evening films was offered at a reduced fee for couples, and as a result of the response, the policy was adopted throughout the state.

Houle reminds us that all of the people in his sample are basically similar in that they all are continuing learners. Their differences are matters of emphasis. Although most of his cases clearly fit into one or another of the three groups, none was completely contained. Educators of adults should find the classifications useful.

THE ADULT LEARNER "Wanted: Culture and Noble Persons"

We boast that we belong to the nineteenth century
  and are making the most rapid strides of any nation.
  But consider how little this village does
for its own culture . . .
We have a comparatively decent system of common schools,
schools for infants only:
but excepting the half-starved Lyceum in the winter,
and latterly the puny beginning of a library
suggested by the state, no school for ourselves . . . .
It is time that we had uncommon schools,
that we did not leave off our education
when we begin to be men and women.   ·
It is time that villages were universities,
and their elder inhabitants the fellows of universities,
with leisure--if they are indeed so well off--
to pursue liberal studies the rest of their lives . . . .
Alas! what with foddering the cattle and tending the store,
we are kept from school too long,
and our education is sadly neglected . . . .
This town has spent seventeen thousand dollars
on a townhouse, thank fortune or politics,
but it probably will not spend so much on living wit,
the true meat to put into that shell,
in a hundred years . . . .
As the nobleman of cultivated taste surrounds himself
with whatever conduces to his culture, --genius--learning--
wit--books--paintings--statuary--music--
philosophical instruments, and the like;
so let the village do,--not stop short at a pedagogue,
a parson, a sexton, a parish library, and three selectmen,
because our pilgrim forefathers got through
a cold winter once on a bleak rock with these.
To act collectively is according to
the spirit of our institutions . . . .
New England can hire all the wise men in the world
to come and teach her, and board them round the while,
and not be provincial at all.

That is the **uncommon** school we want.
  Instead of noblemen, let us have noble villages of men.
  If it is necessary, omit one bridge over the river,
go round a little there,
and throw one arch at least
over the darker gulf of ignorance which surrounds us.

--Henry David Thoreau, 1854

UNDERSTANDING ADULT NEEDS

Rather than studying those who have been failures in life it is encouraging to find a student of life-fulfillment, of those who have made the most of their lives. A. H. Maslow emphasizes that the need for self-actualization is one of the motivators for each human being.[10]

Maslow arranges the human needs in a usable heirarchy, with the **survival** needs as basic, first to demand fulfillment. It is Maslow's contention that until the basic needs are cared for, the individual will not seek higher levels of gratification. Next comes **safety** needs such as shelter, housing, and protection from physical harm. Only after achieving this level will the person pursue love and belonging needs, as a general rule. At the next level are **self-esteem** needs which when satisfied, can lead on to the level of **self-actualization**, the highest level of **self-fulfillment**. Psychologists such as Carl Rogers, Kurt Lewin, Gordon Allport, and Erik H. Erikson have spent their lives gathering evidence that the need for more complete human development is a universal human desire. Program planners can build programs on the Maslow heirarchy of needs, helping adults find richer lives in their climb up the ladder to **self-actualization.** See Chart on next page

A helpful exercise is to list program titles which can be developed out of the stair-step of Malow's heirarchy of human needs. For example, nutrition courses, jogging, weight-watchers, and tennis lessons can all be drawn from the need for satisfying basic physiological needs.

Another view of adult development and learning is that of Alan B. Knox, who has summarized and synthesized information from hundreds of studies from diverse fields in the biological, social, and behaviorial sciences, drawing on physiology, sociology, psychology, and education.[11] Knox has organized his findings around six major topics: the [1] context for development; [2] performance of adults in family, education, work, and community roles; the [3] physical condition of adults; [4] their personality; their [5] learning of new competencies; and [6] interrelationships among those several factors that affect adult functioning--learning.

Some will find the Knox writings useful in gaining a broader perspective on their own personal development. Program planners will find it useful in preparing persons for the helping professions, or continuing education. Knox admits that many of his generalizations reflect the experience of primarily middle-class white Americans, since adult life tends to reflect the societal context in which it occurs. He urges further research from various social classes, minority groups, and from numerous countries.

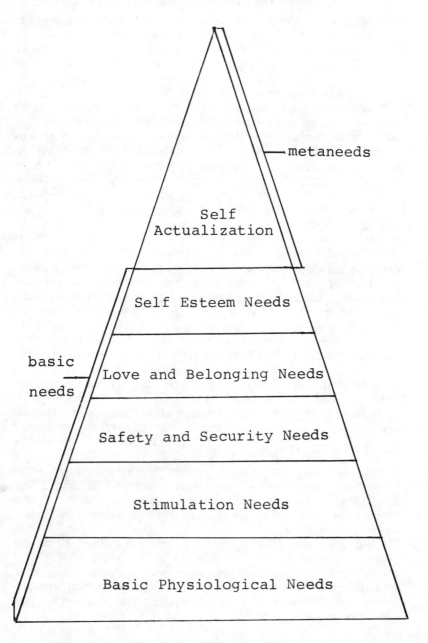

Maslow's Human Needs Hierarchy

metaneeds

Self
Actualization

Self Esteem Needs

basic
needs

Love and Belonging Needs

Safety and Security Needs

Stimulation Needs

Basic Physiological Needs

Knox wisely recognizes that most adult learning occurs outside educational institutions.[12]

METHODS OF STUDYING THE ADULT LEARNER

Educators of adults are continually looking for new ways to understand better the adult learner who appears in their classes or discussion groups. What are some of the methods that can be used effectively in studying the learner? The learner's needs and interests can be examined through the many methods developed by social scientists for social investigation.

Interviews with the students will yield much data about the wishes and interests of adult students. Another source is employer interviews or visits to the factories where the employees are engaged in productive activity. The author has observed that one of the most effective courses on communications resulted from the university instructor's paying a visit to the plants where he was allowed to learn of the kind of problems faced by front-line supervisors, for he was teaching foremen how to communicate more effectively with their employees.

Direct observations by the instructor will reveal many facts about social relations, tensions, and work habits. The visit also develops a rapport with prospective students for it shows concern with their problems. The well-structured questionnaire will provide information that may be referred to repeatedly; students usually are quite willing to write about themselves, their interests, problems, and objectives for taking a course. Interest questionnaires will elicit information about the recreational interests, reading habits, and philosophical outlook and reveal the students' value systems which are important for the instructor to know from the outset if there is to be a desired behavior change which is the essence of the learning process.

Dr. Ralph W. Tyler, an authority on curriculum, advises the use of tests in studying the learner, "particularly tests of present status in skills, like reading, writing, mathematics, in knowledge, in attitudes, and in problem-solving abilities."[13]   It should also be remembered that in most institutions there is a cumulative record of the students' achievement through the years. This is readily available to the instructor who has the initiative to request the material from the appropriate office - most often that of the registrar.

Often educational objectives can be inferred from data gathered about the students. For example, if it is discovered that most of the students in the class have not completed high school, such information might suggest to an adult education administrator that there is a need for a sequential program for high school completion.

HOW DO WE LEARN ABOUT THE ADULT STUDENT?

Every educator of adults wants to know as much as possible about the adult he is teaching. Each of us needs to develop methods of acquainting ourselves with the student in as effective and rapid a way as possible.

This author finds it effective to have at the beginning of each new class a carefully planned period of time to get acquainted. This takes the form of having each person fill out a personal data sheet. The student is asked to keep an extra copy of the form to use in his classes. In adult education classes I have found this method an effective initial way of learning a great deal about the learner, expectations from the course, reading habits, educational background, way of writing, and very often a considerable amount about the value system. The level of expectation, both of the teacher and of the student, is carefully reviewed in light of answers to the questionnaires.

Following the completion of the form, each student is asked to visit for five minutes with the person next to him or her.

This method has proved to be an effective icebreaker and a way to establish a good climate for learning. Name cards are given to each person to fill out and place before him or her. Adult classes meet in a seminarlike atmosphere, preferably in a square or around a circular table, where each can see the other students and the instructor. A good physical arrangement makes for more effective interaction and group participation.[14]

A great deal can be learned about your students from these oral introductions. Graduate students have reported this to be an exceedingly useful method of finding common interests and possible areas for paper topics and group research projects. Maximum use should be made of the intermission of the periods last for two or more hours.

If the instructor is provocative, raising pertinent questions, discussion among the students during the break will encourage intellectual cross-fertilization and raise additional questions for discussion. To provide the climate for learning, the opportunity for questioning, and self-evaluation for students is a major task for the teacher of adults, whether in a formal or informal setting.

A perspective on understanding adult needs is that of developmental tasks. This perspective emphasizes that people have specific "tasks" at each stage of their lives. The following chart summarizes these tasks and potential program response by Adult Education.

PERSONAL DATA SHEET

Name ———————————— Address ———————— Phone ————

Occupation (present or intended) ————————————————————————

Name of spouse ———————— Number of children ———————— Ages ————

Schools you have attended and degree earned:

Pertinent work experience:

Have you participated in an Adult Education Class before?
  If so, describe:

Expectations: What would you like to obtain from the course?
  State five objectives you have for the course.

Member of organizations - list:

Family activities, including hobbies:

Magazines you read regularly:

Books you have read in the last year:

What would you like to be doing 5 years from now?

What would you like to be doing 10 years from now?

(Sample Information Sheet)   From: Dr. Walter Wernick
                                              Associate Professor of Education
                                              Northern Illinois University
                                              DeKalb, Ill. 60115

Name
Address
Telephone
Teaching Position
Teaching Experience
Work Experience
Undergraduate School and Major
Graduate Courses Already Completed
Other Related Information

1.   What do you expect to learn from this course?

2.   What kind of "student-image" do you have of yourself?

3.   In what ways do you think the instructor of this course can help you the most?

Says Dr. Wernick: "This form is really quite simple, but in large classes the information a teacher needs can be collected quite easily."

ADULT LIFE CYCLE TASKS/ADULT CONTINUING EDUCATION PROGRAM RESPONSE

Developmental Stages	Tasks	Program Response	Outcomes Sought
Leaving Home 18-22	1. Break psychological ties. 2. Choose careers. 3. Enter work. 4. Handle peer relationships. 5. Manage home. 6. Manage time. 7. Adjust to life on own. 8. Problem solve. 9. Manage stress accompanying change.	1. Personal development, assertive training workshops. 2. Career workshops, values clarification, occupational information. 3. Education/career preparation. 4. Human relations groups. 5. Consumer education/homemaking skills. 6. Time/leisure use workshop. 7. Living alone; successful singles workshops. 8. Creative problem solving workshops. 9. Stress management, biofeedback, relaxation, TM workshops.	1. Strengthened autonomy. 2. Appropriate career decisions. 3. Successful education/career entry. 4. Effective social interaction. 5. Informed consumer, healthy homelife. 6. Wise use of time. 7. Fulfilled single state, autonomy. 8. Successful problem solving. 9. Successful stress management, personal growth.
Becoming Adult 23-28	1. Select mate. 2. Settle in work, begin career ladder. 3. Parent. 4. Become involved in community. 5. Consume wisely. 6. Homeown. 7. Socially interact. 8. Achieve autonomy. 9. Problem solve. 10. Manage stress accompanying change.	1. Marriage workshops. 2. Management, advancement training. 3. Parenting workshops. 4. Civic education; volunteer training. 5. Consumer education, financial management training. 6. Homeowning, maintenance workshops. 7. Human relations groups, TA. 8. Living alone, divorce workshops. 9. Creative problem solving workshops. 10. Stress management, biofeedback, relaxation, TM workshops.	1. Successful marriage. 2. Career satisfaction and advancement. 3. Effective parents; healthy offspring. 4. Informed, participating citizen. 5. Sound consumer behavior. 6. Satisfying home environment. 7. Social skills. 8. Fulfilled single state, autonomy. 9. Successful problem solving. 10. Successful stress management, personal growth.
Catch-30 29-34	1. Search for personal values. 2. Reappraise relationships. 3. Progress in career. 4. Accept growing children. 5. Put down roots, achieve "permanent" home. 6. Problem solve. 7. Manage stress accompanying change.	1. Values clarification. 2. Marriage counseling and communication workshops; human relations groups; creative divorce workshops. 3. Career advancement training, job redesign workshops. 4. Parent-child relationship workshops. 5. Consumer education. 6. Creative problem solving workshops. 7. Stress management, biofeedback, relaxation, TM workshops.	1. Examined and owned values. 2. Authentic personal relationships. 3. Career satisfaction, economic reward, a sense of competence and achievement. 4. Growth producing parent-child relationship. 5. Sound consumer behavior. 6. Successful problem solving. 7. Successful stress management, personal growth.
Midlife Reexamination 35-43	1. Search for meaning. 2. Reassess marriage. 3. Reexamine work. 4. Relate to teenage children. 5. Relate to aging parents. 6. Reassess personal priorities and values. 7. Adjust to single life. 8. Problem solve. 9. Manage stress accompanying change.	1. Search for meaning workshops. 2. Marriage workshops. 3. Mid-career workshops. 4. Parenting: focus on raising teen-age children. 5. Relating to aging parents workshops. 6. Value clarification; goalsetting workshops. 7. Living alone, divorce workshops. 8. Creative problem solving workshops. 9. Stress management, biofeedback, relaxation, TM workshops.	1. Coping with existential anxiety. 2. Satisfying marriage. 3. Appropriate career decisions. 4. Improved parent-child relations. 5. Improved child-parent relations. 6. Autonomous behavior. 7. Fulfilled single state. 8. Successful problem solving. 9. Successful stress management, personal growth.
Restabilization 44-55	1. Adjust to realities of work. 2. Launch children. 3. Adjust to empty nest. 4. Become more deeply involved in social life. 5. Participate actively in community concerns. 6. Handle increased demands of older parents. 7. Manage leisure time. 8. Manage budget to support college-age children and ailing parents. 9. Adjust to single state. 10. Problem solve. 11. Manage stress accompanying change.	1. Personal, vocational counseling, career workshops. 2. Parenting education. 3. Marriage, personal counseling workshops. 4. Human relations groups. 5. Civic and social issues education. 6. Gerontology education. 7. Leisure use workshops. 8. Financial management workshops. 9. Workshops on loneliness and aloneness. 10. Creative problem solving workshops. 11. Stress management, biofeedback, relaxation, TM workshops.	1. Job adjustment. 2. Civil letting go parental authority. 3. Exploring new sources of satisfaction. 4. Effective social relations. 5. Effective citizenship. 6. Better personal and social adjustment of elderly. 7. Creative use of leisure. 8. Sound consumer behavior. 9. Fulfilled single state. 10. Successful problem solving. 11. Successful stress management, personal growth.
Preparation for Retirement 56-64	1. Adjust to health problems. 2. Deepen personal relations. 3. Prepare for retirement. 4. Expand avocational interests. 5. Finance new leisure. 6. Adjust to loss of mate. 7. Problem solving. 8. Manage stress accompanying change.	1. Programs about nutrition, health. 2. Human relations groups. 3. Preretirement workshops. 4. Art, writing, music courses in performing and appreciation; sponsored educational travel. 5. Money management training. 6. Workshops on aloneness and loneliness, death and dying. 7. Creative problem solving workshops. 8. Stress management, biofeedback, relaxation, TM workshops.	1. Healthier individuals. 2. Effective social skills. 3. Wise retirement planning. 4. Satisfaction of aesthetic urge; broadening of knowledge; enjoyment of travel. 5. Sound consumer behavior. 6. Adjustment to loss, fulfilled single state. 7. Successful problem solving. 8. Successful stress management, personal growth.
Retirement 65+	1. Disengage from paid work. 2. Reassess finances. 3. Be concerned with personal health care. 4. Search for new achievement outlets. 5. Manage leisure time. 6. Adjust to more constant marriage companion. 7. Search for meaning. 8. Adjust to single state. 9. Be reconciled to death. 10. Problem solve. 11. Manage stress accompanying change.	1, 4, 5, 6. Workshops on retirement, volunteering, aging; conferences on public issues affecting aged. 2. Financial management training. 3. Health care programs. 7. Religious exploration. 8. Workshops on aloneness and loneliness. 9. Death and dying workshops. 10. Creative problem solving workshops. 11. Stress management, biofeedback, relaxation, TM workshops.	1, 4, 5, 6. Creative, active retirement; successful coping with life disengagement; public policies responsive to needs of aged. 2. Freedom from financial fears. 3. Appropriate health care. 7. Help in search for life's meaning, values of past life. 8. Fulfilled single state. 9. Philosophic acceptance of death, help in caring for dying and handling of grief. 10. Successful problem solving. 11. Successful stress management, personal growth.

© 1977 by Vivian Rogers McCoy, Director, Adult Life Resource Center, Division of Continuing Education, University of Kansas

VOCATIONAL STUDENTS

A unique subgroup of adult learners are vocational students. In a comprehensive study of occupational students in the Arizona Community Colleges, John H. Ahlen[15] found the following:

1) The students are older than the average community college student.

2) Greater than 60% of the students have no intention to transfer to a four-year institution.

3) Six out of every ten students attend only as part-time evening students enrolled in two courses that require an average of approximately five class hours per week.

4) About 38% of all students never graduated from high school, and only 20% had previously attended a four-year college or university as a full-time student.

5) Of those who graduated from high school, 79% of vocational students ranked in the upper or middle one-third of their high school graduating class.

6) Three out of four students were employed either part-time or full-time while attending a community college. Seventy-four percent of all students were employed for 30 hours, or more, each week and 56% were the head of a household.

7) The persons having the most influence on student attendance were: 1) spouse; 2) employer; and 3) parent.

8) The three most important factors influencing students to attend a community college were: 1) educational programs; 2) low cost; and 3) nearness to home.

Although it is precarious to generalize from the study of one state, some useful observations can be made for adult educators dealing with vocational students. The community college is serving an older population, most of whom do not intend to transfer to a four-year institution, who are attending part-time, and who ranked in their upper or middle one-third of class rank.

Adult educators must have quality educational programs, keep the cost low, and have offerings near the home of the adult student in occupational programs. We can make use of the findings that spouse, employer, and parent influence attendance, and counselors can solicit support from these sources if we are to have persisting, successful students in our vocational programs.

THE SELF-MOTIVATED LEARNER

Many persons learn on their own. Allen Tough has found that adults spend a remarkable amount of time each year working at their major efforts to learn. And this is often on their own.

"Remember me, Professor? I took an incomplete in your writing course twenty years ago when I got married".

Tough says that a typical learning effort requires 100 hours, and the typical adult conducts five of them per year, (500 hours altogether). A few of these learning projects rely on instructors and classes, but Tough says, "70% are self-planned and others rely on friends and peer groups."[16]

Tough claims the picture of adult learning projects has emerged largely in the 70's. Concisely, a learning project is "a highly deliberate effort to gain and retain certain definite knowledge and skill, or to change in some other way. To be included, a series of related learning sessions (episodes in which the person's primary intention was to learn) must add up to at least seven hours."[17]

The definition was so designed as to include the broad range of major learning efforts. Numerous methods can be included--reading, observing, listening, attending class, reflecting, practicing, getting answers to questions--the primary intention for the experience must be to gain and retain certain definite knowledge and skill. Self-planned learning, classroom learning, learning directed by a friend or a group of peers, or learning by programmed instruction are all included. These include a facinating diversity of energy.

The years of the 1970's saw a growth in innovative practices focused on the person learning alone, not relying on a class or an instructor. There are many examples such as: learning contracts, learning exchanges, independent study, individual self-planned learning as a primary procedure in an academic course, behavioral self-control, and some books published commercially to assist the individual learner plan and execute his learning projects.

Persons responsible for professional development have experimented with special procedures designed to help individuals conduct their own learning. Some examples include adult education graduate students (Malcolm Knowles), medical education (McMaster University, Canada). Medical doctors (Leonard Stein), and ministers, who learn through a booklet. Tough reports that during the recent decade several public libraries have worked cooperatively to provide more intensive help for individuals working on adult projects.

What is the most common motivation for an adult learning project? The most common motivation is some anticipated use or immediate application of the desired knowledge or skill. The individual has a task--heating a solar pool, building a piece of furniture, writing a chapter for a book, or hunting up the geneology of the family. The objective is to perform a task efficiently and successfully. Curosity or just wanting to obtain the knowledge for its own sake is less common.

In Tennessee, 466 adults were interviewed in Knoxville and one rural county by Peters and Gordon, who found 91% had conducted at least one learning project during the year. Most learning projects were job-related or recreational, with a limited number doing learning projects for personal improvement, religious, or family relations. [18]

THE INDEPENDENT LEARNER--A GROWING CLIENTELE

American adults are evincing increasing interest in self-educational activities of all kinds and at every educational level. In a 1973 report by the Commission on Nontraditional Study entitled **Diversity by Design**, a representative national sample of adults eighteen through sixty years of age were queried concerning their interest in continuing learning. An impressive 76.8 percent of the sample noted that they were indeed interested in continuing learning, but many were not then actively participating in organized educational activities.

Especially interesting to many adult educators should be some of the problems cited by would-be learners as obstacles to learning.[19] For example, 35.1 percent of the sample, representing twenty-eight million adults indicated that they don't want to go to school full time; 12.0 percent representing 9.6 million stated that "courses I want don't seem to be available"; 6.1

percent or 4.9 million were "tired of school, tired of class-rooms." Many of the obstacles reflected a need for information or counseling services: 16.5 percent representing 13.2 million adults complained of having "no information about where I can get what I want"; 12.5 percent or ten million noted "low grades in the past, not confident of my ability"; and 5.1 percent or 4.1 million admitted "don't know what I'd like to learn or why."

Surely these would-be learners represent a vast group for whom useful educational services might easily be provided.

For those discouraged with the strictures of formal or in-stitutionalized education the library can provide a non-threatening atmosphere, a wealth of resources and the opportunity for in-dividualized assistance without patronization or criticism. Materials may be used at the library or taken home for more leisurely perusal. No requirements, deadlines, or judgments are imposed on the learner. For those in need of further information, the library should be able to be of immediate assistance with its files on educational opportunities for classroom and self-directed learning in the community. [20]

One of the helpful books on self-education is one written by Cyril O. Houle, for forty years on the faculty of the University of Chicago, teaching in the graduate program in adult education. In his book CONTINUING YOUR EDUCATION [21], he stresses Seven Keys to Effective Learning. They are:

1. Act as though you are certain to learn.
2. Set realistic goals -- and measure their accomplishment.
3. Remember the strength of your own point of view.
4. Actively fit new ideas and new facts into context.
5. Seek help and support when you need it.
6. Learn beyond the point necessary for immediate recall.
7. Use psychological as well as logical practices.

INDEPENDENT LEARNING.

The adult who learns independently can find many ways to gain knowledge. Correspondence study has been traditionally the method for persons to learn through distance instruction. I have found teaching by correspondence study a way for the student to learn independently and in depth, but the method takes a high degree of self-discipline, and effective time management on the part of the student. More of this later; let us now con-sider contract learning.

A. Contract learning
A procedure for making the student responsible for his or

196

"My grandson's giving me a watch for graduation."

her growth is to use the contract method of learning. In this approach, the instructor is the tutor, the facilitator, the guide, and the mentor. But the final responsibility for finding the learning resources, the materials, the books, and narrowing the search is the students. The final responsibility for outlining a learning plan, and statement of objectives and the way they will be accomplished remains the students.'

The contract learning plan has been well described by Malcolm Knowles in his **Self-Directed Learning, A Guide for Learners and Teachers**.[22] Knowles describes self-directed learning as "a process in which individuals take the initiative, with or without the help of others, in diagnosing their needs, formulating learning goals, identifying human and material resources for learning, choosing and implementing appropriate learning strategies, and evaluating learning outcomes."[23] Learning need not imply isolation, for Knowles assures there is a lot of mutuality among self-directed learners.

Knowles contrasts self-directed learning with the more traditional idea of "teacher-directed learning." He thinks that the body of theory and practice on which self-directed learning is based may be labeled "androgogy". The word comes from combining the form **andr** of the Greek word **aner** (meaning man). Androgogy is therefore, defined as the art and science of helping adults (Knowles says maturing adults) to learn.[24]

197

There is much to be said for the idea that the adult learns best what he or she most wants to learn. Self-directed learning assumes that the human being grows in capacity with experience, to be more self-directed as an essential part of the process of maturing. In contract learning, the learner's experiences become an expanding resource for learning which can be exploited along with the resources of many experts.

It is Knowles' contention that teacher-directed learning assumes that students are primarily motivated by **external** rewards and even punishments, such as awards, grades, degrees, and the fear of failure. Self-directed learning, however, assumes that learners are motivated by **internal** incentives - for example, curiosity, the motivation of accomplishment, and the wish to achieve.

Knowles concedes that the attitude of the learner is the primary consideration. I have found this true in using contract learning with graduate students in adult education classes. We are so "teacher-directed" in our conditioning by years of "classroom assignments" that it is often a major psychological adjustment for adults to take responsibility for their own learning procedures. My experience is using contract learning is that the best students in the class enjoy the process immensely, and become over-achievers, and that poor students flounder, and reach out for directedness from the instructor. Every facilitator/teacher should experiment with contract-learning in an adult environment, to evoke the most effective learning, with which he or she feels confortable. Knowles advises that "if self-directed learners recognize that there are occasions on which they will need to be taught, they will enter into those taught learning situations in a searching, probing frame of mind and will exploit them as resources for learning without losing their self-directedness."[25]

Diana Worby, a mentor in the English and Humanities program at Empire State College, Suffern, New York utilized the learning contract as an alternative to other forms of independent study. She describes as the essential support, four important guidelines in the learning contract:
  1) the student's general educational purposes;
  2) the specific purposes of the particular contract being written;
  3) actual learning activities to be undertaken;
  4) the criteria by which the work will be evaluated.

Like Knowles, she provides a sample contract from which can be used or adapted to the local learning situation.[26]

This author used the following contract for graduate students in an internship or practicum.

PROJECT OUTLINE FORM - **Practicum**
Internship

Adult Education Workshop
Arizona State University

Dr. Roger W. Axford
Assoc. Prof. Adult Education

Please complete and sign **two** (2) copies of this form. Your instructor will sign and return one copy to you. In this way both of us will have a record of what you have agreed to complete. (Give details)

STATEMENT OF OBJECTIVES (What do you plan to do?)

PLANNED ACTIVITIES (How do you plan to complete your activities?)

CRITERIA FOR EVALUATION (How will you know when you are done? i.e., completion of a paper, log of activities, etc.)

Signed:

_____   _____
(Your signature)   Roger W. Axford

_____   _____
(date)   (date)

199

B. Correspondence Study

This author is an advocate of the efficacy of correspondence study as a method of in-depth learning. The method assumes the maturity of the student, and calls for regular communication between mentor and student. With increased communications links, correspondence study can be combined with questions and answers by telephone, dialogue, computer utilization, library projects, and a modified form of contract learning.

The National University Extension Association, the major national association of public and private institutions offering extension and continuing education, publishes a **GUIDE TO INDEPENDENT STUDY**. This guide offers a listing of sixty-five institutions, accredited colleges and universities throughout the United States which offer correspondence study. This is an invaluable tool for adult counselors and directors of adult education. Included in the guide are listings of courses for College and University credit; courses for graduate credit only; courses for high school, and elementary school credit; as well as non-credit Certificate Program courses.

Independent study departments are especially interested in providing courses which will meet the needs of the physically handicapped. Usually, the vocational rehabilitation division of most state departments of education pay the cost of fees and books for handicapped students wishing to take independent study. The Hadley School for the Blind (700 Elm St. Winnetka, Illinois, 60093) offers courses in braille or on tape, some of the courses offered by NUEA institutions. American Citizenship courses have been worked out by the United States Department of Justice, Immigration, and Naturalization Service.

Correspondence Study is especially useful for those with extended stays in foreign countries. The University of Wisconsin Extension Division, with more than 400 courses, prints a special catalogue which describes enrollment procedures, partial payment plans, costs, postage regulations, time requirements, assignments, examination procedure, transcripts, extensions of time, transfers, and library support, and counseling procedures. You can now earn up to 90 hours of credit toward an undergraduate degree through Independent Study at the University of Wisconsin.

For those interested in the many changes that have occurred in Independent Study they should consult the work of MacKenzie and Christensen, **THE CHANGING WORLD OF CORRESPOND-ENCE STUDY**.[27]

200

UNDERSTANDING THE ADULT LEARNER
Summary (1)

The growing interest in adult education was pointed up in a national study by Johnstone and Rivera, with the finding that many people learn on their own. The typical adult student is described. We learned how the adult learner is different with Roby Kidd's three points: 1) adults have more experiences, 2) different kinds of experiences and 3) adult experiences are organized differently. Jacob Getzel's four conditions present in adult learning can be useful for the teacher of adults, in better understanding the adult learner. Cyril O. Houle's classification of the adult student into the 1) goal-oriented, 2) activity-oriented, and 3) learning-oriented, will aid adult program planners to provide for each type in educational institutions if we are to be successful.

UNDERSTANDING THE ADULT LEARNER
Summary (2)

Alan Knox's study on **Adult Development and Learning** describes the context of development; performance of adults in family, education, work and community roles; physical conditions of adults' their personalities; learning of new competencies; and interrelationships among several factors affecting adult functioning -- learning.

To understand adult needs we examined A. H. Maslow's heirarchy of human needs, learning that the highest level is self-actualization, self-fulfillment. We found that Rogers, Lewin, Allport, and E. Erikson spent their lives studying human development, with important implications for adult educators in program planning. A profile of the adult learner is provided from the study by Solomon Arbeiter with an emphasis on major trends in adult learning, and the potential clientele of adult learners. Demographic statistics are provided by the National Center for Educational Statistics.

UNDERSTANDING THE ADULT LEARNER
Summary (3)

The need to serve the vocational and high risk students in community college is pointed up in a study by John H. Ahlen. The three most important factors influencing students to attend a community college were: 1) the educational programs, 2) low cost, and 3) nearness at home. Seventy-nine per cent of vocational students studied rank in the upper or middle one-third of their

"Did you ever take into consideration that I might have
already reached my goal in life?"

MOTIVATION IS THE KEY!

high school graduating class, and six out of ten students attend
on a part-time basis, with 74% of all students employed for 30
hours or more each week. Responsibility is a key word for the
"new" community college student, with 56% listing that they
are the head of the household in the Ahlen study.

The Adult Life Cycle Tasks, with the Adult Continuing Education Program Response developed by Vivian Rogers McCoy
is a useful tool for program planners, whether working individually or in groups.

The self-motivated learner is considered through the studies
by Allen Tough. We examined the "adult learning project" and
the resources that are necessary for the adult to learn on his/

her own. The independent learner is considered by the use of contracts, with Malcolm Knowles work on **Self-Directed Learning** as a suitable guide both for learners and teachers. Mutuality is the key to the use of contract learner, says Knowles. Andragogy is explored, with consideration of external and internal incentives for learning examined. The author presents a Projest Outline Form for contract learning in an internship or practicum setting, easily adaptable for independent study. Correspondence study is described as distance education. The importance of the library cannot be overemphasized as a resource for the independent learner.

Our conclusion is that we cannot fully understand the predicament of the adult learner unless we stay abreast of the occupational trends and the educational requirements of the times. Junior colleges and community colleges, voluntary agencies, public schools, universities - all will have to find ways of discovering the interests and needs of adult learners and ways of programming for those needs. Various media need to be combined to break the distance barrier, for proximity and propinquity will be primary factors in determining whether adults take advantage of learning opportunities.

Radio, television, telelecture, correspondence study, and media not yet marketed or invented will have to be combined to facilitate the continuing education of adults for a fuller and more abundant life for the individual and for a more productive and peaceful society.

QUESTIONS

1. How would you describe the typical adult education student as found in the Johnstone and Rivera study?
2. How are adults different according to Roby Kidd.
3. How would you utilize Jacob Getzels "conditions present in adult learning" in working with adults?
4. As a program planner how would you incorporate Cyril Houle's classification of the types of adult learners in your offerings?
5. What kind of adult learners did Thoreau hope we could cultivate?
6. Why is Thorndike's study of **ADULT LEARNING** (1928) important?
7. How would you utilize Maslow's heirarchy of human needs?
8. What are some of the major findings (trends) in Arbeiter's profile of the adult learner.
9. How would you make use of Vivian Rogers McCoy's ADULT LIFE CYCLE TASKS with program response?

10. What does Canadian Allen Tough mean by "adult learning projects"? How do you see adult educators tying in with these projects?
11. What do you think of contract learning? How would you develop a self-directed learning project?
12. What are the advantages and disadvantages of correspondence study?
13. How should the library be utilized by adult educators? What resources are there for the independent learner?

BIBLIOGRAPHY

Axford, Roger W., and Robert W. Schultz. "A Yearning for Learning - While Earning" **Training and Development Journal**, Vol. 23, No. 3 (March 1969), pp. 10-13.

Berelson, Bernard and Gary A. Steiner. **Human Behaviro: An Inventory of Scientific Fingsings**. New York: Harcourt, 1964. (Chapter 5, "Learning and Thinking:: esp. pp. 157-168, 192-235.)

Birren, James, **Handbook of Aging and the Individual**, Chicago: U. of Chicago Press, 1959 (Chapter 18, "Theories of Learning and Aging"l Chapter 19, "Age and Learing - Experimental Studies"; Chapter 20, "Intelligence and Problem Solving.")

Broschart, James - **A Synthesis of Selected Manuscripts About the Education of Adults in the United States**. Washington, D.C.; Unpublished Manuscript prepared for the U.S. Office of Education, 1976.

Brunner, Edmund deS., et al. **An Overview of Adult Education Research**. Chicago: Adult Education Association, 1959. (Chapter 2, "Adult Learning.")

Burton, William H. "Basic Principles in a Good Teaching-Learning Situation," **Phi Delta Kappan**, March 1958.

Carey, James T. **Why Students Drop Out, A Study of Evening College Student Motivations**. Center for the Study of Liberal Education for Adults, 1953.

(The) Crnegie Commission on Higher Education. **Toward a Learn-**
(The) Carnegie Commission on Higher Education. **Toward a Learning Society**. New York, New York: McGraw-Hill Book Company, 1973.

Carp, Abraham - et al., "Adult Learning Interests and Experiences," Chapter Two in **Planning Non-Traditional Programs**, K. Patricia Cross, John R. Valley, and associates; San Francisco, California. Jossey-Ball Publishers, 1974.

Cross, Patricia K. - **Beyond the Open Door**, New Students in Higher Education, Jossey Bass, Inc. Pub. 615 Montgomery St. San Francisco, Cal. 94111 (1974)

This book is a study of the interests, abilities and aspirations of the new students available in adult education. Its purpose is to determine what educational experiences college should offer them. It makes some predictions about who will go to college. She gives key characteristics of new students.

Getzels, Jacob. Filmstrip, "Learning Theory and Classroom Practice in Adult Education," University of Michigan Microfilms (Filmstrip and tape). Produced by the Center for the Study of Liberal Education for Adults.

Godbey, Gordon, **Applied Andragogy**, Continuing Education, Penn State, 16802, 1979

Grabowski, Stanley - **Adult and Continuing Education: The Next 10 years.** ERIC Clearinghouse on Career Education. Information series 114, 1977. 26 pp.

Futurism for adults and continuing education in the next 10 years is the focus of this information analysis paper intended for adult educators and researchers. Topics discussed include: the field and issues/impact on future, alternative education. The conclusion emphasizes that the future of adult and continuing education is an optimistic one and that there will be more demand for adult educators who will be more like brokers, planners, and counselors, developers, and linkers than the traditional teachers they have principally been in the past.

A Guide to Needs Assessment In Community Education. USOE, 1976. 30pp.

The purpose of the monograph is to suggest methods for the conduct of a community education needs assessment. Such an assessment should; 1) help the applicants to determine the status of the community in terms of quality of life; 2) provide the applicant with an information base to serve as a guideline for planning and development; 3) encourage the applicant to initiate community education through the assessment process by involving the community in the proposal application. Bowers provides models to achieve these goals.

Guilford, Dorothy M. - "The NonCollegiate Sector; Statistical Snapshots of Adult Continuing Education," address presented at the 29th National Conference on Higher Education, sponsored by the American Association for the Higher Education, 1974.

Houle, Cyril O. - **The Design of Education**, San Fransicso, Cali. Jossey-Bass Publishers, 1972.

Houle, Cyril O. "Who Stays and Why"?, **Adult Education**, Vol. 14, No. 4 (Summer 1964). (Version for adult students is **Continuing Your Education**, McGraw-Hill, 1964. See also Houle, **The Inquiring Mind.**)

Johnstone, John W. C. The presentation by Dr. Johnstone is based on findings from the book with Ramon Rivera, **Volunteers for Learning**. Chicago: Aldine Press, 1965.

Kimmel, Ernest - **The Characteristics of Adult Learners**, Princeton, New Jersey: unpublished manuscript prepared for the College Board, 1976.

Knowles, Malcolm - **The Adult Learner: A Neglected Species**, Houston, Texas: Gulf Publishing Company, 1973.

Knox, Alan B. - **Adult Development and Learning**. A Handbook on Individual Growth and Competence in the Adult Years for Education and the Helping Professions.

Brings together all current, tested knowledge of adult development and learning, including information about the circumstances under which adults learn most effectively, the development and learning are affected by family roles, social activities, education, occupation, personality, and health. 700 pages.

Contents: 1. Development During Adulthood. 2. The Context for Development. 3. Family Role Performance. 4. Education, Work, and Community Performance. 5. Physical Condition. 6. Personality During Adulthood. 7. Adult Learning. 8. Women's Role. 9. Adjusting to Change Events. 10. Perspective on Adulthood. Jossey-Bass, San Francisco, 1977.

Kuhlen, Raymond G. (ed.). **Psychological Backgrounds of Adult Education**. Chicago, Center for the Study of Liberal Education for Adults, 1963. Notes and Essays, No. 40 (Chapter 2, "Adult Capacities to Learn." CSLEA publications can be obtained from Syracuse University, Syracuse, N.Y.)

Miller, Harry L. **Teaching and Learning in Adult Education**. New York: Macmillan, 1964. (Chapter 2, "Some Crucial Conditions for Learning," Chapter 3, "Significant Behavioral Changes for Adult Education.")

National Advisory Council on Adult Education. **A Target Population in Education**, Washington, D.C.; U.S. Government Printing Office, 1974.

National Center for Education Statistics, **The Condition of Education**, Washington, D.C.: U. S. Government Printing Office, 1976.

Newell, J., and Kahn H. **Community Education Advisory Council**, USOE, 1977. 35pp. and appendix

The Newell and Kahn work can best be described as a thought piece. The authors examine the ways in which schools may innovatively serve their communities' needs within the next 12 years. The work discusses the secondary uses of facilities, equipment, and personnel rather than the traditional primary educational functions of the schools.

Reardon, Francis, Garber, Elizabeth M., and Flautz, John, **Needs of the Lifelong Learner**, The View of Agents and Consumers, Pennsylvania Department of Education, April, 1977
  The authors conducted a survey to explore lifelong learning needs in Pennsylvania. The primary needs included: limited requirements for admission of educational programs to encourage broad participating; widespread availability of academic and vocational counseling; and development of tests to supplement the CLEP tests for crediting experience. Additional needs were financial aid for lifelong learners and part time students; more accessible courses; remedial courses; and some type of reciprocity for credit transfer to allow students to move easily from school to school.

Reiss, Mary L., ASSESSING THE EDUCATIONAL NEEDS OF NEW YORK STATE ADULTS: IMPLICATIONS FOR PROGRAM DEVELOPMENT, N.Y. State education Department, Marcy, 1978.

Review of Educational Research, Vol. 23, No. 3. (June 1959), issue on Adult Education, (Chapter 4. The Psychology of Adults; esp. pp. 249-251. The June 1965 issue is devoted to Adult Education.)

Rhyne, Dwight C. "Variations on a Theme by Thorndike," **Adult Education**, Vol. 12, No. 2 (Winter 1961).

Sjogren, Douglas D., and Alan B. Knox. **Age and Learning in University Adult Education**. Adult Education Research, University of Nebraska, 1963. (mimeo; also available as Knox and Associates, "Adult Learning," **Abstracts of Research**.)

Sorenson, Herbert. **Adult Abilities**, St. Paul: U. of Minnesota, Press, 1938.

Thorndike, E. L. **Adult Learning**. New York: Macmillan, 1928.

Tough, Allen - **The Adults Learning Projects**, Ontario, Canada; The Ontario Institute for Studies in Education, 1971.

Wientge, King M., and Philip H. DuBois. **Factors Associated with the Achievement of Adult Students**. St. Louis; Washington University, 1964. (A research report submitted to Cooperative Research Branch, U. S. Office of Education).

Wirtz, Willard - **The Boundless Resource**, A Prospectus for an educational-work Policy, Produced by the National Manpower Institute New Republic Book Co., Inc. Washington, D.C. 1975.
  The central doctrine of this Prospectus is that the key to bring education and work closer together is not so much in any particular programs as in developing truly collaborative processes among those in charge of these functions, including the public.
  See especially the Who and What of Adult Education, p. 97.

207

Young Ken - The Basic Steps of Planning. Pendell Pub. 1978.
pp. 24.

The Basic Steps of Planning is based on the belief that
those persons who know where they want to go in life and
what it takes to get there have a much better chance of
succeeding than those who are not sure of where they are
going and why. The booklet is designed to explain the planning process and to serve as a guide in assisting people
to understand the general nature of the process.

Experiential Learning - A Bibliography

The ERIC Clearinghouse on Higher Education abstracts and
indexes the current research literature on higher education for
publication in the National Institute of Education' monthly **Resources in Education** (RIE). Readers who wish to order ERIC
Document Reproduction Service, Post Office Box 190, Arlington,
Virginia 22210. When ordering, please specify the ERIC document (ED) number. Unless otherwise noted, documents are available in both microfiche (MF) and hard/photocopy (HC).

ADDITIONAL RESOURCES ON THE ADULT LEARNER

ACTION. "University Year for Action." Press release. Wash-
ington, C.D.: ACTION Office of Public Affairs, n.d.
Aronstein, Laurence W. and Olsen, Edward G. Action-Learning:
Student Community Service Projects. Washington, D.C.: Assoc-
iation for Supervision and Curriculum Development, 1974. ED
093 859. MF - $0.75; HC - $1.85.
Averill, Lloyd J. "Competence as a Liberal Art." Address to
Summer Workshop, Ottawa, Kansas 1974 .
Bailey, Stephen K. "Career Education and Higher Education."
Educational Record 54 (Fall 1973): 255-259.
Bell, T. H. "Remarks." **The Chronicle of Higher Education 9**
(January 20, 1975): 6.
Berg, Ivar. **Education and Jobs: The Great Training Robbery.**
New York: Praeger Press, 1970.
Bevan, J. M. "Apropos of Experiential Learning." Paper pre-
sented to the conference of the Society for Field Experience
Education, Atlanta, Georgia, October 12, 1974.
Bok, Derek, **Daedalus** 103 (Fall 1974): 159-172.

Brewster, Kingman, Jr. "Announcement of the Five Year B.A. Program." New Haven: Yale University, 1965.

————. "The Involuntary Campus and the Manipulated Society." Educational Record 51 (Spring 1970): 101-5.

Buckle, Suzanne and Leonard. "Learning From the Urban Environment." Mimeographed paper at the Urban Studies Curriculum Conference. Hartford, Connecticut: Trinity College, June 1972.

California State Legislature. Assembly Bill No. 3973. Sacramento California, 1974.

Carnegie Commission on Higher Education. Less Time, More Options. New York: McGraw-Hill, 1973.

————. Toward a Learning Society. New York: McGraw-Hill, 1973.

Chicago State University. Business Laboratory Program. Program brochure. Chicago, Illinois: Chicago State University, 1975.

College Placement Council. "Liberal Arts Students and the Job Market." The Chronicle of Higher Education 10 (May 5, 1975): 9.

Cooper, Harlan. "Internships in State and Local Government in the South." Mimeographed. Atlanta, Georgia: Southern Regional Education Board, 1974.

Cooperative Assessment of Experiential Learning Project. "The Assessment of the Achievement of Interpersonal Skills." Draft manual. Princeton: Educational Testing Service. 1974.

Cross, K. Patricia, "The Integration of Learning and Earning: Cooperative Education and Nontraditional Study." ERIC/Higher Education Research Report No. 4 Washington, D.C.: American Association for Higher Education, 1973. ED 080 100. MF -$0.75; HC-$3.15.

Davis, Douglas P. "Undergraduate Externships." In Let the Entire Community Become Our University, edited by Philip Ritterbush. Washington, D.C.: Acropolis Books, 1972.

"Developments in service-learning in the South." Regional Spotlight. Atlanta, Georgia: Southern Regional Education Board, Nov./Dec., 1972.

Duley, John. "Cross-Cultural Field Experience." In Implementing Field Experience Education, edited by John Duley. San Francisco: Jossey-Bass, 1974.

Eberly, Donald J. "Diakonia Paideia and the Resource Development Internship Programs." In Service Learning in the South. Atlanta, Georgia: Southern Regional Education Board, 1973.

————. An Agenda for Off-Campus Learning Experiences. Menlo Park, California: Stanford Research Institute, 1969.

————. "Service-Learning: the Road Ahead." National Service

Newsletter (December 1974): 2.

Feldman, Marvin J. "The Relevance Gap in American Education." **The Conference Board Record 9** (June 1972): 28.

Ford, Gerald. Commencement Address, Ohio State University, Columbus, Ohio, September 3, 1974.

Gardner, John W. "The Universities and the Cities." **Educational Record 50** (Winter 1969): 5-8.

Goldstein, Michael B. "Student-Community Involvement: An Evaluation." **Public Management 51** (May 1971): 16.

Graham, Richard A. "University Year for Action." **Change 4** (February 1972): 7.

―――――. "Voluntary Action and Experiential Education." **Journal of Voluntary Action Research 2** (October 1973): 186-193.

Havighurst, Robert J.; Graham, R.; and Eberly, D. "Action-Learning: A New Option for American Youth." In **Let the Entire Community Become Our University**, edited by Philip Ritterbush. Washington, D.C.: Acropolis Books, 1972.

Hedlund, Donald D. "Reflections on Political Internships." **PS 6** (Winter 1973): 19-25.

Heiss, Ann. **An Inventory of Academic Innovation and Reform**. A technical report sponsored by the Carnegie Commission on High Education. Berkeley, California: Carnegie Foundation, 1973.

Hennessy, Bernard C. **Political Internships: Theory, Practice, Evaluation**. University Park, Pennsylvania: The Pennsylvania State University, 1970.

Hirschfield, Fobert S. and Adler, Norman M. "Internships in Politics: The CUNY Experience." **PS 6** (Winter 1973): 13-18.

Hitchcock, James. "The New Vocationalism." **Change 5** (April 1973): 46-50.

Hochstrasser, Donald. "Experiential Education in the University: A Component of Higher Education." Arnold, Daniel et al., "Experiential Education: New Direction for an Old Concept." Papers delivered to the 81st annual meeting of the American Psychological Association, Montreal 1973.

Hodgkinson, Harold L. "Developmental Curricula." In "New Approaches to Undergraduate Education," edited by Bradley H. Sagen. Background papers prepared for the eight regional conferences sponsored by the Midwest Regional Council of the American Association for Higher Education, Washington, D.C.: American Association for Higher Education. October 1972. ED 077 374. MF-$0.75; HC-$1.85.

Hook, Sidney. "John Dewey and His Betrayors." **Change 3** (November 1971): 22-26.

Jarrell, Donald W. "Professional Development: Get Them Early." **Training in Business and Industry 2** (February 1974).

Keeton, Morris. "Dilemmas in Accrediting Off-Campus Learning." In **The Expanded Campus**, edited by D.W. Vermilye. San Francisco: Jossey-Bass. 1972.

Kiel, David H. "Student Learning through Community Involvement: A Report on Three Studies of the Service-Learning Model." Atlanta, Georgia: Southern Regional Education Board, 1972 ED 080 051. MF-$0.75; HC-$4.20.

Knowles, Asa S. and Associates. **Handbook of Cooperative Education**. San Francisco: Jossey-Bass, 1971.

Lyons, Charles C. "Experiential Education: One Point of View." In **Off-Campus Education: An Inquiry**, by Peter Meyers and Sherry L. Petry. Atlanta, Georgia: Southern Regional Education Board, 1972. ED 078 124. MF-$0.75; HC-$1.50.

Lyons, Charles C. "Experiential Education: One Point of View." In **Off-Campus Education: An Inquiry**, by Peter Meyers and Sherry L. Petry. Atlanta, Georgia: Southern Regional Education Board, 1972. ED 080 052. MF-$0.75; HC-$1.50.

Marland, S. P. Jr. "Voicew from the Real World." Washington: Paper presented at the conference of the Colleges of Arts and Sciences, 1972. ED 078 124. MF-$0.75; HC-$1.50.

Meyer, Peter and Petry, Sherry L. **Off-Campus Education: An Inquiry**. Atlanta: Southern Regional Education Board, 1972.

Murphy, Thomas P. **Government Management Internships and Executive Development**. Lexington, Massachusetts: D. C. Heath and Company, 1973.

Nader, Ralph. Conference Address. Atlanta, Georgia: Society for Field Experience Education, Oct. 13, 1974.

Newman, Frank, et al. **Report on Higher Education**. U.S. Department of Health, Education, Welfare. Washington, D.C.: U.S. Government Printing Office, 1971.

Quinn, Mary Ellen, and Sellars, Louise, "Role of the Student." In **Implementing Field Experience Education**, edited by John Duley. San Francisco: Jossey-Bass, 1974.

Ritterbush, Philip C. "Experiential Education and the University." Mimeographed. Wallpack Village, New Jersey, March 10, 1974.

—————. "Learning Fields." In **Options for Learning**, edited by C. Kathryn Shelton et al. Lexington, Kentucky: Office for Experiential Education, 1974.

—————, ed. **Let the Entire Community Become Our University**. Washington, D.C.: Acropolis Books, 1972.

Sagen, H. Bradley. "The Professions: A Neglected Model for Undergraduate Education." Iowa City: Paper presented to Midwest Regional Conferences of the American Association for Higher Education, 1972.

Seidel, Robert A. and Kerwin, Cornelius M. "Public Service Internships: Two Baltimore Experiences." Mimeographed. Baltimore, Maryland: Department of Political Science, Johns Hopkins University, 1974.

Sexton, Robert F. and Stephenson, John B., "Institutionalizing Experiential Education in a State University." In **Implementing Field Experience Education**, edited by John Duley. San Francisco: Jossey-Bass, 1974.

Shapek, Raymond A. "Experiential Education and Service - Learning Internships in Texas" In **Continuing Education for Texas**, edited by Anthony C. Neidhart. San Marcos, Texas: Southwest Texas State University, 1974.

Sigmon, Robert L. "From Adolescence to Adulthood: the Young and the Establishment." Mimeographed. Raleigh, North Carolina: North Carolina Internship Office, August, 1974a.

————. "Public Service Internships - An Institutional Design." In **Let the Entire Community Become Our University**, edited by Philip C. Ritterbush. Washington, D.C.: Acropolis Books, 1972.

————. "Service-Learning: An Educational Style." In **Service-Learning in the South**. Atlanta. Georgia: Southern Regional Education Board, 1973. ED 086 076. MF-$0.75; HC-$1.50.

————. "Service-Learning in North Carolina." In **Implementing Field Experience Education**, edited by John Duley. San Francisco: Jossey-Bass, 1947b.

Smith, Donald A. "The Objective for Field Placement." **Journal of Cooperative Education 10** (May 1974): 17.

Steiger, Representative William. House Education and Labor Committee Report, Washington, D.C.: U.S. Government Printing Office, February, 1973.

Stephenson, John B. and Sexton, Robert F. "Experiential Education and the Revitalization of the Liberal Arts." In **The Philosophy of the Curriculum: The Need for General Education**, edited by Sidney Hook, Paul Kurtz and Miro Todorovich. Buffalo: Prometheus Books, 1975.

Trudeau, Pierre Elliot. "Opportunities for Youth." Ottawa, Canada: Department of State, 1971.

University of Dayton. "Project Interface." Program Catalogue. Dayton, Ohio: University of Dayton, 1970.

Van Aalst, Frank and Waters, R.O. "Liberal Arts and Career Education at St. Mary's College of Maryland." Mimeographed. St. Mary's, Maryland: St. Mary's College, 1974.

Williams. Shelton L. "Policy Research in Undergraduate Learning." **Journal of Higher Education, 45** (April 1974): 296-304.

Work in America. Report of a Special Task Force to the Secretary of Health, Education and Welfare, U.S. Department of Health, Education and Welfare. Cambridge, Massachusetts:

MIT Press. 1973.

Yankelovich, Daniel. **The New Morality: A Profile of American Youth in the 70s.** New York: McGraw-Hill, 1974.

1 John W. C. Johnstone and Ramon J. Rivera, **Volunteers for Learning**, Aldine, Chicago, 1965.

2 John W. C. Johnstone and Ramon J. Rivera, **Volunteers for Learning**, Aldine Publishers, Chicago, Ill. 1965 p. 78 (A comprehensive national study of adult learning activities in the U.S. sponsored by the National Opinion Research Center at the University of Chicago.)

3 Arbeiter, Solomon, "Profile of the Adult Learner", College Board Review, No. 102, Winter 1976-7. Used by permission. (Dr. Arbeiter is Program Planning Officer for the College Board)

4 Roby Kidd, **How Adults Learn**, Association Press, 1975, p. 45-46.

5 James T. Carey, **Why Students Drop Out: A Study of Evening College Student Motivations**, Center for the Study of Liberal Education for Adults, Chicago, 1953. See "Threat of Failure" in Cross, Patricia, **Beyond the Open Door**, Jossey-Bass Pub. San Francisco, 1974 pp. 18-31.

6 Jacob Getzels, from a filmstrip and tape recordings, University of Michigan Microfilms, Ann Arbor, Michigan. Also in **Learning Theory and Classroom Practice in Adult Education**, Report on a Conference on Instruction, Syracuse University' Sagamore Conference Center, May 1956, University College, Syracuse University, pp. 7-8.

7 Cyril O. Houle, **The Inquiring Mind**, U. of Wisconsin Press, Madison, 1961.

8 Houle, **op. cit.**, p. 24.

9 **Ibid.**, p. 43.

10 A. H. Maslow, **Motivation and Personality** (New York: Harper and Brothers, 1954).

11 Knox, Alan B., **Adult Development and Learning**, (A Handbook on Individual Growth and Competence in the Adult Years for Education and the Helping Professions), Jossey-Bass, Inc., Publ. San Francisco, Cal. 94111, 1977.

12 **Ibid.**, p. 5.

13 Ralph W. Tyler, **Basic Principles of Curriculum and Instruction**, U. of Chicago Press, Chicago, Ill., 1950, p. 9.

14 See **Architecture for Adult Education**, a graphic guide for those who are planning physical facilities for adult education. Adult Education Association Commission on Architecture, Washington, D.C.

15 Ahlen, John H., "Identification of High Risk Occupational Students in Arizona Community Colleges" (Unpublished, Ph. D. dissertation, Arizona State University, 1979.)

16 Tough, Allen, "Major Learning Efforts: Recent Research and Future Directions," Ontario Institute for Studies in Education, 252 Bloor St. West, Toronto, Canada M5S 1V6.

17 **Ibid.**, p. 2.

18 John M. Peters & Susan Gordon, Adult Learning Projects: A study of adult learning in urban and rural Tennessee. Knoxville; University of Tennessee, 1974.

19 Commission on Non-traditional Study, **Diversity by Design** (San Francisco: Jossey-Bass, 1973), p. 21.

20 Birge, Lynn, "The Evolution of American Public Library Services to Adult Independent Learners." (Unpublished Dissertation) Arizona State University, 1979. p. 250.

21 Houle, Cyril O. **Continuing Your Education**, McGraw-Hill, N.Y., 1964, pp. 17-36.

22 Knowles, Malcolm, **Self Directed Learning**, Association Press, N.Y., 1975.

23 **Ibid.**, p. 18.

24 **Ibid.**, p. 19.

25 **op. cit.**, p. 21.

26 Worby, Diana, "Independent Learning: The Uses of the Contract in an English Program." Life-Long Learning: The Adult Years, Adult Education Association, U.S.A., Feb. 1979, p. 32.

27 MacKenzie, Ossian, and Edward L. Christensen, **The Changing World of Correspondence Study**, Penn State Press, 1971.

Chapter XIV:

A PHILOSOPHY FOR
ADULT EDUCATION

An excellent plumber is infinitely more admirable than an incompetent philosopher. The society which scorns excellence in plumbing because plumbing is a humble activity and tolerates shoddiness in philosophy because it is an exalted activity will have neither good plumbing nor good philosophy. Neither its pipes nor its theories will hold water.
-John W. Gardner, **Excellence: Can We Be Equal and Excellent Too?**, Harper, New York, 1961

The educator of adults must cultivate a philosophy which will allow him to keep up with rapid technological changes, to adapt to the differing needs of our society, and to live at some peace with himself. I once heard the educator-historian Fred Harvey Harrington, president of the University of Wisconsin, warn his faculty: "Don't attempt too little, and don't attempt too much!"

Those of us who have worked in the field of continuing and adult education know that the development of a workable and viable philosophy of education is slow in coming. Wisdom is not easily come by, takes years of experience, and develops slowly. But with persistence, study, an open mind, and much listening, reading, observation, and discussion with those with more experience and knowledge, we can come to a philosophy of adult education that will benefit both the educator of adults and the thousands of persons who will take part in the institutional programs.

Many adult educators find it difficult to develop a clear image of adult education. This is understandable because of the diverse programs and aims of the field. But if we are to find meaning and increasing significance in our planning of programs, we must cultivate a philosophy for adult education.

Our **goals and aims** will remain unfocused unless we **philosophize** about our **purposes**, our **values**, our **aims** for ourselves and our society. For each of us, our **value system shines** through our programs, and our programs represent our objectified philosophy.

It is the responsibility of the educator of adults to search for a meaningful philosophy of education, both for himself or herself and for the institution through which he works. Jack London says:

It is our thesis that the adult educator, in his search for his personal and occupational identity, must philosophize and engage in philosophical inquiry if we are to succeed in our **search for meaning** and relevance in our work and in our lives. While all of us want to live significant and constructive lives, too many of us are confused, bewildered, and empty of hope - a condition that weakens our leadership ability within the educational enterprise.[1]

In working with educators, and more particularly with administrators of adult programs, there is sometimes a reluctance to discuss the philosophy behind the institutional purposes and objectives of the program. Even some teachers of adults shy away from a penetrating discussion of philosophy. We cannot escape our obligation to examine our system of values to determine where we would like our society to move and identify the kind of persons to whom we hope to bring the better life.

A **philosophy distinguishes** a person as an educator. "As the possession of spoken language distinguishes man from the brutes, so the awareness of his philosophy can be said to distinguish the adult educator from the worker in adult education," [2] say John Walker Powell and Kenneth D. Benne in a discussion of philosophies of adult education. They recognize that there will be conflicting philosophies among educators of adults, and tend to polarize these around two main themes, **the developmental** and the **rationalist**. The **rationalist** viewpoint represents a system of values which **elevates the intellect**, the **wisdom** of the ages, the belief that man should be steeped in the refinement of the ages. **Robert Maynard Hutchins** and the Great Books Foundation represent this point of view.

However, the **developmental philosophy** takes the point of view that education is a dynamic process and views education as a **means to an end**. Emphasis upon the **interrelationships** of people, the **community development** concept, the group dynamics represented in the growth of human relations laboratories such as that at Bethel, Maine,[3] are characteristics of the developmental philosophy. (see chart)

EVERY PERSON A PHILOSOPHER

The educator of adults may attempt to be **eclectic** in philosophical outlook, incorporating a number of approaches to the attainment of the good life, both for himself or herself and for

SCHEMATIC REPRESENTATION OF CLASSICAL PHILOSOPHIES*

	ONTOLOGY	EPISTEMOLOGY	AXIOLOGY	IMPLICATIONS FOR EDUCATION	PRO-PONENT
Idealism	A world of mind of ideas, spiritual reality We must cultivate the soul. Unite ourselves with the spiritual reality to which we belong	Truth as Idea Arrive at truth by reason and intuition	The imitation of the absolute self. To arrive close to the ideal, to neglect the ideal. **Values** are absolute and **unchanging**.	Use approved subject matter. The teacher is an ideal to be emulated. Use symbols and ideas for absorption and discussion. Exact knowledge from the student Deduction.	Plato, Hegel
Realism 1. national classical religious 2. natural or scientific	A world of things The world is natural, rational and spiritual	Truth is an observable fact. One must have definite knowledge to adapt to the universe. An idea is true or valid when it corresponds with those aspects of the world it attempts to describe.	Values are well defined Virtues must be learned Moral standards and habits must be learned.	Subject matter of the Great Books Discipline Initiative rests with the teacher.	Aristotle Locke, Hume, Mill Rousseau
Pragmatism	A world of experiences. The material world exists in its own right but it is not permenent nor independent of people.	Knowledge is a transaction between man and his environment. People make knowledge. The meaning of an idea lies in its consequences. Ends and means are reciprocal, flexible and revisable.	Values are relative and impermenent. Values are those that advance human welfare. Value of critical intelligence.	Child should experience problem solving learning experiences. From concrete to abstract. Learner motivated by interests. Teacher is guide and assistant.	Dewey Peirce James
Existentialism	A world of existing. People make themselves when they act. Life is a movement toward death. People die totally free and apart from any universal system. By itself the universe is meaningless.	Knowledge is a matter of personal choice, an activity, a grappling with basic problems of existence. People inbue the universe with individual meaning. The world is concrete and when we impose meaning we subtract knowledge.	Values are individual. Values are passionate, active commitments.	Use whatever works Revise-induction Student is an individual and should be treated as such. Students have total freedom. Teach passionate concern Creative Individuality.	Sartre, Buber Jaspers Camus

* Thanks to Alice Williams for assistance with this list.

clientele. But it is our responsibility, the adult educator's, to attempt continually to refine and cultivate a more profound and meaningful philosophy of adult education.

In talking about mankind, Karl Jaspers emphasizes the relevant role of the philosophy of the educator. "Philosophy exists wherever thought brings men into an awareness of their existence . . . For no man thinks without philosophizing - Truly or falsely, superficially or profoundly, hastily or slowly and thoroughly. In a world where standards prevail, where judgments are made, there is philosophy." [4]

What, after all, is the purpose of education if it is not to help a person cultivate a philosophy of life which is satisfying and which justifies a vocation and life?

Our devotion to the concept of lifelong learning is a part of our belief that mankind can be improved, that we can learn, that society can be recast. In discussing education with learned persons of various professions, I find that their philosophy of education shines through their conversations. While discussing education, Lawrence B. Perkins, a leading architect who is responsible for some of the most imaginative designs in school architecture in the Twentieth Century, stated, "The essence of education is incompletion. A person who has completed his education is no longer educated. A measure of education is the awareness of an increased number of things that lie ahead of you." [5]

ESSENTIALISTS VERSUS PROGRESSIVES

A great deal of discussion and controversy goes on between the essentialists and progressives, between the child psychologists and the subject-matter specialists, between the Rickovers and Bestors, and the National Education Association, between this school group and that over the highly controversial question of the basic source from which objectives shall be derived. This is basically the question we deal with in program planning.

The progressives emphasize the importance of studying manuals to find out what kinds of interests they have, what problems they encounter and what purposes they have in mind. The progressive sees information gained from studying the individual as providing information for the basic source from which to select objectives. The progressive therefore tends to fall in the camps of the "planning with" point of view.

The essentialist, contrariwise, is very much impressed with the large body of knowledge collected over many thousands of years the so-called cultural heritage, and emphasizes this as the fundamental source for deriving objectives. The essentialist takes as objectives the basic learnings selected from the vast cultural heritage of the past and tends to give them a hierarchy of values. The methodology tends to result in the "planning for" point of view.

Sociologists and many anthropologists who are concerned with the changing cultural patterns in our society and the pressing problems of our contemporary life see in an analysis of contemporary society the basic information from which objectives should be derived. They view educational institutions as agencies for helping people to deal effectively with the critical problems of contemporary life. If they can determine what are the basic contemporary problems, then the objective of the educational agency is to provide those skills, attitudes, and points of knowledge which will help people deal intelligently with these contemporary problems.

On the other hand, the educational philosophers recognize that there are basic values in life which must be transmitted from one generation to another through education. The latter results largely in persons "planning for" so as to instill those values which are thought to be most worth perpetuating and they see educational philosophy as the basic source from which objectives are to be derived.

EDUCATION AS SELF-EDUCATION

Dr. Carl Rogers, eminent psychologist and father of nondirective counseling, takes the point of view that basically no person can "teach" another person, but that if persons truly learn they will teach themselves. The president of the University of Cincinnati, Walter Langsam, takes a similar point of view in a discussion with a group of students reported by the Milwaukee Journal; he says only the individual can truly educate himself, regardless of the influences that may assist in the process. "It is doubtful that anyone can educate anybody else. Rather, education is something that happens to the student while he is working on a subject or subjects." [6]

Langsam contends that the good teacher can present material interestingly and even create an atmosphere that is stimulating, but whether the student learns effectively or does not absorb knowledge remains fundamentally and finally with the student. If educators of adults hold this point of view regarding self-education, they will approach their institutions of learning, their organizations of program, and their instructional staffs quite differently from the traditional administrators who see their roles as dispensing "knowledge." Teaching will be a process of assisting the adult in methods of self-education.

Paul **Douglass** has devoted a major work to a consideration of **teaching for self-education** as a life goal and has based his philosophy upon the thinking of the noted educator, William S. Learned. Douglass charts specific ways for higher education to shift the emphasis from requirements of courses completed to the new awakening of a lifelong intellectual pursuit of **curiosity**. It was Learned's purpose as an educator to encourage the habit of self-education which would continue throughout life as an ongoing activity. His philosophy included the thought that the genuine service of the true teacher is that of a friendly critic, shedding light on a path toward a student's goal by providing for his work under a wholesome personal setting.[7]

Fortunately, more universities are recognizing that adults should be able to pace their learning and have set up **special** degree programs for the mature adult. The Bachelor of Liberal Studies Degree at the University of Oklahoma is one such program for adults that permits and encourages students to proceed at a pace best suited to their level of learning. Considerations are made for ability and motivation **for independent study**, and students are allowed to program according to the time available. The objectives of the BLS degree break sharply from traditional resident, credit-hour programs. Set up to assist the adult in his self-education, the University states its philosophy of the program:

The BLS degree program is designed to give the **mature adult:**

Better understanding of his own personality and potential.

Better understanding of the behavior of individuals and groups.

Knowledge of his own and of other contemporary cultures.

A historical view of man's development - social, intellectual, scientific, artistic, and religious.

Increased appreciation for some of the great literary, scientific, and artistic works of man.

Ability to read, interpret, and evaluate the works of scholars, and to understand the methods of investigation within the broad areas of humanities, social sciences, and natural sciences.

Knowledge of the humanities, natural sciences, and social sciences in sufficient depth and breadth to enable the student to understand relationships among these broad areas of knowledge.

Better understanding of the problems of man in the Twentieth Century and of the probable direction and effect of political, economic, and technological change.[8]

The head of the honors program at Southern Illinois University, philosophor Dr. Claude Coleman, makes a plea for the stable society and the integrated man:

> Today our society suffers from a plethora of splendid splinters - fractional adults who never become men and women in any real sense of the word. I had better define my term, perhaps. Ask who someone is and the reply invariably comes back, "Why, he is a plumber," or a "surgeon," or an "economist," or a "geographer," or a "dean," or a "policeman" - not a man at all but only a splinter.

Giving examples from his experience, Coleman states: "Most scholars work long hours turning out scholarly articles for other blind scholars to read in their own fields. They are finely trained scholars, but they are not men. They are fractions of men."[10]

Coleman recognizes the danger of producing fine scholars rather than whole people. He laments the situation in our society where the skillful dentist sounds off in the barbershop concerning political situations about which he or she has little knowledge and, unfortunately, reveals as great an, or greater, ignorance than the barber's. Occasionally, departments within a university think they gain applause from their colleagues by deprecating scholars or departments in other colleges. The tragedy of narrow scholarship points out the need for broadly educated persons who are appreciative of the wholeness, the unity of knowledge.

It is a tragic commentary on our age of specialization when persons of letters are unable to talk intelligently outside their own specialty. A physician in Racine, Wisconsin, was talking to a group of undergraduates about the relationship between psychiatry and education. He lamented that so many members of the medical profession are not more liberally educated men. Jocularly he commented: "Did you ever spend an evening socially with a group of surgeons? When you get beyond the viscera, they're lost!"[11]

SCHOOLING AND EDUCATION

A friend gave me a copy of a sign he kept next to his desk where his colleagues in the university could see it plainly. The sign read: "Are you educated or just schooled?" The question, prominently displayed, continues to be a source of intellectual stimulation and often begins a philosophical discussion of training versus education, schooling versus education, and the values that underlie continuing education.

Mortimer J. Adler of "Great Books" fame speaks of the difference between schooling and education:

I can hardly remember what I used to think when I had the mistaken notion that the schools were the most important part of the educational process; for now I think exactly the reverse. I am now convinced that it is adult education which is the substantial and major part of the educational process-the part which all the rest is at best-and it is at its best only when it is-a preparation.[12]

Adler wishes we could distinguish between schooling and "adult education," because the public image is one of an unfortunate connotation. By "schooling" he would imply the development and training of young, while for Adler "education," leaving off the "adult," would signify the learning which is done by mature men and women. Youth, he claims, is the obstacle, for "the young cannot be educated."

The protected life and artificial existence of the young stand in the education which Adler would make a part of the real education. Only the adult can value this because of an experience from which to make judgments. The child is trainable, but children in school are not educable. "Only in the mature soil, soil rich with experience-the soul in the mature person-can ideas really take root."[13]

What is the objective of all our schooling and of our education? Is it not maturity, wisdom, the ability to get the most out of life? Is it not to gain more understanding, insight, compassion, and a deeper comprehension of the nature of the world and of the people who live in it?

To the question, "When does education stop?" author James A. Michener, in speaking to a group of students at Macalester College, assured the graduating students, "It doesn't!"

During his war days, Michener had become impressed with observing the top officers off duty. He observed that some of the officers used their free time to educate themselves in new fields. One of his officers spent six hours each day learning French. When asked why he spent so much time learning a language when he had no immediate use for it, he replied, "How do I know where I'll be sent when the war's over?" It was at that time Michener began thinking seriously about his own self-education and began writing what later became **Tales of the South Pacific**. Regarding reeducation, he says:

I know now that the good work of the world is accomplish ed principally by people who dedicate themselves unstintingly to the big, distant goal. Weeks, months, years pass, but

222

the good workman knows that he is gambling on an ultimate achievement which cannot be measured in time spent. Responsible men and women leap to the challenge of jobs that require enormous dedication and years to fulfill and are happiest when they are so involved. This means that men and women who hope to make a real contribution to American life must **Re-educate** themselves periodically or they are doomed to mediocrity.[14]

We are never wise enough to stop learning, and the agencies of adult education and their administrators must develop a philosophy which will result in programs that will institutionalize the ongoing learning process. Even if we have learned a subject, we need to continue to use it to make it viable.

Ideas which we receive in our schooling must be given life. If the body requires exercise to stave off atrophy, even more does the mind need feeding and stimulation. Therefore, means for learning must be provided for adults in forms that are readily accessible. Home libraries, recordings, and the home computer for information retrieval in the form of a console similar to our television set will make opportunities for learning as available as the switch of the dial.[15]

Some of our leading encyclopedia companies are experimenting with methods of bringing information into our homes through economical, efficient, and effective methods. Fortunately most people with healthy minds can continue to learn and grow intellectually as long as they live.

Those of use who have worked in the field of continuing and adult education know that the development of a workable and viable philosophy of education is slow in coming. Wisdom is not easily come by, takes years of experience, and develops slowly. But with persistence, study, an open mind, and much listening, reading, observation, and discussion with those with more experience and knowledge, we can come to a philosophy of adult education that will benefit both the educator of adults and the thousands of persons who will take part in the institutional programs.

Some of the sources of philosophy outlined in the accompanying chart are useful in considering ways in which objectives and values may be distilled for an adult education program. The program philosophy will be the result.   See Chart on next page

PUBLIC SCHOOL ADULT EDUCATORS' SURVEY

In a study of the public school adult education programs of Northern Illinois, an examination of the view of the director as to the philosophy of his program is revealing. From the study it was found that the directors conceived of the program as serv-

ADULT STUDENTS	DIRECTOR OF ADULT AND CONTINUING EDUCATION	INSTITUTION OF ADULT EDUCA-TION	SOCIETY	THE ADULT EDUCATOR'S ADVISORY BOARD

Values and Objectives
of the
Adult Education Program
THE PROGRAM PHILOSOPHY

"Schooling must needs be not merely preparation for life but living itself, and thus EDUCATION." John Dewey

"A government resting on the principle of popular suffrage cannot be successful unless those who elect and who obey their governors are educated." William H. Lighty

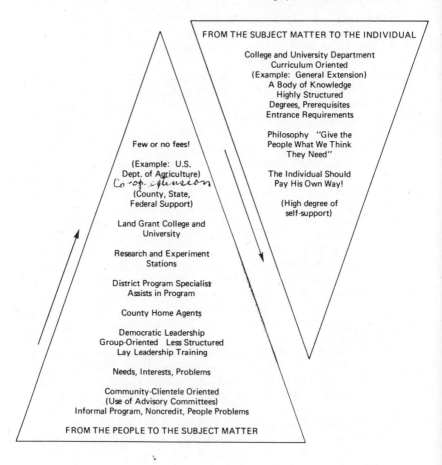

FROM THE SUBJECT MATTER TO THE INDIVIDUAL

College and University Department
Curriculum Oriented
(Example: General Extension)
A Body of Knowledge
Highly Structured
Degrees, Prerequisites
Entrance Requirements

Few or no fees!

(Example: U.S.
Dept. of Agriculture)
Co-op. extension
(County, State,
Federal Support)

Land Grant College and
University

Research and Experiment
Stations

District Program Specialist
Assists in Program

County Home Agents

Democratic Leadership
Group-Oriented   Less Structured
Lay Leadership Training

Needs, Interests, Problems

Community-Clientele Oriented
(Use of Advisory Committees)
Informal Program, Noncredit, People Problems

FROM THE PEOPLE TO THE SUBJECT MATTER

Philosophy   "Give the
People What We Think
They Need"

The Individual Should
Pay His Own Way!

(High degree of
self-support)

224

ing adults primarily for the purposes of leisure time and recreation, the cultivation of vocational skills, continuing education and cultural development, and community services.

The study was based upon replies from 47 high school districts in the state and was a fairly representative sample. In almost no case in the study did the director express the philosophy of the program as being that of leading the students into new areas where they did not currently feel an educational need. A summary of the findings follows:

THE DIRECTORS' VIEW OF THE PURPOSES OF THE ADULT PROGRAM

	Number of Times
Leisure time use and recreation	33
Vocational skills development	27
Continuing education and cultural development	26
Community service	25
Self-improvement	15
To use facilities	3
Public relations	3
Expand upon the cardinal principles of education	1

FINANCING REFLECTS THE PHILOSOPHY OF EDUCATING ADULTS

The method by which a program of educating adults is financed is basic to the understanding of the nature of the enterprise. It is axiomatic to say that the way the educational institution is financed will have a major influence on the philosophy adopted by the persons administering the program for continuing education. In fact, if a sharp look is taken at the agency of adult education, the philosophy will be reflected in the way the program is financed.

For example, if the public educational institution takes the point of view that all adults have the right and obligation to learn throughout their lifetimes, the program of the high schools, colleges, and universities will be budgeted so that all persons will have equal access to the learning experiences. Questions need to be asked to determine what philosophy is maintained by those advocating adult and continuing education:

Chart of the Contrasting Philosophy of Adult Education and Continuing Education

1. Primary consideration - problem situations.
2. Student-oriented - adult learner a living textbook.

3. Program or curriculum built around the student's **needs and interests**.
4. Highest resource value is learner's own experience. Knowledge brought to bear upon it.
5. We learn what we do.
6. Primary emphasis upon work, recreation, family life, improved community life.
7. Situation approach means learning process is in a setting of life's reality.
8. Search takes adult to discovery in areas most desired.
9. Teacher is a counselor, guide, supervisor, encourager, inspirer, knowledgeable resource.
10. Adult pursues interest, specific needs, problem areas, helps with developmental tasks.
11. Experience the text of truth and validity - **learner's living** notebook and textbook.
12. Noncredit-oriented.
13. Student-defined curriculum.
14. Immediate **usefulness** of information.
15. Discussion developing socializing group activity.
16. **Earning a living** and making a more creative life.
17. Self-supported - service-oriented to clientele.

Youth Education and Degree Curriculum

1. Primary consideration - subjects.
2. Book- and content-oriented, accumulated wisdom and knowledge,
3. Student required to adject himself to predetermined curriculum.
4. Much vicarious substitution of others' experience.
5. We learn what we hear and read.
6. Primary emphasis upon courses, degrees and examinations.
7. Academic, often related to the past, often removed from present application.
8. Search defined within limits of instructors or teachers.
9. Teacher is fount of wisdom, knowledge, often dispenser of information.
10. Student pursues catalog prescribed set of courses and rigid requirements.
11. Published textbooks, professors, and syllabi are authority, a priori.
12. Credit-oriented.
13. Professor defined curriculum.
14. Future utilization of learning.
15. Lecture imparting information and data.
16. Achieving an advanced degree or preparing for a specialization.
17. State-supported - curriculum-oriented to state purposes.

SUMMARY

We have seen that each educator of adults must develop a philosophy with which he or she can live comfortably and effectively and which represents his or her value system. Each of us can obtain this from reading, life experiences, professional associations, and from institutional orientation. We know there are conflicting value systems and therefore conflicting philosophies of adult and continuing education. But we must philosophize, as we do when judgments are made.

We have examined the idea that self-education is an objective of adult education and have contrasted schooling and education. We have examined the dangers of overspecialization and the need for the cultivation of wisdom. We know that education never stops, and we examined the need for reeducation and remaining active intellectually to keep the mind alert. We then described a framework for the sources of a philosophy for adult education. We finally examined the various ways of financing adult education programs and found that the philosophy of the agency influences the financing, and that the financing in turn has a profound effect upon the philosophy and functioning of the agency.

We concluded by comparing the philosophy of adult and continuing education with that of programs for youth which prepares for life, giving the tools for lifelong learning.

QUESTIONS

1. How would you describe your philosophy of adult education?
2. How do you think a person's philosophy distinguishes him/her as an educator?
3. Discuss "the essence of education is incompletion".
4. How do you react to the idea that "only the individual can truly educate him/herself"?
5. How would you program for the idea "teaching will be a process of assisting the adult in methods of self-education".
6. What are the dangers of "over-specialization"? What do you mean by an "educated" person?
7. How would you make a distinction between "training" (schooled) and education?
8. What are the implications of Michener's concept of "re-education" for adult educators?
9. How would you build a program from the bottom up, from the people, rather than imposing curriculum from above?
10. What are the implications of more "leisure time use and recreation" for adult education programs?
11. How does the financing of programs reflect the philosophy of an adult educator? Illustrate.

12. How would you contrast adult continuing education with education for youth?

BIBLIOGRAPHY

Adler, Mortimer J. "Adult Education," from a lecture, Copyright 1952, The Great Books Foundation, Chicago

Axford, Roger W. "Needed: A Clearer Philosophy for Training and Development," Adult Leadership, February 1966. (an examination of the training and development of adult educators in light of a higher educational level, technological change and cultural lag, creativity, and innovation in programming, and personal growth.)

——————. "W. H. Lighty -- Adult Education Pioneer," unpublished Ph.D. dissertation, University of Chicago, 1961.

Berdyaev, Nicholas. Slavery & Freedom, N.Y. Charles Scribner's Sons, 1944. (Discusses various forms of slavery: war, state, property, money)

Bergevin, Paul. A Philosophy for Adult Education, Seabury Press, N.Y. 1967.

Blakely, R. J. "Adult Education Needs a Philosophy and a Goal," Adult Education, Vol. 3, No. 1 (November 1952).

Cross, Patricia. Accent on Learning. Jossey Bass, San Francisco, 1976.

Curti, Merle. The Social Ideas of American Educators, Scribner, 1960. Report of the Commission of the Social Studies Part X. See esp. Chapter 3, "Education and Social Reform: Horace Mann."

Diekhoff et al. "The University's Role in Adult Education." Journal of Higher Education, Vol. 26, No. 1 (January 1955).

Douglas, Paul. Teaching for Self-Education, as a Life Long Goal. New York: Harper, 1960.

Dunstan, Mary Jane, and Garlan, Pat. Worlds in the Making. (Probes for Students of the Future) Prentice-Hall, Englewood, N.J. 1970.

Eby, Kermit. The Protests of an Ex-Organization Man. Boston: Beacon Press, 1961.

Fletcher, C. Scott. Address, "The Battle of The Cirriculum" The Fund for Adult Education, Jan. 7, 1958.

Grattan, Harley C. American Ideas About Adult Education. (1710-1951). New York: Teacher's College Press, 1959.

Hesburgh, Theodore M., Miller, Paul A., Wharton, Clifton R., Jr. Patterns for Lifelong Learning. Jossey Bass, San Francisco, 1973. Investigates the concept of education as a lifelong process, open to all. Establishes a philosophic basis for lifelong learning; shows how to expand the role of colleges in adult and continuing education; suggests procedures to be set up, kinds of courses to be offered, type of control and leadership required. Action programs are offered for administrators.

Houle, Cyril O. **Continuing Your Education.** New York: McGraw-Hill, 1964.

Kallen, Horace M. **Philosophical Issues in Adult Education.** Springfield, Ill.: Charles C. Thomas, 1962.

London, Jack. **"A Search for Direction in University Adult Education."** Adult Leadership, October 1966, pp. 110-112.

Lee, Irving. **"The Man Who Knows It All,"** Film - Talking Sense Series. National Educational Television, N.Y. Describes problems of teachableness and the dangers of the "disease of allness."

Michener, James A. **"When Does Education Stop?"** Reader's Digest, December 1962, pp. 153-154.

Mische, Gerald and Patricia. **Toward A Human World Order.** (Beyond the National Security Straitjacket.) Paulist Press, N.Y. Ramsey, J. J. 1977.

Park, Joe (ed). **The Philosophy of Education.** New York: Macmillan, 1958.

Soleri, Paulo. **The Arcology of Paolo Soleri.** (The Bridge Between Matter and Spirit) Anchor Books, Garden City, N.Y. 1973.

Schwertman, John B. **"Adult Education--Ends or Means,"** Adult Education, Autum 1954.

Sharp, Louise. **Why Teach?** New York: Holt, 1957.

Theobald, Robert. **Futures Conditional.** Bobbs Merrill Co. Inc. Indianapolis & New York, 1972 (World Views of Futurists)

Whitehead, Alfred North. **The Aims of Education.** New York: New American Library, 1960.

Zeigler, Jesse H. **Focus on Adults.** The Brethern Press, Elgin, Ill. 60120. 1965 (Motives of Adults, What Causes Change, the Church, Art, Drama and Fiction, and Impact on Adults.)

1 Jack London, "A Search for Direction in University Adult Education," **Adult Leadership**, October 1966, pp. 110-112.

2 See Smith, Aker, Kidd, Handbook of Adult Education, 1970, Macmillan.

3 The National Training Laboratories sponsored by the National Education Association hold workshops for sensitivity training at Bethel, Maine, and regional centers throughout the United States.

4 Karl Jaspers, "The Present Task of Philosophy," in his **Philosophy and the World**, Regnery, Chicago, 1963, pp. 3-4.

5 Conversation with the author.

6 **Milwaukee Journal**, March 16, 1965, p. 16.

7 Paul Douglass, **Teaching for Self-Education**, Harper, New York, 1960, p. 16.

8 Statement of "The Bachelor of Liberal Studies," College of Continuing Education, University of Oklahoma, Norman, Okla. Adult degree programs are also in operation at Harvard, New York University, Johns Hopkins, Brooklyn College, University of Maryland, Roosevelt University, and Goddard College.

9 Claude Coleman, "We Need Whole Men, Not 'Splinters,' " a speech in author's files.

10 **Ibid.**, p. 1.

11 Leo Lifschutz, M.D., University of Wisconsin, Racine Center, Spring 1959.

12 Mortimer J. Adler, "Adult Education," from a lecture, copyright 1952, The Great Books Foundation, p. 1.

13 **Ibid.**, p. 3.

14 James A. Michener, "When Does Education Stop?" Condensed address delivered at Macalaster, St. Paul, Minn. **Reader's Digest**, December 1962, pp. 153-156.

15 Interview with Maurice Mitchell, President, Encyclopaedia Britannica, Inc., November 2, 1966. Chicago, Ill.; also Videotape, Northern Illinois University, DeKalb, Ill.

Chapter XV:

AN "IDEAL" ADULT EDUCATION TEACHER

It is the supreme art of the teacher to awaken joy in creative expression and knowledge.

-Albert Einstein (1879-1955)

All who teach adults should find great satisfaction in examining the idea of an "ideal teacher." Through many years of working with teachers of adults, and having come from a long line of teachers, I have been building a model of the "ideal adult education teacher."

Whether I amattenting a lecture, listening to a radio address, sitting in on an administrative meeting, or listening to a sermon, I am continually thinking about and critically analyzing teaching and methods of teaching and learning. Each teacher of adults attempts to form a construct of the "ideal teacher" as it pertains to various kinds of groups and classes who are to be informed, inspired, or even enlightened. And even from those who entertain, there is much to be learned. For example, Sam Levenson, himself a teacher of Spanish for fifteen years, has something to teach us about touching people where the experience counts, and I recommend his words of wisdom on education in **Everything But Money.**[1]

BUILDING A CONSTRUCT OF THE IDEAL TEACHER

Each semester I have my students list what they consider the twenty-five most important qualities for the "ideal teacher" of adult education. Few other experiments have proved more enlightening, enjoyable, and revealing of people's values. Teachers of adults seem intrigued with the idea of giving a priority list of qualities most desired in a teacher. They react quickly and enthusiastically. Every teacher can use such a list for self-examination and screening.

Dr. G. Bromley Oxnam, for many years a Bishop of the Methodist Church, tells the story of his interview with Dr. James Harmon Hoose, head of the Department of Philosophy, University of Southern California. Just before graduation Oxnam, who was headed for the seminary, went to Dr. Hoose and said, "Dr. Hoose, what advice would you give a young man going into the ministry?" Hoose looked at Oxnam for a moment and then said, "Scholarship, no mannerisms." But on the day of Oxnam's leaving, to his amazement, he saw Dr. Hoose, with eyes full of light, step down from the streetcar and walk toward him.

Quickly, the 70 year-old professor came to his subject. "Oxnam," he said, "I came down here just to add a word to what I told you a few weeks back-scholarship, sympathy, and no mannerisms." Bishop Oxnam never forgot the comments for the visit, though he never saw Dr. Hoose again. These three characteristics are often mentioned by adult educators.

Below is a list of qualities enumerated by my graduate students in adult education as being important for the "ideal adult education teacher":

1. Shows fairness
2. Has sense of humor
3. Possesses fund of knowledge
4. Is good speaker-communicates well
5. Likes people-informal
6. Is good organizer-uses Lesson plans
7. Counsels students
8. Is a good listener
9. Is an enthusiastic teacher
10. Varies methods of teaching
11. Is observant
12. Knows students' interests
13. Has neat appearance
14. Uses visual aids
15. Stimulates discussion
16. Raises questions
17. Knows sources of information
18. Is professional in relationships
19. Relates well to students
20. Considers individual differences
21. Suggests further study
22. Has confidence in students
23. Is well prepared
24. Motivates learning
25. Maintains interest in subject

Any teacher of adults would do well to use such a list periodically to check on progress.

Drawing on his thirty-nine years of experience as a teacher, George Herbert Palmer, Professor of Philosophy at Harvard University, wrote a small book called **The Ideal Teacher.** Palmer contends that in life there is no learning nor human excellence which is not useful for teachers. He asks the question, "What are the characteristics of the teacher without which he must fail and which, once his, will almost certainly insure his success?" Although a teacher may possess as many more qualities as he likes, in fact the more the better, Palmer claims four to be fundamental:

An aptitude for empathy
An already accumulated wealth of wisdom.
An ability to invigorate life through knowledge.
A readiness to be forgotten. [2]

I have discussed the above qualities with graduate classes, and have added some elements. From this comes keys for teaching adults:

1. EMPATHY

2. WEALTH OF WISDOM

3. ENTHUSIASM · · · INVIGORATE LEARNING

4. READINESS TO BE FORGOTTEN

Empathy

Too few persons understand the profound task of the teacher. Many think the teacher is to be a walking encyclopedia. To be a fountain of knowledge is an admirable quality, to be sure, but the primary job of the teacher is to impart knowledge, not merely to acquire it. If we are content to keep knowledge to ourselves we cannot be true teachers. There must be a desire to see the student grow, expand horizons, and even surpass the teachers in talent. As Palmer proposes, it is the "passion to make scholars" that is evidence of the excellent teacher. Empathy and imagination are key qualities.

For a time I worked among the Native Americans of Oklahoma. I treasure the saying attributed to the chief: "I shall refuse to judge another brave until I have walked for two moons in that brave's moccasins." That is empathy. The teacher who has

233

empathy, the qualities of projection and empathy will be able to consider first the needs of the students - or, as Palmer says, "His head will be full of others needs."

Any teacher of adults should be prepared to acknowledge other factors that affect learning and stretch imagination for ways to compensate for them. A few examples will illustrate the point.

The adult art student who has had a sharp argument with his wife before coming to class is not going to be moved by the sheer beauty of a classroom "prop". The adult woman trying to get background information on a current foreign policy matter is going to be less than attentive if one of her children has a temperature of 104 degrees. The man studying group dynamics isn't going to concentrate as hard, knowing that he really should be prepared the next morning to tell his boss why sales in his area fell off 20 percent the previous month. These are not unusual examples. These are "facts of life" that adult educators must weigh in maintaining rapport with students; and the instructor must be there to boost the morale or suggest alternate routes until the crisis is over.

Accumulated Wealth of Knowledge

Of all teachers, the teacher of adults has the greatest obligation to be a liberally educated person. As teachers, there is no knowledge about which we should not be curious. Admittedly we can know but a small fraction of the accumulated wisdom of the world, but knowledge of all types is in our province and wisdom is a key objective.

Like a well-designed building, our knowledge must have a foundation and a depth that may not show on the surface on in our conversational speech. We should be clutching at information, new ideas, and wisdom at every opportunity, in continuous learning.

Enthusiasm. . . the Ability to Invigorate Life Through Knowledge

Teachers of adults are obliged to make "enthusiasm" a must in their teaching. For adults, by and large, come voluntarily to learn. We must keep adults interested, curious, and informed or they will lose interest and drop out. There is too little research on why adults drop out, but it is a topic that needs more investigation. [3] The key to the kingdom of adult programming is the teacher with the ability to invigorate life through knowledge. James T. Carey, in his study of why students drop out, indicated that 52 percent of the students said that "something about the college" led to their decision to drop out. Putting together the

234

categories, they were: courses not available, 27 percent; financial reasons (which imply some suggestion about the universities' policies), 17 percent; and dissatisfaction with the college, 8 percent. The remaining responses related to the self and totaled 48 percent, adding together job causes, 20 percent; health reasons, 5 percent; and miscellaneous reasons not connected with the university, 23 percent.⬥

Adult students often are reluctant to put on a questionnaire that the instruction was unpalatable. I know adult students who would rather drop out than complain that the instruction is inadequate, poorly organized, or not up to required standards of teaching.

I have learned to love history. It was not always so. I had a professor of history who droned through his classes as though the guillotine of the French Revolution were rasping at his throat. Undoubtedly, if I had studied harder I might have learned to enjoy despite the drone. He did a disservice to teaching and to higher education.

Now that I am older, I think he may have had low blood pressure or was forced by his parents into higher education. But he would have benefited education and the field of history if he had possessed enough enthusiasm to make history live.

Contrariwise, I had a speech professor who could make opening the door a dramatic enterprise, worth coming to class just to see. And she was nearly blind, accompanied by a seeing-eye dog. But she loved to teach speech, worked her students hard, and was loved and appreciated for her fondness of her subject - a quality that shone through daily.

Who among us has not had a teacher who evidenced the vitality and enthusiasm of her subject.

A Willingness to Be Forgotten

On this point I have received more controversy and discussion than any dealing with the qualities of an ideal teacher.

Just as most persons dislike discussing death or forced retirement, teachers don't like to think they are going to be forgotten. And in some outstanding cases each of us does remember a teacher vividly. But "willingness" is the keyword. Our task is to become the prod for questioning, the spark for curiosity, the goad for learning. If we are "remembered" that is frosting on the cake, but it is not our main objective.

Unless the teacher has the quality to be selfless in the sense of doing good without having to be noticed or repaid, the person is in the wrong profession. Palmer reminds us that "the love of praise is almost our last infirmity."[5] There is hardly a more crippling weakness for a teacher. But there is no more true promise than "He that loses his life will find it." The true teacher lives for students and for the wisdom and knowledge which the teacher is privileged to impart. An instructor is a channel through which flows the distilled wisdom of the ages and the "glory of the lighted mind." And for the teacher of adults, there is the same sense of adventure and sometimes a more dangerous life.

Life is a great gamble. Which of us knows whether our students have taken to themselves our best points? One student will learn one thing from us and another, something we hardly dreamed of. Some of our students will be ready to receive, and on others it will be as though we are casting pearls before swine. A phrase learned in my childhood and of unknown origin is most applicable: "Nor can any noble thing be wealth except to a noble person." Our task is to give the most opportunities for learning possible and have the faith that enlightenment and our efforts may affect a life positively.

When we think of the more than fifty teachers many of us have had through the years, we realize we are a composite of contributions and inspiration imparted by a host of scholarly saints. Now let us examine some of the human desires which must be kept in mind in dealing with either students or teachers of adults.

The teacher who wants to understand students will do well to remember the basic four wishes of each adult coming into class:

Recognition
Response
Security
New Experience

Putting this thought another way, Dr. Louis Raths, identifies ten key components of the nature of good teaching: [7]

1. Teaching as telling
2. Teaching as security giving
3. Teaching as clarifying
4. Teaching as group-unifying operations
5. Teaching as the diagnosis of learning difficulties
6. Teaching as the making of curriculum materials
7. Teaching as helping students learn how to learn
8. Teaching of enrichment of the community
9. Teaching as participation in the total school program
10. Teaching as "marking"

236

Experience with teaching adults bears out the fact that adults like to learn of their own progress. Usually, they do not like to have their progress compared with that achieved by others. Therefore, teaching as "marking" is a necessary part of credit classes only. Since many adult classes are of a not-for-credit nature, the individual self-analysis of progress in a subject is primary for teachers of adults. A section on evaluation will point up techniques for seeing whether the students have progressed or feel they have benefited from the educational experience. Such evaluations come in many forms: verbal, written, and observation of mastery of a subject where there is manual skill involved. What is more pleasing to an instructor than to see a student successfully apply knowledge to life?

A self-appraisal for the teachers of adults is useful to "check up on ourselves." Such a scale is printed for the use of those who want to improve as adult educators. See chart on page 239

GOALS AND OBJECTIVES FOR A TEACHER OF ADULTS

To gain an overview of the large and heterogeneous field of adult education, agencies, programs, processes and methods.

To become acquainted with the literature of the field.

To exchange experiences with teachers and program planners in the field of adult education.

To learn of the resources on the local, state, national and international levels.

To become familiar with some of the history of the agencies and their leaders.

To experience some methods and processes of adult education.

To learn of the pioneering being done in new programs and methods.

To study at least one agency of adult eduation in depth.

To deepen commitment to the continuing education of oneself and other adults.

To learn of ways to motivate people to lifelong learning.

To develop a more comprehensive philosophy of adult education based on the learnings of and the associations made in classes or the community.

To learn about theories of adult learning and ways they might apply to programming.

To examine the problems of financing adult education.

To examine ways of program planning, sources of ideas and evaluative techniques.

To develop a personal library of adult education materials.

The ideal teacher of adults will have a clearly defined set of objectives. He or she will be a continuous learner in the process of becoming and striving to achieve a self-imposed set of objectives. Listed are some of the goals that any dedicated instructor of adults, on whatever level, will try to achieve during the person's reading, training, or professional career.

"No, actually it's about teaching."

Self-Rating Sheet for Evening Instructors

At the close of every session, rate it in terms of the accomplishment
of each of the qualities of a good group learning situation.
Use the following rating scale:

3 = in this respect I was notably successful
2 = in this respect I was moderately successful
1 = in this respect I was unsuccessful

Qualities of a Good Class Meeting	Sessions																
	1	2	3	4	5	6	7	8	9	10	11	12	13	14	15	16	17
1. Did I have a basic plan for the session but use it flexibly?																	
2. Did all members of the group understand both the immediate and ultimate goals of the course?																	
3. Were the methods and procedures used as varied as possible?																	
4. Was there a good social feeling in the group?																	
5. Did I use the experience of the members of the group to make my teaching real and vital?																	
6. Did I reflect in every way my conviction of the importance of broad values?																	
7. Was I aware of the special needs and concerns of each individual in the group?																	
8. Did I provide support and reinforcement for the students who need it?																	
9. Was the physical setting as attractive and comfortable as I could make it?																	
10. Do I know everyone's name?																	
Total score																	

SKILLS FOR TEACHING ADULTS

Teaching adults requires specific skills:

1. ESTABLISHING A LEARNING SET: The instructor's ability
to create in students a cognitive and affective predisposition
to engage in a given learning activity.

2. LOGICAL ORGANIZATION: The instructor's skill in arranging and presenting course content and learning activities so
that students understand the relationships among the various
topics, ideas, issues, activities, etc., covered in the course.

239

3. PACING: The instructor's skill in introducing new topics or activities at an appropriate rate and in spending enough, but not too much, time developing those topics or activities.

4. ELABORATION: The instructor's skill in clarifying or developing an idea or topic..

5. EXPRESSION: The instructor's skill in using verbal (voice tone, inflection, pitch, emphasis) and nonverbal (facial expressions, gestures, body movements) techniques to increase the power and meaning of his/her communication.

6. ASKING QUESTIONS: The instructor's skill in using various questioning techniques at appropriate times and for a variety of instructional purposes.

7. RESPONDING TO QUESTIONS: The instructor's ability to answer questions clearly and concisely and with an appropriate emotional tone.

8. STUDENT PARTICIPATION: The instructor's skills in facilitating student participation in class discussions and in leading those discussions in fruitful directions.

9. CLOSURE: The instructor's abilities to integrate the major points of a lesson or unit of instruction, to establish a cognitive link between the familiar and the new, and to provide students with a feeling of accomplishment.

10. EVALUATION: The instructor's skills in specifying the criteria for evaluation, in designing valid and reliable evaluation procedures, and in providing adequate feedback to students about their progress.

11. LEVEL OF CHALLENGE: The instructor's skills in selecting course objectives, content, and activities which challenge students' conceptual abilities but which are not too difficult for students to master.

12. METHODS AND MATERIALS: The instructor's ability to use various teaching methods effectively and to provide variation in cognitive behaviors, classroom activities, and instructional materials.

13. CREATIVITY: The instructor's ability to use creative and imaginative teaching strategies.

14. MANAGEMENT: The instructor's skill in performing the organizational and administrative tasks in providing learning experiences for students.

15. FLEXIBILITY INDIVIDUALIZATION: The instructor's ability to deal with differing interests and abilities among students in his/her class and to respond constructively to student suggestions, criticisms, comments about his/her teaching strategies.

16. INTERPERSONAL RELATIONS: The instructor's ability to relate to people in ways which promote mutual respect and rapport.

17. LEARNING ENVIRONMENT: The instructor's abilities to create and maintain an atmosphere conducive to student involvement (overt and/or covert) and learning.

18. ENTHUSIASM/INSPIRATION: The instructor's abilities to conduct and direct learning activities in a dynamic manner and to stimulate interest and excitement in course content and activites.

19. PERSPECTIVES: The instructor's ability to establish a frame of reference for concepts, issues, ideas, etc., and to expand that frame of reference to include an increasingly wider variety of viewpoints, implications, and relationships.

20. VALUE CONTEXT: The instructor's abilities: a) to identify explicitly his/her own values and to clarify the implications of those values in the selection and interpretation of subject matter; b) to explore other values and their implications as they relate to his/her subject matter; and c) to help students clarify their values and recognize the implications of those values for their personal and professional conduct.

Source: Clinic to Improve University Teaching, a multi year project funded by the Kellogg Foundation and conducted through the University of Massachusetts. Dr. Michael Melnick directed the project. This list is contained in the 1975 annual report. Thanks to Dr. Mark Rossman, Department of Higher and Adult Education, Arizona State University for making these available.

THE TEN COMMANDMENTS OF GOOD TEACHING [8]

Thou shalt have a genuine love for people and an ability to identify with them and their problems.

Thou shalt be unashamedly curious, and never afraid to ask questions.

Thou shalt develop a specialty in a field of knowledge, and a breadth of knowledge in numerous fields.

Thou shalt practice self-discipline, self-respect, and an ability to live with one's self and enjoy the solitude.

Thou shalt invigorate life with hobbies and recreation, for these keep one from becoming a pedantic bore.

Thou shalt cultivate the ability to listen, as well as to give counsel, for much learning is done with the bended ear.

Thou shalt cultivate the skills of cooperation, for more persons fail for lack of ability to get along with others than from lack of knowledge.

Thou shalt cultivate a professional attitude and outlook, identify with the teaching profession, help to recruit those who love to learn and to teach, and help exclude those not worthy of the high calling called "teaching."

Thou shalt practice the patience of Job?

Thou shalt cultivate an inquiring mind, be committed to continuing education and lifelong learning, and have a willingness to be forgotten.

IN-SERVICE FOR ADULT EDUCATION TEACHERS

Teachers of adults need in-service training and opportunities to learn effective techniques for teaching adults. Administrators will do well to acquaint their teachers with the literature of the field. Subscriptions to magazines such as **Lifelong Learning** and **Adult Education** will be of assistance and acquaint the new teacher of adults with the programs in the field, some of the successes, and the results of current research.

An example is a newsletter published by the National Association for Public School Continuing and Adult Education, 'Techniques," which is devoted to "What New Teachers of Adults Want to Know." Each issue is devoted to a special topic such as legislation, teaching methods, audio-visual techniques, or topics related to teaching adults more effectively. Teachers of adults should feel a responsibility to contribute to the professional literature and become involved in the research studies being carried on in universities. The ideal teacher of adults will become acquainted with the literature, join the appropriate adult education professional association, and learn all that can be from visitations, interviews, and swap sessions at conferences and institutes. Like Alice in Wonderland, we have to run "just to stay in the same place."

TECHNÍQUES

for teachers of adults

Vol. VI, No. 1,

WHAT NEW TEACHERS OF ADULTS WANT TO KNOW

If you are teaching adults for the first time--or if you are a relative newcomer to the field--you may be puzzled and concerned about many aspects of your new job. This issue of Techniques is devoted to answering some of the questions which come up most often in talking to teachers or leaders of adult groups. Because of limited space, the answers will be short. If you wish more detailed answers on any of these topics, or if they suggest other topics, pass them on to your director as the basis for a new or expanded in-service education program in your school. NAPSAE can help by supplying information on methods and materials.

Q. I've been teaching children in day school. What is different about teaching adults?

A. Most adults attend an adult class because they want to, not because they have to. They are self-motivated. Yet, because many adults doubt their ability to study and learn, or because they fear exposure and ridicule, they need constant re-motivation. If the course does not meet their needs, they may not say so. They simply don't come back. Adults come to class with background knowledge and opinions on many subjects. Even if they are learning to read and write, they have held jobs and raised families. They have something to contribute, as well as many things to learn. Give them opportunities to communicate their knowledge and experience to the rest of the class. It will boost their self-esteem, and the other students (as well as you, the teacher) will benefit.

Q. This is my first year teaching adults. Frankly, I am worried. What if some of them know more than I do?

A. This is one of the great rewards of teaching adults. In some classes it is perfectly possible that some students will know more about some things than any other student--or than the teacher. The teacher's opportunity then is to take time, early in the course, to inventory student resources and then make these a part of the year-long learning process.

Q. How should I start off my first class session?

A. As all experienced teachers of adults know, the first few classes of each term are crucial ones for grabbing and holding the interest of the students. The first few minutes of the first session of the year should be devoted to giving students a feeling that they are part of a warm, informal, and friendly group...that they can speak up comfortably...that they are accepted and not criticized...that they are not alone but that everyone is in the same boat. One way of doing all this is to embark on a discussion of what each student wants to learn--and why. This can be followed by talking about ways the students would like to relate to each other: who is to decide--and how--if someone monopolizes the teacher's time--or if the teacher seems to be spending too much time on materials which have already been covered.

 National Association for Public School Adult Education, 1201 Sixteenth Street, N.W., Washington, D. C. 20036

243

TEACHER'S PROCESS PLAN

Course: Teacher:
Semester:

AT THE OPENING SESSION:
1. How will you introduce yourself? How will you describe your perception of your role, your special resources and limitations, your availability for consultation, etc.?

2. What procedures will you use to engage the students in becoming acquainted with one another in terms of their work, experience, resources, interests, etc.?

3. What other procedures will you use to establish a climate of mutual respect, collaborativeness rather than competitiveness, informality, security, warmth of relationship with you, supportiveness, etc.?

4. How will you engage the students in examining, clarifying, and influencing the objectives of the course?

5. How will you acquaint the students with your plan of work for the course and their responsibilities in it?

6. How will you help them prepare to carry the responsibilities you expect of them?

7. How will you acquaint the students with the resources (material and human) available to them for accomplishing their learning objectives?

8. What learning activities will you suggest the students engage in between the first and second sessions of the course?

9. What physical arrangement of your meeting room do you prefer to facilitate interaction among the students and between them and you?

IN SUBSEQUENT SESSIONS (indicate which session when appropriate):
1. How will you engage the students in diagnosing their individual and collective needs and interests regarding the content of the course?

2. How will you engage the students in formulating learning objectives based on their diagnosed needs and interests?

3. What specific learning strategies (methods, techniques, devices, materials, etc.) do you propose using in this course?

4. How will the students be involved in selecting and participating in these strategies?

5. What procedures and tools will you use for helping students assess their progress toward their objectives?

6. What procedures and tools will you use for evaluating learning outcomes at the end of the course?

7. If appropriate, how will grades be arrived at?

8. What procedures and tools will you use for getting feedback from the students periodically and at the end regarding the quality of this learning experience?

9. What content do you expect to be acquired through this course (including knowledge, understanding, skills, attitudes, and values)?

SUMMARY

We attempted to build a construct of the "ideal teacher" and suggested ways of involving adult learners in defining those qualities. We examined George Herbert Palmer's four qualities considered fundamental for good teaching: vicariousness, a wealth of knowledge, and ability to invigorate learning, and a readiness to be forgotton, with examples for illustration. We also considered W. I. Thomas' four basic wishes as useful for being a good teacher of adults: recognition, response, security, and new experience.

A self-rating chart for instructor's of adults was presented, which can be adapted to local situations. Some goals and objectives for the teacher of adults were enumerated, which can be utilized for an introductory course in adult education or for in-service training. "The Ten Commandments of Good Teaching" is presented as a springboard for discussion. Some professional journals are suggested to aid in keeping up in the field, for both the practioner and the researcher. Skills for teaching adults are offered as a means of checking for ways to improve pre-service or in-service education.

245

QUESTIONS FOR DISCUSSION

1. How would you prepare persons to become and "ideal adult education teacher?"
2. Who is the teacher that stands out most in your memory? What qualities did that person possess?
3. What skills would you most like to cultivate to become a better teacher of adults?
4. Where would you turn for resources to help teachers of adults improve their teaching?
5. How would you set up an in-service training program for part-time or full-time teachers of adults? Any useful visuals? Case studies?
6. How do you deal with the self-directed learner? What are the different roles you play as an adult educator?
7. How do you go about systematically trying to become a more effective teacher of adults?

BIBLIOGRAPHY

Berman, Louis M. (ed.). **The Nature of Teaching.** Madison: U.of Wisconsin Press, 1963

Buscaglia, Leo. **Love.** Fawcett Books, C.B.S. Publications, 1972.
——————. **Personhood, A Journey to Your Soul,** Charles B. Slack, Inc. 6900 Grove, Thorofare, New Jersey, 08086.

Byers, Loretta, and Elizabeth Irish. **Success in Student Teaching.** Boston: Heath, 1961.

Carter, Phillip, and Verl Short. **Speaking About Adults...and the Continuing Education Process.** DeKalb, Ill: Department of Adult Education. Northern Illinois University, 1966.

Conant, James B. **The Education of American Teachers.** New York: McGraw-Hill, 1963.

Daigneault, George H., and D. B. Gowin. **The Part-time College Teacher.** Center for Study of Liberal Education for Adults, 1961.

Diekhoff, John S. **The Domain of the Faculty.** New York: Harper, 1956.

Douglass, Paul. **Teaching for Self-Education.** New York: Harper, 1956.
Harper, 1960.

Freire, Paulo. **Pedagogy of the Oppressed,** Seabury Press, N.Y. 1970.

Gardner, John W. **Self Renewal,** N.Y.: Harper & Row, 1963.

Garrett, Henry E. **The Art of Good Teaching.** Philadelphia: McKay, 1964.

Hall, Budd L. and J. Roby Kidd. **Adult Learning: A Design for Action.** Elmsford, N.Y.: Pergamin Press, Inc., 1978. The book consists of 24 papers by adult educators that were prepared for an international conference in Tanzania. The central theme of the work is the development of a design for adult education and adult education programs that recognize the centrality of the participation of people in planning and implementing development decisions for the future.

Houle, Cyril O. **Continuing Your Education. New York: McGraw-Hill, 1964.**

Jersild, Arthur T. **When Teachers Face Themselves.** New York: Teachers College Press, 1955.

Klevins, Chester. **Materials and Methods in Continuing Education.** Klevins Publications, N.Y. Los Angeles, 1976. Lib. Cong. No. 76-44122.

Kidd, J.R. **How Adults Learn.** New York: Association Press, 1959.

Knowles, Malcolm S. The Modern Practice of **Adult Education: Andragogy Vs. Pedagogy,** Association Press, N.Y. 1975.

McLagan, Patricia. **Helping Others Learn: Designing Programs for Adults.** Reading MA: Addison Wesley Pub., 1978. The monograph is designed for people who design, deliver, and develop programs. To the author, helping others learn involves designing at least some extra degree of "learnability" into programs. How this is accomplished is the subject of the monograph.

Olsen, E. and P. Clark. **Life Centering Education.** Pendell Pub. 1977. Life Centering Education is a call to action on the crucial problem of developing a functional plan for sequential, cumulative, and realistic individual and group learning experiences based on the fact that there is only one species of human on our planet, and that it is an endangered species. The book proposes a curriculum based upon enduring life concerns and related problems of living.

Palmer, George Herbert, **The Ideal Teacher.** Boston: Houghton, 1910. (A Classic)

Paulston, Rolland, ed. **Non-Formal Education: An Annotated International Bibliography.** Praeger Press, 1972. Non-formal education is defined as structures, systematic, non-school educational and training activities at relatively short duration in which sponsoring agencies seek concrete behavioral changes in fairly distinct target populations. It is education that does not advance to a higher level of the hierarchical formal schooling. Includes Orientation and Basic Issues, Area Studies, Organizations Conducting Programs, Target

Learner Populations, Program Content, Instructional Methodologies and Materials, Reference Materials and Publications.

Pemberton, Frank. **Education After Dark.** Harvard Today, Autumn 1963.

Pleasures in Learning. Selected Essays. Washington, D.C.: Center for Study of Liberal Education for Adults. 1961.

Seaman, Donald. **Adult Education Teaching Techniques.** ERIC, Career Information Series #110. 1977.

A review and synthesis of research on effective techniques for teaching adults at different educational and occupational levels is presented in this information analysis paper intended for continuing and adult educators in education, industry, and government. The operational framework of the review is based on Verner's classifications and definitions of the terms adult education, method, technique, and device.

Sharp, D. Louise. **Why Teach?** New York: Holt, 1957.

Tough, Allen. **The Adult's Learning Projects: A Fresh Approach to Theory and Practice.** OISE, 1971.

Tough's work is based upon research findings on the adult learner. Employing the findings and implications of the studies, all of which focus on the adult's learning projects, he provides a fresh approach to theory and practice in adult education and learning. This approach is already proving useful for the researcher and the practitioner. The work encompasses the entire range of deliberate adult learning, self-planned learning and private lessons as well as courses and workshops.

Verduin-Miller-Greer. **Adults Teaching Adults,** Austin, Texas, Learning Concepts, 1977.

Whipple, James B. **Especially for Adults.** Notes and Essays No. 19. Washington, D.C.: Center for Study of Liberal Education for Adults, 1947.

Whitehead, Alfred North. **The Aims of Education.** New York: Macmillan, 1929.

Winegartner, Charles & Neil Postman. **Teaching As A Subversive Activity.** Delacorte Press, N.Y. 1969.

Yamamoto, Kaoru. **Teaching: Essays and Readings.** Houghton-Mifflin Boston, 1969. The What, Why, Where and how of Teaching Effectively. Teaching styles and learning.

1 Sam Levenson. **Everything But Money,** Simon and Schuster, New York, 1966.

2 George Herbert Palmer. **The Ideal Teacher,** Houghton. Boston, 1910, p. 7.

3 James T. Carey. "Why Students Drop Out: A Study of Evening College Student Motivations." Center for the Study of Liberal Education for Adults, 1953.

4 **Ibid.,** p. 19.

5 George H. Palmer, **op cit.**, p. 26.

6 W. I. Thomas. ————————

7 Louise M. Berman (ed.), **The Nature of Teaching.** U. of Wisconsin Press, Madison. 1963, p. 8.

8 Roger W. Axford, **Wisconsin Education Journal,** 1963; **Florida Education Journal.** 1964.

9 Appreciation to Malcolm Knowles, Dept. of Adult and Community College Education. North Caroline State University.

Chapter XVI:

THE EXTENSION-OUTREACH FUNCTION

"Schools are not the ultimate formative force. Social institutions, the trend of occupations, the pattern of social arrangements, are the finally controlling influences in shaping minds... Effective education, that which really leaves a stamp on character and thought, is obtained when graduates come to take their part in the activities of adult society."

John Dewey, 1930

Every great university has as its mission three basic function:

1. Teaching
2. Research
3. Public service--extension

The landgrant institutions such as Michigan State University and the University of Maine have sometimes been described as the milkstool of higher education. As these institutions have gained in stature in the past hundred years since the Merrill Act of 1862, many have surpassed the traditional Ivy League schools, largely due to state and federal financial support based on public service, in helping to solve society's problems.

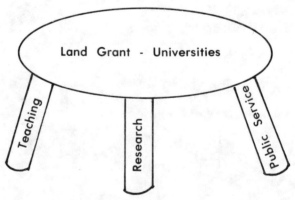

The Milkstool of Higher Education

PRO-ACTIVE VS. RE-ACTIVE

It is the responsibility of an Extension Division or a Department of Continuing Education to anticipate needs, rather than merely to respond to needs in the community. To be **pro-active** rather than **re-active** is the key to leadership in the field. For example, a proactive university would seek out situations, such as hospitals or other social service agencies, in which to offer inservice training, rather than waiting for those agencies to come to the university with a request.

When the field worker or extension agent is in touch with agency needs, community contacts, and program potential, the creative adult education leader is growing, and the agency will gain the confidence of the community.

OUTREACH FUNCTION--CONTINUING AND ADULT EDUCATION

A model for the organization of a Continuing Education Division is illustrated by the circular chart on page   Input from citizens is continually welcomed, and this can be encouraged by the use of an advisory committee.[1]   Often the advisory committee is made up of both faculty members and members from the community. This is an excellent way of informing faculty of community needs, as well as of gaining insight into the talents available for community service. However, promotion and tenure in colleges and universities are not always associated with extension and public service, so faculty must be supported by the top administration of an institution if the effort is to be successful.

It is worthy of note, however, that many universities have chosen as their president leaders from the field of University Extension, as illustrated by the University of Maine, the University of New Hampshire, and the University of Missouri, to name but a few. There is a recognition of community outreach serving the needs of the wider community outside the ivy walls of academia, as a leading function of an institution of higher learning. It is not enough to discover knowledge (research); it must be disseminated and put to work in the marketplace. If the colleges and universities become removed from the basic problems of the people, new institutional forms will arise to meet those needs.

Institutions, like people, mature and grow. Though some grow by planning, most grow "like Topsy". Often when a new function, a new grant, a new program is to be added to a college or university it is "tacked on" to the Extension Division. This is why we find summer sessions, English language programs,

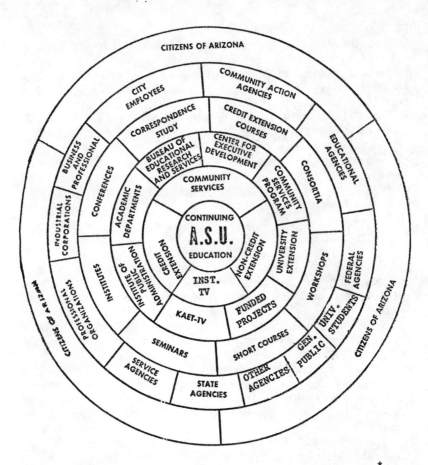

MODEL FOR CONTINUING EDUCATION *

* Thanks to Dr. Dennis Kigin, Dean, Division of Continuing Education, Arizona State University.

Elderhostels, and other often significant programs added to an Extension Division. Some activities, like radio and television, have grown from being an arm of Extension into full blown departments with their own staffs and budgets.

An example of the "mature" Continuing Education Division is that of the Michigan State University organization, which is headed by assistant deans as shown in the following chart. It is this author's thinking that an Assistant Dean for Continuing Education in each college of a university is necessary for effective program. Unless there is a person, specifically designated

252

for the outreach function, continuing education and community service are neglected in favor of research or residence teaching. An Associate or Assistant Dean, funded by both Extension and the resident college, will see to it that faculty and classes get off the campus. Without such a person "Everybody's business is nobody's business." Michigan State University, through the leadership of President Emeritus John Hannah, Dr. John Holden, and the Directors of the Kellogg Continuing Education Center, has built a commitment to University Outreach into the MSU system. Similarly, the University of Wisconsin has reorganized its Extension Division and has a Division of Outreach, headed by a Provost with responsibilities state-wide. For many years this was headed by a seasoned adult education leader, Dr. Wilson Thiede.

NON-CREDIT ACTIVITIES

An important aspect of Outreach is instruction on a non-credit basis. In a study of non-credit activities in institutions of higher learning, it was found that, in non-credit adult and continuing education activities in U.S. colleges and universities: 1. adult and continuing education activities were offered by 2,225 colleges and universities during 1975-6 which represented 102% INCREASE from 1967-68. 2. two-year colleges constituted 44.6% of the total institutions offering adult and continuing education, accounting for 47.3% of total registrations, 3. registrations in adult and continuing education activities offered by colleges and universities in 1975-6 totaled 8.8 million, which was 56.5% increase from 1967-68. 4. public institutions reported 89.1% of the registrations for 1975-76; and 5. the largest registrations were reported for courses in business, management, education, health professions, and fine and applied arts.

It is significant that the CONTINUING EDUCATION UNIT (described on next page) was used in 1975-76 to record the extent of the adult and continuing education activities by 798 of the 2,225 institutions which offered such activities.[2] The continuing education unit is being used more extensively with short non-credit courses now in the allied health fields, and in professional continuing Education.[3]

WHAT THEY ARE!

The Continuing Education Unit (CEU) is a nationally recognized, standard unit of measurement which is awarded for every ten contact hours of participation in an organized, continuing education experience, under responsible sponsorship, capable direction and qualified instruction.

The CEU was developed by a national task force under the joint sponsorship of the National University Extension Association, the American Association of Collegiate Registrars and Admissions Officers, the U. S. Civil Service Commission, and the U. S. Office of Education. After an extensive review of nationwide continuing education programs, the task force arrived at a way to recognize and record a person's participation in qualified programs - the Continuing Education Unit.

Under the CEU system, each person participating in qualifying programs has a permanent, strictly confidential record on file listing the programs completed and accumulated units of credit. At ASU, this record is continually updated as additional CEU's are earned. A person may receive his/her cumulative record or have it sent to persons he/she designates at any time.

While the CEU was not designed to be equated with academic credit or to be applied toward an academic degree, many business firms and other organizations have recognized the CEU as an input in considering persons for promotion, salary increases, transfers, etc. This recognition implies that some form of useful learning takes place when a person attends a continuing education program, even though he/she may not have taken tests, written papers, or given oral reports which were evaluated.

The cumulative record of CEU's awarded at ASU is maintained in the Summer Session and Extension Office. By contacting this office (602) 965-6563 a personal record of these units can be sent to you or to someone you name. A minimal fee is charged for this service.

WHAT THEY ARE NOT!

The Continuing Education Unit is not equivalent to Academic Credit given by accredited colleges and universities. It is not accepted by most colleges and universities as credit toward a degree, ASU included.

While some organizations granting CEU's require recipients to take and/or pass tests, write papers, or make oral presentations which are evaluated before "credit" is given, this is strictly a local requirement and is not specified as a national standard. Local deviations such as these appear to be permissable and up to the descretion of the agency sponsoring the specific program.

In the Center for Executive Development at ASU, CEU's are not granted to persons completing only a portion of a program. They are given only to those participants who have completed the program by meeting the specific attendance requirements outlined in the brochure or communicated orally or in writing at the outset of the program.

CEU's are not issued for short conferences. However, CEU's and fractional parts of CEU's are given for participation in seminars without regard to the length of the program.

The CEU does not imply any "quality" level of achievement. It should not be equated with "pass-fail" now being given in some academic courses at the collegiate level. It is given as an attendance-participation award and carries no assurances   learning has taken place.

For additional information regarding Continuing Education Units (CEU's) write or call:

Center for Executive Development
College of Business Administration
Arizona State University
Tempe, Arizona 85281
Phone (602) 965-3441

ADMINISTRATION OF CONTINUING EDUCATION--A functional Approach

The traditional administrative theory concept dealing with functions of an organization is the functional approach theory. Gulick and Urwich have described this in their work with the National Agricultural Extension Center at the University of Wisconsin. [4]

The effective administrator will use as a checklist the functions sometimes described as POSDCORB. This is an acronymn taken from the initials of the administrative responsibilities of the adult education administrator. They are:

Planning -- Without planning, outlining the goals for the Division, and the methods to accomplish them, chances are little will be achieved.

Organizing -- This involves a formal structure to carry out desired goals.

Staffing -- The selection and development of personnel. The personnel function is paramount, and a chief administrator will consider this, along with in-service training.

Directing -- "The buck stops here" is part of directing. The arduous task of decision-making is a key to effective administration. Giving instructions, effectively defines "the leader."

Coordinating -- Checking on the functions delegated to personnel, and seeing that people work together effectively. Team-building is important.

Reporting -- Reporting upward, and reporting downward. Keeping colleagues informed, superiors, subordinates, the community, all are important for good morale. Annual reports are a protection and a way of informing superiors of needs and accomplishments.

Budgeting --This includes accounting, financial planning, studying cost effectiveness, accountability, and control. A studying cost effectively, accountability, and con- A program that is self-supporting will be approach- in a different way than one with subsidy. Soft money (grants) may require special staff contacts of a non-tenure nature.

DELEGATION

A key administrative principle is that responsibility for a task demands the necessary delegation. Nothing is more frustrating than having a task assigned without the adaquate responsibility for fulfilling the job.

Dr. James Harlow, a leader in theory of administration, emphasizes that organization is, at any particular time in the life of an enterprise, the standing plan by which distribution of work load is dispersed among members of the institution. This is a key decision-making function.[5]Many an administrator has failed, for the lack of the courage or the faith to delegate responsibility. Picking good staff, using their strengths, and then letting them fly with imaginative ideas is the basis of successful programming in extension and in continuing education. Morale can often be measured in terms of effective delegation.

ADMINISTRATION OF OUTREACH TO MINORITY POPULATIONS

Outreach also includes affirmative action. Institutions of higher education may neglect minority groups either because of tradition, cultural bias, or distance factors. We need to use the outreach function of colleges and universities to bring knowledge to remote geographical areas. A good example of working effectively to bring educational services to remote areas is that of the University of Regina, a plan worked but by Extra-Session Credit Division of the Department of University Extention. A model for serving Native-Americans is presented--an agreement for offering off-campus classes.

UNIVERSITY OF REGINA - SASKATCHEWAN INDIAN FEDERAT-
ED COLLEGE WORKING AGREEMENT FOR OFF-CAMPUS
CLASSES*

P R O C E D U R E S

1. The Bank Councils in consultation with the Saskatchewan
Indian Federated College and the Saskatchewan Indian Community   College, assess the student needs in their community.

2. The Saskatchewan Indian Community College makes an official
request for classes from the University of Regina via the
Saskatchewan Indian Federated College with copies to the
Department of Extension.

3. When both the need for a class and the availability of an
instructor is reasonably certain, the class is established
so that students may register in it. All off-campus classes
must be established through the Extra-Session Credit Division, Department of Extension, University of Regina.

4. The Saskatchewan Indian Federated College in consultation
with the Band Councils, will make recommendation regarding instructors for off-campus classes. When faculty members
(teaching as part of regular load) are involved in instructing off-campus classes, no further approval is required. However, when sessional lecturers or University Faculty on over-
load are required, mutual agreement between the Saskatchewan Indian Federated College and the University of Regina
must be obtained using the Department of Extension as a
vehicle for administering the approval process. A letter of
recommendation from the Saskatchewan Indiana Federated
College together with a letter from the appropriate faculty,
along with a current Sessional Lecturer Information (S.L.I.)
form or curriculum vitae must be forwarded to the Department of Extension. In turn, approval is obtained from the
Vice-President for subsequent appointment.

5. The procedure outlined above would put in place the following:
   a. the students would identify with the Saskatchewan Indian
   Federated College and the University of Regina;

   b. either the University of Regina or the Saskatchewan
   Indian Federated College would employ the instructor,
   subject to approval procedure (4) above;

c. the Saskatchewan Indian Community College would pay the University of Regina for 15 tuitions regardless of class size when the University of Regina is employing the class instructor;

d. the Saskatchewan Indian Community College would be responsible for the costs of decentralizing instruction.

*Thanks to James Carefoot, Extra-Session Credit Division, Department of University Extension, University of Regina, Regina Canada (S4S OA2)

Structure of the University of Regina

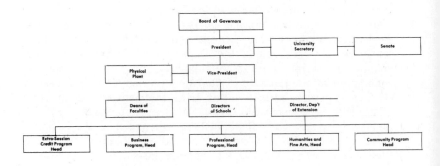

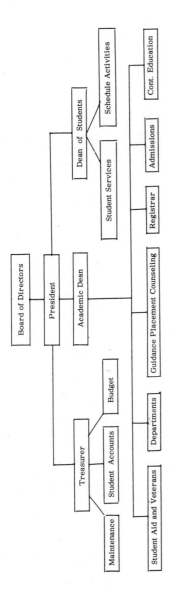

Board of Directors

President

Treasurer — Academic Dean — Dean of Students

Maintenance — Student Accounts — Budget — Student Aid and Veterans — Departments — Guidance Placement Counseling — Student Services — Schedule Activities — Registrar — Admissions — Cont. Education

Director of
Continuing Education
1. Evening College
2. Summer School
3. Enrichment Programs
4. Conferences, Workshops
   Institutes

Treasurer - charges and payments
Maintenance - facilities and parking, etc.
Student Accounts Fees and tuition; special arrangements
   for deferred payment
Budget - obvious
Department and Faculty - Staffing; approval for
   course and part-time faculty;
Registrar - record keeping; drop/add process, transcript;
Admissions - matriculation application; admittance to
   degree candidacy; transfer of credit;
Scheduling and activities - availability of facilities;
Guidance and Placement and Counseling - Center use
   for evening students; referrals;
Student Aid and Veterans - referrals for help;
Other institutional offices:
   Public Relations and Publicity - Brochures,
      Newspaper writeups, etc.
   Food Service - scheduling of meals for on-campus
      workshops
   Word Processing Center - mailings, duplicating
   PrintShop - printing of brochures, forms, etc.

Provided by Callistas Milan,
   Director of Evening School,
   Saint Vincent College
   Latrobe, Pa.

259

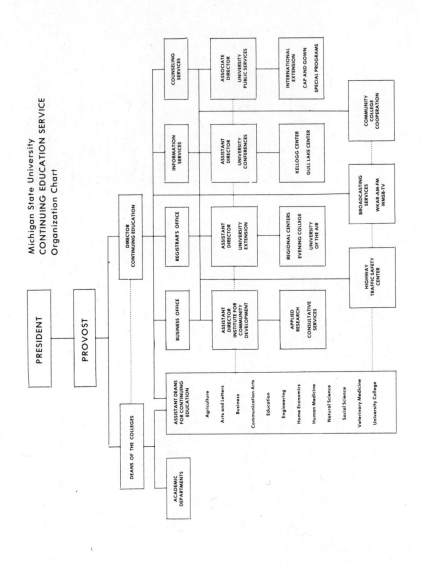

Michigan State University
CONTINUING EDUCATION SERVICE
Organization Chart

PRESIDENT

PROVOST

DIRECTOR
CONTINUING EDUCATION

DEANS OF THE COLLEGES

ACADEMIC
DEPARTMENTS

ASSISTANT DEANS
FOR CONTINUING
EDUCATION

Agriculture
Arts and Letters
Business
Communication Arts
Education
Engineering
Home Economics
Human Medicine
Natural Science
Social Science
Veterinary Medicine
University College

BUSINESS OFFICE

ASSISTANT
DIRECTOR
INSTITUTE FOR
COMMUNITY
DEVELOPMENT

APPLIED
RESEARCH
CONSULTATIVE
SERVICES

REGISTRAR'S OFFICE

ASSISTANT
DIRECTOR
UNIVERSITY
EXTENSION

REGIONAL CENTERS
EVENING COLLEGE
UNIVERSITY
OF THE AIR

INFORMATION
SERVICES

ASSISTANT
DIRECTOR
UNIVERSITY
CONFERENCES

KELLOGG CENTER
GULL LAKE CENTER

COUNSELING
SERVICES

ASSOCIATE
DIRECTOR
UNIVERSITY
PUBLIC SERVICES

INTERNATIONAL
EXTENSION
CAP AND GOWN
SPECIAL PROGRAMS

HIGHWAY
TRAFFIC SAFETY
CENTER

BROADCASTING
SERVICES
WKAR-AM-FM
WMSB-TV

COMMUNITY
COLLEGE
COOPERATION

260

THE OUTREACH EXTENSION WORKER

Persons interested in extension might ask, "What does the extension worker do?". One of the best ways to understand the many roles of the extension agent, and this can be applied to the now developing "urban extension agent," is to examine the roles played by the outreach agent. E. Weldon Findlay has developed a typology for extension agents, which can be used for training, evaluation, and role definition. Since many of the Extension Divisions are combining general and cooperative extension, such as in Missouri and Wisconsin, it would be well for Deans and Directors to use Findlay's typology for consideration in job descriptions, job analysis, and in-service education. Although the role behaviors are for "Cooperative Extension Agents" they have applicability for a broader range of outreach agents.

A Typology of Role Behavior
of County Cooperative Extension Agents [6]

1. Cooperative Extension System--Understand the nature of the Cooperative Extension Service as a public educational system and adheres to its structure, processes, and evolution within a hierarchy of systems, with emphasis on performance at the level of complex adaptive systems. This involves an understanding of how a system functions as a whole by virtue of the interdependence of its elements, including systemic structure and linkage, psychological system, personality or self-system, socio-cultural system, administrative system, and systemic processes.

2. Development of a Philosophy--Understands and influences the variables relevant to the process whereby individuals place value on objects, qualities, and evidence within the environment and establish beliefs and values as guides to system relationship and the behaviors relative to the evaluation of differences. This involves such elements as variables, variability, affective behavior, and evaluation.

3. Development of Systems--Understands the evolvement of individual systems and promotes their growth toward structural, cognitive, and affective maturity through adaptation and adjustment to environmental variables. This involves such elements as development, adaptation, and deviance.

4. Professionalism--Understands the meaning of behavior associated with professionals, acquires and exercises this behavior, including the sequence of acts or responses which have professional orientation and may be understood as assigned goals and purposes.

5. Learning Process--Understands general theories and conditions of learning and cognitions central to individual growth and development, and adjusts them to environmental conditions. Involved here are such elements as learning, conditions of learning, cognitive growth and development and learning controls.

6. Motivation of Client Systems--Understands the process of motivation, involving a meaningful learning set, and exercises a disposition to incorporate new material into the cognitive structure essential to meaningful receptive learning. Involved are such elements as need, value, motive, and interest.

7. Programming--Understands and executes the process of programming purposeful change and the related processes of problem-solving, situational, directional, and strategy analyses.

8. Learning Experiences--Understands and executes the process of purposeful learning, including the selection of desirable learning outcomes and means to achieve them. These may be in the cognitive, affective, or psychomotor realms, and involve such elements as educational objectives, hierarchy of objectives, content, and the abilities to achieve useful learning outcomes.

9. Diffusion of Knowledge--Understands and executes the process of imparting, exchanging, or transferring factual information in the form of knowledge, skills, values, ideas, concepts, and principles in system development, control, and maintenance of system development, control, and maintenance of system viability. This includes such sub-elements as communication and communication processes.

10. Adoption of Innovation--Understands and executes the process of influencing adoption of innovation, including the stages and techniques associated with influencing behavioral change in client systems and the elements, conditions, methods, and guidelines associated with teaching and purposeful learning involving learning situations, communication media, technological content, and guides to effective educational influence.

11. Appraisal of Innovation--Understand and executes the factors and stages in the process of evaluating the adoption of innovation by the client system, involving such major elements as instructional media, variability, measurement, transfer, need, motive and value.

12. Management of Resources--Understands and performs the management of administrative functions and processes through which systems maintain viability and affect developmental change. Involved here are such elements as the judicious use of means to achieve ends, decision-making, planning, organization, facilitation, direction, leadership, guidance, mediation, personnel development, controlling, and coordination.

THE ADMINISTRATION'S DILEMMA

If he's friendly with the office personnel, he's a politician.
If he keeps to himself, he's a snob.

If he works on a day to day basis, he lacks foresight.
If he had long-range plans, he's a daydreamer.

If his name appears in the newspapers, he's a publicity hound.
If no one has ever heard of him, he's a nonentity.

If he requests a large appropriation, he is against economy.
If he doesn't ask for more money, he's a timid soul (or stark mad).

If he tries to eliminate red tape, he has no regard for the system.
If he insists on going through channels, he's a bureaucrat.

If he speaks the language of education, he's a cliche expert.
If he doesn't use jargon, he's illiterate.

If he writes for the educational journals, he's neglecting his work.
If he has never written an article, he hasn't had a thought of his own
for twenty years.

If he is late for work in the morning, he's taking advantage of
his position.
If he gets to the office on time, he's an eager beaver.

If the office is running smoothly, he is a dictator.
If the office is a mess, he's a poor administrator.

If he holds weekly staff meetings, he's in desperate need of ideas.
If he doesn't hold weekly staff meetings, he doesn't appreciate
the value of teamwork.

If he spends a lot of time with the Board, he's a back slapper.
If he's never with the Board, he's on his way out.

If he goes to conventions, he's on the gravy train.
If he never makes a trip, he's not important.

If he tries to do all the work himself, he doesn't trust anybody.
If he delegates as much as possible, he's lazy.

If he takes his briefcase home, he's trying to impress the Board.
If he leaves the office without any homework, he has a sinecure.

If he enjoys reading this description, he's facetious.
If he doesn't think it's clever, he's entitled to his own opinion.

Thanks to - - Center for Indian Education - Arizona State University

OUTREACH/DISTANCE EDUCATION--THE OPEN UNIVERSITY
When Harold Wilson retired as the Prime Minister of Great Britain in 1976, he listed as one of his main achievements in office the success of the open university. The open university has been described by some as a correspondence university. But it is much more. It is combining radio, television, tutorial instruction, experimental learning kits, correspondence material, telephone visits with faculty, and the summer seminars.

The Open University grew out of a vision of Jennie Lee and Harold Wilson, both leaders in the Labor Party in 1963. It was a University of the Air that was initially proposed, and which grew into the Open University. It was their hope that this media would attract many from the working classes. Actually, the majority attracted have been teachers, who want degrees to upgrade their positions in the profession. The aims of the proposed new institution were spelled out in the Report on the Open University Planning Committee which was presented in 1969. Correspondence, with largely part-time students, was the objective. The Open University was to provide post-experience courses for those with professional experience, and for working people who wished to change their jobs in mid-career.

The Open University has seen excellent progress since 1971 when it enrolled 19,581 students. With now more than 55,000 students enrolled, the University is well established as a form of distance education available to farmers, housewives, and miners, or whosoever will take the time and discipline to learn.

By 1978, the Open University was already the largest British university in the United Kingdom. Compared to other industrialized countries, the Open University is not large, but in 1977 it had more than 55,000 student enrolled and was still growing.

The University has a Royal Charter, and has the standard pattern familiar to British university faculty of appointing eminent academic faculty to its examining boards. It is these faculty who make sure that the standards of all the British degrees are of top quality. A special emphasis is put upon the writing ability of the instructors which are engaged by the Open University, for this is imperative for distance education.

Radio and television were to be the primary media for this distance education university. It was hoped that the working class would take advantage of the cultural offerings via the air. These boradcasts take up only five to eight percent of the student study time; books are still the major source for study materials, and the Open University runs a major book publishing operation, drawing on the talent of all the British universities for texts and materials. Home experimental kits are used by science students. The students are largely independent learners working mostly in their homes, and sending lessons to tutors for suggestions and for corrections. In an interview with one of the tutors who was teaching a sociology course for the Open University, this author found the University of London faculty member meeting on a regular basis with a group of 6 to 8 students at Kent. He was impressed with the seriousness of the adult students.[7]

Are there entrance requirements for the Open University? Unique in the British system of higher education, the Open University has no entrance requirements. About one-third of the students have been admitted without the formal qualifications which other British universities require.

The geographic distribution is fairly well dispersed throughout all parts of Britain, with students in Scotland, England, and Wales. This comprises about 55 million people from which the Open University draws its students.

The timetable is flexible, with the calendar year beginning in January and final examinations being given in November. There are no conventional class timetables. Fortunately, students can progess at their own pace, with students taking from two to eight years to earn a degree.

The Open University operates on a credit system different from any other university. For a pass degree, six credits are required, and eight credits are demanded for an honors degree. Normally, a one-credit courses requires ten hours of student time per week, or a total of about 350 hours. For students with specific professional qualifications, credit exemptions are granted.

Flexibility of time and space is the advance of the Open University. It is possible to progress at one's own pace. Students can retake failed courses. They can drop in after they have dropped out. The essential course materials are available for general sale, and may be bought in units or blocks.

How are faculty engaged and in what form? The teaching is done with a high degree of centralized staff. The central academic staff works, not just as individuals, but as part of the Open University faculty team. They prepare correspondence courses which are printed, and also broadcast programs, and each course is replayed on radio or television for a total of four years. There is a large counseling and teaching staff employed part-time, and students meet with counselors at the local study centers. In each of the courses students have course tutors who mark papers, and return essays with suggestions for further study. Tutors are available for week-end tutorial classes.

Because of the increasing enrollments, the cost benefits of the Open University are being realized. By 1977 the enrollment had soared to 55,000 part-time students, with 1,900 full-time employees and several thousand part-time counseling and teaching staff members. The expense of large lecture halls, theatres, campus upkeep are not needed. It is economical education, and the Labor Party sold it on the basis of high quality, yet economical methodology. Although the failure rate is close to 30%, the costs are relatively low for part-time education. The Open University has produced graduates more economically than the conventional British universities. The system is being emulated in Israel and elsewhere.

The broadcasting is a fairly expensive component of the distance education carried on by the Open University. Because of the expense of quality programming by television and radio, the university has not yet reaped all the potential economies of large-scale economies. The number of students could be doubled, while increasing the cost only 50 percent.

There are numerous reasons for the cost-effectivenss of the Open University as compared with other British universities. British universities are predominately residential. The residential accommodations for students attending 30 weeks out of fifty-two is expensive. Ordinary British universities have expensive teaching arrangements. Course materials are produced centrally, by a relatively small faculty. In 1977, while one British academic in a traditional university taught eleven full-time students, one Open University faculty member taught an average of 180 part-time students. Capital costs are saved, plus savings on instructional expenses.

THE EXTERNAL DEGREE

The Open University has its counterpart in the United States in the external degree. Pennsylvania State Univversity, University Park, Pennsylvania was one of the first state universities to take initiative on the External Degree. In 1972 the Commission on External Degree programs reported the need for opportunities for adults to earn degrees from Penn State through part-time studies. That same year President John W. Oswald, in an address to the University Faculty Senate, said, "There have emerged over the past years in nearly all colleges and university, including Penn State, what now appears to be artificial and sometime arbitrary rules, regulations, and procedures separating students who are enrolled part-time from those enrolled for full-time study; students on campus from those off campus; students taught in the daytime from those taught in the evening; and students who learn independently from those who learn in classrooms. These rules and regulations tend to handicap students not only as they move from short-range to long-range educational goals at Penn State, but as they move to other colleges and universities throughout the state and nation to complete their studies."

"The Senate response to these issues, in my opinion, can be within a wide range. As a very minimum response, I ask that the Senate consider and take action on the recommendations of the Commission on External Degrees relative to admissions, residency, and graduation requirements for extended degree opportunities for part-time students. In so doing, I hope you will enact legislation which will permit the colleges to make available existing associate or baccalaureate degree programs to part-time students and/or, as time and resources permit, to develop new ones. While this initial action would not assure the full establishment of extended degree opportunities, it would provide the enabling legislation under which the colleges could act responsibly."

Other universities followed the lead of Penn State and established Committees and Commissions on External Degrees which give flexibility to learning for the part-time student.

THE OUTREACH FUNCTION

Summary

Teaching, research, and public service--the outreach function often called extension, are the three missions of great universities. The Morrill Act of 1862 funded land grant universities to see to it that agricultural and home economics knowledge was extended off campus. This outreach function was institutionalized in cooperative extension, which in many universities is combined with general extension in a Division of Continuing Education. Community Colleges often call this function of outreach "community service", which includes non-credit courses, seminars, institutes, and cultural events.

As adult educators we are reminded to be pro-active, rather than re-active. That means taking initiative, of discovering community needs, looking for program possibilities, and taking leadership in program development.

A number of models for continuing education are offered, one for a large university, one for a small liberal arts college. Michigan State University with its pattern of "Assistant dean" for Continuing Education in each college is pointed to as a viable model for getting the outreach function budgeted, and performed. It is suggested that "everybody's responsibility is nobody's responsibility", and the outreach function must be built into the institution with a commitment at the presidential level. A checklist for administering the outreach function is offered: planning, organizaing, staffing, directing, coordinating, reporting, and budgeting. Delegation, with the authority to carry out responsibility, is a key to good administration of continuing education.

A sample agreement for off-campus classes is offered, which can be adapted to the local scene. A Canadian pattern of offering the outreach function is presented which involves 13 community colleges, 3 technical institutes and 2 universities. In order to understand the functions of the extension worker, the outreach person, a typology of role behaviors for extension agents developed by Weldon Findlay is presented which can be used with adaptation in urban or general extension.

The development of the British Open University is described, including the methodology of tutorial, correspondence study, learning kits, and other media. The flexibility of the program is the advantage, meeting head-on the problem of time and space. An external program for adults, the outreach function is primary for the growing number of persons studying at home or at locations in Scotland, England, and Wales. The use of local learning centers and part-time counseling and teaching staff are vital to the success of the Open University. The economy of the Open University was examined as well as the maintaining of quality in distance education. Underdeveloped countries will do well to examine this model of distance teaching, which has been emulated in Isreal as is told in the story of "Isreal's Everyman--A Second Chance to Go to College."

QUESTIONS FOR DISCUSSION

1. How would you build support for the outreach function of a college or university?
2. How would you distinguish between pro-active and reactive approaches to community problems? Illustrate.
3. How would you draw an organization chart for an Extension Division in a small college? For a university of 35,000?
4. What are the advantages of an ASSOCIATE DEAN in each college responsible for the continuing education/outreach function of the institution. If this is a split appointment with University Extension what are the implications?
5. How would you utilize the POSDCORB acronym in administratopm? Illustrate each area of responsibility as it applies to an adult education administrator.
6. What are some of the advantages of the Open University? Is it cost effective? How would you decide whether to advise a student to become involved in an open university program?

Bibliography
READING AND RESOURCES

Alfred, Harold. **Continuing Education in Action''** Residential Centers, Wiley and Sons, 1968.

Anderson, Thomas H., and Scott B. York, **Characteristics of Extramural Students in a Large Midwestern University,** University of Illinois Press, Urbana, 1971.

Anderson, Thomas, and Paul H. Tippy. **An Exploratory Study of Correspondence Students,** University of Illinois Press, Urbana, 1971.

Bebout, John E. **The Idea of Urban Extension Service.** New Brunswick:Rutgers, The State University, January 1963, mimeograph.

Bonniwell, H. Thomas **A Historical Analysis of Non-Credit Adult Education Program Development at the University of Georgia, 1804-1968.** Georgia University, Athens, 1969.

Bricker, George W. **Bricker's Directory of University-Sponsored Executive Development Programs: 1971 Supplement.** Bricker Publications, 1970.

Burch, Glen. **Challenge to the University,** Center for the Study of Liberal Education for Adults. Chicago, 1961.

Chickering, Arthur. **Empire State College Learning Contracts, Report of President's Advisory Committee on Academic Quality,** Empire State College, State University of New York, Saratoga Springs, 1973.

Christensen, Edward, and O. MacKenzie. **The Changing World of Correspondence Study: International Readings,** 1971 (LC 5915 M3).

Conner, W. **Student Turn-over in Short University Extension Courses,** Studies in Adult Education, 5:1, pp. 43-57, April, 1973.

Dressel, Paul L., and Mary Thompson. **Independent Study,** 1973. (LE 1049 D73).

Essex, Diane L., and Thomas H. Anderson, **Some Correlates of Success in Correspondence Study,** 1972.

Gould, Samuel B., and Patricia K. Cross. **Explorations in Nontraditional Study.** 1972 (LB 2360 E9X)

Green, J. Earl. **What Students Think of Off-Campus Classes: More Evidence of That Old Question.** New Campus, 27: pp. 37-42, Spring, 1974.

Harrington, Fred. **The Future of Adult Education, (New Responsibilities of Colleges and Universities),** Jossey Bass, San Francisco, Cal. 94111, 1977.

Harrison, Paul C., Jr., and Carl A. Lindsay, **Inventory of Continuing Education Activities in Pennsylvania Institutions of**

270

Higher Learning for the Academic Year 1969-1970: Final Report, Pennsylvania State University, University Park, April, 1971.

Harter, Donald. Reaction of State of New York Students Toward Independent Study Courses, State University of New York, Saratoga Springs, December, 1969.

Hesburgh, Miller & Wharton, Patters of Lifelong Learning, Jossey-Bass, 1973.

Hook, Sidney. The Idea of a Modern University, Prometheus Books, 1974. Buffalo, N.Y. 14215

Houle, Cyril O. Residential Continuing Education. Syracuse University, Publications in Continuing Education, 1971.

Houle, Cyril O. The External Degree. 1973 (LB 2381 H68).

Hyde, R. Abner, Goal, Congruence and Organizational Efficacy in Two Merging Adult Education Centers, University of Tennessee Press, Knoxville, 1969.

Johnstone, John W. C., and R. J. Rivera. Volunteers for Learning: A Study of Educational Pursuits of American Adults, Alpine Publishers, Chicago, 1965.

Kelsey, L. David, and C. C. Hearne, Cooperative Extension Work, 3rd ed., Comstock Publishing Assoc., Ithaca, NY, 1963.

Kliment, Stephen A., and Jane Lord. Build If You Must, But Consider...2. Non-Campus Facilities. Planning for Higher Education, Society for College and University Planning, Vol. 3, No. 2, April 1974.

Knoell, Dorothy and Charles McIntyre, Planning Colleges for the Community, Jossey-Bass, 1974. San Francisco.

Kreitlow, Burton W., and Teresa MacNeil. A Model for Educational Improvement in Extension: Theoretical Paper Number 26, University of Wisconsin Press, Madison, April, 1970.

Lengans, J. Paul. Selected Concepts from Educational Psychology and Adult Education for Extension and Continuing Educators. Syracuse University Publications in Continuing Education, 1971.

Liveright, A. A. Adult Education in Colleges and Universities, Center for the Study of Liberal Education for Adults, Chicago, 1960.

Livingston, Donald E. Adult Education in the Units of the Montana University System, Ed. D. Dissertation, Arizona State University, Tempe 1969.

MacKenzie, Ossian. Correspondence Instruction in the United States, 1968 (LC 5951 M3).

Martin, Kevin. How to go to High School or College by Mail. Frederick Fell, Inc., February 1969.

Miller, James R., and Robert W. McCormick. A Theoretical Model to Improve the Extension Education Outreach, Behavioral, Business, Management and Systems Concepts, Research Series

271

in Agricultural Education, Ohio State University, Department of Agricultural Education, Columbus, January 1972.

Nelson, Nancy. **Prisons and Colleges.** Adult Leadership, 23:12, 6/75.

Penfield, Kathleen, R., **Public Service Vs. Academic Values: University Extension in Conflict.** Adult Education, 25:2; pp. 107-124, Winter, 1975.

Peterson, Renee and William. **University Adult Education,** Harper & Row, New York, 1960.

Porter, Lee. **Faculty Perceptions of Continuing Education at Syracuse University,** New York Publications Program in Continuing education, Syracuse University, March 1970.

Rouch, David B. **Priorities in Adult Education,** Adult Education Association of the U.S.A.

Report of the Policy Statement Committee, The National University Extension Association, n.d., Washington, D. C.

Sanders, H. C., **Cooperative Extension Service, (S544 S2).**

Shannon, Theodore J., and Clarence A. Schoenfield, **The University Extension** (LC 6 219 S5) (Primary Reference). 1967.

Simpson, Bert K. **Analysis of the Understanding, Acceptance, and Implementation of the Purposes of Title I of the Higher Education Act of 1965.** United States International University, San Diego, Ca., June 1970.

Smith, Ruby Green. **The People's Colleges,** Cornell University Press, Ithaca, N. . 1949.

The Contemporary University: U.S.A. Daedalus, Fall, 1964.

The Cooperative Extension Service: A Nationwide Knowledge System for Today's Problems, Colorado State University, Cooperative Extension Service, Ft. Collins, July 1974.

Today's Critical Needs and University Extension, American Association of State Universities and Land-Grant Colleges, Division of General Extension, Washington, D. C., 1961.

Urban Extension. A Report on Experimental Programs Assisted by the Ford Foundation (LC 66 27861). 1970.

Vermilye, Dyckman W. **The Expanded Campus, Current Issues in Higher Education.** Jossey-Bass, San Francisco, 1974.

Vermilye, Dyckman W. **Lifelong Learners - A New Clientele for Higher Education.** Jossey-Bass, San Francisco, 1974.

Vermilye, Dyckman W. **Learner Centered Reform.** Jossey-Bass, San Francisco, 1975.

Vermilye, Dyckman W. **Individualizing the System.** Jossey-Bass, San Francisco, 1976.

Verner, Coolie, and Alan Booth. **Adult Education,** The Center for Applied Research in Education, New York, 1964.

Wedemeyer, Charles A. **Toward an Extension-Oriented Research Environment - - A Paradox, A Model and a Proposal,** NUEA

Spectator, 35:10, pp. 8-13, December 1972.

Perry, Walter. **The Open University.** San Francisco: Jossey-Bass Publications, 1977. 298 p.

Ferguson, John. **The Open University From Within.** New York: New York University Press, 1976. 165 pp.

Tunstall, Jeremy. **The Open University Opens.** Amherst: University of Massachusetts Press, 1974. 191p.

"Case for Educare and the Open University," **Saturday Review World,** Vol. 1, (August 24, 1974), pp. 74-5.

ERIC, "Excellence, Equality, and the Open University." ED 149 684

"Economics of the Open University," L. Wagner. **Higher Education,** Vol. 6, (August 1977), pp. 359-81.

"New Roles for the University: the British Experience," M. Pinto-Duschinsky. **Journal of Education,** Vol. 159, (May 1977), pp. 43-54.

"Counseling and Advisory Service for Adult Learners: an Open University Perspective," D. Stewart & M. Richardson. **International Review of Education,** Vol. 23, No. 4, 1977, pp. 425-37.

"Thinking in Response to Print; Open U. Reading Diploma," M. Hoffman. **The Times Educational Supplement,** 3289, (July 14, 1978), pp. 41-45.

"Students' Reactions to Tutoring by Telephone in Britain's Open University," E. Williams. Vol. 15, (October 1975), pp. 42-6. **Educational Technology.**

Fletcher, Marjorie A., "The Open University of Great Britain: Its Influence on Non-traditional Education in the United States." Drexel Library Quarterly, 11 April 1975 pp. 2-3.

* Appreciation for assistance by Gerard Pasquerell.

International Adult Education - - Bibliography

Bawtree, Vicky, Ed. Ideas and Actions, the bimonthly bulletin of FAO's Action for Development Program, devotes Issue 124, 1978/5, to the work of the ICAE Participatory Research Network. Ideas and Action is published in English, French and Spanish editions and is available free from FAO, 00100 Rome, Italy.

Adult educators in Botswana have been using popular theatre to involve large groups of people in community and development issues. These experiences are being documented in a sweies of reports from the Institute of Adult Education, University College of Botswana, P.B. 0022, Gaborone.

Educacion de Adultos en America Latina, prepared and published by the Latin American Program of the International Council for Adult Education, 1977, 199 pages, $10.00 (postage included). First director of over 400 professions and 200 institutions engaged in adult education and training Latin America. In Spanish with introduction and description in English. Order from: Consejo Internacional para la Educacion de Adultos, Oficina Regional, Apartado Postal 682, San Jose, Costa Rica

Hall, Budd L. ICAE Director of Research Analysis of Tanzania's "Man is Health" campaign - and titled Mtu ni Afya: Tanzania's Health Campaign, has been published by the Clearinghouse on Development Communication, Academy for Development. The 74-page book can be obtained free of charge from Clearinghouse, 1414 22nd Street, NW, Washington, DC 20037, USA.

Hall, Budd L. and J. Roby Kidd, eds. **Adult Learning: A Design for Action,** contains selected papers from the International Conference on Adult Education and Development, Dar es Salaam, Tanzania, in June 1976. The 340-page book is available from Pergamon Press (Headington Hill Hall, Oxford, England) and its distributors.

Hall, Budd L., Director of Research, International Council for Adult Education. Mtu ni Afya: Tanzania's Health Campaign. Published by Clearinghouse on Development Communication, Academy for Educational Development, 1978, 74 pages. No charge: Distribution funded by the U.S. Agency for International Development. Describes and analyzes how the Man in Health campaign came about, how it was planned, what its underlying methodology was, and what impact it had; and examines the case for mass radio study-group campaigns as an integral and continuous part of national development strategies. Order from Clearinghouse on Development Communication, 1414 22nd Street, N.W., Washington, D.C. 20037, USA.

Edin and Edward Hutchinson, Later Learning: Fresh Horizons in English Adult Education. Published by Routledge & Kegan Paul Ltd., 1978, 200 pages, (pounds) 7.20 post included. Describes the fresh start in education provided, particularly for women, through the Fresh Horizons courses at London's City Lit Centre for Adult Education (1966-74); details about these older learners from their own statements; implications of the Fresh Horizons experience for the extensive provision of full and part-time non-residential courses for adult learners. Order from: Routledge & Kegan Paul Ltd., Broadway House, Newton Road, Henly-on-Thames, Oxon, England RG9 IEN and, 9 Park St., Boston, Mass. 02108, USA-Oxford University Press (Canada), 70 Wynford Drive, Don Mills, Ontario, Canada M3C

1J9

Jones, H. A. and A. H. Charnley, Adult Literacy: A Study of its Impact - Published by the National Institute of Adult Education, 1978, 121 pages, (pounds) 1.00 (U.K.) and (pounds) $1.50 overseas (postage included). Adult students and volunteer tutors were partners in this major research project into various aspects of the first three years' activity of the U.K. Continuing Adult Literacy Campaign. Written for tutors, organizers and administrators in the field, and provides a basis for informed discussion of future developments in adult literacy schemes. Order from (cash with order): National Institute of Adult Education, 19B DeMontfort Street, Leicester, England, LEI 7GE - also available from: Canadian Association for Adult Education, 29 Prince Arthur Avenue, Toronto, Canada M5R IB2.

Kassam, Yusuf. The Adult Education Revolution in Tanzania - is the first comprehensive record of the remarkable achievements of the country's adult education program between 1969 and 1976. The 114-page book is available for KS 20 from: Shungwaya Publisher, Box 49162, Nairobi, Kenya.

Kidd, Roby and Gordon Selman, Eds. Coming of Age: Canadian Adult Education in the 1960s, - Published by the Canadian Association for Adult Education, 1977, 400 pages, $13.95 hardcover, $8.95 paperback. The third anthology to document developments in adult education through republished writings by 65 different authors that reflect the significance of the decade for national concerns and for increased recognition of adult education.

MacBride Commission - The Unesco International Commission for the Study of Communication Problems. Interim Report and two annex documents. Available from Unesco, Place de Fontenoy, 75700 Paris, France.

Dr. Mohl E. - Dine Saber, Director - General, Arab League Educational, Cultural and Scientific Organization (ALECSO). Development and Adult Education in the Arab States: An Analysis of Some Issues. Published cooperatively by the International Council for Adult Education and ALECSO, 1977, 55 pages, $6.00 surface mail, $7.00 airmail. Examines basic concepts for a contemporary understanding of the cultural, political, economic and education situation of the Arab world; focuses on cultural change and education, literacy and adult education, and the role of women in integrated development. Order from: International Council for Adult Education, 29 Prince Arthur Avenue, Toronto, Canada M5R 1B2 and Arab League Educational, Cultural and Scientific Organization, 1 Shihab Street, Dokki, Egypt.

1 See ORGANIZATION AND EFFECTIVE USE OF ADVISORY COMMITTEES, OE-84000 Trade and Industrial Education, Office of Education, U. S. HEW, Bulletin No. 288, Series No. 71, U. S. Government Printing Office. Also **Guidelines for School-Community Advisory Councils**, Flint Michigan and Advisory Committee What? Why? Who? How? When? Where?, Arizona State Division of Vocational Education, Phoenix, Az. Useful - Samuel M. Burt, THE STATE ADVISORY COUNCILS ON VOCATIONAL EDUCATION, Washington D.C.: The W. E. Upjohn Institute for Employment Research, 1101 17th St. N.W. 1969) Individual copies free upon request.

2 Kemp, Florence B. "Non-Credit Activities in Institutions of Higher Education for the Year Ending, June 30, 1976" Supt. of Documents, U. S. Government Printing Office, Wash. D.C. 20434 (Stock No. 017-080-01841-1) National Center for Educational Statistics, 1978.

3 Zabezensky, Ferne, "Participation in P.A.C.E. Continuing Education Activities by Arizona Medical Technologists in 1974, (Ph.D. dissertation) Arizona State University. 1975.

4 Gulick, Luther and Lyndall Urwick, Papers on the Science of Administration in Extension, National Agricultural Extension Center for Advanced Study, Madison, Wisconsin, 1959, pp. 31-58.

5 Harlow, James, "Is Reorganization Necessary, in Clark, Robert C. and Roland H. Abraham, **Administration in Extension**. National Extension Center for Advanced Studies, Madison Wis. 1959, pp. 59-73.

6 Findlay, E. Weldon, "Curriculum Development for Professional Leaders in Extension Education" (Ph.D. dissertation, Cornell University, 1969).

7 Taped interview with Mr. D. Butterworth, London University, August, 1973.

Chapter XVII

PROGRAMMING IN ADULT EDUCATION

No term or idea in the whole of adult education is quite so widely used, nor quite so elusive in precise meaning as the term program. Yet none is so important since it is around this word and the idea or rather the activity that it represents that the vast variety of specialized interest that make up contemporary adult or continuing education coalesce.

> -Alan M. Thomas (Executive Director, Canadian Adult Education Association), in Gale Jensen et al. (eds.), **Adult Education: Outlines of an Emerging Field of University Study,** Adult Education Association, 1964, p. 241.

PLANNING "WITH" AND PLANNING "FOR" IN PROGRAMMING

The problem with which we have to deal is basically one of understanding and organizing the curriculum or program as we call it in adult education. Ralph W. Tyler for many years, Director, Center for the Study of the Behavioral Sciences, Palo Alto, California, has thrown considerable light on this subject by his study of the problem of curriculum and program construction:

Before we consider the question of planning "with" or "for" in adult education, we have to examine some fundamental questions underlying all program planning and curriculum building:

What purposes should the institution or agency seek to attain?

What educational experiences can be provided that are likely to attain these purposes?

How can these educational experiences be effectively organized?

How can we determine whether these purposes are being attained?[1]

The answers to the above questions will vary from institution to institution, but the questions themselves are fundamental for any educational program in attacking the problem of program planning and methodology.

Goals & Objectives

Many educational programs do not have clearly defined goals. In some cases one may ask a teacher just what are the objectives of the course. One may **not** get a satisfactory reply. An instructor may say that primarily one is teaching social studies because it is essential to a well-rounded education. Undoubtedly some excellent educational work is being done by "artistic teachers" who do not have a clear conception of objectives or goals but do have a sense of what is good teaching, what materials are valuable, what topics are most worthwhile, and what methods help develop topics effectively with and for the students. Some teachers have an intuitive ability to present material interestingly or have gained the ability through the years.

However, for most teachers, if an educational program is to be well planned and continued improvement is to be made, it is vitally important to have some clear conception of the **goals** These educational aims and objectives become the criteria for choosing materials, outlining content, developing procedures for instruction, and evaluating. The various aspects of the educational program are basically means to accomplish our educational purposes or aims-which we call **objectives** in programming.

EDUCATIONAL OBJECTIVES
TYLERIAN STRUCTURAL FRAMEWORK FOR CHOOSING EDUCATION OBJECTIVES (With and For)

Study of Learners	Study of Society	Study of Specialists
Filter through	Philosophy of education	What is most valuable
Filter through	Educational Psychology	What is possible to learn
		Related Experiences

In the final analysis, objectives are matters of choice. The goals of a program must, therefore, be the considered value judgements of those responsible for the educational institution and representative of it. A carefully thought out and comprehensive philosophy of education is, therefore, necessary to guide in making these judgments since individuals reflect the educational philosophy of institutions.

In the past I have directed a project of Latin American teachers from Venezuela and the Dominican Republic here in the United States. The purpose of this program was to study the compre-

278

hensive high school in order to reconstruct educational systems for a more democratic inclusion of a larger number of young people in the now highly "academic" and traditional curriculum. I found some of these teachers had a most difficult time conceiving of program planning other than a rigid, highly structured, authoritarian "planning for" approach that they experienced in their homeland. Curriculum in these countries came from a centralized Ministry of Education and was uniform throughout the nation. Regardless of what school you might be in on a certain Tuesday morning, you would find each eighth-grade class studying the same material with little room for adaptation for individual needs and differences. This pattern, it appears, brought to the fore in administration those of a highly authoritarian philosophy and character. Among the teachers (I was again and again told) in Latin American education there was little room for flexibility, creativity, and adjustability for different levels of learning. I found there was less of a tendency to ask fundamental questions and more of an attempt to look for easy, pat answers that would work in a uniform pattern. The least understandable aspect of American education for the Latin American educators was the close interplay in the school-community relationship. The most easily understood was the central offices of the public schools and the State Department of Public Instruction. This illustrates the "planning for" approach as contrasted with the "planning with" approach of democratic education.

CONDITIONS OF ADULT LEARNING-SOME REASONS FOR "PLANNING WITH"

1. **Understanding and accepting objectives and procedures** -when the learner understands and accepts the objectives and methods of the program, the person is better able to focus his attention on the relevant parts of the learning experience.

The Ideal Situation

Teacher's objectives

Common objectives of
learning experience

Learner's objectives

2. **Making ideas available.** A primary responsibility of a true "teacher" is to make learning experiences and ideas avail able. To develop a "learning situation" is the role of the teacher, remembering that each may get something quite different from the experience. We are most accustomed to an "authority" as the common source of ideas (lecturer, panel

of experts, resource person). The teacher himself should be a resource and should know how to involve learners in growth experiences.

3. **Integrate ideas with the learner's past experience.** By knowing something of the learner's past experience it may be possible to make current experiences more meaningful. For example, unless we understood that most academically oriented institutions do not have electives in underdeveloped Latin American areas, one could have a session of guidance and completely miss the fact that this is meaningless unless one has an elective system of education with **choices to be made!** If you have to build and execute a program for adults, a discussion of methodology is much more meaningful if you have experienced the problem firsthand. The leader or teacher can build bridges between new ideas in a new situation and the known experience of the learner; through participation and questions he can evaluate whether he is "getting through" and he can validate progress toward learning.

SOURCES FOR PROGRAM PLANNING

I. Studies of the Learners Themselves as a Source of Educational Objectives

We think of education as the process of helping people to change their patterns of behavior. When we view education in this way, it should be clear that educational objectives are changes in behavior that an educational agency attempts to bring about in its participants. Studies of the learners themselves should seek to **identify needed changes in behavior patterns** of adults which the educational agency is trying to produce.

Havighurst and Orr, the authors of the booklet "Adult Education and Adult Needs."[2] start with the assumption that "the goal of adult education is to help people live better" and raised the question, "What does 'living better' mean and how can education help people do it?" In order to get one kind of answer to these questions, they went to a group of people and asked them to tell what their daily life consisted of and what **seemed important to them**.

They scrutinized the answjs in light of what social philosophers have said concerning the good life in America, and on sophers have said concerning the good life in America, and on that basis they made judgments concerning the degree of success which the various people whom they studied achieved in their adult years. They studies people between ages 40 and 70. From the study of middle-aged people grew the following set of developmental **directions in which a person should grow if he is to be useful and happy after age 50.**

1. **Valuing wisdom versus valuing physical powers.**
2. Emotional expansion versus emotional constriction.
3. Mental flexibility versus mental rigidity.
4. Expansion of interests beyond the work role.
5. Body transcendence versus body preoccupation.

In a discussion of adult needs and developmental tasks, the authors define developmental tasks as the "basic tasks of living." The developmental tasks are set for us by three forces:

The expectations of values of our society.
The maturing and then the aging of our bodies.
Our own personal values and aspirations.

Havighurst and Orr describe the following social expectations and social roles which imping upon an adult in modern society. These roles have a limited number of areas of behavior and have a profound implication for program planners:

Parent	User of leisure
Spouse	Church Member
Child of Again Parent	Club or association member
Homemaker (male or female)	Citizen
Worker	Friend

II. Developmental Tasks as a Basis for Program Planning

In working with adult groups, i have found the developmental task concept of Robert J. Havighurst exceedingly valuable. In evolving programs at the University of Wisconsin, we used this framework for considering how adults could benefit from the program, and programs were considered in the light of how they might contribute to the maturity of the adult, and at least a partial achievement of a developmental task. Inexperienced program planners, with either volunteer groups or with credit classes, may find the framework the author has developed from Havighurst developmental tasks of middle-aged adults useful. (See following page)

If we are to have effective program planning, it is necessary to understand the special characteristics of adults. We often fail because we think of our planning in terms of methods and procedures used with children. Schmidt and Svenson point out that the adult learner differs from the child learner in

281

THE DEVELOPMENTAL TASKS OF MIDDLE-AGED ADULTS by Dr. Robert J. Havighurst University of Chicago	PROGRAM SUGGESTIONS by Dr. Roger W. Axford—Associate Professor of Education, Director of Adult Education Northern Illinois University, DeKalb, Illinois
The Task:	Program:
1. Help adolescent children become happy and responsible adults.	Understanding the Adolescent (one course)
2. Work out new satisfactions in marriage relationship.	There is apparently no course whose content is designed to assist adults directly in this task. No doubt husbands and wives attend programs together as a means of meeting this task. We have in some instances encouraged couple attendance by reduction of fee for husband and wife.
3. Working out relationships with aging parents.	Planning for Retirement series
4. Creating beautiful and comfortable home.	(The following seem remotely related): The Meaning of Art—Art Appreciation—Creative Design
5. Reaching the peak of the work career.	Many programs in the Vocational field are designed primarily to increase specific competencies or vocational skills: Course for Office Secretaries—Strength of Materials Economic Reasoning for the Layman—Engineering Refresher Leadership Skills (Commerce)—How to Plan Your Investments Planning for Savings Improvement and Profit—Steward Training—Labor Looks at Civil Liberties Comparatively, we seem to have more programs in this area. Whether they meet the problem of this task is another question.
6. Achieving mature social and civic responsibility.	Problems of Africa—Crisis in the Middle East—Leadership Training—Intergroup Relations in the Community—The World Around Us—Public Speaking—Midwest Seminar on Foreign Policy
7. Accepting and adjusting to physiological changes of middle age.	Planning for Retirement series.
8. Making an art of friendship.	We probably provide the medium through which a number of people make new friendships and continue old ones. No doubt some of the people we reach have been interested in attending programs as one means of reaching satisfaction in this task.
9. Creative use of leisure.	Art Courses—Planning for Retirement—Juvenile Writing Philosophy—Gateways to Music—Evaluating Your Invention Documentary Films—Language Courses for Travelers—Travel Courses—Many Wisconsin Idea Theater Courses
10. Becoming and Maintaining active Club or association membership.	Leadership Training—Public Speaking—Adult Education Institute (for Federated Women's Clubs)—BIPS Programs (program notes, etc.)
11. Becoming and maintaining active church membership.	Early New Testament Times—Church Music Conference Church Music Workshop—Theater in the Church—Religious Drama Workshop

several respects which have implications for methodology in adult education:

1. The adult learner has more experience and a different quality of experience to contribute to the learning situation.
2. The adult learner is ready to learn different things from the youthful learner because he faces different developmental tasks (e.g., parenthood).
3. The adult learner tends to be more **autonomous**, therefore less comfortable in a dependent role.
4. The adult learner is usually interested in the **immediate usefulness** [4] of new knowledge (practical application).

III. The Community Survey in Program Planning

Each year adult educators become aware of the importance of understanding the community as a basis for program planning in adult education. If the program is built around the real-life problems and interests of the area served, support will come from those who pay for the service.

The adult educator will use every device to better understand the potential clientele, for he or she is helping to mold the character of the community and the leadership for the future. Dr. Samuel E. Hand, for many years State Supervisor of the Adult Education of the Florida State Department of Education and now a professor of adult education at Florida State University, has pointed out four basic reasons for systematic study of the community by educators of adults for program planning:

1. Sociologists have long recognized that the community exercises great influence on the development of the human personality.

2. Democratic society depends for its existence upon citizen participation, and no better way has been found to achieve widespread and enlightened citizen participation than through involvement in the study of community problems.

3. Great social problems can be, and usually are, illustrated within the context of community life, and it is at this level that they can best be understood and dealt with by the ordinary individual.

4. Communities differ and an educational program designed for one community will not necessarily accommodate the needs of another. Every community deserves, and in fact requires, its own individually tailored program. [5]

283

The outline suggested by Hand for studying the community includes the following:

History and setting of the community
The people
The labor force
The economic structure
Sources of information
Local government
Health

School finance
Social problems
Religious composition
Housing
Recreation
Library
Community groups

The value of such a survey is that the adult educator will acquire information about the programs and resources of the community which will help him answer important questions, such as, "What problems exist in the schools and community about which citizens should be concerned?" and, "What other agencies are in adult education and in what form?" and, "What gaps exist in the community for program possibilities?" and, "Where should our agency apply its efforts in order to make the most pronounced contributions?"

Sometimes one of the agencies of the state government will assist a community in doing a self-survey. The Division of Children and Youth of the Wisconsin Department of Public Welfare assisted a number of counties to involve citizens in examining their communities. Walworth and Racine counties were studies in some depth, utilizing citizen committees. The participants realized that if the citizens themselves did the study with the assistance of professionals in methodology, the citizens will vote more wisely and may do something about their own community problems. A sample survey/needs assessment instrument is provided in Appendix D.

WHAT KIND OF PROGRAMS FOR ADULTS?

In a statement, "Canada's First Plan for Continuous Learning," Canadian adult educators attempt to plan a course ahead for adult education.[6] Speaking to the school boards of Canada, they suggest that at least five kinds of adult programs be considered:

Those designed to make people feel confident in the basic reading and writing skills.

Those designed to upgrade the educational achievements of individuals so that they can take further training in business and industry or, if they wish, proceed to university study.

Cultural programs designed to broaden the horizons

284

and enrich the lives of individuals.

Vocational courses and programs designed to update previous education or training; and

Besides specific courses, adult education could and should provide vocational and educational counseling and coordinate extension services in the whole area served by a school.

E. T. Marriott, chief Administrative officer, Halifax Municipal School Board and chairman of a committee of the Canadian association to study the role of school boards in adult education, feels that the public school is the primary agency for adult and continuing education. Says Marriott:

The days when one's formal education was over when he left school are no more. From the standpoint of pure economics, it would appear that our present and future public schools are the most obvious institutions to offer adult and continuing education. The administrative necessities are already established, the buildings are regularly used only about five hours a day and facilities for teaching academic, commercial, and limited vocational subjects have been provided, and trained teachers are available. Adults have accepted the fact that they must pay for the education of their children. They would welcome the dividend of receiving useful education themselves.[7]

Because program planning is important in the process of adult and continuing education, it is valuable now to ask questions, "Where does the administrator get new and creative program ideas?" Undoubtedly, educators of adults will develop techniques through the years, but the author has found certain methods useful for cultivating program ideas which may save time and energy for the newcomer to the field. Now let us examine some of the ways in which a new director of adult education might answer the question, "How shall I cultivate program ideas?"

HOW TO CULTIVATE PROGRAM IDEAS

A good program planner has to be creative. He or she must continually keep eyes, ears, and mind open always receptive to new ideas. But where do we turn for new ideas, program potential, and people? Where do we uncover possibilities for new courses, lecture series, or institutes?[8]

In many years of programming for adults, I have found numerous sources for new ideas. I regularly carry with me a note pad and write down ideas that need to incubate. (3 x 5 cards are useful - one idea per card). Occasionally a program idea will spring up from the most unexpected source. For example, I paid a visit to a journalist friend who writes features for the women's page in one of America's largest and most highly respected newspapers, the **Milwaukee Journal.** Dorothy Witte Austin asked, "What are you doing to prepare people for their visit to Europe?" I responded that I had just recently made a file on a person who is a specialist on Italy and was interested in helping people learn more about the countries they visit. "How to Prepare for Your European Tour" was the brainchild in embryo. The result: not only did we get a specialist from each country for the University-sponsored series, but three of the lecturers either were born in the country chosen or had spent a major part of their lives in the area which they described. Eight Friday evenings in the late spring were chosen, bringing the series close to the summer tours. Most the speakers were aware that a picture is worth a thousand words, so they illustrated the lectures with colored slides. One husband-and-wife team of artists had just returned from a year in the Scandinavan countries, bringing to their lecture samples of folk arts and craft. Our bonus for the series was a two-page weekly spread in the **Milwaukee Journal** written by the journalist who had sparked the idea, complete with photos. She never missed a lecture. The payoff was the Sunday newspaper stories which reached thousands throughout the state of Wisconsin.

Speaker's directories are an excellent source of talent. Occasionally I have found a faculty member who has a specialty or avocation which I had not known about. For example, an English professor lists "Censorship" and "Civil Rights" as topics he will debate or discuss. "Christian Faith and Science" is a topic favorite with a philosophy professor. Many public libraries carry a card file of speakers and topics which specialists will talk about. One caution: observe the person in action to be sure he or she is articulate, relates well with adults, and knows the subject. Where possible, check out the speaker's ability with others who have heard the lecturer. Some adult education councils produce a "Speakers' List," such as the **Speakers of Consequence** booklet published by the Chicago Adult Education Council. Such a booklet is a worthy project for your council if no such directory now exists.

Book reviews, feature stores, and newspaper clippings are important to enrich your "idea file." Interviews with idea people such as artists, writers, and actors have brought to birth some of our most imaginative programs in adult education. I cull news releases for unusual visitors in this country. Periodically I find a program gold mine in the person of a

"Visiting Professor" from abroad. For example, Dr. John Harrison, associate director of Extra-Mural Study from the University of Leeds and author of **Learning and Living, 1790-1960,** a history of the adult education movement in England, was visiting the University of Wisconsin. Harrison agreed to speak to our Racine Adult Education Roundtable and describe ways in which our programs for adults in the United States differ from or are similar to the British offerings. His description of the Worker's Education Association in England and the administrative organization of British adult education was new to many of our adult educators. The gathering offered new ideas for more than thirty professional adult educators.

A study of catalogs of the various agencies of adult education from around the state, the country, and the world is a rich source for program ideas and material. Our program planners pass along clippings taken from catalogs gleaned from numerous extension divisions. Time spent analyzing programs of comparable agencies of adult education proves to be time well invested. Duplication may be eliminated, and trends may be observed by careful examination of bulletins and announcements in your area. At conventions, a visit with program people, "How do you do it?" sessions, and examination and collection of swap-shop literature may be your best investiment of time.[9]

Advisory committees are a good source both for program ideas and for being assured of an interested clientele when the program begins. Often the advisory committee will provide the clientele, especially important if you depend upon volunteer attendance. Subject area advisory committees (such as Nursing Education) develop community leadership when well organized and are a "bank" of ideas in program planning. Brainstorming with faculty and staff already involved in the program will give feedback and new program suggestions which will keep administrators closer to the needs and interests of adults.

Faculty members often want to make suggestions, and a listening ear will give a good pulse count on the health of the developing program. Democratic involvement of the faculty in program planning can be a sure morale builder if properly administered.

Broad interests and wide reading on the part of the administrator will keep the program planner abreast of the times. There is no substitute for regular hours in the library. If a half day or a day can be set aside for reading, writing, and planning, the dividends in quality programs will warrant the investment of time. Occasionally consultants can prove exceedingly useful. Although sometimes an expense, consultation should be built into the adult education budget. Wise consultants can bring objectivity and a detachment which can prove productive and eco-

---

Adult Student Questionnaire
University of Wisconsin Extension Division—Milwaukee
600 West Kilbourn Avenue, Milwaukee, Wisconsin 53203

HERE ARE SOME QUESTIONS ONLY <u>YOU</u> CAN ANSWER . . . AND WE NEED YOUR HELP!

To be effective, continuing education programs must always remain closely in touch with the current interests and needs of adults in the communities they serve. As a participant in this semester's programs, you can be an invaluable source of help to us if you will take a few minutes to give us the answers to the questions below. Your reward will be still better programming in the future.

1. Through what source did you hear of the class you are now attending?

( ) Newspaper ad	( ) Trade or professional group
( ) Radio or TV	( ) Employer
( ) Bulletin board at _____	( ) Public library
( ) Friend	( ) School board bulletin
( ) University mailing	( ) Had to seek out information
( ) Previous course	( ) Other: _____

2. What do you hope to gain from the course?
   _____
   _____

3. What are future courses you might take? (No obligation)
   _____
   _____

4. If you were in charge of preparing programs, what additional courses would you offer?
   _____
   _____

   What changes would you make in present courses or procedures?
   _____
   _____

5. What are your hobbies or special interests?
   _____

6. What are most convenient class hours for you? _____

7. What is most convenient location for you?   ( ) Kenwood Campus
                                               ( ) Downtown Campus

Your name _____ Date _____

Class you are currently attending _____

Home address _____ Telephone _____

City and State _____ Zip _____

Occupation _____ Age _____

Employer _____ Address _____
                    1 2 3 4 5 6 7 8
Education (circle highest year) 9 10 11 12 13 14 15 16 17 18 Degree: _____

One way to study student interests—the questionnaire.

New scientific information can prove grist for new programs for adults. Specialized information resulting from research is needed by business and industry and can result in productive conferences and short courses for updating knowledge. Beware, however, of possible pitfalls in areas such as foreign affairs. A current topic may be exhausted through overexposure to the subject via the radio, TV, or the newspapers. Periodically, questionnaires or interest finders may assist in learning what adults consider most important. However, indication of interest and the actual enrollment with payment of a fee are two quite different things, as many an adult education program planner has woefully learned.

A weakness of some agencies of adult education is an attempt to be all things to all people. This is no more possible for an agency than it is for a person. The question the adult educator must ask is: "What can my institution do better than any other agency in my community or region?" The public school, the university, or any agency of adult education should do only those programs for which it is best suited. Often an agency in the community has a special resource or a program gap which needs to be filled. Collaboration with other agencies may bring about the success of a needed program. Cooperation, coordination, and exchange of information are basic to community improvement. The educator of adults who can be a catalyst of need and talent in our society is the true "urban agent."

To examine and analyze results of research pertaining to adult learning may prove valuable to the planner of programs. When I studied a client analysis, a self-study of a sister educational institution in a city of a million persons, immediately I became aware of our differing traditions and emphases. Census data can prove helpful in finding out who are the potential clientele for your programs, especially if interpreted and refined by a knowledgeable sociologist often available at the local university. One of the Wisconsin specialists in "women's education" is using census data as a basis for future programs, now that she knows the number of college graduates in the area surrounding the university. Also, she now knows how many women in the area are high school dropouts, how many have had some college work, and how many are heads of households or are working.

A service that adult educators can render is to familiarize their community with the current films which can be used by Community Colleges, labor unions, churches, and voluntary organization. Often the Film Library of a University will consider it an opportunity to show new films they have bought, in order to get circulation. I found the University of Michigan Media Department willing to cooperate in a Film Festival for the National Adult Education Association. We were able to provide program planning personnel with new ideas for making visual the area that interested them. For example, a film series on Aging can be used by R.S.V.P., American Association for Retired Persons, gerontology program planners, and continuing education faculty from a school of nursing.

There is no one source for program ideas, rather there are innumerable sources. The only limitation is the imagination of the program planner and his sensitivity to community needs. Agency boards, university administrators, and adult education administrators must be made more aware that developing program ideas takes time, training, money, and experience - but, above all, imaginative programs demand a climate of experimentation and creativity. Fortunately, because we believe in continuing education and lifelong learning, we can all grow in the ability to discover and cultivate new program ideas.

PROGRAM DEVELOPMENT

Get the program **idea** down on paper! Develop a program planning form. On page 294 is a form for asking the right questions when preparing a **program** for adults. You may want to adapt the form to your local institution, but is is useful to be sure you anticipate answers to the needs of the activity: who, what, when, where, why, and who pays? Such a form can keep the program planner out of trouble! It will also save many phone calls.

An organization chart is useful to know what is being planned by which department of the agency. An illustration of the program plan for one state agency is given as an example of the areas which the Illinois Junior College Board hopes to see developed in the years ahead. Where does your program fit in your organization chart?

The conference and institute programs in continuing education are growing rapidly and tapping the talents of many persons in education, industry, business and the professions so that it's difficult to keep up with this facet of man's insatiable desire to "keep learning."

CONTINUING EDUCATION DIVISION
UNIVERSITY OF MAINE
WORKSHEET FOR BUDGETING INFORMAL PROJECTS

University of Maine   Center or Bureau _____ Date _____

Submit one copy to State Director of the Continuing Education Division on all projects except those for which uniform fee has been established.

Name of Project: _____

Group Served: _____

Project Date(s): _____ Location: _____

ESTIMATED EXPENSES

PROMOTION	AMOUNT	POST-PROJECT CHARGES	AMOUNT
Planning (inc. travel)	$	Proceedings, writing & edit	$
Brochures & Advertising		Printing of proceedings	
Mailing-postage, clerical		Mailing proceedings	
Other		Evaluation questionnaire	
		Certificates	
		Other	

INSTRUCTION		TOTAL DIRECT COSTS	
Project chairman*		OVERHEAD (Computed % of	
Speakers (No.)		direct costs)	
Instructional materials		Percentage recommended	
Projectionist/Film rental		%	
Notebook covers, mimeo		Breakfasts ( )	
Lab materials & supplies		Lunches ( )	
Other		Dinners ( )	

SPECIAL FEATURES		EXPENSE—GRAND TOTAL	
Entertainment, tours, etc.		ESTIMATED INCOME	
Complimentary meals			
Housing for registrants		Estimated enrollments:	
Tickets, name tags			
Extra clerical help		maximum _____	
University transport		minimum _____	
Rental of space, janitor		Recommended fee per	
Other		individual $ _____	
		or per group $ _____	
		Income from	
		Registrations	
		Sale of proceedings	
ADDITIONAL COMMENTS:		Other	
		INCOME—GRAND TOTAL	
		NET INCOME	
*Salary/Honorarium and travel costs		NET LOSS	

Person Submitting Worksheet _____

Front of worksheet.

291

Final Costs

CONTINUING EDUCATION DIVISION
UNIVERSITY OF MAINE
FINANCIAL STATEMENT ON INFORMAL PROJECT

Center: _____ Date: _____

Submit one copy to the State Director of Continuing Education Division <u>after</u> completion of project.

Name of Project: _____

Group Served: _____

Project Date(s): _____ Location: _____

ACTUAL EXPENSE

PROMOTION	AMOUNT	POST-PROJECT CHARGES	AMOUNT
Planning (inc. travel)	$	Proceedings, writing & edit	$
Brochures & Advertising		Printing of proceedings	
Mailing-postage, clerical		Mailing proceedings	
Other		Evaluation questionnaire	
		Certificates	
		Other	
INSTRUCTION		TOTAL DIRECT COSTS	
Project chairman*		OVERHEAD (Computed % of	
Speakers (No.)		direct costs)	
Instructional materials		Percentage recommended	
Projectionist/Film rental		_____%	
Notebook covers, mimeo			
Lab materials & supplies		Breakfasts ( )	
Other		Lunches ( )	
		Dinners ( )	
SPECIAL FEATURES		EXPENSE—Grand Total	
Entertainment, tours, etc.		ACTUAL INCOME	
Complimentary meals			
Housing for registrants		Number registered	
Tickets, name tags		Fee charged:	
Extra clerical help		Individual $	
University transport		or Group $	
Rental of space, janitor			
Other		ACTUAL INCOME	
		ACTUAL NET INCOME	
		ACTUAL NET LOSS	

*Salary/Honorarium
and travel costs   Administrative Head _____

Used by permission of John M. Blake, Director of Continuing Education, University of Maine

Back of worksheet.

DATE _____

TOPIC _____

COURSE _____ INSTITUTE _____ CONFERENCE _____

SUGGESTED DEPARTMENT _____

INSTRUCTOR _____ TEL NO. _____

LOCATION _____ ROOM NO. _____

NO. OF SESSIONS _____ HOURS _____

BEGINNING DATE _____ TIME _____ DAY _____

Topic: ⟶_____ Lecturer _____

Social Security No. _____

COOPERATING AGENCIES _____ TEL NO. _____

CONTACT PERSON(S) _____ TEL NO. _____

ADDRESS _____

FEES _____ BILL _____

PROMOTION _____ MAILING LIST _____

INITIATOR _____

COPIES SENT TO:

_____
INSTRUCTOR

_____
CONTACT PERSON

_____
EXTENSION DIRECTOR

_____
DEPARTMENT HEAD

Questions that must be answered in order for a program in adult education to be organized and executed effectively. This has proved to be a useful program guide.

ADULT PROGRAM DEVELOPMENT*

Some concerns to remember in program planning and development are:
I. Overall Concerns
   A. Democratic concept - all participants are to be equally served.
   B. Regional and area needs differ - assess and/or survey real needs.
   C. Administrational function often determines success of program.
II. Availability of Programs
   A. Non-credit course tailored to special needs
   B. Credit course
   C. Short term education for special needs of special information
   D. Conferences, seminars, and workshops designed to inform special clients
   E. Forum or lecture series to discuss issues or gather information
   F. Home instruction for confined clients via correspondence courses, TV, radio, newspapers, or other non-traditional techniques.
   G. Consultants to address special short term needs.
III. Determination of Facilities Useful for Programs
   A. Traditional type of educational program in non-traditional facility.
   B. Traditional type of educational program at a non-traditional time
   C. Non-traditional educational program in unique setting
IV. Survey of Available Resources
   A. Local government - recreation programs, service agencies, fire departments, police departments, city maintenance crews
   B. Local civic service groups - Elks, Eagles, Kiwanis, Rotary, B.P.W., Boy/Girl Scouts, Red Cross
   C. Religious/church organizations
   D. State government - Arizona Department of Economic Security, Department of transportation, Attorney General's Office
   E. State professional organizations - Arizona Education Association, Arizona Bar Association, Arizona Medical Association, Arizona Board of Accounting
   F. Federal agencies - Social Security, HEW, . . .
V. Development of Resource File
   A. 4 x 8 card file with pre-printed information:

1. names of people (organizations, groups)
2. address and telephone contact person
3. type and kinds of assistance available
4. people with special skills or techniques
5. subject matter resources
6. equipment availability (transportation, A/V, training)
7. facilities by type and special service

B. Develop lists of possible funding sources

VI. Survey of Clients
A. Socio-economic survey (age, sex, income, race, ethnic composition, number, types of common interests/experiences)
B. Educational levels
C. Previous services offered
D. Services offered by whom
E. Services offered where
F. Organizational structure for services
G. Types of promotion/advertising done
H. Determine what they say they need
I. Determine what other sources say they need
J. Determine resources available
K. Develop

VII. Evaluation

* Used by permission - Dr. George L. Lepchenski, Assistant Campus Dean, Lake Havasu City Campus, Mohave Community College, Arizona

STEPS IN PROGRAM PLANNING
1. Establish planning committee and/or advisory committee.
2. Identify problems or discover needs of the particular group.
3. State objectives in such a way that they imply changes in behavior of individuals.
4. Determine the subject areas.
5. Determine the criteria for selecting the instructional staff.
6. Select the instructional staff.
7. Determine the methods of presentation.
8. Select the instructional materials.
9. Develop pre-conference activities such as a suggested list of readings, study materials, assignments, radio and/or TV programs, publicity, and mailing lists.
10. Relate objectives, methods, and individual participants to problems and needs.
11. Construct a budget.
12. Establish cost.
13. Select participants for the program

14. Inform the prospective participants (promotion).
15. Register the participants.
16. Orient the instructional staff to theprogram.
17. Orient the participants to the program.
18. Arrange the facilities and services to be rendered.
19. Observe the group; i.e., the continuing concern with adult learning and the many aspects of the dynamics of group endeavor.
20. Develop evaluative instruments to measure the effectiveness of the particular program in the light of stated objectives.
21. Administer the evaluative instruments.
22. Develop post-conference activities such as home study, readings, assignments, follow-up, and/or radio programs, proceedings.
23. Analyze and report the results of the evaluation.
24. Prepare a final report on the program including financial statement.

PROGRAM DESIGN: TIME SEQUENCE

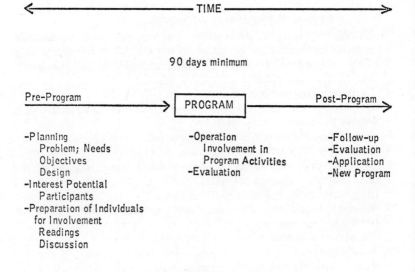

<------------------------- TIME ------------------------->

90 days minimum

Pre-Program   → | PROGRAM | ———— Post-Program →

-Planning
  Problem; Needs
  Objectives
  Design
-Interest Potential
  Participants
-Preparation of Individuals
  for Involvement
  Readings
  Discussion

-Operation
  Involvement in
  Program Activities
-Evaluation

-Follow-up
-Evaluation
-Application
-New Program

Voluntary versus Involuntary Participation
A Primary Consideration

For those of us who have had to work with adults who come to a program out of their voluntary interest, we know that developing a program in this manner or having a captive audience are **two quite different things.** If your program depends upon continuing the interest of a group, it would behoove you to involve the learners in their program planning at the early stages.

Those who work in cooperative or general extension know that adults feel they should be taken in on the objectives of the course and want to participate in the success of the outcome. To have the participants in a class feel a responsibility for the success of a program is an art well worth cultivating for adult educators. If you have a structured classroom where students are there because they **must** be, you may be sure of attendance, but you can seldom be sure of the amount of learning and retention.

Informal orientation sessions can prove to be of inestimable value for "loosening up" the adult, so that there will be participation and a give-and-take. It is well known that the adult learner reacts not only to planned learning experiences but to the total setting in which learning takes place, the **gestalt.** I feel quite certain that more "real learning" often takes place in the clashing of ideas during the coffee break than in the more structured classroom sessions in my adult education classes. Adult students will try out ideas on each other if the academic climate permits.

The Dilemma Facing Adult Educators

A central problem in successful programming is to identify accurately what people want, think they need, and actually do need, and to incorporate these into a realistic, well-organized, and concerted series of forceful activities.11 The dilemma for the educator is how to reconcile what is seen as a need for preserving the integrity of the subject matter and the institution, as contrasted with involving people in the kind of educational experiences they see as meaningful.12

This states the dilemma of adult educators. They must find areas of interest to adults which will attract them to the program. If they are in an institution of higher learning, they must in addition find subject matter that will attract faculty or teachers to do the instruction. This is a part of the art of program and curriculum planning necessary to be an effective administrator.

Scott C. Fletcher, for many years president of the Fund for Adult Education, in a speech to the Oklahoma Adult Education Association, argued that the curriculum for adult education should be built around the "Four Roles in Life." He suggests that the view of continuing education as remedial is based on the misconception that education is a "concluded achievement" instead of an "endless process".

Fletcher contends that a more accurate conception is that the most serious deficiency is the lack of insatiable curiosity and a need for a systematic program of "boundlessly extending one's knowledge and understanding." ▨ Arguing that no education is as practical as a comprehensive continuing liberal education, Fletcher offers the following four life roles as a basis for building a curriculum or program for educating adults:

Decisions as an individual
Decisions in the home
Decisions on the job
Decisions as a citizen

Using this framework for programs for adults, the adult educator then brings skills into focus with the best vision of the learner. The task is to organize, design, and execute situations for maximum learning. The capacity to learn must be emphasized - not just the advancement of learning about subjects and current issues. The task of the educator is to help the adult formulate objectives and to take an active part in the process of re-education. The adult must continually be made aware that the learning process is something that happens within the individual, and must be initiated internally with the help of the educator.

SUMMARY

We examined Ralph W. Tyler's approach to curriculum planning: purposes of the institution, what experiences provided to attain these purposes, how are experiences effectively organized, and how can we know purposes have been attained. We looked at studies of the learners as a source for educational objectives. We contrasted a "planning with" approach to a "planning for" methodology in program planning.

Havighurst's Developmental tasks are considered as a basis for program organization. The community survey is suggested as a way of getting program ideas, and Samuel E. Hand's approach to community study is suggested.

Various techniques for Cultivating Program ideas including Speaker's Directories, advisory committees, and consultants are presented. Program sheets are presented, along with some concrete steps in program planning and development. Fifty steps to a successful conference are presented as a check list for the program planner.

➡️50 STEPS TO A SUCCESSFUL CONFERENCE ●

WEEKS BEFORE CONFERENCE	30 29 28 27 26 25 24 23 22 21 20 19 18 17 16 15 14 13 12 11 10 9 8 7 6 5 4 3 2 1 0 1 2 3 4 5
1. Suggest program	
2. Define audience	
3. Determine needs	
4. Contact associations/publications	
5. Interview potential attendees	
6. Review available lists	
7. Review previous critiques*	
8. Write previous attendees*	
9. Review competitive programs	
10. List subjects (10 to 50)	
11. Draft theme/title	
12. Determine price	
13. Establish program budget	
14. Select coordinator/moderator	
15. Check conflicting programs	
16. Determine location/dates	
17. Prepare subjects/speakers list	
18. Invite speakers, follow w/phone	
19. Select and order mailing lists	
20. Select publication list/publicity	
21. Prepare/send first press release	
22. Contact accepting speakers weekly	
23. Design brochure	
24. Edit bios/abstracts as received	
25. Prepare brochure copy	
26. Get printing quotations	
27. Send final copy to artist	
28. Approve brochure for print	
29. Print brochure	
30. Establish inquiry procedure	
31. Order workbooks	
32. Prepare workbook materials	
33. Send labels to mailing house	
35. Start mailing	
36. Prepare/send more press releases	
37. Establish registration procedure	
38. Determine speaker time schedule	
39. Review A/V requirements	
40. Select on-site personnel	
41. Prepare on-site materials	
42. Send welcome letters	
43. Arrive at location	
44. HOLD CONFERENCE	
45. Prepare final class list	
46. Send attendee certificates	
47. Correspond with speakers	
48. Correspond with attendees	
49. Correspond with attendee firms	
50. Evaluate critiques	
WEEKS BEFORE CONFERENCE	30 29 28 27 26 25 24 23 22 21 20 19 18 17 16 15 14 13 12 11 10 9 8 7 6 5 4 3 2 1 0 1 2 3 4 5

* = repeat programs only   ➡️ = start activity   ● = complete activity

50 STEPS TO A SUCCESSFUL CONFERENCE

©1976 Bureau of Business & Technology, Inc., 101 Park Avenue, New York, New York 10017 • 212-889-5315

Used by permission of Jerome Prager

299

PROGRAMMING

Questions
1. How would you program "with" the mature adult?
2. How would you go about developing a set of objectives for a course?
3. How would you find out about your adult learners?
4. How would you use Havighurst and Orr's "adult needs" for program planning? Developmental tasks?
5. How would you approach a credit vs. non-credit offering in program planning?
6. How would you use Tyler's structural frame for choosing "educational objectives?"
7. How would you use a needs assessment? A Community Survey, in planning an adult education program? Census data?
8. How would you cultivate program ideas?
9. How would you use the program form in developing your program?
10. How would you use the list of residential centers listed in the back of the book?

Bibliography

Alford, Harold. **Residential Centers for Continuing Education: A Design for Lifelong Learning.** New York: Wiley, 1968.

Bergevin, Paul, et al. **Adult Education Procedures.** Greenwich, Conn.: Seabury Press, 1963.

Brower, Stephen L. **Dilemma of Adult Educators,** Journal of Cooperative Extension (Summer 1964), p. 114.

Chancellor, John. **Helping Adults to Learn, The Library in Action.** Chicago: American Library Association, 1939.

Dyer, John. **Ivory Towers in the Market Place.** Indianapolis: Bobbs-Merrill, 1956.

Fletcher, Scott C. **The Battle of the Curriculum.** Washington, D.C.: Fund for Adult Education, 1958.

Hand, Samuel E. **An Outline of a Community Survey for Program Planning in Adult Education,** Bulletin 71F-1, Division of Vocational and Adult Education, State Department of Edcation, Tallahassee, Fla., March 29, 1960.

Havighurst, Robert J., and Betty Orr. **Adult Education and Adult Needs, Center for the Study of Liberal Education for Adults,** 1956.

Houle, Cyril O. **The Design of Education.** San Francisco, Jossey Bass. 1972. Provides a systematic blueprint--or design--for planning, setting up, implementing, reconstructing, improving, and evaluating adult and continuing eudcation programs--a workable system that can be tailored to fit any educational situation for any kind of student. Adult learning situations are classified into categories; step-by-step procedures for putting programs for each category into effect are provided. An annotated bibliographic essay is included. Contents: 1. Credos and Systems 2. Fundamental System 3. Four Cases 4. Categories of Educational Situations 5. Development of Program Design 6. Major Program Reconstruction. 7. The System in Perspective.

Houle, Cyril O. **The External Degree.** San Francisco, Jossey Bass. 1973.

Knowles, Malcolm (ed.). **Handbook of Adult Education.** Washington, D.C.: Adult Education Association, 1960, p. 82.

Knowles, Malcolm. **Modern Practice of Adult Education. Association** Press, 1977 (Outlines a practical procedure for organizing a program)

Leagans, J. Paul. **A Concept of Needs.** Journal of Cooperative Extension (Summer 1964), p. 90.

Morgan, Barton; Holmes, Glenn; and Bundy, Clarence. **Methods** in Adult Education, Interstate Printers and Publishers, Inc. Danville, Ill. 1963. (deals with various participation techniques)

Siegle, Peter E., and James B. Whipple. **New Directions in Programming for University Adult Education.** Chicago: Center for the Study of Liberal Education for Adults, 1957.

Smith, Aker, and Kidd. **Handbook of Adult Education. Mac-**Millan, N.Y. 1970. (See Part III, Program Areas, p. 397)

Snow, Robert H. **Community Adult Education.** New York: Putnam, 1955.

Tyler, Ralph W. **Principles of Curriculum and Instruction.** Chicago: U. of Chicago Press, 1950, pp. 1-2

Ziegler, Jesse H. **Focus on Adults.** Elgin: Brethren Press, 1965.

FOOTNOTES CHAPTER 17

1 Ralph W. Tyler, **Principles of Curriculum and Instruction**, U. of Chicago Press, 1950, pp. 1-2.

2 Robert J. Havighurst and Betty Orr, "Adult Education and Adult Needs," Center for the Study of Liberal Education for Adults, Washington, D.C., 1956.

3 Malcolm Knowles (ed.), **Handbook of Adult Education**, Adult Education Association, U.S.A., Washington, D.C.: 1960, p. 82.

4 **Ibid.**

5 Samuel E. Hand, "An Outline of a Community Survey for Program Planning in Adult Education," Bulletin 71F-1, Division of Vocational and Adult Education, State Department of Education, Tallahassee, Fla., March 29, 1960.

6 **Adult Education**, Vol. 3, No. 5 (June 1966).

7 **Ibid.**, p. 2.

8 See Alex F. Osborn, **Applied Imagination**, 3rd ed., Scribner's, New York, 1963.

9 Roger W. Axford, "How to Survive a Convention," **Adult Leadership**, Vol. 11, No. 9 (March 1963), pp. 265-267.

10 Roger W. Axford (ed.), **College Community Consultation**, Enlightenment Press, Dekalb, Ill., 1967.

11 J. Paul Leagans, "A Concept of Needs," **Journal of Cooperative Extension** (Summer 1964), p. 90.

12 Stephen L. Brower, "Dilemma of Adult Educators," **Journal of Cooperative Extension** (Summer 1964), p. 114.

13 Scott C. Fletcher, **The Battle of the Curriculum**, Fund for Adult Education, 1958.

Chapter XVIII

PROMOTING THE
ADULT EDUCATION PROGRAM

Effective publicity requires having a nose for news, a talent for assembling it, and tenacity to carry through to the right media.

-The Quill, a magazine for journalists
published by Sigma Delta Chi

The best adult education program in the world may die a silent death for lack of promotion. The idea that the world will beat a path to the door of the man who has invented a better mousetrap may be true in some fields, but, unfortunately, does not often apply to our field. After a quality program is in operation and clientele has been built, then the promotional task becomes increasingly simplified. But the people must know what is available to them **before** they can partake of the wealth of knowledge represented in many excellent programs of adult and continuing education.

THE BIG FOUR AND THE FUNDAMENTAL FIVE

It is an axiom that voluntary programs require promotion and publicity. One experienced adult educator, Ralph Rohling, Office of the Illinois Superintendent of Public Instruction, puts it this way: "We are competing with the big four: beer, booze, bowling and the boob tube!"

The means of promotion may be as simple as a word-of-mouth campaign, a radio announcement, an item in the college newspaper, or an article in the women's column. But the people **must** know! The fundamental five of the journalistic field is as basic today as it was when the first newspaper went to press: **Who? What? When? Why?** The seasoned educator of adults will learn the various methods of promoting programs and will develop the skill most productive for the particular community. The most effective educators of adults have their fingers on the pulse of the communications media in their communities and know many of the reporters, radio announcers, and other media men by their first names. Fortunate is the program planner who has a part-time or full-time promotion person on the staff of the agency of adult education.

Mailing lists and former students are the best potential for future programs, and the mature adult program will have built up a clientele of continuing learners who can give advice, disseminate information and suggest new program areas.

HOW ADULT EDUCATORS LOOK AT AND USE PROMOTION

Some testimonies from persons working in the field will throw light on the way adult educators look at promotion.

"Promotion is one of the most difficult tasks in adult education," says Mary Ann Diller, a seasoned educator of adults in Danville, Illinois, and head of a successful program. "My personal philosophy concerning this phase of adult education is to use every possible medium to promote until the public is completely saturated with publicity-then publicize again." [1]

Jack Jillson, journalist and publications editor, Northern Illinois University, says:

Targeting the message is important, and the accuracy and completeness of the information are imperative for the success of the publicity. One error in dates may cause immeasurable administrative headaches. Careful proofreading by the program administrator will save many errors. [2]

One of the unique promotional devices was that used by librarian Ethel Brann at Lake Geneva, Wisconsin. She approached the two banks in the city and got their cooperation in sending the announcement of spring and fall courses with the bank statements. She found that the Lake Geneva Adult Education Council had a good response to this method of promoting offerings of cultural activities, university courses, and programs of voluntary agencies. Although Lake Geneva is a small town, fourteen adult education agencies cooperated.

In Southern illinois, E. Dean Browning at Alton uses grade school children to get announcements to parents. Says Browning:

As for promotion, before each semester we send information to the local newspaper, local radio station, plant bulletin boards, advisory committee members, and service organizations. We send booklets to all fourth- and fifth-graders in the system each fall to take home to their parents, and we send flyers and booklets to all industrial plants, job shops, and garages in the area. [3]

The brochure seems to be the most widely used medium for for informing adults of learning opportunities, outside of the newspapers. "We have brochures," continues Browning, "at the beginning of each quarter which are mailed throughout the area to those who have been enrollees, to school administrators, and the like. All area papers carry announcements of Mrs. Araminta Bigelow's observations on the value of word-of-mouth promotion: "Word of mouth seems also to be important in the advertising." [4]

Inside of brochure.

Outside of brochure.

Some adult educators have to pay for newspaper advertising, while others have it contributed as a public service. While Richard G. Graves, Director of Adult Education at Waukegan, Illinois, sends out more than 42,000 direct-mail announcements of his night-school bulletin; he also has the cooperation of the local newspaper. "In addition to the mail distribution, we publicize heavily in a local daily newspaper during the registration periods. We do not pay for any advertising outside of direct mail," Graves said. [5]

Ralph R. Rowe, Harvey, Illinois, reports that his adult education office uses the local newspaper to publicize the program and that the agency has had increased enrollments each year. He feels that an active and complete adult education program is one of the best ways of getting taxpayers into the schools. When courses are tailored to the interests and needs of the people of the community, the people will support the adult program.

In Champaign, Illinois, a university town, radio and TV are utilized to promote the adult education story. C. E. Summerville reports that they use the local papers with stories and pictures. But in addition, "We also use the TV and radio media."

Floyd C. Tompkins, for many years Director of Adult Education in the oldest public junior college in the United States, reports that he uses a multimedia approach for telling the story of adult education offerings. Recognizing the difficulty of adequate promotion, Tompkins says, "I am sure that you will find that publicity is no small job. In fact, we think that 'word of mouth' is the best publicity that can be had. We use the radio the newspaper, and also the monthly school report to students."

Gunnar Fransen, Rockford's Director of Public School Adult Education, in Illinois' second largest city, reports that besides brochures which list time, place, and cost of all the courses; he uses newspaper stories, advertisements, television spot announcements (donated as a public service), and an educational committee of various social, civic, industrial, and business organizations.

At one of the Northern universities the training directors, personnel groups, women's clubs, and numerous voluntary organizations are used to tell the story of adult education offerings, including university extension courses, lectures, and radio courses offered during the day and the evening. The university radio station is used for spot announcements to promote the courses to be offered adults on and off the campus.

In Wisconsin, the Milwaukee Council for Adult Learning, representing more than forty agencies of adult education, held one-day conference dealing entirely with the problems and possibilities for telling the adult education story more adequately.

The group annually cooperates with the two major newspapers of the city to produce a Sunday supplement in the **Milwaukee Sentinel** and the **Milwaukee Journal** supported by advertising.

307

The Wisconsin Library Association, through the leadership of an adult educator, Beryl E. Hoyt, held a conference at Lake Geneva, Wisconsin, called a "Public Relations Workshop." These conferences involved newspaper personnel, adult education specialists from the University of Wisconsin, and local library board members. The purpose of the conference was to make the leaders of libraries and the news media more aware of how better to tell their message-how to promote the adult education story.

WE MUST DRAMATIZE OUR WORK

Relating the plot of Sidney Kingley's play, **Dead End**, Milton R. Stern, author of **People, Programs and Persuasion**, tells of a summer night in Manhattan when one of the Dead End kids peered over the garden wall at Sutton Place. Jumping down and stretching out both arms, the youth sweeps into an elaborate strut and yells to his buddies, "Look at me, fellas; I'm dancin'!"

A live, vital program of adult education may be likened unto a vibrant, colorful, aesthetic dance, and the director of adult education may be thought of as the "producer." What adult educators must do, even more than people in other kinds of educational activity, is to call attention to the program...to **dramatize our work.** To Stern, that is what promoting adult education means: using publicity, advertising, direct mail, personal contact, all of these, so that adults enroll in classes, visit cultural events and involve themselves in the life of learning in the community. He describes promotion as the "most pragmatically American of undertakings. If a particular gambit succeeds, then it has been proven worthwhile-at least for the time being." [6] Any adult educator who has the ability to put himself or herself in the place of the reader, listener, the potential partaker of the adult education activity will communicate. As Stern points out, an amateur is message-centered, and a professional is audience-centered.

PROMOTION: 50 PERCENT OF THE BATTLE

Although you may have one of the best programs in the world, if no one knows about it, the cause is lost. "Promotion is 50 percent of the battle," says Ralph Rohling. He adds:

My experience is that some very excellent courses will go for a while, then die off, and then will become popular again. For example, we had rapid reading and it was well attended. Then the attendance fell off. The same with teaching the Russian language. But we kept the rapid reading in the bulletin, and soon it was well attended again. [7]

WHAT'S IN A NAME?

Through years of offering courses, I have found that the title of a course is of utmost importance. For example, in a University Extension offering, we list the course as Family Financial

Management with a topnotch economist instructing. The course failed for lack of adequate enrollment. The next semester we listed the course as How to Manage Your Money, with identical course content and the same instructor, and the program was oversubscribed. What's in a name? A great deal! Perhaps the difference between a course's succeeding and failing.

Titles are very important (says Rohling). For example, if you offer **Basic Electronic Circuitry**, the course may not go, but if you call the same content **TV Assembly and Repair**, adults will flock to take the course. Another from my experience, call a course **Solid-State Electronics**, and the course may not make it. But if you call it **Transistors and Diodes**, men will enroll for the course. I changed **Auto Shop I** to **Engine Tune-Up** and it went well. The title showed the course was for someone who wanted to work with his hands. We deal with practical-minded people; they want to get their hands greasy. The titles have to be in the vernacular of the people, so they understand them.

Promotional material must be put in the language of those who are to be attracted. We must have the ability to project our program offerings in an attractive manner, without the least diluting the content of the course. And good promotion can be the "fun" side of administration.

ANALYSIS OF INFORMATION SOURCES USEFUL

Periodically, every agency of adult education should do some market research. The wise adult educator will try to find out where and how people found out about the program. For example, in the Green Bay area of Wisconsin, a study was made of the sources of information which lead to participants' enrolling in adult education activities in Brown County. The tabulation verified my contention that most persons learn about an adult education activity from another person. Publicity seems to reinforce this method. Of 2,855 persons responding, 1,049, or 36.54 percent, learned of the program from another person. (See accompanying chart. [8])

A STUDY OF PROMOTIONAL TECHNIQUES

While working in a city of over a million people, a group of Wisconsin adult educators found that although we used a number of media for telling the story of offerings in adult and continuing education, only a small percentage of the adult population was involved at any one time. Attempting to learn more of how people found out about our program, we undertook research to try to more intelligently find our public and to inform them more effectively. Our limited research was done on the basis of 742 responses.

Sources of Information Which Led to Participants' Enrolling in Adult Education
Activities in the Green Bay Area

Upper figure: Percentage
Lower figure: Actual number

	Story in *Press-Gazette*	Announcement on television	Announcement on radio program	Announcement mailed from adult education agency	From another person	Other	No response	Total number of participants	Total number of responses	Number of multiple responses
Vocational and Adult School	23.01			12.46	43.09	18.32	2.68			
	275	4	1	149	515	219	32	1,187	1,195	8
Green Bay Center University of Wisconsin	30.05			25.90	17.62	24.87	1.55			
	58			50	34	48	3	192	193	1
Cooperative Extension Service	11.00	1.35	1.35	10.49	46.86	9.98	18.95			
	65	8	8	62	277	59	112	586	591	5
Kellogg Public Library	2.33	1.36	1.36	1.17	17.70	65.18	10.89			
	12	7	7	6	91	335	56	512	514	2
YMCA	24.59	5.74	.82	12.30	44.26	11.48	.82			
	30	7	1	15	54	14	1	122	122	0
YWCA	18.18	1.82		9.09	33.64	11.82	25.45			
	20	2		10	37	13	28	110	110	0
Neville Public Museum	8.90	5.48	.68	2.72	27.88	42.84	10.88			
	13	8	1	4	41	63	16	146	146	0
Totals	16.47	1.25	.63	10.31	36.54	26.16	8.64			
	473	36	18	296	1,049	751	248	2,855	2,871	16

We examined four media, each of which had been used with some success: a catalog of courses, newspaper advertising, group-course mailings, and individual course mailings. The findings of the survey are as follows:

Catalog: Direct-mail promotion to the general adult education list through the catalog produced 51 percent of the keyed

310

responses. The Director of Publications advised on the basis of this response that the catalog should be considered the best medium at that time. A schoolboard catalog accounted for 8 percent and involved no expense to the university.

Newspaper Advertising: The Adult Education Supplements of the **Milwaukee Journal** and **Sentinel** produced 9 percent of the 10.9 percent response attributable to newspaper advertising.

Grouped Course Mailings: Of the groups' course mailings, we found the mailings to women in the greater Milwaukee area most successful, accounting for 19 percent of the keyed response. This was a flyer including women's daytime learning, art courses, music, and counseling sessions. This response was no surprise, since the lists used were of women who had actively expressed an interest in continuing education. It was suggested that the women's list be added to the General Education List. The other group-course self-mailers yielded 4 percent, such as Engineering, Commerce, and Nursing Continuing Education. It was recommended that a centralized list with great selectivity be maintained with at least one full-time person utilizing equipment which would rapidly allow selectivity for lists.

Individual Course Mailings: This included such mailings as the Chicago Symphony subscriber's invitation list for Symphony Concert Previews (mimeographed, with 15 responses). A flyer on "Trees and Plants for Cities and Suburbs" brought only three responses from the mailing, although the class was well attended. It was recommended that we should continue such mailings where interest is a special interest. It was suggested, however, that where interest is diffuse and hard to pinpoint, we would be better off taking a small announcement ad in a broad newspaper medium than using direct mail trial and error.

Although many agencies use direct mail extensively in adult education, it appears that few educational institutions use professional counsel or employ a specialist on their staffs for this purpose. This is a weakness. In visiting university extension divisions throughout the country, I know of few places where direct-mail expertise is employed in a systematic fashion. The University of California and Marquette University are among the few I know using direct-mail professionals for some of their promotional programs, although undoubtedly there are more.

ADULT EDUCATION IS NEWS

I have found that adult education, like elementary and secondary education can be news. In Wisconsin, the author approached the Associated Press and found the AP people receptive to a series of articles dealing with the growing participation of adults in continuing education. The articles were carried for a period of two weeks, one per day, and reached thousands of people through sixteen newspapers which used the series. Called "Never Too Old to Learn," the articles brought response from businessmen, educators, and persons interested in learning more about agencies offering programs.

While teaching for Florida State University, I found the same interest in the growing field of adult education. The Florida Associated Press assigned me to write a series, again entitled "Never Too Old to Learn," and the topics included:

Opportunities await if you yearn to learn.

Florida Institute for Continuing University Studies takes University to Students.

Extension service plays changing role.

Adults earn one out of ten high school diplomas.

Opportunities beckon to women.

Adults live in to study.

Illiteracy in state is above U.S. average.

Libraries are big factor in education.

The series was released from St. Petersburg by the **St. Petersburg Times**, and was carried by twelve major papers throughout Florida. I received letters from persons wanting to complete their high school education, calls from adults desiring to learn of opportunities to update their training, and even inquiries from persons retiring from military service who decided they would like to go back to school and get a degree. The Florida Institute of Continuing University Studies, the off-campus agency for taking university courses throughout the state at that time published the series as a booklet, "Never Too Old to Learn," and distributed it to educators and the general public upon request. [9]

THE ADVISORY COMMITTEE AS A PROMOTION
MEDIA

The advisory committee, made up of persons who know the program area and the persons who should benefit from an adult education program, is a gold mine for getting the word to the right people. I have seen programs filled with participants because the advisory committee helping to structure the sessions knew where the people were who would most benefit. They knew mailing lists and the names of keepers of the lists. Often they volunteered to have the envelopes addressed in their offices if they "felt involved."

The success of a musical series may depend upon involving the secretary of the community orchestra, the chairperson of the women's federated clubs, the symphony series chairperson, or the local music consultant of the public schools.

Don't try going it alone! If you do, you may also find yourself alone on opening night of the adult program series.

A kindling of self-interest and effective efforts toward professional success as vital factors in the promotion of virtually any project must also be applied to adult education. Courses tailored and targeted to the interests and needs of a particular community will bring support for the adult program if wisely promoted.

Then comes the challenging problem of how to reach most effectively the potential public with an attractive series of academic offerings. Among the successful publicity channels are distribution through direct mail, with bank statements, through school children, by brochures, by newspaper advertising, by individual flyers, through distribution of catalogues at supermarket checkout counters, in Sunday supplements, on TV, and by word-of-mouth advertising. Each media has its special impact, and no one method is a panacea for the educator of adults. The secret is multiplicity of effort.

COOPERATING FOR EFFECTIVE PROMOTION

Because few adult educators have extensive experience with promotional techniques such as direct mail, advertising campaigns, news articles, radio and TV promotion, and because few have at their disposal the professional advice and counsel necessary, groups of adult educators would be wise to come together to learn all they can about techniques of promotion, publicity, and public relations.

The entire field staff of the University of Wisconsin Extension Division, comprising more than forty full-time adult educators, spent two days in a workshop dealing with publicity and promotion. A direct-mail expert was brought in. Case studies of different approaches to methods of interesting a special public were examined. For example, the man who worked with the group had sold brushes, including push brooms for cleaning factories. His direct-mail program had replaced nineteen salesmen. But he found that in an area of the South, although personal letters went to the individuals responsible for purchasing from the president of the company, no sales came from these factories. A visit to the area disclosed the fact that no brooms are used in the mills of this Southern region-because sticks with carpeting attached are more effective for collecting lint and tufts. Mailing to this target area was of course discontinued.

As educators, we must periodically take the same kind of hard look at our promotion. Educational institutions are notoriously wasteful in using amateur methods to try to tell and sell their story. By groups of adult educators coming together to examine promotional methods and to seek modern and professional techniques for promoting a quality product, we will be able to serve the public better. It would be an economical move for a number of adjacent institutions working in adult education to engage a direct mail or promotion firm to handle their mailing lists and campaigns and to develop interest finders. Such money would be well spent, although private institutions will undoubtedly find this easier to accomplish than public institutions. Some uneasiness may come from the fear that conservative elements of taxpayers would charge the institution with going "Madison Avenue," not realizing that the minor investment, as in business, brings greater returns. Public institutions too often consider that if adults want to learn, they will somehow find out about offerings and will beat a path to the door of the academic Mecca, regardless of the distance from the adult learner. Promotion, propinquity, and public awareness are essential to a successful program of adult education.

Councils of adult education, developing state organizations within the National Association for Public Continuing and Adult Education, and the Adult Education Association, U.S.A., can take initiative in sponsoring such workshops for promoting more effectively the adult education story. We must have the faith that if the people know, they will go and grow intellectually.

Where there is not always the availability of a professional public relations person, an adult educator is often forced to write "copy" for the local newspaper or stations. This could be an entire chapter in itself, but the adjoining table of twenty hints from Wallace Wikoff, a veteran newspaper man who later joined the public information department of a large university, may serve to guide such an adult educator.

Wikoff also warns-and we use the verb advisedly - that the adult educator who feels he or she can substitute academic language for journalese in writing stories for local editors is doing adult education a great disservice.

TWENTY QUESTIONS FOR A NEWS WRITER

1. Are there unnecessary words, sentences, paragraphs?
2. Am I sure of my "facts"?
3. Have I presented all sides?
4. Have I properly identified everyone in the story?
5. Have I given enough background for the reader to under-

stand?

6. How does the story relate in importance to the total number of stories destined for that issue?
7. Are there any double meanings that will confuse the reader?
8. Am I editorializing?
9. Am I using "loaded" words?
10. Have I checked all of my spelling?
11. Am I using common English or relying on the language of my profession?
12. Should this have been a straight story or a feature?
13. Would direct quotes improve my story?
14. Am I bowing to a pressure group?
15. Am I injecting my own self-interest or bias?
16. Am I being repetitious?
17. Am I guilty of the "halo effect"?
18. Am I being fair to my readers? my editor?
19. Have I researched properly?
20. Will I be proud to admit that I wrote the article?

The above list was designed for the reporter who has to write all types of stories and "compete" with other reporters for space. The listing, is applicable here because it will help the adult educator understand the problems of the press. Most of all, it will train the adult educator to "speak their language."

AN ANNUAL RECRUITING PLAN

The plan described herein is a complex, interrelated series of sub-plans. The sub-plans are each designed to be pursued more or less separately, but together comprise a comprehensive multi-phased attack. The sub-plans are as follows:

1. The School District Plan - designed to involve all district employees in the recruitment process.
2. The Under 20 Plan - designed to recruit those recent high school grads who are under 20 years of age, and are thus reimbursable.
3. The Institutional Plan - to identify new institutional markets and sell management on the development of a program.
4. The Advertising Plan - to develop a "theme" which will focus community attention on Continuing Education Programs.
5. The Brochure - Similar to successful brochures in the past.
6. The Assistant Principal's Plan - to concentrate upon former and current students (the old "Bird in the Hand" trick) and walk-in registrations.

7. The War Department - to monitor the registration process, and build morale of personnel.
8. The Census Tract Plan - to prioritize specific areas for efficient door-to-door recruiting by centralized teams.

When viewed as a total entity, the plan is a cohesive sophisticated approach to the recruitment of adult students.

- - -

**Thanks to Dr. Thomas Rosenthal, Adult Education Program, Pontiac, Michigan

SCHOOL DISTRICT INVOLVEMENT PLAN

Responsible Administrator:
Description
This plan will involve all school district employees and related groups as recruiters for the credit/non-credit Continuing Education Program. The purpose of this plan is to:
1. Identify potential adult education students and refer them to the Continuing Education Department for follow-up by a professional adult educator.
2. Have school district personnel serve in the capacity as an advisory recruiting committee.
3. Develop a total school district commitment for support of adult education.
Specific groups or individuals to be involved might include the superintendent, executive board, management teacm, coordinating council, elementary/secondary principals, Title 1 commitee, PTA, and community aids.

Implementation
April   Identify all school groups to be contacted.
April   Develop a presentation for these groups regarding adult education, specifics on how they can assist, and what it means to them.
May-June   Set up several groups or multigroups presentations to:
            1. Solicit letters of support
            2. Select recruiting laiasons for each group.
            3. Select recruiting advisory council members.
July-Sept. Follow-up through regularly scheduled advisory council meetings through fourth Friday.
October   Develop an evaluation of the effectiveness of this plan.

316

UNDER 20 PLAN

Responsible Administrator:

Description

This plan will involve the identification of high school graduates and high school drop outs for the school year (from Pontiac Northern, Pontiac Central, and Pontiac Catholic). These students, who are under 20 as of September 1, will be identified and sent one of two letters of invitation letting them know that they are eligible to take classes in the Pontiac Adult Education Program. The letter to High School Grads will describe the new college preparation program, vocational education, and other educational opportunities available to them free of charge. The letter to the drop outs will describe our high school completion program, alternative education program, C/COAP, G.E.D., vocational, and other services such as placement, testing and counseling that is available to them. A postage paid return card will identify those students who are interested. In August, a phone call or home visit will be conducted from a central operation.

time Line

March	Contact each of the schools to obtain lists of graduates and high school drop outs.
April	Prepare mailing labels and envelopes.
May	Conduct an inservice meeting for all high school counselors to let them know of this new program; ask for their assistance.
June	Mail information and return card to all grads and drop outs.
August	Have a central recruiting team contact each student when it conducts its house-to-house campaign in August.
August	Each positive response will be followed up by an Assistant Principal contact for enrollment.

INSTITUTIONAL/INDUSTRIAL PLAN

Responsible Administrator:

Plan Description

This plan is to focus attention upon programs operated in institutional and industrial settings. The growth and development of programs currently in operation, as well as the potential establishment of new programs are the major goals.

Through April 8 Potential growth areas should be identified and prioritized and key contact persons i-

317

dentified.

April 11-May   A team of 2 administrators meet with contact persons for each operational program to discuss:
1. Plans for advertising, enrolling, and attendance of students.
2. Specific plans to expand the existing program.

April 11   A presentation be developed to illustrate the advantages of a Continuing Education program for an institution or industry. The presentation to include:
1. A display book
2. Specific handouts illustrating program components.

April 11-May   A team of 2 administrators meet with representatives of identified institutions or industries to initiate new programs.

May-June   Follow-up on the best prospect for new programs and/or expanded programs. Begin implementation of new and/or expanded programs. This should be done by the team of administrators.

June   Establish specific plans for recruitment at each program site.

WAR DEPARTMENT

Responsible Administrator:

Description

This plan is designed to continually monitor the enrollment progress and to create an environment and/or climate conducive to maintaining a high level of motivation for all recruiters during the month of September. To accomplish this a room similar to a political headquarters will be established at Eastern. All recruiters and/or Assistant Principals for Continuing Education will report three days each week at a specific time to turn in all enrollment forms. Enrollments for each Assistant Principal will be charted. This time will also be used for mini inservice sessions, pep talks, brainstorming, and problem solving. In order to accommodate all involved staff, an early morning session and a late afternoon session will be conducted each day.

Time Line

July   Plan the specific operation of the war room including such things as personnel needs, decor, charts, mini inservice sessions, pep talks, and other specifics to insure its success.

318

August   Set up the war room.
September   Implement the use of the war room.

1977-78 RECRUITMENT ADVERTISING
Responsible Administrator:
Plan Description

The primary goal of the advertising campaign is to systematically develop a specific theme which would ultimately form community attention on Continuing Education. The theme must be creative and attention getting. Further, the campaign should be separated into two distinct phases as follows:

1. **Build-up campaign** - The impetus of this phase is to begin to draw attention and elicit curiosity. This phase will "tease" the collective curiosity of Pontiac residents and begin to direct their attention toward the peak-time campaign.

2. **Peak-time campaign** - Designed to acutely focus attention. This phase should coordinate with brochure release and other key events near the end of August.

Time Line

April   Theme identified - developed
May   Materials developed and ordered
                     1. Graphic layout - design.
                     2. Billboard location, etc.
                     3. Locations for posters identified.
July 15-Aug. 19   Lead-up campaign operational - billboards, posters, etc.
Aug. 22-Sept. 30   Peak period campaign operational - this should coordinate with brochure mailing.

ASSISTANT PRINCIPALS FOR
CONTINUING EDUCATION
RECRUITING PLAN
Responsible Administrator:
Plan Description

The primary functions of Assistant Principals in the overall recruiting plan are as follows:

1. Recruiting current and past students.
2. Follow-up on interested individuals as identified by centralized plans.
3. Implement an opening registration plan for the efficient processing of "walk-in" students.
4. Development of a plan to insure that those students registered attend class.

319

Time Line

April-May   Prior to the end of the current semester the following steps should be completed:

1. Pertinent fall information given to all current students.
2. Current students should be asked to complete "interest" cards.
3. Current students asked to refer friends and relatives for summer contact.
4. Specific graduates identified as potential recruiters. A mailing should be prepared for a "preferred client", advanced mailing of brochure, etc.

Aug. 25-Sept. 9   An efficient system to contact interested persons identified by the central plans should be developed and implemented by each Assistant Principal.

Sept. 2-30   An efficient system for processing walk-in registrants is essential.

Sept. 12-30   A follow-up system for "no-shows" must be implemented.

CENSUS TRACT RECRUITING

Responsible Administrator:

Plan Description

Each street in the city will be identified by census tract number. The residents living on each street will be identified house by house using Bressler's. Every student in our program living within the school district will be identified street-by-street.

Recruiters will be identified to work in a central recruiting program. These may be CETA personnel, and possibly teacher assistants and career advisors. They will be inserviced in door-to-door recruiting techniques.

Streets will be listed by census tract so that the streets with the highest percentage potential of non-high school adult graduates will be first. Recruiters will recruit utilizing these prioritized street guides and will operate from a central recruiting base. Their function will be to contact each potential non-grad household to inform them of the adult education opportunities open to them. They will not enroll students, but will complete an information form which will indicate interest on the part of potential students. These forms will be turned in to the central office daily and in turn will be given to the Assistant Principal either closest to the potential student, or the Assistant Principal whose program the student indicates he/she wishes to attend.

The adults who are already in our program and living in a target neighborhood, will be used by the recruiter to obtain referrals of other neighbors who might be interested in our program. The recruiter will also be responsible for follow-up of the high school grad program and the drop out program.

After the adult has indicated interest, the Assistant Principal will follow up to insure that the adult has in fact enrolled and has been in attendance in his program.

Time Line

March 1-15	Identify each street by census tract.
March 15-30	Copy each street resident list out of Bress-
April 1-15	ler's. Analyze census tract data to determine the priority for home contact for each street.
April 15-May 30	Identify all potential door-to-door recruiters.
June 1-15	Contact by letter and phone all potential recruiters outlining their summer responsibilities.
June 1-15	Plan a comprehensive three day recruiter inservice.
June 17-19	Recruiter Inservice.
June 20-Aug. 30	Recruiters will be involved in the door-to-door student indentification plan. 1. Recruiters will meet centrally every day to be given their recruiting assignment for the day. 2. Potential student cards will be turned in each day.
September	All potential adult students will be contacted by a professional adult educator for enrollments.

BROCHURE

Responsible Administrator:
Description

The brochure will be similar to the previous brochure in kind and format consisting of 12 to 16 pages, 2 colors and in newsprint.

Time Line

April 22	Preliminary course schedule will be developed by the Assistant Principals and be ready.
April 22-May 15	Review process will each Assistant Principal will take place to finalize the brochure content.

May 23	Brochure course and program content will be finalized.
May 23-June 16	Brochure design and layout will take place.
June 16	Brochure will be finalized and copy ready.
July 14	Brochure will go to the printer.
August 1	Brochure will be delivered to schools for recruiting.
August 1-14	Preview copies of the brochure and a letter will be sent to all identified potential adult education students.
August 30	Bulk Mailing of the brochures will be mailed to all residents in the area using both American Mailers and the Postal Patron method.

TIME LINE FOR RECRUITING PLAN

March

March 1-15	Identify each street by census tract.
March 15-30	Copy each street resident list out of Bresslers.
March 1-30	Contact each school to obtain list of graduates and high school drop outs.

April

April 1-15	Analyze census tract data to determine the priority of home contact for each street.
April 1-30	Identify all potential door-to-door recruiters.
April 1-30	Identify all school groups to be contacted.
April 1-30	Develop a presentation for these groups regarding adult education specifics, how they can assist, and what it means to them.
April 1-30	Prepare mailing labels and envelopes.
April 11-30	Establish a team of two administrators to meet with contact persons for each operational program to discuss plans.
April 11-30	Specific plan to expand existing program presentation.
April 11-30	Identify institutions for new programs.
April 11-30	Identification of student presently in program who may help in various fashions.
April 1-30	Identify "Theme".
April 22	Preliminary course offerings in.
April 22-May 15	Review schedule with Assistant Principals.
April 15-May 30	Identify all potential door-to-door recruiters.

May

May 1-June 30	Set up several group and multi-group presentations.
May 1-30	Inservice for high school counselors seeking assistance and support.
May 1-June 30	Follow-up on new or expanded programs.
May 1-30	Continuing utilization of previous students.
May 1-30	Materials developed and ordered.
May 1-15	Continued review of Assistant Principals' class schedules.
May 23	Brochure course and program context finalized.
May 23-June 16	Brochure design and layout.

June

June 1-15	Potential recruiters contacted to outline summer responsibilities.
June 1-15	Plan comprehensive three day recruiter inservice.
June 17-19	Recruiter Inservice.
June 20-Aug. 30	Door-to-door identification plan
June 1-30	Continue group presentations.
June 1-30	Mail information and return card to all grads and drop outs.
June 1-30	Continue follow-up of new and expanded programs.
June 1-30	Establish specific plans for sight recruitment.
June 16	Continue preparation of brochure.
June 16	Brochure copy ready.

July

July 1-30	Recruiters involved in door-to-door identification plan.
July 1-30	Follow-up through regularly scheduled advisory council meetings through Friday.
July 1-30	"War Room" prepared.
July 15-30	Lead-up campaign operational.
July 14	Brochure to printer.

August

August 1-30	Continued recruiter door-to-door identification plan.
August 1-30	Continue advisory council meetings.
August 1-30	Central recruiting team contacts students with Assistant Principal contacts to those positively responding.
August 1-30	"War Room" set up.

August 25-30	Each Assistant Principal should have efficient system of implementation to contact interested persons.
August 22-30	Peak period of campaign operational.
August 1	Brochures delivered to schools.
August 1-14	Preview copies of brochure mailed to identified students.
August 30	Mass mailing of brochures.

September

September 1	All potential students contacted by professional adult educator.
September 1	Continued advisory council meetings.
September 1	Implement "War Room".
September 2-30	An efficient system of processing walk-in registrants.
September 12-30	Follow-up on "no shows".
September 1-30	Peak period of campaign operational.

October

| October 1 | Evaluation of campaign procedures. |

1977/78 VACATION CALENDAR

Responsible Administrator:

Plan

The recruiting plan necessitates that a uniform calendar for administrators, secretaries, teachers and other staff be developed. This is to insure that all staff members are available at the proper times to implement the recruiting plan and open the programs smoothly. The following vacation calendar will be adopted.

Assistant Principals

The Assistant Principal/Continuing Education 216 day contract calendar will begin on Monday, August 1, and will end on Monday, June 26. The following dates will be vacation days:

September 5	Labor Day
November 24-25	Thanksgiving Break
Dec. 21 - Jan. 3	Christmas Break
March 24-31	Easter Break
May 29	Memorial Day

Any weekend or regularly scheduled vacation days that may be necessary to work will be taken off at the end of the calendar year.

Program Supervisors

The Program Supervisor 221 day calendar will be identical to the Assistant Principal's calendar with the exception of an additional five days built into the calendar to specifically help provide coverage for those programs that may operate outside of the regular schedule adopted for both regular day school and Continuing Education. An example may be OCC class registration over the Christmas break.

Assistant Directors and Supervisors

The Assistant Director 231 day contract will be identical to the Assistant Principals' calendar with the exception that the additional 15 days will be scheduled so that at least one Assistant Director or the Director is on duty throughout the summer and all vacation periods to provide for administrative department coverage at all times.

Secretaries/Assistant Principals/Continuing Education

Secretaries will work the same calendar as their immediate supervisor with the exception being when a secretary's work year is longer than her supervisor's work year. These additional days are to be scheduled so the secretary will report to another administrator during this period. Secretaries should be on a 1:00 p.m. to 10:00 p.m. schedule.

Full Time Continuing Education Teachers

The teacher work year will begin August 25, and will end May 22. The following are non-work days within the work calendar period:

September 5	Labor Day
November 23-25	Thanksgiving Break
December 21-Jan. 3	Christmas Break
March 24-31	Easter Break

Part Time Continuing Education Teachers

Part time Continuing Education teacher's employment will consist of 30 weeks during the time classes are in session plus a pre-service meeting on September 8. The following will not be work days for part time Continuing Education teachers:

November 21-25	Thanksgiving Break
Dec. 21 - Jan. 3	Christmas Break
January 16-27	Semester Break
March 24-31	Easter Break

NOTE: The following promotion ideas are submitted by Al Mc Pherson. Mr. Mc Pherson is with Detroit Adult Education. He is also a member of Michigan's joint MAPACE - MCSEA "You Can" committee.

The key to a successful promotion is to give yourself plenty of advance time to get all aspects of the program operating. And, enlist other community leaders and business associates to support the effort.

With this in mind, the promotion can be broken down into three major parts:

1. Contact community leaders and business associates.
2. Plan press conference and/or "kick-off" event.
3. Set promotion activities into action (ads, radio, TV, press releases, etc.)

I. CONTACT COMMUNITY LEADERS AND BUSINESS ASSOCIATES

Community leaders, friends and business associates will be valuable in helping you publicize and support the program. A personal visit or phone call (followed by printed information) a best bet for those you know well. A cover letter accompanied by printed information will serve for other industries and individuals, and will help if time is a factor. You should be prepared to show samples of material listed under "Promotion Activities."

Your target area for this cooperative effort will include:

City Government leaders
Welfare Department leaders
Business leaders
Labor organizations and trade unions
Youth group heads (YMCA, YWCA, etc.)
Church groups and leaders
Local Board of Education leaders
Police organizations
Libraries
Poverty agencies or groups
Other Educators
Local college administrators
Hospital administrators
An advertising agency friend or PR friend might be willing to give "public service" assistance.
Leaders of local bus and transportation companies
Any company or business that sends out bills or statements might be willing to include the information flyer in its billing. Include utility companies, banks and department stores.

Those you contact will be able to suggest further outlets for the promotional materials. And, they should be encouraged to use all promotional pieces listed in "Promotional Activities."

326

In addition to explaining education programs, the above groups should be offered posters, flyers, cards and other materials. Company bulletin boards, lunch rooms, restaurants, bank counters, store windows, etc. are prime targets for promotional materials. Remember, you must "sell" them on helping you promote. "You Can" like you would sell them on products or services. Most firms do not yet know or understand the importance of adult and community education.

II. PLAN PRESS CONFERENCE AND/OR KICK-OFF EVENT
A kick-off conference (press conference or press party) will lend importance to your campaign and will allow press groups to ask questions. It will also act as a starter for your campaign (that will be supported by your efforts in print ads, radio and TV).

Where possible, a spokesman should be asked to head a "You Can" committee. He (or she) could be a sports figure, a prominent businessman, an educator or a church leader. In conjunction with, or instead of a spokesman, your local government can designate a "You Can" day or week. This could be used as a kick-off "key" for your campaign.

A press conference that announces the beginning of "You Can" day (or week) gives you, or your spokesperson, the chance to personally promote the TV series. Coverage in local community newspapers as well as in larger dailies, will serve as a good base on which your full-media promotion can begin.

Your initial press release can be localized to include your kick-off event. This press release should be sent to all news media including radio and TV.

Your press conference or kick-off event should happen a few days (no more than a week) before your full-media campaign (radio, TV, print ads, etc.) And, in some cases, they might start simultaneously. If a press conference or kick-off event is not feasible, the press release explaining the TV series should start one or two weeks prior to the start of the full media coverage and should be followed by other releases (shorter) every two weeks until you feel all papers are aware of your efforts.

In addition, your spokesman, or you, should appear on TV talk shows, and radio shows and discuss the adult education program and its aims. Don't be bashful - you are selling "You Can" - so give it all the "gusto" you can...sell it like you would a product.

PROMOTION ACTIVITIES
One of the most important aspects of a promotion is to have

an "identity". Using the "You Can" logo on **all** materials (ads, flyers, posters, etc.) is therefore, quite important. Here's a suggested rundown of materials.

1. Press Releases

   As mentioned earlier, a press release must be localized for the activity you plan (Kick-off event, You Can Week, or as an initial informational tool to press, radio and TV people). All releases should be sent to any of the following in your area:

   All newspapers

   All local magazines

   Educational publications (Local Board of Education)

   Industrial or business publications (such as employee newspapers, flyers or magazines)

   TV stations (local talk show personalities)

   Radio stations (news shows and local talk shows)

   Any company, business or organization that sends a bill stuffer (local telephone, electric or water company, etc.). They might include a short blurb in a current issue. Most of these publications need at least two months notice. Subsequent releases could feature stories on teachers in the program, subjects offered or any local tie-ins with the subject matter.

   The point is: Keep as much news about your program before the press as possible and localize the news, when possible. A suggested follow-up release: A "personality" story on one of the students taking courses.

2. Print Ads

   An advertising agency friend will be valuable in telling you which papers reach the audience you're aiming for and what publications are best for the area you cover. As in radio and TV, you should be asking for public service (free space) or an interview. Consider the following:

Daily, local and community papers
Educational publications
Welfare publications
Sports publications
Company and union newspapers
Coop advertising (where local advertisers insert the "You Can" slug in their aids, at no charge)

Again, the print ad campaign needs to be aimed. So advice on which publications can do the best job for the money is necessary. (Sometimes contacting a large scale local advertiser is a good idea.)

3. Radio Commercial

You should approach local radio stations to place your commercial on a "Public Service" basis. No charge to you for public service spots. The FCC encourages radio stations to boradcast public service commercials. And most stations are very cooperative. But it's good to keep in mind that there are many public service organizations competing for air time.

A "60" commercial is fine, but shorter versions such as 10 sec. or 30 sec. "spots" could also be prepared and submitted.

4. TV Commercial

What applies for radio applies for TV public service messages. You should contact the Community Affairs Director at the TV stations. Also keep in mind that short TV spots are the easiest to get on the air (10 second, 20 second or 30 second... but not 60 second). Thirty second seems to be the most acceptable.

5. Posters

The poster can be a way of "blanketing" your area with the message. Enlist all your contacts in getting the posters out. And, you might want to consider printing it in several sizes to fit different applications.

Boy Scout groups, Girl Scout groups, church groups and any youth organizations might be enlisted to help distribute the posters.

6. Flyer or Brochure

The flyer will carry more detailed information than the poster and can be printed as a "fold" piece or as one side of an 8 x 10 sheet of paper. It will include a coupon that can be filled out and mailed in. Possible outlets:

Local Board of Education
Local Department of Labor
Employment agencies

329

Police Departments and police community groups
Welfare Departments
Unemployment agencies of government
Youth groups (YMCA, YWCA, etc.)
Church groups
Offered to local companies (telephone, electric, water or department stores) that include bill inserts in their bills and whole envelopes would hold the flyer as a separate insert. You should consider the size of local billing envelopes before your flyer is printed so the flyer can be constructed small enough to fit into any of the envelopes.

7. Counter Top Card (stand up with pocket)
This would be used where a continuing display of the brochure for giveaway would be desirable. Display in:
All local businesses (especially those with counter tops or table areas
All government agencies (especially Post Office and Unemployment Offices)
Police Department
Libraries
Labor union offices
Train and bus stations

8. Tent Cards
This would be used on tables in lunchrooms, cafeterias or or restaurants or in any location where a larger display was not appropriate. You could contact large businesses who maintain employee lunch or dinner facilities and ask if they are willing to pay the cost of printing.

9. Transit Display
Two outlets are possible: car cards in busses or subways and large outdoor billboards. The transit company and billboard company might contribute the space.
Bus and subway cards are approximately 11 inches by 28 inches. Billboard ("30" sheet) is about 115 inches by 259 inches. Billboards in disadvantages neighborhoods would be best.
Contact them early since space is usually rented far in advance.
In large transportation centers, illuminated displays are usually available from the individual center.

10. Postage Indicia
Many businesses or organizations utilize postage meters and most are willing to cooperate in promoting programs such as the high school series. The message must be short. You will have to pay for the metal "dies" or "slug" unless the sponsoring company agrees to pick up the tab.

330

11. Advertising Specialties

The "You Can" logo and thought provoking copy have been used successfully on bumper stickers, pens, decals, rulers, badges, balloons, litterbags, book covers, placemats, napkins, portfolios, car signs and other items.

FACE TO FACE RECRUITMENT

A recruiter campaign was conceived under the basic premise that present Adult Basic Education students and graduates are the best recruiters. Two types of recruiters were used: those students paid as paraprofessionals who recruit door to door, and ABE student volunteers who spread the message of ABE to their friends, relatives, and neighbors, and participate actively in special projects to obtain students throughout the year. The following is, in part, the plan used in Midland, Michigan which could be implemented to serve any local situation:

Paid Recruiters

After a short by intensive sales type training program, students litterally "knock-on-doors" in target areas within the city and throughout the country, for live interested prospects. They also visit specific people who had been referred by agencies and the schools in their area. The recruiters were really "salesmen" for the ABE program. Due to an average distance of fifteen miles between classes outside the city, potential students who are members of the immediate community near the outreach centers are employed as recruiters. Information derived on possible students is then turned into the Continuing Education office at a "weekly recruiter meeting" during the month of September.

Follow-up is extremely important in gaining students. Each prospective student referred by a recruiter receives a telephone call from the coordinator explaining details of the ABE program, encouraging the prospect to ask questions. By answering these questions openly, it alleviates many of the fears regarding attendance in ABE, and is also part of the selling program.

Finally, recruiters are responsible for bringing the students to the first class or meeting the student at the initial session. "Knowing a familiar face" is most important and alleviates many fears, which of course makes the first step into the classroom easier.

Volunteer Recruiters

Often ABE students will volunteer to help with special recruitment projects. This gives students a sense of belonging and self-confidence-goals of the ABE.

"You Can" bumper stickers are distributed at the orientation meeting which is held after an informal potluck 'Getting to Know You" dinner. Students from the previous year are asked to remember their uneasiness at their first meeting and do everything possible to help new students feel welcome.

At the second meeting, a "You Can" portfolio containing recruiment materials is distributed to each student, followed by a five minute "pep talk" explaining the benefits of the overall program. Students are proud of their involvement in the ABE program. They carry these folders with them everywhere and seem to be eager to answer questions. Volunteers are also encouraged to "Each One Bring One" through the use of "You can" incentive awards for outstanding recruiting. These incentives can be small wall plaques or certificates for an "outstanding" job. If you budget permits even inexpensive cameras, handbags or wallets, these are good incentives.

One interesting and productive project accomplished by ABE student volunteers was the construction of a booth in the form of the red "You Can" School House for use at County Fairs. A volunteer recruiter and member of the ABE Advisory Commitee should be in attendance at all times to answer questions, take names for follow-up calls, and give away helium filled "You Can" balloons, or other inexpensive promotional items.

Recruiters, fortified with "You Can" materials and specialty items, contributed more than any other factor to the growth of Midland's ABE program.

THE FUTURE OF "YOU CAN"

John R. Colbert, Director of Adult Basic Education, Pontiac Michigan School district.

Adult and Community Education programs have been at work meeting the needs of the Adult Community in education and leisure time activities for many years. This particular service is not limited to a few cities in one state or even a few of the fifty states. Today Adult and Community Education programs are being operated in most towns and cities throughout the United States. These programs though varied in nature to meet the needs of the local citizens have one common goal.

EDUCATION AS A LIFELONG PROCESS

In order to cooperatively work toward this goal in every community throughout the United States it seems almost a necessity to have developed a unity in the image of what Adult and Community Education stands for.

For many years different states and communities in the United States have had different logos (an emblem that is identified with a product) that was Adult and Community Education to them. Unfortunately many years went by with many different communities using different logos. This in many ways separated Adult and Community Education programs from one geographic area to another.

Identity is important in order to know where you might find the service you are after. With the highly mobile adult population in the United States in 1974 people freely moved from town to town and state to state. Adult and Community Education needs to be ready to cope with this highly mobile population. Why not tie Adult and Community Education together nationally with a National Publicity Campaign centering around a logo. Wouldn't this make it easier for prospects to identify an Adult and Community Education program from one state to another?

In 1972 the State of Michigan initiated a campaign that was designed to unify Adult and Community Education in that state. A logo was used that put together a symbol for the educational institution (Little Red School House) and a positive phrase (YOU CAN).

The development of the logo for Michigan was carefully designed in order to give flexibility to the use of the logo. The important concept was the use of the logo on as many items in the Adult and Community Education program as possible.

YOU CAN had a fast and very positive growth in Michigan. From Michigan in 1974 it began to spread to other states in the United States. The idea of a national identity for Adult and Community Education began to be a reality.

Looking into the future, Adult and Community Education will develop into a force that will become more visible and as a result serve more of the millions of adults around the United States that wish to enrich their life through education. It is also evident that a national unity will enable adult and community educators to become the viable political force they need to become in order to finance programs that will keep pace with a society in change.

A COLLECTION OF SOME RECRUITING PROCEDURES
IN ADULT EDUCATION

I.   GENERAL SUGGESTIONS:
     The best time for distribution of printed materials is about three weeks in advance of the program. The program should be built with a slogan, title, symbol, distinctive letter etc. for long-term identification. Adults are

more likely to participate if the fundamental questions of who, what, where and why are told in the materials. The adult educators should make and maintain personal contacts with the representatives of the news media.

II. POINTS TO CONSIDER IN PRINTING AND ADVERTISING PROGRAMS:
   1. Purpose of the program
   3. Nature of the sponsors of the program
   4. Leaders of the activities
   5. Cost to the participant
   6. Location of the program
   7. Procedures for enrolling

III. DISTRIBUTION OF PRINTED MATERIALS:
   1. Send home with children from school
   2. Industrial plants
   3. Job shops
   4. Libraries
   5. Educational officers of military establishments
   6. Welcome wagon ladies
   7. Barbershops and hairdressers, laundromats and grocery stores
   8. Bank statements, light and water statements
   9. Settlement houses
   10. Unemployment, welfare and public health centers
   11. Scout meetings
   12. P.T.A. Meetings
   13. Housing authority receipts
   14. Lodges, ethnic and veterans organizations
   15. Vocational rehabilitation
   16. Head-start programs
   17. Legal aid organizations
   18. Mailing lists
      a. Union membership
      b. High school dropout lists over a number of years
      c. Business and professional societies
      d. Present and past adult education students
      e. Business and industrial lists
      f. Alien registration and naturalization lists
      g. Vocational rehabilitation lists
      h. Welfare lists
      i. Cooperative extension lists

IV. NEWSPAPER RECRUITING PROGRAMS:
   1. Plan a schedule of advertising - consult your newspaper editor
   2. Use a relatively large number of small ads
   3. Have eye-catching headlines

4. Make ads easy to read and specific in detail
5. Notify reporters of programs and submit properly written accounts of activities
6. Utilize neighborhood papers, shoppers guides, ethnic papers in addition to regular daily and weekly editions.

V. RADIO AND TELEVISION PROGRAMS:
1. Submit news stories and notify of programs well in advance.
2. Use spot announcments, consider timing.
3. Present interviews with staff and participants.
4. Use telecourses involving the broadcasting of class sessions.
5. Utilize ethnic oriented stations.

VI. POSTERS AND DISPLAYS
1. Utilize windows and lobbies of stores and theaters
2. Use laundromat bulletin boards
3. Consider booths and displays in county fairs, state fairs and parades.
4. Utilize industrial plant entrances and cafeterias
5. Display at P.T.A. meetings
6. Utilize lodges, fraternal and veteran's buildings
7. Displays in food stamp offices
8. Posters in barbershops and hairdressers shops
9. Posters on busses
10. Posters in driver's license offices
11. Posters and displays in labor union halls
12. Posters and displays in neighborhood grocery stores
13. Displays and posters in public health centers.
14. Displays and posters in employment centers.
15. Posters with envelope of pre-addressed postcards requesting more AE information.

VII. WORD OF MOUTH (considered the most effective single method)
1. Teachers in AE and in public school programs
2. Employers
3. Church leaders
4. Neighborhood and plant sound trucks and speaker systems
5. Former students
6. Telephone committees (invitations and reminders)
7. Community workers, social workers, welfare workers, postmen, and milkmen.
8. Influential neighborhood and community leaders - local politicians.
9. VISTA workers
10. Driver's examiners
11. Bartenders

12. Speaker's bureau (carry AE message to organizations)
13. Paid recruiters
14. Advisory councils

VIII. MISCELLANEOUS RECRUITING SUGGESTIONS:
   Advertising signs on adult education building (avoid com-
   merical concept) Develop open-house programs including the
   holding of civic, fraternal and other group meetings in
   the AE facilities. Remember, a good program will develop
   recruiters - testimonials are often effective recruiting
   devices. Provide transportation and lighted parking lots and
   make this known in your advertising.

PROMOTING THE ADULT EDUCATION PROGRAM

QUESTIONS
1. How would you utilize the Big Four and the Fundamental
   five in your promotional program?
2. How would you most effectively use an advisory committee
   in promoting specific programs; the general problem?
3. Why do you feel there is much truth in Mary Ann Diller's
   comment, "Promotion is one of the most difficult tasks in
   Adult Education?"
4. What are different approached to the use of radio for promotion?
5. How would you cultivate the media as an adult educator?
6. How can persons with limited budgets utilize TV for promotion?
7. How would you organize a "Public Relations" Workshop?
8. How do you dramatize your adult education work?
9. What are some attractive names for courses you have developed?
10. What kind of market research would you recommend?
11. How would you utilize a model for promotion of the Univer-
    sity of Wisconsin Extension Division?
12. Recruiting is bound up with promotion. How would you use
    the annual plan developed for recruiting suggested by Dr.
    Thomas Rosenthal?

SUMMARY
   Promotion may save the life of an excellent program. People
must know what is available to them in adult education, and the
various media let people know. The Who? What? When? Where?
and Why? are the fundamental five for the adult educator, and
knowing the media persons in the community is important.
   The advisory committee is a useful technique for getting the
word to the right people and involving the potential clientele

336

in program planning. Many devices are used by adult educators to let their people know about adult education offerings: newspapers, radio, plant bulletin boards, and service organizations. Word of mouth is often the most effective method of spreading the word about a course or program offered to adults. The brochure is still the most widely used medium for informing adults about learning opportunities. Sunday supplements in major newspapers prove useful in large cities to tell the adult education story and announce courses. To dramatize the story of adult education is one of our tasks, and adult education was likened unto a vibrant, colorful aesthetic dance.

The importance of the course title was described. One title may not attract a clientele, while another more descriptive title may draw a large class. A great deal depends upon the name of the course.

Analyzing the sources of information which adults use to learn of adult education activities is important, and an example of such a study was described. We learned that in many states adult education is news. Agencies will do well to cooperate in joint promotion. Workshops in promotion methods was advocated. Professional adult education groups will benefit by sponsoring such institutes on promotion techniques. Finally, twenty questions for a news writer gave useful questions to be asked by adult educators in preparing copy for the mass media.

BIBLIOGRAPHY

Blakely, Robert J. **How to Read a Newspaper: A Guidebook.** Chicago: Field Enterprises, 1967.

49 Ways Direct Advertising Can Be Put to Work in Your Business. New York: Direct Mail Advertising Association, Inc. (n.d.)

Making Your Publicity Work-Handbook. Women in Communication, P.O. 33131, Phoenix, Az. 85067. $6.50, 1979

McElreath, Mark, **Developing a Strategy for Adult Education Via Mas Media,** Adult Education, Vol 25, No. 1 1974

Organization and Effective Use of Advisory Committees. Washington, D.C.: U.S. Department of Health, Education and Welfare Pamphlet OE-86009; Vocational Division Bulletin No. 288, T & I Education Series No. 71. (n.d.)

Publicity Handbook, A Guide for Publicity Chairmen. Chicago: Consumer Information Service.

Schoenfeld, Clarence. **The University and Its Publics: Approaches to a Public Relations Program for Colleges and Universities.** New York: Harper, 1954.

————. **Publicity Media and Methods, Their Role in Modern Public Relations.** New York: Macmillan, 1963.

So, You've Been Elected Publicity Chairman. Los Angeles: Occidental Life Insurance Company of California.

Stern, Milton R. **People, Programs, and Persuasion; Some Remarks About Promoting University Adult Education.** Center for Study of Liberal Education for Adults, Notes and Essays, No. 33, 1961.

"The Effective and Profitable Use of Industrial Direct Mail Advertising." Sales brochure. New York: McGraw-Hill

FILMS

"Never Too Old To Learn," produced by Phoenix Community College. Phoenix, Arizona, 85067   29 min. (Order from Director of Evening Division.)

"The Skillmakers," produced by the Milwaukee Vocational, Technical, and Adult Schools, Milwaukee, Wisconsin. 29 min. (Order from Director of Public Relations.)

"To Teach a Child", 29 min. - from your Community School Director

"I Can- -" A film showing what adult education did for a worker. Geared to public school adult education. From National Association for Public Continuing and Ad. Educ. Washington, D.C.

FOOTNOTES CHAPTER 18

1 From selected quotes from Directors of Adult Education throughout the state of Illinois, 1965. (Author's files.)

2 Interview with Jack Jillson, Feb. 27, 1967, DeKalb, Ill.

3 Illinois Survey of Adult Educators, **op. cit.**, p. 1.

4 **Ibid.**, p. 2.

5 **Ibid.**, p. 1.

6 Milton R. Stern, "Look At Me, Fellas: I'm Dancin'!" Speech to Milwaukee Council for Adult Learning, Jan. 17, 1963.

7 From an interview at DeKalb, Ill., Jan. 6, 1967.

8 William D. Dowling, "Characteristics of Adult Education Participants in Green Bay, Wisconsin" (mimeo), 1963.

9 Roger W. Axford, "Never Too Old to Learn," Continuing Education Department, Board of Higher Education, Tallahassee, Fla., 1965.

Chapter XVIV

FUNDING ADULT EDUCATION

There is a great deal of discussion among adult educators as to whether local programs should pay for themselves or be supported by subsidy. Some citizens take the point of view that because adults earn more, by in large, that they should pay for any adult or continuing education. Most non-credit courses both in the public schools and in the universities and community colleges pay their own way.

It is this author's point of view that public support of public adult education is a good investment. The G.I. bill was probably the best investment we have made in ourselves, in higher education, and in increased taxes from increased earning power.

Very often the administrative costs of the adult education program are borne by the public institution. For example, most departments of continuing education, or extension must pay their way for program costs, but the administrative costs such as deans and secretarial help is underwritten, much like the undergraduate program is financially underwritten.

Some public school adult education programs are administered on a pay-as-you-go basis. The adult basic education programs are usually supported by federal monies administered through the states.

Funding of conferences and institutes is usually on a break-even basis. Residential adult education centers are expensive, and occupancy varies from 50 to 100%. Often there is a tug-of-war between the program planner and the residential center manager. One is program oriented; the other is anxious to keep the rooms filled, regardless of the quality of the program. The director of a Kellogg Continuing Education Center will usually be happy to discuss his financial dilemma.

The federal government is one of the largest purveyors of adult education in our society. More than 240 federal programs are involved in some way in supporting continuing education activities for adults. It is reported that the combined allocation for the programs which are labeled as continuing education, adult education, or lifelong learning is nearly $14 billion, and it is growing. It is difficult to distinguish that part which is specifically labeled as learning opportunities for adults. Very often a total figure will be support dollars earmarked for learning activities, a part of which involves adults.

Manpower training programs represent the largest number of federal programs, as mentioned earlier in the book, financing continuing education opportunities for adults. These amount to about one-fifth of total federal dollars involved in learning opportunities for adults. Monies supporting manpower training is channeled mostly through institutions, individuals, direct training activities of federal agencies, state agencies, or a combination of institutions and individuals.

Programs supporting special-purpose activities total about 4 percent of the federal appropriations affecting lifelong learning. The monies going to cooperative extension amounts to about 70 percent of these dollars, with funds going directly to land-grant universities, the adult aspect of vocational education making grants to the states, and adult basic education grants made mostly to state departments of education.

FEDERAL POLICIES REGARDING CONTINUING EDUCATION FOR ADULTS

The federal government does not have a comprehensive or fully integrated federal policy regarding life-long learning. Richard W. Jonsen has made some general observations regarding those federal policies:

1. The provision of adult learning opportunities appears to be something for which the federal government has been willing, perhaps by default, to bear some responsibility. It is unclear whether the magnitude of that responsibility is as great as **the share of the burden carried by the federal government** for elementary-secondary and postsecondary education.

2. Federal activity has developed in response to various problems, primarily those of critical manpower needs and problems of disadvantaged populations. The emphasis in most cases has been on preparation of practitioners in specific fields (medical, social services, rehabilitation services, geriatrics) or on the development of marketable skills in disadvantaged populations (the handicapped, the poor, welfare recipients, the unemployed).

3. In spite of federal initiatives, education is traditionally and constitutionally a state responsibility. This locus of responsibility is more specific (and frequently articulated in state constitutions) in the case of elementary, secondary and post-secondary education than it is for education for adults. [2]

Well over half of the federal funding for adult learning activities supports postsecondary institutions or their students. The Veterans' Administration with its educational benefits is a leading program illustrating individual support. Support for generalized learning

340

activities for adults as contrasted with learning activities for college-age students is small.

Also limited are monies for research or experimental programs. Some funds for research on adult learning are provided by the National Institute for Education. Venture capital is provided in limited amounts for such as the Fund for the Improvement of Postsecondary Education. One of the creative programs was funding provided for experimental projects to stimulate extension and outreach programs, called the Community Service and Continuing Education Program (Title I of the Higher Education Act). The weakness of that program was the lack of extensive dissemination of the results of the projects. Many continuing education divisions will look back and find that they had as their beginning one of the Community Service and Continuing Education grants.

STATE POLICIES FOR FUNDING CONTINUING EDUCATION

Despite much discussion and study by the states regarding the question of how lifelong learning activities should be funded, there is no comprehensive policy that has emerged for funding continuing education for adults. Efforts by the states have resulted in the development of new programs and services such as external degree programs, adult learning centers, independent study programs, and a limited amount of aid for the part-time student. Lifelong learning for adults is still not a high priority for most states, and none has developed thus far a comprehensive state policy for learning opportunities for adults. State appropriations have been increasing for the provision of opportunities for lifelong learning but this varies from state to state.[3]

The breakdown for consideration of funding learning opportunities for adults breaks down into: 1) Public Elementary-Secondary Education, 2) Postsecondary Institutions, including Community Colleges, Four-Year Colleges and Universities, and Continuing Education Agencies, 3) Financial Subsidy to Individuals (the most extensive form of state subsidy to individuals for learning opportunities is the state student aid program), 4) The Private Sector (not all of these learning activities are self-support),

Jonsen found that pricing and funding practices dealing with lifelong learning was neither uniform nor well categorized. He did discover however, that:

-- Most but not all noncredit activities are self supporting.
-- The self supporting aspect of noncredit activities is affected by external governmental support.
-- Tuitions vary between on and off campus / credit and noncredit activities and within these categories.
-- Since state subsidy policies vary, the resulting charge to the participant will be as dependent upon location or time of

341

offering as upon the nature of the activity.

-- The availability of subsidies to individuals for adult learning activities will depend upon the type of activity (e.g., some manpower training areas enjoy federal subsidy), economic and employment status, state of residence, employer or union membership. [4]

It is worthy of note to observe the percentage of learners participating in learning activities provided by differing types of sponsors:

PERCENTAGE OF LEARNERS PARTICIPATING IN LEARNING ACTIVITIES PROVIDED BY VARIOUS SPONSERS

	1969	1972	1975
Public grade school or high school	15.1%	14.0%	11.0%
Two-year college or voca-tional-technical in-stitutions	11.9	16.3	17.7
Private trade or business school	11.5	8.9	3.7
Four-year college or university	21.7	21.4	19.1
Employer	17.4	16.6	15.3
Community organization	11.9	12.7	10.5
Labor organization or professional associations		5.5	6.1
Private tutor		6.0	6.9
Government agency			8.0
Hospital	3	4	
Correspondence school			3.6
Other	19.3	9.4	19.3
Not reported	.4	.6	.4

Source: Bureau of the Census, Survey of Adult Education: Current Population Survey, May 1975 (Washington, D.C., U.S. Department of Commerce, 1977)

PRICING STRATEGIES AND TACTICS FOR THE MARKETING OF ADULT EDUCATION COURSES: A WORKSHOP FOR PRACTITIONERS [5]

INSTRUCTOR:

Marvin E. Lamoureux, M.B.A., Ed.D.
Dean of Instruction
Vancouver Community College:
Vancouver Vocational Institute
Vancouver, B.C., Canada

COURSE GOALS:

(1) To introduce the participant to the nature of pricing as perceived by the economist, psychologist, accountant and marketing manager.

(2) To have the participant understand two popular cost accounting approaches to course pricing: absorption-costing and contribution costing.

(3) To have the participant understand a marketing management approach to course pricing and the latter's use of cost accounting data and methods.

(4) To have the participant complete and discuss various course pricing case studies. The cases will be the workshop component of this program and should aid the participant to understand, in a practical sense, the background to the development of a personal course pricing strategy and related tactics.

COURSE OUTLINE:

Hour One: INTRODUCTION

(1) Introduction to the concept of a price strategy and related tactics.

(2) Introduction to pri ing as perceived by four disciplines: economics, psychology, accounting and marketing.

Workshop Case #1: "John Kenneth Galbraith Comes to Town"

Hours Two and Three: THE ABSORPTION - COST APPROACH TO GUIDING A PRICE DECISION

Workshop Case #2: "This Course Won't Go Unless It Pays For Itself Completely!"

Hour Four: THE CONTRIBUTION - COST APPROACH TO GUIDING A PRICE DECISION

Workshop Case #3: "Total cost allocation is all well and good, but this course is a go as long as its identifiable (variable) costs are covered and there is a chance for some, even a minimal, contribution to overhead (fixed) costs!"

Hour Five: THE MARKETING APPROACH TO GUIDING A PRICE DECISION

Workshop Case #4: "Why don't we look at our adult participants as a collection of distinctive mini-markets and price accordingly?"

Workshop Case #1
JOHN KENNETH GALBRAITH COMES TO TOWN*

As a keen student of economics, a lover of popular guest lecturers, and a wise adult education administrator, you have decided to combine these interests and will be bringing a foremost economist to your institution.

You've decided to "promote" a lecture featuring John Kenneth Galbraith.

Remembering your administration classes, you realize that you must ascertain what kind of market there is for attending such a lecture, what kind of prices they are willing to pay, the promotion needed to inform the market, and finally, the expected cost - revenue outcome.

From a survey, you gather the following information:
- 500 persons would be willing to attend paying an entrance price of $20.
- 700 persons would come if the entrance price was $16.
- 800 persons would come if the price was $12.
- 1,000 persons at a price of $10.
- 1,500 persons at a price of $8.
- 2,000 persons at a price of $6.

The next thing that you do is to figure out your costs. They are as follows:

Fee for Galbraith	$2,000
Travelling, living and other expenses for Galbraith	1,000
Rental of hall for 1,000 persons	500
Rental of hall for 2,000 persons	1,000
Promotion expenses	1,000
Personnel required for attendance at lecture hall	350
Pro-rated institutional costs are $1.00 per PARTICIPANT	

*Case materials developed by Mr. Paul Bridge, M.B.A.: Project Director for Small Business Administration Extension Courses, Vancouver Community College, Vancouver, B.C., Canada

1. Using your knowledge of demand analysis, determine which price you should charge to generate maximum profits.
2. You are pricing the same event, only now, instead of being a profit-maximizing entrepreneur, your objective is to charge your audience as little money as possible but assess a markup of 20% on the price of the ticket to cover any unplanned outcomes and/or contribute to any non-appropriate overhead. Using the same information, with what size audience are your

average total costs at a minimum? What are your costs at this point? If you were then going to charge a 20% markup for your profit, what would this markup be?

3. Again, you are pricing the same event, only now, as a comfirmed adult education capitalist, you want to "skim the cream off the market" (since you feel you are in a monopoly position). You decide you can change three or four different prices for a lecture depending on where persons sit in the ahll. To skim the cream off the market, what prices would you charge? How many persons would you charge at that price? What would your total profit be?

4. Determine the number of participants needed to break-even and state fgures in blank column.

re: 2

Total Costs = Fixed Costs plus Variable Costs

Average Total Costs = $\dfrac{\text{Total Costs}}{\text{Quantity}}$

Unit Price	Quantity (Demand)	Total Costs	Average Total	$ATC	Breakdown By Participants
$20	500	$5350	$\dfrac{\$5350}{500}$	$10.70	
$16	700	$5550	$\dfrac{\$5550}{700}$	$ 7.93	
$12	800	$5650	$\dfrac{\$5650}{800}$	$ 7.06	
$10	1000	$5850	$\dfrac{\$5850}{1000}$	$ 5.85	
$ 8	1500	$6850	$\dfrac{\$6850}{1500}$	$ 4.57	
$ 6	2000	$7350	$\dfrac{\$7350}{2000}$	$ 3.68	

Markup = 20% of sales
   = 20% of $3.68
   = 74¢

therefore: ticket price = $3.68 + .74 = $4.42

     or $4.50 to "round off".

345

Would charge:	Revenue
500 persons at $20	$10,000
200 persons at $16 (700 - 500)	3,200
100 persons at $12 (800 - 700)	1,200
200 persons at $10 (1,000 - 800)	2,000
500 persons at $8 (1,500 - 1,000)	4,000
500 persons at $6 (2,000 - 1,500)	3,000
Total Revenue	$23,400

INCOME STATEMENT

Total Revenue		$23,400
Less: Variable Costs	$5350	
Fixed Costs	2000	
Total Costs		7,350
Total Profits		$16,050

Re-capitulation

Procedure	Number of Participants	Ticket Fee	Total Revenue	Total Costs	Profit
#1	700	$16.00	$11,200	$5550	$5650
#2	2000	$ 4.50	$ 9,000	$7350	$1650
#3	2000	Variable	$23,400	$7350	$16,050

Workshop Case #2
"THIS COURSE WON'T GO UNLESS IT PAYS FOR ITSELF COMPLETELY"

Ms. Mary Becker, Continuing Education Director for the East Hampton, Washington School District (including the community college) was entering a new budget year and faced with the normal anxiety related to program planning. Everyone had ideas based on past successes and failures as well as future expectations. She had, however, very good co-workers who could handle all facets of the programming function except one: the pricing function. Decisions about course pricing were a constant battle among the school district's chief financial officer, herself and the program planners. After each session with the latter individuals she would think to herself: "What am I running, a private profit-making adult education institution to pay for school district administrators, a welfare-type of operation to serve the whole community, or whatever?"

"There had never been a policy decision about pricing, but there was one about my surplus at year end--it goes to the general fund." Each year she had to bargain for a start-up cash-flow and budget to at least break-even (pay for all expenses). However, since the Continuing Education Services Dept. had been the fastest growing school district department (with both elementary and secondary attendance dropping) she had continuous pressure to "make more money".

The facts of school district financial life were becoming clearer, especially this year. A greater portion of the school district's overhead had been placed in her "readjusted" budget. She was, in effect, now asked to pay for more of the school district capital and operating expenditures (albeit hidden in her budget) and still

347

launch enough courses, with enough participation, and adequate revenue to make a year-end surplus.

Exhibit #1 reflects her yearly budget. This includes her programming, office salaries, supplies and "readjusted" overhead expenses. It does not include expenses directly related to the presentation of any specific course. The latter expenses are "added-on" and stated in the final year-end budget.

Exhibit #2 reflects the distribution by hours of the courses put on the previous year. Ms. Becker expects a 12% increase in the number of courses for each category.

Exhibit #3 reflects the average distribution of participants for each course that was a successful "Go" in each hourly category. Ms. Becker expects the same average attendance this year as last.

Given the above information:

(1) Develop a course pricing formula using the absorption-cost method.

(2) Indicate the expenses you would allocate to each of the above course categories.

(3) If Ms. Becker was asked to "come through with a 10% surplus", would that change #1, #2 above? Explain.

(4) Indicate three problems associated with the use of the absorption-cost approach to course pricing.

EXHIBIT #1

PROJECTED EXPENSES FOR THE BUDGET YEAR

	BUDGET
**DEPT 418 CENTER ADMINISTRATION	
*NON-INSTRUCTIONAL SALARIES	
0560 418 NON-INSTRUCTIONAL SENIOR OFFICERS	22,800
0562 418 NON-INSTRUCTIONAL SUPPORT STAFF	11,600
0563 418 NON-INSTRUCTIONAL SUP STAFF TEMP-OVERTIME	2,000
0569 418 ALLOCATED OVERHEAD	21,600
	58,000
*OTHER EXPENSES	
0626 418 ADVERTISING	4,000
0627 418 ROOM RENTAL	12,000
0628 418 GENERAL SUPPLIES	3,000
0630 418 PROGRAM DEVELOPMENT	3,000
0635 418 BOOKS PERIODICALS FILMS ETC	1,000
0651 418 TRAVEL & CONFERENCES	1,500
0652 418 TRAVEL LOCAL MILEAGE ALLOWANCE ONLY	500
0659 418 MEETINGS & HOSTINGS	250
0682 418 MEMBERSHIPS	100
0692 418 PROFESSIONAL DEVELOPMENT	300
0775 418 EQUIPMENT RENTAL - OTHER	1,000
0795 418 REPLACEMENT OF EQUIPMENT	1,000
	27,650

TOTAL ALL EXPENSES   85,650

EXHIBIT #2

DISTRIBUTION OF COURSES BY COURSE CONTACT HOURS

HOURLY SEGMENTS	"NO-GO" COURSES	"GO" COURSES	TOTAL COURSES
1-6	5	47	52
7-8	3	30	33
9-10	6	60	66
11-13	7	71	78
14-15	4	34	38
16-19	3	27	30
20-25	9	92	101
26 or more	2	20	22
TOTALS	39	381	420

EXHIBIT #3

DISTRIBUTION OF AVERAGE COURSE ENROLLMENT PER HOURLY COURSE SEGMENT

HOURLY SEGMENTS	NUMBER OF "GO" COURSES	AVERAGE ATTENDANCE
1-6	47 courses	142 participants
7-8	30	47
9-10	60	33
11-13	71	32
14-15	34	28
16-19	27	18
20-25	92	20
26 or more	20	19
	381 courses	

349

"Total Cost Allocation is all well and good, but this course is a "Go" as long as its identifiable (variable) costs are covered and there is a chance that for some, even minimal contributions, to overhead (fixed) costs!"

Ms. Mary Becker has been approached by a program planner to conduct a 12 hour cost accounting up-grading course. This course would prepare prospective C.P.A. aspirants for the upcoming state board examination. An instructor is available for $25.00 per class contact hour. Materials for the class will be $5.00 per student. The newspaper advertisement will cost $125.00. Registration materials are $2.50 per student. Audio-Visual materials are projected to cost $35.00 (including a textbook for the instructor). Brochures, other printed material, mail and postage will be $82.50. As the instructor has already given such a course and has prepared lecture and problem sets no programming salary will be necessary for the said instructor.

Problem:

1) Determine the fixed (overhead) expenses for this course based on the allocation formula you developed in the previous case (Workshop Case #2). Do not include the 10% surplus factor.

2) Determine the variable (direct) expenses identified with this course.

3) Using the absorption-cost approach, determine a break-even course fee. Do not include surplus factor.

4) Using the contribution-cost approach, determine a course fee price and state the contribution margin.

ILLUSTRATIONS OF THE RELEVANCE OF THE CONTRIBUTION APPROACH

| Dropping a Course |

Assume that there are three programs each composed of a group of courses. Management is considering dropping program C, which has consistently shown a net loss. The predicted income statements follow:

(See Chart on page 351)

PROGRAMS

	A	B	C	TOTAL
Fees	$50,000	$40,000	$10,000	$100,000
Variable expenses	29,500	28,000	7,500	65,000
Contribution margin	$20,500(41%)	$12,000(30%)	$ 2,500(25%)	$ 35,000(35%)
Fixed Expenses	16,500	9,000	4,500*	30,000
Operating Surplus	$ 4,000	$ 3,000	$(2,000)	$ 5,000

*Includes Program Planner's salary of $2,000

Assume that the only available alternatives are to drop Program C
or to continue with Program C. Assume further that the total assets
invested will not be affected by the decision. Thus, the issue becomes one
of selecting the programming combination that will provide a maximum surplus.
Comparisons follow:

INCOME STATEMENTS	KEEP PROGRAM	DROP PROGRAM	DIFFERENCE
Fees	$100,000	$90,000	-$10,000
Variable expenses	$65,000	$57,500	-$ 7,500
Fixed expenses	30,000	28,000	- 2,000
Total Expenses	$95,000	$85,500	-$ 9,500
Operating surplus	$ 5,000	$ 4,500	-$ 500

The data above reveal that dropping unprofitable Program C would make
matters worse instead of better. Why? Because all the fixed expenses would
continue except for the $2,000 that would be jarred loose through discharging
a program planner. Program C now contributes $2,500 toward the coverage of
fixed overhead; thus, the net effect of dropping Program C would be to forego
the $2,500 contribution in order to save the $2,000 salaries. The result would
be a $500 drop in overall surplus from $5,000 to $4,500.

Another important alternative besides the two discussed above is the
possibility of dropping Program C, keeping the programmer and using the vacant
facilities to expand, say, Program A to satisfy its expanding demand. If this
happened, and if fees of Program A are expanded by $10,000, surplus would
increase by $1,600 as follows:

	TOTAL KEEP PROGRAM C	TOTAL DROP C PROGRAM MORE A	DIFFERENCE	
			DROP C	MORE A
Fees	$100,000	$100,000	-$10,000	+$10,000
Variable expenses	$ 65,000	$ 63,400	-$ 7,500	+$ 5,900
Fixed expenses	30,000	30,000		
Total Expenses	$ 95,000	$ 93,400	-$ 7,500	+$ 5,900
Operating Surplus	$ 5,000	$ 6,600	-$ 2,500	+$ 4,100

351

Workshop Case #4

"Why don't we look at our adult participants as a collection of distinctive mini-markets and price accordingly?"

Mary Becker had just completed two concurrent courses: a marketing management course and an advanced seminar on adult education program planning. During the courses' presentation she became aware of two apparent parallel concepts which she had always thought existed, but they were never discussed or used by herself or her program planners when it came to the development of a course or program of courses.

On the one hand, adult education literature stated that unlike elementary or secondary education, adult participants presented a diversity of backgrounds, including: (1) age structure; (2) educational levels; (3) work experiences; (4) life experiences; (5) institutional expectations; (6) course expectations; (7) economic backgrounds, and; (8) reasons for participation.

Marketing literature also noted that no company's market is truly homogenous. In fact it is really a grouping of heterogenous or mini-markets. And, the company that realizes this fact gears its decision-making to such a consequence, and produces products or services to meet the needs of the mini-markets.

"The latter concept", recalled Mary, "was called market segmentation". She furthermore noted that: "they not only subdivide the potential market by demographic criteria (age, sex, income, education, etc.), but also by life styles, experiences and expectations". In discussions with the marketing course instructor Mary simply said: "once you have split your total market into the mini-markets, so what! That is, what do marketing managers do with the information?"

The instructor responded: "that this is the beginning foundation because if you know who your buyers are, where they would like to buy; what literature (newspapers, magazines, etc.) they read, plus some knowledge of competitive and consumer expected price ranges, then you can consider the marketing of the product or service".

"In other words you feel more confident about the four-p's."

"The four-what!" exclaimed Mary.

"The price of the product or service, the place or places where your customers would like to purchase it and where it would be advantageous to offer the product; the type of promotion which will appeal to them, and finally the form that the product should take. In your instance it would be course content, materials, course length, etc."

"In other words," said the instructor, "once you accept the concept of market segmentation, no product or service, and in your case an adult education course, is just presented to the so-called 'total potential market'. In fact, all four elements of the four-p's must be presented as a coherent whole--the product or service is as important as the price, as where the product is made available, as the promotion that attracts the customers''.

Problem:

(1) Reflecting on your own adult education organization, can you think of three distinct mini-markets? Please state a descriptive phrase or title for each mini-market and a short paragraph describing each market.

(2) Given the ''4-p's'' (product, place, promotion, and price), would you think of one adult education course that you would present to all three groups and how the marketing tactics would vary for each market.

FUNDING (SUMMARY)

Subsidy of local programs versus self-support is a source of extensive debate among adult educators. It was observed that most non-credit continuing education courses offered by colleges and universities are provided on a pay-as-you-go basis.

Often administrative costs of continuing education divisions are underwritten by the public institution. Private adult education institutions are expected to make a profit, being proprietary institutions. Residential centers for continuing education have the dilemma of trying to maintain quality programs of adult education, while at the same time trying to keep the rooms filled.

We know that funding the adult education operation is a key to success. Now the federal government is one of the largest sources for funding, with billions of dollars being spent for continuing education in many forms and numerous agencies.

We found that manpower training gets a lion's share of the financing for continuing education. We found that the federal government does not have a comprehensive, integrated federal policy regarding lifelong learning. Federal activity developed mainly in connection with problems dealing with the disadvantaged, and critical manpower needs. Emphasis has been mostly in preparing practitioners in specific fields such as social services, geriatrics, and the medical and allied health fields. Despite federal initiatives, education is traditionally and constitutionally the responsibility of the state. Much funding is done through state departments of education getting federal monies for categorical programs.

There are limited monies for research and experimental programs dealing with adult education. Some research funding has come from the National Institute for Education, dealing with adult learning. There is need for more monies for dissemination of the findings of research, and successful programs working with adults.

Robert Pitchell has pointed up the need for financial support for part-time students.

Richard W. Jonsen found that pricing and funding practices dealing with lifelong learning are neither uniform nor well categorized. Most but not all non-credit offerings are self-supporting. There is a need for more subsidy for adult learning activities, credit and non-credit. Coordination is needed both at the state and national level to stretch the dollar. A model for state organizational coordination was presented.

Since marketing strategies, and pricing are so important for the success of adult education programs, a suggested workshop for practitioners is presented with some actual cases for discussion.

An extensive annotated bibliography dealing with financing lifelong learning presents some of the issues for funding part-time students, and some ideas for building the concept of lifelong learning into the fabric of our society.

QUESTIONS:
1. Should noncredit activities (such as community service courses in the community colleges) be subsidized?
2. Should subsidies to individuals be limited to full-time students or broadened to part-time students meeting the criterion of need?
3. Should continuing education units (CEU's) be subsidized?
4. Should there be categorical funding such as in the Community Service and Continuing Education programs (Title I, Higher Education Act)?
5. Should subsidies to individuals be limited to use at collegiate or postsecondary institutions? (Denmark, Sweden, England subsidize non-formal adult education activities such as in the Danish Folk Schools)
6. Should labor education be subsidized, or must unions pay their own way?
7. What are the advantages and disadvantages of subsidy for university extension divisions? Why should cooperative extension be subsidized federally, and through state funds but not general extension?
8. What are the possibilities for coordinating the diverse agencies offering lifelong learning, and programs of continuing education in the various states? How can federal subsidy assist in that coordination?

The argument is made by some that adults should pay their own way. Yet, our best investment in terms of human resource development, and the eventual generation of tax revenue, was the training provided by the G.I. Bill.

Financing Lifelong Learning: Annotated Bibliography *

Abert, James G. "Viewpoint: Money for Continuing Education."
Change 5 (October 1973): 8, 9.
   Author proposes a "National Continuing Education Trust",
a vehicle for financing continuing education. "Funds for the
trust would accumulate in the form of individual entitlements,
and might be keyed to social security numbers" (p. 8). Suggests
several ways for financing the trust.

Academy for Educational Development, Inc. **Never Too Old to
Learn.** A report submitted to the Edna McConnell Clark Foundation. New York: Academy for Educational Development, Inc.,
1974.
   Discussion of innovative programs that encourage older
people to enroll including programs that offer free or reduced
tuition. Discussion of financing educational programs for older
people.

American Council on Education. Committee on the Financing
of Higher Education for Adult Students. **Financing Part-time
Students: The New Majority in Post-secondary Education.** Report
of the Committee on the Financing of Higher Education for
Adult Students to the Office of Governmental Relations. American
Council on Education. Washington, D.C.: American Council
on Education, 1974.
   State that while part-time students now represent over half
of the students in postsecondary institutions, they are discrim-
inated against in receiving financial aid. Find that proposals
for financing postsecondary education tend to be directed toward
an undifferentiated population but with direct or implied emphasis
on full-time regular students.

Bengelsdorf, Winnie. **Women's Stake in Low Tuition.** Washington,
D.C.: American Association of State Colleges and Universities,
October 1974.
   Case made for lowering tuition. Discusses inequitable treatment of men and women and full- and part-time students in
higher education financing policies. Suggests ways for working
to support lower tuition.

Benson, Charles S., and Hodgkinson, Harold L. **Implementing the
Learning Society.** San Francisco: Jossey-Bass, 1974.
   Support entitlement plan available to all persons, independent
of age or income. Grants would provide four years of income
support and the equivalent of two years' tuition. Purpose is to
free college access from influence of social class and improve
efficiency of higher education.

355

Berstecher, Dieter, and Hecquet, Ignace. "Cost and Financing Problems in University Education." In A University of the Future, pp. 77-129. By Dieter Berstecher et al. The Hague: Martinus Nijhoff, 1974.

In Part II of this chapter, "Sources and Methods of Financing: Possible Alternatives and Implications", discuss various sources for funding universities (the student, private or public companies, and local or central public authorities) and financing methods. One method discussed involves individuals contributing to an "educational fund". "One possible solution would be to allow the individual to distribute the foreseeable cost of his successive training periods over the whole of his working life. The individual would regularly pay his contribution to an 'education fund' and would draw from this fund the costs of his period of education" (p. 112).

Broschart, J.R. "A Synthesis of Selected Manuscripts about the Education of Adults in the United States." Prepared for the Bureau of Occupational and Adult Education, United States Office of Education, February, 1976.

Synthesis of study documents relating to the concept of lifelong learning. Includes section dealing with barriers to learning, including that of cost.

Bushnell, David S. **Needed: A Voucher Plan in Support of Continuing Education.** Alexandria, Virginia: Human Resources Research Organization, August 1973.

Due to new emphasis on career education, increased job competition, and technological changes forcing job changes. author sees a greater need for ensuring lifelong learning opportunities. Author sees the enactment of legislation to set up a voucher program as ensuring lifelong learning opportunities.

The C.I.C. Study of the non-Traditional Student. Iowa City, Iowa: Division of Extension and University Services, The University of Iowa, 1973. Report No. 1: **University Credit and Degree-Earning Opportunities for Adults,** by Robert F. Ray.

Recommend that institutions give due consideration to the financial needs of the part-time student. Fee schedules should be reviewed to provide equal treatment for the part-time student.

Carnegie Council on Policy Studies in Higher Education. **The Federal Role in Postsecondary Education: Unfinished Business 1975-80.** San Francisco: Jossey-Bass, 1975.

Among recommendations relating to student aid and related programs, the Council recommends restructuring of the Basic Educational Opportunity Grants program, gradually becoming an entitlement program; supports structuring the loan program along the lines of the National Student Loan Bank recommended by the Carnegie Commission in 1970; and recommends removing restrictions of aid to part-time students, permitting part-time students to be eligible for aid on a pro-rated basis for all federal student aid programs.

Carnegie Commission on Higher Education. **Higher Education: Who Pays? Who Benefits? Who Should Pay?**
New York: McGraw-Hill, 1973.

To aid the economically disadvantaged student, the Commission recommends an expansion of federal student aid, including full funding of the Basic Opportunity Grants program, and a gradual increase in tuition charges in public institutions except for lower-division students. Recommends the establishment of a National Student Loan Bank that would ". . .permit borrowing up to a reasonable limit that would reflect both tuition charges and subsistence costs. Loan repayments should be based upon income currently earned, and up to 40 years should be permitted for repayment" (p. 121).

Carnegie Commission on High Education. **Less Time, More Options: Education beyond the High School.**
New York: McGraw-Hill, 1971.

Recommend that all persons after high school graduation have two years of education placed "in the bank" for them to be used whenever they want. List five ways this could be accomplished including ". . .by adding to social security a program for 'educational security' to be paid through payroll taxes on employers and employees, with the benefits to be available on application after a sustained employment" (p. 21).

Carnegie Commission on High Education. **Toward a Learning Society: Alternative Channels to Life, Work and Service.**
New York: McGraw-Hill, 1973

In chapter 4, "New Funding for Postsecondary Education", discuss alternative means of financing lifelong learning, including state or federal programs of tuition credit for two years of postsecondary education, paid educational leave, privately funded programs and publicly funded programs, including federally sponsored endowment plans. In Chapter 5, reconfirm recommendation to establish a program whereby two years of postsecondary education would be placed "in the bank" for every person after graduation from high school, to be withdrawn at any time.

Carnegie Council on Policy Studies in Higher Education. **Low or No Tuition, the Feasibility of a National Policy for the First Two Years of College.** San Francisco: Jossey-Bass, 1975.

Analyze proposals for low or no tuition in the first two years of public postsecondary education. Conclude that achievement of the above through state action is improbable and through federal action, most difficult. Also conclude that the federal government give highest priority to those programs to which it is already committed.

Cartter, Allan M. "**The Need for a New Approach to Financing Recurrent Education.**" Berkeley, California, 1973.

As a means of financing recurrent education, author proposes a "personal social insurance account," available to each individual at the age of eighteen. Throughout the individual's lifetime, the accounts could be drawn against for educational purposes, up to an amount equal to 1/2 of the tuition for four academic years. Monthly subsistence payments could be drawn (equal to 1/2 of an individual's average earnings in the preceding five years) after five years of employment. "Any time after age 60, any unexpended balance in one's account could either be exhausted as a terminal employment leave benefit, or added to one's OASI (old age and Survivors Insurance) balance and reflected in higher pension benefits" (p. 13). Funding would be provided by a $10.2 billion transfer from existing programs and every employed person would have an annual 4 percent surcharge on earned income.

Christoffel, Pamela, and Rice, Lois. **Federal Policy Issues and Data Needs in Postsecondary Education.** Final Report to the National Center for Educational Statistics. Washington, D.C.: Government Printing Office, 1975.

One of the issues identified is that of federal support of recurrent education. See a need for data to identify those who wish to participate in recurrent education but do not, analysis of barriers to participation in adult education, and data on charges incurred by student participants and how these charges are met. "Statistics which describe what portion of these charges are paid by the students themselves, by employers, or by other persons or organizations are necessary for Federal Planners reviewing student financial assistance programs, as well as for their consideration of alternatives" (p. 33).

College Entrance Examination Board. College Scholarship Service. Panel on Financial Need Analysis. **New Approaches to Student Financial Aid.** Report of the Panel on Student Financial Need Analysis. By Allan M. Cartter, Chairman. New York: College Entrance Examination Board, 1971.

Panel states that while a steady broadening of the GI Bill concept to include more groups would be a desirable goal, it is doubtful that movement towards this goal will become a reality due to the demands upon public and private funds for the foreseeable future (p. 80).

Commission on Educational Planning (Alberta). Walter H. Worth, Commissioner. **A Choice of Futures.** Edmonton, Alberta: L. S. Wall, 1972.

Report advocates lifelong learning. The Commission sees a greater need to tie together work and education. States that a voucher system is unlikely for the foreseeable future but should monitor voucher systems elsewhere. See the possibility of employers contributing to an educational fund to cover employees' tuition fees and other expenses associated with leaves for formal learning experiences. Report includes a discussion of the possibility of setting up an educational bank, entitling individuals to a certain number of years of schooling at public expense. At present time, the Commission emphasizes financing education through the provision of grants.

Commission on Non-Traditional Study. Samuel B. Gould, Chairman. **Diversity by Design.** San Francisco: Jossey-Bass, 1973.

To broaden educational opportunities for adults, the Commission recommends providing greater financial support for adult students. **"Financial support (either scholarships or loans) should be provided to all postsecondary school students on which they may draw according to their educational needs, circumstances of life, and continuing or recurrent interests in improvement.** If this recommendation were to be made a reality, the entire span of years of an individual from completion of secondary school to death would be regarded as a single period of time. Every individual would receive as a right a predetermined number of dollar credits which he could either use up immediately for college, defer for later use, or balance out according to his needs for initial and deferred education" (pp. 24-25). As a first step in reform, the Commission suggests the revision of existing student-aid programs to better meet the requirements of lifelong education.

Goldman, Ralph M. **"Lifespan Educational Insurance: A Proposal"** In **Alternative Futures in American Education; Appendix to Hearing on H.R. 3606 and Related Bills to Create a National Institute of Education before the Selected Subcommittee on Education,** pp. 241-47. U.S. Congress, Committee on Education and Labor, Committee Print. Washington, D.C.: Government Printing Office, 1972.

Honey, John C., and Hartle, Terry W. **A Career Education Entitlement Plan: Administrative and Political Issues.** Prepared for the Department of Health, Education, and Welfare, The National Institute of Education. Syracuse, New York: Educational Finance and Governance Center, Syracuse University Research Corporation, April 1975.

Discuss existing and proposed entitlement schemes (Basic Educational Opportunity Grant Program, GI Bill for Vietnam veterans, New York State's Tuition Assistance Plan, the proposed plans of Norman D. Kurland, Herbert E. Striner, and Charles S. Benson and Harold L. Hodgkinson) and then deal with administrative issues and political considerations of an entitlement program. Two proposals for pursuing the entitlement idea are offered: (1) to initiate a several-year experiment with a limited sample of recipients, (2) to build on existing entitlement activities of the federal government and several of the states.

Kirschner Associates, Inc. **"Summary Report; An Analysis of Selected Issues in Adult Education".** Prepared for Office of Planning, Budgeting and Evaluation, Office of Education, U.S. Department of Health, Education, and Welfare, February 1976.

Project identifies and explores various policies for the federal government concerning the education of adults. Among policy issues discussed are: policies dealing with the level of federal support of adult education and policies concerning systems for delivering adult education. Conclude that larger federal budgets are required if the national goals for the education of adults are to be met. Under the discussion of systems for delivering adult education, discuss means of support including direct funding, vouchers, and tax incentives. State that "given the variety of financial approaches and the substantial sums of money involved, this area too deserves policy consideration to the extent possible using the data collected in this project" (p. 15)

Klein, William A. **"A Proposal for a Universal Personal Capital Account."** University of California at Los Angeles, February 1974.

Proposes a plan, entitling individuals eighteen or over to an account which could be drawn against for educational and certain medical services. Allows for persons over sixty-five to draw upon any remaining amount (with accumulated interest) to purchase an annuity.

Kurland, Norman D. **"Financing Lifelong Learning: An Approach to an Age-Neutral Educational Entitlement."** Study of Adult Education, New York State Education Department, Albany, New York, 5 February 1975. (ED 113 457)

A shorter and updated verson of "Financing Lifelong Learning: Proposal for an Age-Neutral Educational Entitlement Program", November 25, 1974. Proposes that an entitlement be granted annually to every adult to be used for a broad range of educational activities. Unused entitlement would remain available throughout the individual's life and would earn interest at a rate to be specified.

Kurland, Norman D., and Comly, Lucy T. **"Financing Lifelong Education: Next Steps in Exploring the Entitlement Approach."** Study of Adult Education, New York State Education Department, Albany, New York, 9 December 1975.

Proposes activities for further exploration of the entitlement approach including production of papers along 14 study topics, development of proposals for further work, and maintenance of a national clearinghouse function for entitlement-related explorations.

Kurland, Norman D., and Comly, Lucy T. **"Financing Lifelong Learning: Rationale and Alternatives."** Study of Adult Education, New York State Education Department, Albany, New York, 8 April 1975. (ED 113 456)

Presents rationale for financing lifelong learning and examination of seven alternatives including: (1) State financing of leadership positions, (2) State financing of information and counseling services, (3) State aid to institutions, (4) institutional incentive grants, (5) extension of State student aid to part-time and non-credit students, (6) an entitlement approach, and (7) tax incentives.

Levine, Herbert A. "Labor-Management Policies on Educational Opportunity." Paper presented at the Recurrent Education Conference, Session 6. Industry Worker Concerns in Recurrent Education, Georgetown University, Washington, D.C., 21 March 1973.

Of the many types of educational opportunity programs offered in collective bargaining agreements, paper concentrates on tuition-refund programs, union-industry education and training funds, and paid educational leave.

Levine, Herbert A. "Paid Educational Leaves: Implications for Work and Education in America." In Second National Conference on Open Learning and Nontraditional Study, **Conference Proceedings; Designing Diversity '75**, pp. 173-178. Compiled by C. Edward Cavert. Lincoln, Nebraska: University of Mid-America, 1975.

Discusses the various ways in which industry finances their employees' education. Includes tuition refund programs, cents-per-hour educational and cultural trust funds, scholarship benefits for children of members, and paid educational leave.

Levine, Herbert A. "Summary Statement." Presented at the Conference on Foreign Legislation on Paid Educational Leave: Implications for the United States, Woodrow Wilson House, Washington, D.C., 17, 18, 19 September 1974.

Summarizes the discussions of the Conference which dealt

with: "(1) the recent actions of the International Labour Organization on Paid Educational Leave; (2) the attempts to increase educational opportunity through National and State Legislation and private practice, including collective bargaining in France, Germany and England; (3) some of the more forward-looking American educational opportunity plans currently being offered as unilateral company or international union plans and/or as these programs developed through the collective bargaining process" (p. 2).

Lytle, R.J. **Liberty Schools: A Parent's Voucher Plan.** Farmington, Michigan: Structures Publishing Company, 1975.

In the chapter entitled "Higher Education", proposes financing higher education through entitlements made to every person over eighteen years of age". . .representing his fair share of the total tax dollars spent on higher education" (p. 133). The purpose of the entitlement would be to enable the student to choose among the various types of education, and not be forced into enrolling in the least costly. Colleges and universities could be required to". . .provide scholarships in some relation to their income from gifts and endowments, thus providing. . .similar leverage for the poor. . ." (p. 135).

McClure, Peter. "Grubstake: A Radical Proposal." **Change** 8 (June 1976): 30, 38-44

Proposes a voucher system granting each individual at age eighteen or upon high school graduation the sum of $10,000 or more to be used for increased take-home pay, further education, or financial investments.

Medsker, Leland et al. **Extending Opportunities for a College Degree: Practices, Problems and Potentials.** Berkeley, California: Center for Research and Development in Higher Education, University of California, Berkeley, 1975.

Report of a study of various postsecondary adult programs offered in a variety of systems and institutions. Chapter VIII, "The Economics of Extended Degree Programs" includes findings of how students met educational expenses. Chapter XI, "Suggested Guidelines for Implementing Extended Degree Programs - Finance" includes suggestion that consideration be given to a voucher-type system to aid adult and part-time students.

Mushkin, Selma J., ed. **Recurrent Education.** Washington, D.C.: U.S. Department of Health, Education, and Welfare, National Institute of Education, 1974.

Consists of papers deriving from the Georgetown University Conference on Recurrent Education, March 1973. Includes a section which deals with the "Financing and Politics of Recurrent Education."

National Advisory Council on Extension and Continuing Education. **Equity of Access: Continuing Education and the Part-Time Student.** 9th Annual Report. Washington, D.C.: National Advisory Council on Extension and Continuing Education, 1975.

In addition to the Council's recommendations relating to Title I of the Higher Education Act of 1965, the Council recommends, in Recommendation Seven, that amendments be made to the student financial assistance provisions of Title IV of the Higher Education Act to support needs of adult part-time students. This includes a proposed amendment to broaden the "basic opportunity grant program" to include part-time students attending on less than a half-time basis.

New York. State University of New York. University Task Force on Part-Time Students. **State University of New York and the Part-time Student; A Report of the University Task Force on Part-time Students.** Albany, New York: University Task Force on Part-time students, February 1976.

In chapter 5, "Financing Part-Time Education", the Task Force urges the development of a five-year plan to lower per-credit-hour tuition to 1/30th the tuition charged to full-time enrollment. State that steps should be taken to provide equal access to financial aid for the part-time student. Suggest possible alternate financing strategies.

New York. University of the State of New York. Board of Regents **Education beyond High School: The Regents Statewide Plan for the Development of Post-Secondary Education, 1972.** Albany New York: University of the State of New York, State Education Department, November 1972.

In "Part IV: Noncollegiate Post-Secondary Education", recommend that "student financial aid programs incorporate additional provisions for adults who wish to continue their education beyond high school" and "students be permitted the choice of applying financial assistance to any post-secondary educational programs in the State, including non-collegiate programs." (p 180)

New York, University of State of New York. Board of Regents. **Postsecondary Education in Transition; the Regents 1974 Progress Report on "Education beyond High School: the Regents Statewide Plan for the Development of Postsecondary Education, 1972"** Albany, New York: University of the State of New York, November 1974.

Includes recommendations aimed at extending access to postsecondary education for adults. Includes recommendations to broaden the Tuition Assistance Program to include part-time students, to eliminate the provision in the Tuition Assistance Program which excludes students who graduated prior to

January 1, 1974, and to enable all adults in comparable economic circumstances to qualify for student aid.

New York. University of the State of New York. State Education Department. Bureau of Research in Higher and Professional Education. **The "Voucher System" and Higher Education in New York State.** Albany, New York: The University of the State of New York, Autumn 1970.

Focuses on the "voucher system" as it may be used in New York State to finance higher education. This report explores the historical background, examines the Hansen and Weisbrod Plan,". . .applies it to New York State, and discusses the advantages and disadvantages, implications, administrative needs, and estimated costs" (p. 2)

Nolfi, George J. "Analytical Framework for Comparative Policy and Program Analysis of Alternative Proposals for Federal Programs of Educational Entitlement." Prepared for submission to the Ford Foundation. University Consultants, Inc., Cambridge, Massachusetts, 18 October 1973. Revised 6 November 1973. Draft

Discusses the problems surrounding the discussion of the entitlement concept and the need for a comprehensive analysis of the implications of alternative entitlement program designs through comparative analysis of results of alternative programs within a fixed budget constraint" (p. 1)

Nolfi, George J. "Design for Open Learning: Implementing a Network of Existing Educational Resources." In Second National Conference on Open Learning and Nontraditional Study, **Designing Diversity '75; Conference Proceedings,** pp423-441. Compiled by C. Edward Cavert, Lincoln, Nebraska: University of Mid-America, 1975.

Part I includes eleven rules for effecting research, design, pilot-testing and implementing expanded open learning. Part II summarizes two program initiatives in Massachusetts: the Adult Recurrent Education Entitlement Voucher Program and the Regional Education Opportunities Center program.

Nolfi, George J. "Proposal for a National Adult Recurrent Education Entitlement Voucher Program: Financing Open Learning and Continuing Education through Selective Entitlement." Testimony presented before the Subcommittee on Postsecondary Education, House Committee on Education and Labor, Washington, D.C., 25 September 1975.

In Part I, "Context and Rationale: the Need for Public Policy and Investment", states that while many adults are being served by current continuing education opportunities, two major groups are not: "Disadvantaged Clientele" and "Second-Chance Clientele." Believes that federal subsidy should be targeted on these two groups. "Public policy and investment should therefore be selective and compliment, not supplant the existing provate investment" (p. 6) Argues in favor of choosing selective entitlement vouchers rather than universal entitlements. In Part II proposes a specific plan (adapted from the state plan now pending in the Massachusetts legislature) for financing adult continuing and recurrent postsecondary education.

Nolfi, George J. "Setting and Criteria for the Design of an Effective Public Policy of Educational Entitlements." Presented to the Seminar on Entitlements convened by the Office of the Assistant Secretary of Education, Washington, D.C., 21 July 1975.

"This paper presents: (1) a brief review of the origins of the Adult Recurrent Education Selective Entitlement Voucher Proposal now pending in the Massachusetts Legislature; (2) a discussion of several key facts which constitute the general background and setting of the questions of adult educational entitlement; and (3) a set of criteria for the design of effective public policy and programs of adult educational entitlement" (p. 1)

Nolfi, George J. **State-based Adult Recurrent Education Entitlement Voucher Program: Financing Open Learning and Continuing Education through a Selective Entitlement.** Cambridge, Massachusetts: University Consultants, Inc., 1974, 1975.

An analysis of the rationale and design of the proposed legislation pending in Massachusetts, (the Adult Recurrent Education Entitlement Voucher Program) and its applicability to other states.

Nolfi, George J., and Nelson, Valerie, I. "The Implementation and Operation of a State-based Adult Recurrent Education Entitlement Voucher Program to Finance Open Learning and Continuing Education". Paper #2 in **Plan for an Open Learning Network in Massachusetts.** Cambridge, Massachusetts: University Consultants, Inc., July 1974. Working Paper.

Elaboration of the specific operational design for the "Adult Recurrent Education Entitlement Voucher Program"

Nolfi, George J., and Nelson, Valerie I. **Strengthening the Alternative Postsecondary Education System: Continuing and Part-time Study in Massachusetts.** 2 vols. Cambridge, Massachusetts: University Consultants, Inc., 1973.

The initial proposal for proposed legislation in Massachusetts, the "Adult Recurrent Education Entitlement Voucher Program"; vouchers to be awarded to adults with priorities placed on those of low previous education and low income.

Panel on Financing Low-income and Minority Students in Higher

Education. **Toward Equal Opportunity for Higher Education; Report.** New York: College Entrance Examination Board, 1973.

The panel recommends a federal grant program that would entitle full-time and part-time students from lower-income families to direct grants, up to $2,000 annually. Students in this program would also receive vouchers to purchase supplementary services (tutorial programs, etc.) in the amount of $35/month.

Peterson, Richard E. et al. **Postsecondary Alternatives: Meeting California's Educational Needs; A Feasability Study.** Second Technical Report: **Inventory of Existing Postsecondary Alternatives,** by Marcia B. Salner. Sacramento, California: Assembly Publications Office, September, 1975.

Report describes postsecondary, part-time educational opportunities available in California. Part I describes opportunities by educational segment (community colleges, University of California, independent colleges, etc.). Part 2 gives an overview of the programs. Among author's conclusions are that access for part-time students could be extended by changing state policy to extend financial aid to needy students who wish to study in part-time, off-campus degree programs, and to give incentives for the University of California to establish part-time, pro-rated fees.

Pitchell, Robert J. "Financing Part-Time Students." In **Lifelong Learners - a New Clientele for Higher Education,** pp. 40-46. Edited by Dyckman W. Vermilye. San Francisco: Jossey-Bass, 1974.

Reports discrimination in financing the part-time student by collegiate institutions, state and federal governments. Suggests that few of the current financing plans take a differential approach to postsecondary clientele groups, especially as they relate to part-time students. Proposes five priority alternatives for financing postsecondary education which would aid the part-time student.

Regan, Peter F.; Solkoff, Norman; and Stafford, Walter F. **Recurrent Education in the State of New York.** Recurrent Education; Policy and Development in OECD Countries Series. Paris: Organization for Economic Co-operation and Development, Center for Educational Research and Innovation, 1972.

Comments related to financing recurrent education are included in "Problems Facing Recurrent Education" (pp. 31-32).

Rehn, Gosta. "For Greater Flexibility of Working Life." **OECD Observer** No. 62 (February 1973): 3-7

Recommends an integrated insurance system for transferring income between different periods of life. "Each person would be given a right to draw on his account for purposes of his own choosing in a way that would be similar in a technical sense to the right to borrow on that part of one's private life insurance which is not needed to cover the risk-sharing involved' (p. 4). Whether or not this system is introduced, suggests that each individual, past the age of compulsory schooling, be given a basic study credit to cover living expenses and tuition costs that could be used at any period of his life. The alternative of using the money for other purposes would be available if an individual at a later stage of life had not used it for study.

Reimer, Everett W. **School is Dead: Alternatives in Education.** Garden City, New York: Doubleday, 1971.

In Chapter 10, "Financing Universal Education," proposes a redirection of educational tax funds from educational institutions into a system of personal education accounts. At the level of expenditure at the time of writing this would provide each person with $250 per year to spend on education; at birth, a life-time fund of $17,000. "Putting financial command of educational resources in the hands of learners does not solve all the problems of allocating these resources, but it is an indispensable step toward a solution. Not only the problems of equalizing opportunity across class lines but many other problems. . .become manageable with the aid of this principle. Schools would stand, adjust, or fail according to the satisfaction of their clients. Other educational institutions would develop in accordance with their ability to satisfy client needs. Learners would choose whether to learn on the job or full-time, which skills they wanted to learn at what age they wanted to use their educational resources, and how" (p. 144)

Scribner, Harvey B., and Stevens, Leonard B. "Entitlements for Career Education: A Background Paper." Prepared for the National Institute of Education, April 1975.

Proposes granting entitlements, on the model of the GI Bill, to any person who left school before acquiring a high school diploma. There would be a stipulation that the entitlement ". . .be used for purposes of career education. By 'career education,' the government would mean any legitimate educational pursuit designed to further or enhance the applicant's career or work objectives" (p. 33)

The Second Newman Report: National Policy and Higher Education. Report of a Special Task Force to the Secretary of Health, Education, and Welfare. Cambridge, Massachusetts: The M.I.T. Press, 1973.

Encourage the revision of student aid guidelines to include

a broader age group. Encourage serious study of various methods that could be used to support students returning to school later in life. Recommend that ". . .the Secretary of Health, Education, and Welfare commission a comprehensive analysis of these financing strategies, develop a forum for the public discussion of the competing priorities and diverse interests involved, and develop an effective program of financing of students during recurrent periods of education" (p. 111).

University of Notre Dame. Center for Continuing Education. **The Learning Society; A Report of the Study on Continuing Education and the Future.** Notre Dame, Indiana: Center for Continuing Education, 1973(?)

Recommendations 3 and 4 relate to financing lifelong learning. Under Recommendation 3, suggest that the citizen could receive financial support at any age to guarantee access to educational opportunities, the program accompanied by an income stipend covering a portion of wages lost during participation in education programs. Recommendation 4 encourages changes in public policy to promote lifelong learning including: (1) released time from employment (cost financed through a trust fund fed by employer and employee contributions) and (2) tax credits and tax deductions for individual educational expenses.

Van Dusen, William D. "Financial Aid for Part-time Students: Status and Issues." Report by the Washington Office of the College Entrance Examination Board for the National Advisory Council on Extension and Continuing Education, 1 September 1975.

Identifies problems in providing part-time students equal access to postsecondary education. Summarizes reasons for, and raises questions about, adopting an "age-neutral" educational entitlement.

FOOTNOTES CHAPTER 19

1 Pamela C. Christoffel, **Current Federal Programs for Lifelong Learning,** Washington, D.C. College Entrance Examination Board, 1977.

2 Jonsen, Richard W. LIFELONG LEARNING: STATE POLICIES AND STATE FEDERAL RELATIONSHIPS, PRIORITIES, ISSUES AND ALTERNATIVES. Report No. 113, Sept. 1978, Education Commission of the States, Denver, Colorado, 80295 p. 5.

3 "State Appropriations up 24 Percent in Two Years," Chronicle of Higher Education, Oct. 25, 1976.

4 Jonsen, Richard W. op. cit., p. 11.

5 Used by permission.

Chapter XX

COUNSELING
ADULT LEARNERS

Then said a teacher, Speak to us of Teaching. And he said:
No man can reveal to you aught but that which already lies
half asleep in the dawning of your knowledge.

The teacher who walks in the shadow of the temple, among
his followers, gives not of his wisdom but rather of his
faith and his lovingness.

If he is indeed wise he does not bid you enter the house
of his wisdom, but rather leads you to the threshold of your
own mind.

-Kahlil Gibran, The Prophet

THE NEED FOR ADULT COUNSELING-
A NEGLECTED AREA

A more systematic and well-planned program of guidance
and counseling, particularly with the rapid technological changes
occurring in our culture, is badly needed in our society. Counseling is defined by one counselor as face-to-face interviews conducted in privacy, usually centered in immediate problems, and often
terminated when solutions are found; the process of helping
individuals to better understand themselves in their abilities,
aptitudes, interests, vocational goals, and personal limitations.
With the prediction that persons will change jobs on an average
of at least three times during their lifetime, more adequate
advising for adults is imperative.

In the education of adults, effective counseling is one of the
most neglected areas of development. With the elective system
in our secondary schools, much attention has been given to
guidance programs and to the training and certification of secondary personnel in counseling. But to a large extent adults have had
to seek counsel where they could find it. Too often this has
been from persons with little or no special training in the art
of adult counseling. It is a well-recognized fact that the needs
of adults are different from those of youth.

In many respects business and industry have done a better job
of recognizing the importance of counseling adults than has
education. Directors of personnel, social workers, directors
of adult education, and administrators in voluntary agencies have

been concerned with the well-being of individuals who are maturing. They have felt for a long time that most persons would be happier and work more efficiently if engaged in tasks for which they are best fitted in terms of their abilities and interests. Our increasingly technological society must develop a concern for more adequate counseling and guidance for the young adult, the adult in later years, and the retired person. The extended life span and the increased leisure time available make the counseling function even more demanding for our institutions of learning.

In a recent interview, a representative of the Illinois Junior College Board predicted that very soon the State of Illinois will be spending more than a million dollars per year on the guidance function in the community colleges of the state. Nearly every state in the union is feeling the need for guidance personnel trained in the art of counseling. Our universities are not yet providing adequately trained persons for the growing agencies of secondary education and the many burgeoning agencies of adult and continuing education.

When radical changes come in our society, the individuals who are inadequately trained and vocationally maladjusted suffer the most. Most of the employment services of the various states and the territories have done a remarkable job of assisting both the individual and industries in testing for vocational skills and for placement in jobs most fitting for the adult. Where there are physical and mental handicaps, the vocational rehabilitation departments of the states have helped widows, invalids, and their dependents develop or reclaim skills necessary to make them productive members of our society again.

Some of our universities are making special efforts to provide testing and guidance services to adults as well as to youth. Special programs at the University of Minnesota and the University of Wisconsin give individual counseling and guidance to women interested in refresher courses and re-entry into the labor market. Some agencies of adult education offer vocational testing on a fee basis, but most public institutions are providing some kind of guidance as a public service. Many institutions of learning are offering special reading programs whereby the mature student may improve his skills in reading and become more proficient in comprehension, gain skills in speed reading, and develop effective study habits. Through the skillful utilization of two professors with Ph.D.'s in reading, one Northern university has noncredit reading improvement courses available to the entire student body, youth and adult. Many potential dropouts have been salvaged.[1]

Perhaps a most productive investment would be the development of reading laboratories which could be utilized by adults on a flexible time schedule. Through testing and counseling, the skills which cripple the adult learner could be analyzed and programs developed to bring maximum utilization of talent and ability.

THE TASK OF COUNSELING SERVICES

It is recognized that though the task of counseling is an important one, it is also a difficult one. Many adults have a traditional reluctance to make inquiry of agencies involved with adult education. But economic, political and social changes are creating conditions which are forcing individuals to recognize vocational and educational needs and to seek counsel. Because more adults are identifying with agencies of adult learning of various types, out-of-school youth and adults are beginning to seek organized educational resources to help them discover gaps in their training, and to improve skills where they have problem areas needing assistance. George C. Mann, for many years Chief of the Division of Adult and Continuation Education for the state of California, has estimated from his surveys that 75 percent of the adults enrolling in classes need and want counseling and guidance of some kind.

Once the adult has found a chosen field, he or she usually want to deepen knowledge in a trade or profession. Most adults now recognize that further training pays off in income, prestige, and position. Further personal development will bring benefits in security, wages, respect, self-understanding, and esteem. The adult also needs counsel in problems of part education, in becoming a more adequate partner in the family, and in being a more effective citizen in the community. Often counseling may result in a recognition of the need to study art, music, literature, or modern languages to be used in enriching a travel experience. Emphasis is put upon being able to participate more intelligently in discussion and increased creativity.

Such improved skills will prove beneficial on the job, in human relations, and in self-development. The counselor of adults can guide the inquiring adult to pastures of learning and social and intellectual challenges for growth.

EFFECTIVE COUNSELING DEFINED

W. R. Reilly of the Dade County Public Schools in Florida has defined counseling as the face-to-face interview, conducted in privacy, usually centered in immediate problems, and often terminated when the solution of the problem is found. [2] Counseling is the process of helping individuals to better understand themselves in the light of their abilities, aptitudes, interests, strengths, and limitations. This process enables them to use their education and social potentialities more wisely and, as a result, become increasingly more capable of mature self-guidance.

The effective counselor is the person who can relate well with the adult, help the adult reflect on problems, point out strengths and weaknesses in the adult's approach to self-actualization, and offer suggestions for educational programs, methods, or agencies for fulfilling the goals outlined by the adult. It is dangerous for the counselor to attempt to solve the problems for the client, for there are many subtle motivations that cannot be fully understood without much depth counseling. But the counselor can suggest alternatives, open up new avenues of possible solutions to problems, and suggest educational programs that may assist the adult in enriching life or developing needed skills. Carol Rogers has made the academic community aware of the danger of advising the client, "If I were you, I would ..." The role of the counselor is to help the adult come to wise and mature decisions and to take responsibility for his or her actions.

One of the many purposes of counseling adults is to aid each person in the process of realizing his best self, developing latent talents, discovering new areas of creativity. This may be in formal or informal learning situations. When A. H. Maslow studied creativity among adults, he found that he had to change his outlook regarding creativity as a result of the cases he interviewed. Maslow said:

I first had to change my ideas about creativity as soon as I began studying people who were positively healthy, highly evolved and matured, self-actualizing. Furthermore, I soon discovered that I had, like most other people, been thinking of creativeness in terms of products, and secondly, I had unconsciously assumed that any painter, any poet, any composer was leading a creative life.

But these expectations were broken up by various of my subjects. For instance, one woman, uneducated, poor, a full-time housewife and mother, did none of these conventionally creative things and yet was a marvelous cook, mother wife, and homemaker. With little money, her home was somehow always beautiful. She was a perfect hostess. Her meals were banquets. Her taste in linens, silver, glass, crockery, and furniture was impeccable. She was in all these areas original, novel, ingenious, unexpected, inventive. I just had to call her creative. I learned from her and others like her that a first-rate soup is more creative than a second-rate painting, and that, generally, cooking or parenthood or making a home could be creative while poetry need not be; it could be uncreative. [3]

Maslow found that the self-actualizing individual is more "self-accepting than the average." He is less afraid of his own thoughts

372

and less fearful of being disapproved.

A part of the counselor's task is to help the adult look at himself or herself realistically. To assist the maturing adult become what Rogers has called the "fully functioning person" is another objective. To help the adult see and accept limitations and to discover and cultivate talents is the role of the counselor.

Dr. Martin Bartels, Director of Placement, Northern Illinois University says:

The most important role of the counselor of adults in placement is to assist the client in self-realization. By this we mean acquiring a durable view of his capabilities and how he can release these capabilities in a work-a-day world. This calls for a balance between suggested procedures on the one hand and non-directive counseling on the other. The important goal which is to be achieved is self-realization on the part of the counselee.

I have been challenged by the idea that anyone faced with a problem of reassessing or adjusting his work status could well ask himself what are his immediate goals and what are his goals for the future, say five, ten or fifteen years ahead. The answer to this kind of question frequently brings with it some fascinating discovery of need for educational development. (Interview, February 5, 1967)

In interviewing adults, it is useful for the counselor to keep in mind the thought that we are trying to help the individual find a vocational place in society. What is sadder than finding a person who is a "square peg in a round hole?"

COOPERATIVE VENTURES IN ADULT
COUNSELING

Occasionally institutions can go together in a joint effort to provide adults of the area with advisement and counseling. An example is that of the coordinator of women's continuing education and a university area representative working with the YWCA. Below is an example of interinstitutional cooperation where the adult student is the beneficiary:

UWM PLANS COUNSELING AT YWCA SITE

Educational counseling, a cooperative venture of The University of Wisconsin-Milwaukee Extension Division and the Southwest YWCA, will be offered to men and women of West Allis, Greenfield, Frankline, Greendale and Hales Corners on Thursday, April 1, at the southwest YWCA headquarters, 10712 W. Grange Avenue, Hales Corners.

Murray Deutsch, suburban administrator for the UWM Extension Division; and Miss Dorothy Miniace, Coordinator of

Women's Education, will be available for individual counseling on educational needs and problems from 1 p.m. to 4 p.m. at the YWCA.

Mrs. Arlyne Siehr, Director of the Southwest YWCA, said many persons in the area had expressed interest in acquiring more education, or exploring the possibilities of taking special noncredit courses, but found that problems of time and distance and transportation precluded going to the downtown UWM campus.

Deutsch said the purpose of the counseling would be to discover what the individual educational needs were, and how they could be met. He indicated that the University Extension Division was interested in arranging off-campus seminars in suburban or outlying areas where there was sufficient interest. Several areas have been suggested for seminars, including family living, child development, social issues, and youth leadership. Short courses in arts, science, or literature might be developed on a neighborhood basis, he said, if interest developed.[4]

The adult counselor must develop what Adler has called the **gemeinschaftsgefuhl**, the ability to have for human beings a deep feeling of identification, sympathy, and affection. This quality, it would seem, is a sine qua non, an absolute necessity for the counselor who wants to realte to adults, to advise, to assist in their vocational, academic, and personal problems. The professional counselor knows when emotional blocks are standing in the way of learning and refers the adult to an appropriate agency for other than academic counsel. The wise academic counselor will not attempt to be a family service agency or psychiatrist.

The adult counselor can assist in steering the adult into those learning activities which will help in considering a change in career. Jean-Paul Sartre points to the career choice as the key decision that will largely determine an individual's personality.

There is a drive within the individual which moves him from selfcenteredness across the spectrum of life styles toward altruistic love. However, each step along this path presupposes unsettling experiences, thereby revealing one's individual human nature. It is natural for man to like to project an ideal self, and he finds it painful to have others see beneath his many facades.[5]

The counselor should keep files and current materials on: City-wide agencies offering adult learning opportunities (Many adult education councils or city libraries keep such a file).

Requirements for degree completion and certificate programs in colleges and universities.

High school completion and equivalency (G.E.D.) opportunities.
Adult educators in the community who could assist in program advisement.
Library resources for self-improvement and reading lists.
Placement representatives who can advise on trends in employment.

The counselor who becomes a part of an adult education council or professional group will learn of opportunities available in the community and the sources for assisting adults in programs for self-development, both credit and non-credit.

ADULT TEACHERS AS COUNSELORS

The teachers in the adult classes are often closer to the student than any member of the staff of an adult education agency. The wise administrator of an adult program will take full advantage of this rapport between teacher and student.

Many teachers will welcome assistance and will find useful a pamphlet such as that produced by the National Association for Public School Adult Education entitled "Counseling and Interviewing Adult Students." Discussed are topics such as: "What's Behind the Counseling Idea?" "People Who Need Counseling," and "About Adult Students." A section on "What the Counselor Does" describes interviews, group meetings for discussion of tests and registration procedures, placement and referral opportunities, and training other adult-education staff.

"Group guidance" in advance of enrollment in the adult school is suggested as a useful orientation and a way of developing a sense of belonging among adults. Record-keeping might well be in the hands of the counselor, and people enrolling in noncredit courses could be asked to complete a minimum of forms. A most discouraging picture is that of the adult student trying to become reoriented to a learning situation and then being confronted with a plethora of forms to be filled out before being allowed to enroll. Counselors will do a real service in helping eliminate unnecessary hurdles to adult learning. The psychological factors of "being out of school," "rusty at learning," "away from the books too long," all contribute to the adult's becoming a dropout.

Every method the counselor can develop to increase the adult's self-confidence, encourage attendance, and cultivate the feeling that the institution wants to help in educational pursuits will bring the adult learner back for other learning experiences. The counselor, student, and adult teacher through cooperation can enhance immeasurably the desire for learning.

Effective interviewing is a "must" for the counselor. The ability to listen and to hear what the student **means to say**, as well

375

as what he or she actually says, is what makes counseling an art as well as a science. The objective of the interview is to find out what the student really needs and wants to acquire.

HIGH STANDARDS FOR COUNSELING

The administrator recognizes that adults have many differing counseling needs. These can be met only through a variety of individual conferences and group processes. In order to help the adult achieve personal goals, it is imperative to develop high standards for a successful guidance and counseling program:

The California State Department of Education has outlined certain standards for establishing and maintaining the guidance and counseling program:

1. All members of the staff including custodians, office clerks, and receptionists know the plan that is used for counseling and guidance.
2. Receptionists and office clerks are provided with essential counseling information, since the office staff is responsible for many of the first contacts between the adult and the school.
3. Teachers are instructed in the principles of counseling and guidance in order that they may be prepared to help their students as needs arise. Teachers refer students to the proper person if the situation is beyond their knowledge or resources. They will be alert for students who seem to be in doubt about what courses they should take and refer them to the proper person for assistance.
4. By his example and attitude the administrator creates on the part of his entire staff a sincere desire to assist adults in their efforts to solve their problems.
5. Regardless of the size of the adult program, education program guidance facilities are available to the adult for appraising his individual abilities and aptitudes, evaluating his educational and occupational background, and interpreting his own expressed goals and interests.
6. Permanent records are kept of the scholastic achievements of all students. In addition, a permanent file is maintained for test scores, evaluative statements, and work experience records of students who receive service from the counseling and guidance program.
7. Occupational counseling is a part of the guidance program. Such service required the administrator or his designated assistant to have a thorough acquaintanceship with the business and industrial life of his community in order that information given will be practical and realistic. [6]

LIBRARIES TAKE A STATEWIDE APPROACH TO COUNSELING ADULTS

The public librarians, typically, are thought of as auxiliary aides in the counseling of adults, rather than as professional counselors. They stand ready to back up the professional counselor with appropriate supportive materials such as books, pamphlets, and periodicals. For example, in the state of Wisconsin, such assistance will extend to lending such materials from larger libraries, including the Free Library Commission's General Reference and Loan division.

Understandably, the quality of services offered in the public libraries varies greatly among states. But in the best of them, large and small, librarians maintain community organization files, enabling them to refer patrons to the counseling services of local agencies, both governmental and private. Larger libraries own professional directories and can also relay information about state and national agencies with counseling functions.

The public librarians most often approach the direct counseling service to adults in their reference services and reader's guidance activities. In both of these functions the librarian is concerned with interpreting the expressed needs of library users and counsels them in the appropriate materials which will meet their individual needs.

Coordination of functions occurs through the state library commissions. The state employment services can utilize the library commissions for obtaining materials pertaining to employment opportunities. Librarians offering reference services must be able to understand the questioner's needs and must use judgment in supplying answers suitable to the questioner's use for the material and his background of knowledge.

Reader's advisory services or reader's guidance ranges from a simple request for a book on a particular industry to the preparation of extensive reading programs for personal development and job reorientation. In its best-developed form the reader's guidance service will include frequent discussions between librarian and counselee and will demand on the part of the librarian a sensitive understanding of the processes of individual and social growth.

Wise adult educators will utilize the potential for guidance services provided by the public libraries.

STATE EMPLOYMENT SERVICES PROVIDE MAJOR COUNSELING AID TO ADULT EDUCATORS

The alert educator of adults will utilize the services of many agencies in the community for counseling rather than try to do the job alone. In order to assist every job seeker to find a niche in the labor force, the state employment service, which now exists in every state, provides, in addition to its regular job placement service, special employment counseling assistance.

Often the problem faced by an experienced youth or adult is deciding which occupation he or she is best fitted to enter. The handicapped worker may be forced to change occupations and may need assistance in determining which of the fields he is best suited for. The older worker or the member of the minority group may need special assistance in relating his abilities to available job opportunities. Parolees, returning veterans, and women re-entering the job market after an extended absence may require help in re-entering a previous occupation or selecting a different one. Referral is a function of a seasoned educator of adults.

The specialized services of employment counselors are available to help job seekers overcome these and other obstacles to suitable employment. Every district office of the state employment services has on its staff one or more qualified counselors available to provide counseling assistance without charge to job seekers who wish and need it.

The U.S. Employment Service has developed a General Aptitude Test Battery to assist counselors in assessing the potential skills of job applicants. In addition, up-to-date occupational and labor-market information is available to the counselor to insure realistic vocational planning with the client. Specialized counseling techniques have been developed for assisting older workers, the handicapped, veterans, and special groups. Liaison is maintained with other community services such as libraries and university centers for referrals to and from other governmental and voluntary agencies. The employment service of a community is a useful aid for the educator of adults in learning about training needs and referral possibilities. It can also be utilized for testing where the agency is not equipped for this service.

OTHER INFORMATION AND REFERRAL SERVICES

Vigorous community councils have developed Information and Referral Services which can help persons with problems. In Arizona, the city of Phoenix and Maricopa county cooperated in establishing such a service with a 24-hour phone information service. It was established under a United States Public Health Service grant, but now receives funds from many agencies through the community council.

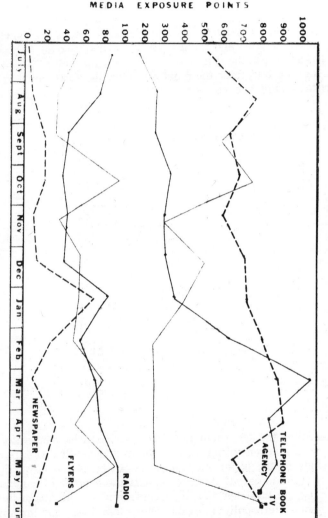

HOW PEOPLE LEARN ABOUT
INFORMATION AND REFERRAL SERVICES

MEDIA EXPOSURE POINTS

PROJECT MONTHS

July Aug Sept Oct Nov Dec Jan Feb Mar Apr May Jun

NEWSPAPER

FLYERS

RADIO

TELEPHONE BOOK

AGENCY

TV

379

For the project year of July 1977 through June 1978, I & R answered 30,717 calls. These cases are analyzed in this annual report on the basis of the top ten problems, area and age of people served, the day and after-hours program, the impact of consumerism, and the usefulness of media exposure. The statistics showed that the average I & R caller was female between the ages of 18 to 34, who resided in the northwest area of Phoenix. Her greatest need was counseling.

Even in a land of abundance and affluence, calls for services showed that in the age range 19-25 years, and 26-55 years, emergency food lead the list.

For the age 56 and older the most pressing need was for housing, with health ranking second. (see chart)

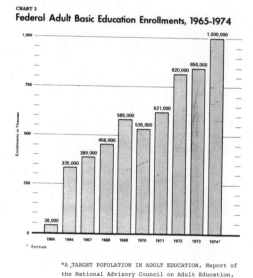

CHART 2
Federal Adult Basic Education Enrollments, 1965-1974

*A TARGET POPULATION IN ADULT EDUCATION, Report of the National Advisory Council on Adult Education, November, 1974

In examining the geographical areas COUNSELING, ranked second in four of the seven areas as a problem. Counseling was listed a first in one of the upper income areas of Phoenix. It is worthy of note that the number of divorces equals the number of marriages in this area. An information and referral service can assist in this highly mobile metropolitan region, where loneliness and instability are rampant. Adult education agencies can do their part in alleviating some of the social problems of the cities.

TOP FIVE PROBLEMS BY AREA

AREAS	PROBLEMS				
	1st	2nd	3rd	4th	5th
	Counseling	Transportation	Emergency Food	Consumer	Legal
N.E. PHX.	Transportation	Landlord Tenant	Recreation	Health	Employment
S. PHX.	Emergency Food	Housing	Transportation	Employment	Health
SCOTS.	Legal	Counseling	Consumer	Employment	Health
TEMPE	Landlord Tenant	Counseling	Legal	Recreation	Employment
MESA	Legal	Counseling	Housing	Consumer	Landlord Tenant
GLEN.	Housing	Counseling	Legal	Employment	Landlord Tenant
ALL OTHER	Consumer	Legal	Counseling	Health	Housing

With this age of consumerism comes increasing consumer problems such as how to deal with "rip-offs", interstate moving problems, mail-order companies, TV repair, real estate and home-building to name a few. I & R sought out and compiled more than 250 consumer-assistance organizations to aid the wary buyr.

Call for Action, an independent, non-profit organization helps consumers through its nationwide network of more than 40 radio and TV stations, and is an adjunct to the I & R consumer program.

Information and Referral also assisted in the Census of the Deaf to isolate the deaf and hard-of-hearing needs in the area. The natural outgrowth of this activity was the placement of the American Deafness and Rehabilitation Association (ADARA) program and its TTY - Teletype assistance program in the I & R headquarters so the deaf who have the TTY could be served on a 24-hour basis.

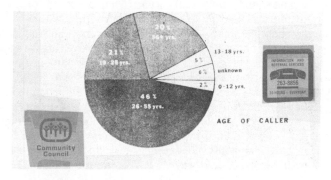

AGE OF CALLER

381

If you do not now have an information and referral service, join hands with your community council, your director of community education, or your librarian. Eliminating duplication of services is one of the selling points, and improved human services is primary. The entire community can benefit from your cooperative efforts.

COUNSELING THE HANDICAPPED

Counseling the handicapped that have been neglected for many years is a growing field for the adult educator. Vocational Rehabilitation has a needs appraisal for the handicapped person, and plans study programs on a one-to-one basis. Departments of Special Education are now including courses from which adult educators may benefit. Federal legislation is mandating that we take cognizance of this important area of service, and staff for more adaquate counseling. More and more handicapped persons are moving into this field, since they have the first-hand experience of knowing the special needs of those who have physical or emotional problems.

INTERNATIONAL OUTLOOK AND SOCIAL CHANGE

The occupational outlook is increasingly taking on an international aspect.[7] More and more people will be taking jobs abroad, and many will be unprepared both intellectually and psychologically. Adults will need and want the kinds of cultural knowledge which will more adequately prepare them to pursue careers effectively in other nations. Language skills will become more important, and the lack of skill in communication or a special language may be the barrier standing in the way of potential success. Adults will have to learn how to live in a foreign culture and to learn what it takes to work successfully in a community thousands of miles from the boundaries of the United States.

Social change will affect adults even more deeply than youth, for youth have been raised in a world of jet planes, Telstar, atomic bombs, and perpetual war. The adult is the one who finds it difficult to accept the new world picture with 2,500-mile per hour space vehicles. The adult is the one who finds adaptation to automation, worldwide TV, and international cooperation more difficult to accept. Many of us were born in the period of national isolation, Model-T Fords, and the one-room school.

Adults will have to learn to live within an urban existence. Three-fourths of the young people of the next decade will be born in metropolitan areas; the large city will be their natural environment. For many adults it is most difficult to accept rapid change. The adult counselor can help his clients to learn to live with change and to accept it as a part of daily living.

A counselor of adults must understand the social changes that are occurring. He or she must understand the adult student, as all attempt to live satisfactorily with a rapidly changing technological civilization and new world order moving toward peace and international cooperation for self-preservation.

SUMMARY

Counseling the adult, we found, is one of the neglected areas in the field of adult education. We found that business and industry have led the way in counseling the adult and leading him to more opportunities for learning. Counseling should be built into the programs of public school, junior college advising, and voluntary agencies. We found that one state plans to expend more than a million dollars on the guidance function within the junior college system. There is a great need for trained persons for this field.

Some universities are accenting testing and guidance services for women, many of whom want to reenter the labor market. Reading improvement and developing more effective study skills are accompanying programs for salvaging potential dropouts and persons crippled intellectually by lack of study skills.

The difficulty of effective counseling was recognized. Because of the need for retraining which accompanies rapid technological change, adults are seeking counsel on how to become more effective wage earners. Recognition of the value of advanced training is now becoming widespread, for the adult sees that training pays off in income, prestige, and position. Personal development brings benefits in security, respect, and self-understanding. In a United Press International release, Gay Pauley reports that "statistically, the holder of a college degree averages an estimated $200,000 more in lifetime earnings than a person without a degree."[8]

Relating well to individuals is a key to effective counseling. Helping the client see strengths and weaknesses, and suggesting educational programs, and making referrals is basic. Maslow and Rogers have given useful information on assisting the individual to self-actualization, to becoming the most effective and skillful person he or she is capable to being. Bartels says the most important role of the counselor of adults in placement is to assist the client toward self-actualization.

In this chapter a review of the resources for adult education was explored. Directories of agencies for educating adults, both formal and informal, were examined, and examples were given. Cooperative ventures between various agencies were explained, and the kinds of iles and current materials an effective counselor should maintain were suggested.

An exploration of the role of the teacher as an adult counselor pointed up the need for an open ear and an open door for the adult student. Interviewing techniques were shown to be the tool required for an outstanding counselor, and the need for higher standards in counseling was emphasized.

A list of certain standards for establishing and maintaining the guidance and counseling program was given in some detail so that the novice may have guidelines for starting correctly. The libraries were described as an excellent auxiliary aid for the adult counselor. Examples of the kinds of assistance available were enumerated.

The state employment services are a major counseling resource for the administrator or teacher of adult programs. Many training programs are now being administered through the Department of Labor and the United States Employment Service. More are going into effect each year. Tests and current occupational data are offered by local offices, and each community can benefit from their services.

Information and referral services are suggested as counseling resources. Given in graphic form is "How people learn about information and referral services" The top five problems are given by age, with emergency food listed highest in the 26-55 age range, and housing highest in the 56 plus years. Counseling ranked second in 4 of 7 areas studied in the Phoenix, Arizona area. The Community Council is suggested as a good source for organizing an Information and Referral Service if one is not in existance in the adult educator' community.

Counseling the handicapped is becoming a larger field of service. Adult Educators need to use the services of Departments of Special Education to gain the skills needed to serve this clientele. Vocational Rehabilitation departments in state government are suggested as useful resources for aid in this area, where training is on a one-to-one basis.

Finally the international outlook was examined and the necessity for guidance and counseling personnel to be aware of rapid social change was discussed. Urbanization is recognized as a leading characteristic of our society, and programs and counseling should be cognizant of the impact of such changes.

QUESTIONS:
1. Why does counseling seem to be a neglected area in adult education?
2. What are some agencies that can assist the adult educator in counseling services?
3. How would you define effective counseling?

4. What does Maslow mean by self-actualization? What would you include in this area?
5. How might you establish a cooperative venture in counseling?
6. How can adult teachers be effective counselors?
7. What are some information and referrals services you can utilize as an adult counselor.
8. What are some of the major problem areas requiring counseling for adults?
9. Why do we need an international outlook as adult education relates to occupational counseling?
10. How can libraries be useful in the counseling process?

BIBLIOGRAPHY

Allport, Gordon W. **Patterns and Growth in Personality.** New York: Holt, 1961.

Bane, J. E. **Guidance in Industrial Education,** bibliography, Ind. Arts and Voc. Educ. 50:12-144 F'61.

Barry, Ruth, and Beverly Wolf. **Modern Issues in Guidance Personnel Work.** New York: Bureau of Publications, Teachers College, Columbia University, 1957.

Bennett, Meraget E. **Guidance and Counseling in Groups.** New York: McGraw Hill, 1963, pp. 218, 224, 241, and 366.

Blum, Lawrence. "Counseling Adults," in Philip Carter, and Verl Short, **Speaking About Adults.** Northern Illinois U., DeKalb, Ill. 1966

Brayfield, Arthur H. **Readings in Modern Methods of Counseling.** New York: Appleton, 1950.

Burmahln, E. F. "How to Counsel with Adults in Business Training Programs," American Vocational Journal, Vol. 30, No. 1 (October 1955)

Campion, H. A. "Counseling Service for Adults," California Journal of Secondary Education, Vol. 28 (December 1953), pp 463-466.

Counseling and Interviewing Adult Students. Washington, D.C.: National Association for Public School Adult Education, 1965.

Gass, G. Z. "Counseling Implications of Women's Cahnging Role," Bibliography Personnel and Guidance, Vol. 37 (March 1959) pp. 482-487.

Hand, Samuel E. **A Review of Physiological and Psychological Cahnges in Aging and Their Implications for Teachers of Adults.** 3rd ed. Bulletin 71-G-1 (April 1957), Adult Education Section, Division of Vocational and Adult Education, State Department of Education, Tallahassee, Fla.

Harris, Chester W. **Encyclopedia of Educational Research.** New York: Macmillan, 1960, pp. 343-345, 347-348, 1039, 1063-1066, 1417-1418, 1422, 1429-1430.

Havighurst, Robert, "The Leisure Activities of the Middle-Aged," **American Journal of Sociology,** Vol. 63 (1957), pp. 152-162.

The Social Competence of Middle Aged People," Genetic Psychology Monographs, Vol. 56 (1957), pp 297-375.

Klein, Paul E. **Counseling Techniques in Adult Education.** New York: McGraw Hill, 1946.

Kuhlen, Raymond G., and G. G. Thompson, **Psychological Studies of Human Development,** New York: Appleton, 1952, pp. 147. 276, 325, and 359.

Lambert, H. S. "Adult Counseling Program," Baltimore Bulletin Educator, Vol. 33 (June 1956), pp 57-60.

Lipman, A. "Role Conceptions and Morale in Couples on Retirement," Psychology Abstracts, Vol. 16 (1961), pp. 267-271.

Lockwood, W. V. "Adult Guidance, A Community Responsibility," Personnel and Guidance, Vol. 31 (October 1952) pp. 31-34.

Logie, I.R. ADULT GROUP GUIDANCE, OCCUPATIONS, Vol. 29 (January 1951), pp. 287-288.

Maslow, A. H. **Motivation and Personality.** New York:Harper, 1954,p. 146.

Toward a Psychology of Being. Princeton, N.J.; Van Nostrand, 1962, pp. 127, 177.

Mathewson, R. H. **Provision of Adult Guidance Services,"** School and Society, Vol. 72 (July 1951), pp. 5-7.

McGowan, John F. **Counseling-Readings in Theory and Practice.** New York: Holt, 1962.

and Porter. **Introduction to Employment Service Counseling** (mimeo), Missouri State Employment Service Training Manual (n.d.).

Miller, L. M. "Guidance for Older People, A Public School Service," **School Life,** Vol. 43 (May 1961), pp. 9-12.

Muro, James J., and Stanley L. Freeman. **Readings in Group Counseling.** Scranton, Pa: International Textbook Company, 1968.

Murphy, Gardner, and Raymond Kuhlen. **Psychological Needs of Adults.** Chicago, Ill.:Center for the study of liberal Education for Adults, 1963.

Neal, R. "Counseling the Off-Campus Woman Student," **Personnel and Guidance Journal,** Vol. 36 (January 1958), pp. 342-343.

Overstreet, Harry A. **The Mature Mind.** New York:Norton, 1959.

Pine, G. J. "Guidance in Our Changing World," **Scholastic Teacher,** 83:0, T & N 8 1963.

Pressey, Sidney L., and Raymond G. Kuhlen. **Psychological Development through the Life Span.** New York:Harper, 1959.

Pine, G.J. "Guidance in Our Changing World," Scholastic Teacher, 83:9, T & N 8 1963

Robinson, F. P. "Guidance for All: In Principle and in Practice," Personnel and Guidance Journal, Vol. 31 (May 1953), pp. 500-504.

Rogers, C. R. "What It Means to Become a Mature Person" National Association of Deans of Women Journal. Vol. 18 (June 1955), pp. 153-157.

Sather, T. D. "Counseling at the Adult Level" Wisconsin Journal Educator, Vol. 83 (May 1951), pp. 13-14.

Snyder, W. V., and J. E. Williams, "Changes in Self and Other Perceptional Counseling," Journal of Counseling in Psychology, Vol. 9, No. 1 (Spring 1962), pp. 18-30.

Snyder, William V., et al. Casebook of Nondirective Counseling. Boston: Houghton, 1947.

Thatcher, John H. Public School Adult Education. (A Guide for Administrators). Washington, D.C.: National Association of Public School Administrators, 1963.

Woody, Thomas. A History of Women's Education in the United States. New York:Science Press, 1929, Vol. II, pp. 90-97.

COUNSELING —Bibliography

Bolles, Richard. The Three Boxes of Life and How to Get Out of Them. Ten Speed Press, 1978. 466 pp. Bolles calls this work, "a book of ideas about school, work, and retirement" -- or the Three boxes of Life." Like his earlier work, What Color is Your Parachute, Bolles provides an entertaining and readable guide on how to integrate these three periods of life in a personally coherent and understandable life/work plan.

Career Education Project. Career development series. Newton, Mass.: Education Development Center, 1975.

Commission on Non-Traditional Study, Diversity by Design. Jossey-Bass, San Francisco, 1973.

Costar, E. Estimation of intelligence and motivation as a screening procedure for programs on PLATO IV. Unplublished doctoral dissertation, University of Illinois, Champaign-Urbana, 1975.

Counseling Adults, The Counseling Psychologist, Div. of A.P.A. Vol. 6, No. 1, 1976

Counseling and Interviewing Adult Students. Washington, D.C.: National Association for Public School Adult Education, 1965.

Diamond, E. (Ed.) Issues of sex bias in interest measurement. Washington, D.C.: U.S. Government Printing Office, 1975.

Farmer, H. Guided Inquiry Group Career Counseling. Champaign, Illinois: University of Illinois, Illini Bookstore, 1974.

Gifford, Jacques. **Problems of Guidance and Counseling in Adult Education.** Council for Cultural Cooperation, 1976, 19 pp. The paper is divided into three parts: 1) The method of guidance and counseling; 2) The contributions guidance and counseling have made to adult education; and 3) the presentation of a methodological approach for the integration of guidance and counseling with the concept of lifelong learning.

Goldman, L. **Using tests in counseling.** New Jersey: Prentice-Hall, Inc., 1971.

Harris, J. "The Computer: Guidance Tool of the Future." Journal of Counseling Psychology, 1974, 21, 331-339.

Healy, C. **Career Counseling in the Community College.** Springfield, Illinois: Charles C. Thomas, 1974.

Holland, J. **Making Vocational Choice: A Theory of Careers.** Englewood Cliffs, N.J.; Prentice Hall, 1973.

McGowan, John F. **Counseling-Readings in Theory and Practice.** New York: Holt, 1962.

Muro, James J. and Stanley L. Freeman. **Readings in Group Counseling.** Scranton, Pa.; International Textbook Company, 1968.

Rogers, C. **On Becoming a Person.** Boston: Houghton Mifflin, 1961.

Rogers, C. Empathic: An Unappreciated Way of Being. The Counseling Psychologist, 1975, 5, 2-10.

Schlossberg, N. "A Framework for Counseling Women." Personnel and Guidance Journal, 1972, 51, 137-143.

Super, D. **Career Development Inventory.** Unpublished inventory. Available from the author at Columbia University, Teachers College, New York City, N.Y., 1974.

FOOTNOTES CHAPTER 20

1 Roger W. Axford and Alice Richardson, "Reading Improvement-Key to Knowledge," **Extension Insights,** University of Wisconsin, Vol. 7, No. 3 (December 1963).

2 W. R. Reilly, "Guidance Services for Vocational, Technical and Adult Education," Dade County (Miami) Public Schools (mimeo), January 1964.

3 A. H. Maslow, **Toward a Psychology of Being,** Van Nostrand, Princeton, N.J., 1962, pp. 127-128.

4 **Milwaukee Journal,** March 30, 1965.

5 Joseph B. Simons, "An Existential View of Vocational Development," **Personnel and Guidance Journal,** Vol. 14, No. 6 (February 1966), pp. 604-610.

6 "Professional Standards for Adult Education Administrators," Bulletin of California State Department of Education, Vol. 24, No. 16 (November 1955), pp. 14-15.

7 Gilbert C. Wrenn, **The Counselor in a Changing World,** American Personnel and Guidance Association, Washington, D.C., 1962.

8 "Degree Ensures $200,000 More Income," **UPI dispatch, DeKalb Chronicle,** March 26, 1968.

Chapter XXI

EVALUATING ADULT EDUCATION PROGRAMS

It seems to be clear from all the evidence that adults, even more than children, are interested in the application of what they learn. Adults seem to be more interested in the directions in which their learning is taking them. The motivation of adults, since they engage in most activities from free choice and not by law, is dependent upon their being convinced that progress is being made toward some goal. For all these objectives evaluation is essential.

> J. Roby Kidd, in **How Adults Learn**,
> Association Press, New York, 1959, p. 295.

Too many of us as educators evaluate like the marksman who shoots an arrow at the tree, then walks to the tree and draws a target around the arrow with a bull's eye at the arrowhead.

How we evaluate—After the fact!

Evaluation is one of the most difficult tasks we have as educators. But it is imperative. We need to know the extent to which we are attaining some of our objectives, which ones we have missed, and where we need to put the emphasis for future learning. Evaluation becomes difficult unless goals are sharp. Since the individual is continually changing, measurements are not always precise. We need continually to be developing more adequate instruments to determine whether we have achieved the objectives for which we are teaching. Even though evaluation is difficult, it must be undertaken to see if we are meeting the needs of the adults in our program.

THE EVALUATION PROCESS-A FACTOR IN MOTIVATION

To know whether we are reaching the objectives which we have set for ourselves in our educational program is the essence of the evaluative process. Adult educator Wilson Thiede has stated that

Knowing where we've been and where we are going-the degree to which we are attaining our goals, the extent to which our efforts are productive-are questions of concern to competent professionals in all areas of life. The process of determining the extent to which objectives have been attained is evaluation. [1]

Before an adequate job of evaluation can be done by educators, we must have clearly stated goals and objectives. Since education is a process of changing persons in desirable ways, we must know what kinds of behavioral changes we want. When objectives are stated in ways that can be qualified, we can build instruments which measure the degree to which we have achieved our objectives and determine whether we need to reteach in light of what we know was not learned. Unfortunately it is difficult to devise ways to measure educational changes, but evaluation must be done and we must continually try to find improved methods of appraising whether the "learner" has truly learned. An evaluative process must be built into the program from the start.

Optimum learning will occur if educators of adults keep in mind the question, "What are the evaluative processes?" A dynamic evaluation requires four points for procedure: (1) a clear goal, (2) an appraisal and knowledge of the present position in relation to that goal, (3) the position at some past time (for example, a pretest), and (4) the learning resources available to be brought to bear upon the desired goal.

Too little thought has been given by educators of adults to the methods of deriving objectives and goals. If at the outset of an educational program a clear set of goals is outlined by the instructor, and if these goals are combined with the stated objectives of the students obtained through a questionnaire, interviews, or check list, the chances of attaining the common goals are far more likely.

I often take the first session of a class to find out what the adult students consider their objectives to be for the course. Then I outline the specific objectives of the program as I see them at the beginning. If there is a convergence on a number of the goals, then we know there is more possibility for success - for achieving mutual objectives. We then have a firm basis for evaluation and the chances for motivation in learning are enhanced.

USING EVALUATION FOR PROGRAM IMPROVEMENT

A novice adult educator may ask, "What is the purpose of program evaluation?" -and indeed some programmers feel threatened when mention is made of "evaluation." The evaluative process may be used as a stepping stone to program improvement, for program evaluation is a means of determining: (1) how successfully the program is accomplishing its objectives, (2) how the participating members are reacting, (3) what can be learned that will make the next program more productive, and (4) whether there have been any real behavioral changes produced.

It takes courage for the teacher of adults or the director of an adult education program to put a measuring stick against a class or program periodically to see if it is accomplishing what was set out for it. Evaluation should be built into the program at certain checkpoints. If the students find that they have not learned certain skills, additional time may be desired to practice those skills. Evaluation may come from employing a number of questions to differing participants in the program: the adult educator examining the program through a self-study; an outside expert examining the agency to see if agency personnel have clearly stated goals and objectives and if they are being attained; the adult teacher doing a self-evaluation to see if he or she had provided the correct learning experiences for students and the conditions for learning; and the students making an evaluation of the teacher.

Each of these will be dealt with, and examples of questionnaires will be given which may be adapted to local adult educational institutions.

Three Principles for Program Evaluation

I. **Instruments for self-evaluation are preferred to evaluation by others.** Most adults like to see their own progress. Ernest McMahon surveyed 1,896 adult students in noncredit university courses with the result that two-thirds or 1,256 wanted both grades and examinations, 189 wanted grades without examinations; 88 wanted an examination but no course grade; only 363 wanted neither grades nor examinations. [2]

Often the adult does not feel comfortable having progress compared with that of another adult. It is extremely important that the adult be allowed a self-evaluation if we are testing for the success of an individual skill or action. For example, if we are trying to help the adult achieve reading comprehension, he or she is apt to want to have himself or herself tested, learn techniques and skills for improvement, and then find out how much progress he or she has made in a specific period of time. A pretest is a useful tool for finding out what needs to be learned and how to pace learning. As McMahon found, mature adults are in favor of tests and self-evaluation, but they do not like to be held up to ridicule or compared with other adults who may be considerably advanced.

II. **Involve program planners in the evaluation process.** Persons who have been involved in planning a program or building a curriculum for a group of learners should benefit from the experience of evaluation of that same program. If a program committee has put together a series of lectures, it can benefit from the task of evaluating whether any learning has taken place. For example, in a class for expectant mothers-after the lectures, demonstrations, and discussions,-if the mother has learned how to care for the newborn child, the real test is whether she can perform the skills she has observed. Life-saving is one of the most dramatic illustration of the evaluative experience, for if the drowning victim has an ill-prepared student,the life-saving evaluation can be disastrous. Parachuting instruction does not allow for a second chance in evaluation. These are instances where one cannot learn by mistakes.

III. **Evaluation should be concerned with outcomes and results rather than activity or energy spent.** Unfortunately, often much activity and energy are put into a learning experience with very few tangible results. Therefore, evaluation should be made in terms of small steps of advancement toward specific objectives. Small successes will keep the adult from becoming discouraged and dropping out of the program. We can take a lesson from the time-study analysts. Industry has learned that large tasks can be more readily learned if work is broken down into **small steps** which can be mastered one at a time. If we can **help** the student learn the fundamental steps and then build on these, we will see more achievement. The wise adult instructor will assist the student in setting short-term goals as well as long-term **goals**.

USING EVALUATION COMMITTEES

An evaluation committee can be an effective tool for appraising the progress of a program. It can also be a fine learning experience for program-planning personnel. The program eval-

uation committee should be responsible for:
1. Assessing the objectives and goals of the program and the effectiveness of the planning.
2. Assessing the learning experiences to achieve these goals.
3. Collecting facts and information on new problems and new needs for consideration in planning for the future.
4. Arrange for instruments for evaluation before, during and after the meeting.
5. Develop techniques for evaluation such as:
   (a) questionnaires,
   (b) interviews with representative participants.
   (c) demonstrations by learners
   (d) roving reporters.
6. Developing a self-evaluation instrument that may be used by the learner.

ADVISORY COMMITTEES IN EVALUATION-SETTING OBJECTIVES AND EVALUATION

As an advisory committee which is used to set up a program can be a useful instrument for goal-setting and for evaluation. If the group can at the outset establish a specific set of learning objectives, the testing at the end of the program or reactions of the learners can give some indication as to the extent that the individuals have made changes in their behavior. If goals are not clear, the chances of obtaining the desired objectives are minimal and haphazard.

For example, in a short course for supervisors in industry, an advisory committee of personnel managers and training directors was asked to outline objectives they considered important for the participants to achieve during the ten-session program, "Business Economics." The reactions were as follows:
1. Developing an awareness of the problems of production and marketing.
2. Understanding an annual report, production figures, production budgets.
3. What is capital and how is capital acquired and stimulated?
4. How does a departmental budget fit for understanding the business organization?
5. How is a business organization financed?
6. What are business cycles and what is the role of money and banking?
7. Understanding scarcity, supply and demand.

8. Understanding the tax structure and its implications for a modern corporation.
9. Developing an appreciation of the implications of business economics and profits.
10. How do businesses come into existence and how do they stay in existence?
11. Understanding the stockholder, dividends, and the stockholder in the organization
12. Understanding the international economic picture and foreign markets.
13. An awareness of wage-and-hour laws, collective barganing and labor-management relations.
14. The how and why of unionism and its evolution.
15. Learning to read the financial page of a newspaper. (Subscribe to a financial periodical and hope the adult will continue to read it.)
16. Understanding the balance of wages and profits.
17. How does the departmental budget fit into the total financial structure of a manufacturing organization?
18. What are the influences of a board of directors? What is their role?
19. What is meant by the mixed capitalistic system?
20. What is the Securities Exchange Commission and how does it function?
21. What is the relation of government to business activity? The government's role in business?
22. Understanding debt, equity, and liability.

"Just tell me which business courses my competitor is taking".

Used by permission of the University of Wisconsin Extension.

On the basis of the above points, objectives for learning in the course were developed by a professor of finance as a part of a sequence of courses for supervisors in industry. By following this procedure, the training directors, the students, and instructor know what is to be learned and the instructor knows the desired course content. All parties know the basis for examining the students for comprehension and behavioral changes. If the instructor knows what is expected and the persons in the class know the goals, the chances of achieving these objectives are increased immeasurably.

SELF-EVALUATION BY THE ADULT INSTRUCTOR

Teachers of adults will do well to check themselves following each class to see if they are maintaining the highest of teaching standards. We have found a self-rating sheet useful in giving instructors an opportunity to ask themselves if they are exemplifying qualities of good class meeting.

At the close of every session, rate it in terms of the accomplishment of each of the qualities of a good group learning situation. Use the following rating scale:

3 = in this respect I was notably successful
2 = in this respect I was moderately successful
1 = in this respect I was unsuccessful

Qualities of a Good Class Meeting	Sessions																
	1	2	3	4	5	6	7	8	9	10	11	12	13	14	15	16	17
1. Did I have a basic plan for the session but use it flexibly?																	
2. Did all members of the group understand both the immediate and ultimate goals of the course?																	
3. Were the methods and procedures used as varied as possible?																	
4. Was there a good social feeling in the group?																	
5. Did I use the experience of the members of the group to make my teaching real and vital?																	
6. Did I reflect in every way my conviction of the importance of broad values?																	
7. Was I aware of the special needs and concerns of each individual in the group?																	
8. Did I provide support and reinforcement for the students who need it?																	
9. Was the physical setting as attractive and comfortable as I could make it?																	
10. Do I know everyone's name?																	
Total score																	

Evening school instructors can be provided the self-rating chart at the time they are given the class list so that they can check themselves on lesson plans, physical facilities, teaching methods, group climate, utilization of student experiences, and rapport with the adult students. An effective administrator of an adult program will give the student a chance to evaluate the instructor in order to obtain feedback for better program planning, and will also give the instructor an opportunity to check on himself or herself. The accompanying self-rating sheet is a useful check list. The rating sheet should be used as a basis for a faculty meeting early in the year to provide discussion of "superior teaching" qualities. Other qualities might be added which are unique to the local institution.

STUDENT COURSE EVALUATION

The University Student Government has prepared the following evaluation sheet to give each student an opportunity to evaluate his respective courses taken this semester at UW-M. The information which you put on this questionnaire will be used solely by the instructor of the course program and also give him a clear insight into student opinion. We would like to point out that you are not required to fill this sheet out, nor is the instructor required to distribute it in his classes; it is completely voluntary. We are confident, however, that through the cooperation of both the students and faculty this evaluation will be successful and will have some definite meaning.

Name of Instructor _____ Course _____

Date _____

I. Student Attitude

  1. How many hours a week do you spend on this course? _____

  2. Is this a required course?   _____

  3. Is this course helping you toward your ultimate goal? _____

  4. Suitability of the size of the class (consider the subject matter and type of class - lecture, lab, etc.)
    Below average _____ Average _____ Above average _____ Excellent _____

  5. The degree to which the objectives of the course were clarified and discussed.
    Below average _____ Average _____ Above average _____ Excellent _____

  6. The agreement between the announced objectives of the course and what was actually done.
    Below average _____ Average _____ Above average _____ Excellent _____

  7. Range of ability in the class (are there too many extremely bright or extremely dull students.)
    Below average _____ Average _____ Above average _____ Excellent _____

  8. Does the final test (if given) have too much bearing on the final grade?
    Below average _____ Average _____ Above average _____ Excellent _____

II. Instructor in Charge of Course

  1. Interest in subject.
    Below average _____ Average _____ Above average _____ Excellent _____

  2. Sympathetic attitude toward students.
    Below average _____ Average _____ Above average _____ Excellent _____

Front of evaluation sheet.

3. Fairness in grading.
Below average_____ Average_____ Above average_____ Excellent_____

4. Presentation of subject matter.
Below average___·____ Average_____ Above average_____ Excellent_____

5. Sense of humor.
Below average_____ Average_____ Above average_____ Excellent_____

6. Self-confidence.
Below average_____ Average_____ Above average_____ Excellent_____

7. Stimulating intellectual curiosity.
Below average_____ Average_____ Above average_____ Excellent_____

8. Method of delivery.
Below average_____ Average_____ Above average_____ Excellent_____

III. Course Material

1. Suitability of the method or methods by which subject matter of the course is presented (recitation, lecture, laboratory, etc.)
Below average_____ Average_____ Above average_____ Excellent_____

2. Suitability of the reference materials available for the course.
Below average_____ Average_____ Above average_____ Excellent_____

3. Suitability of the assigned textbook.
Below average_____ Average_____ Above average_____ Excellent_____

4. Suitability of the amount and type of assigned outside work.
Below average_____ Average_____ Above average_____ Excellent_____

Expected grade in this course_____

Do not sign your name.

Back of evaluation sheet.

THE STUDENT'S EVALUATION OF TEACHING

Every educational institution finds it a distinct advantage to know the quality of performance by its faculty. This is no less true for instructors dealing with adults than for other levels of instruction. Perhaps it is even more essential that the instructors themselves be informed of their own success or failure because improvement depends on knowledge of results, and eliminating faults depends first upon the recognition of them.

Aristotle suggested in his **Politics** that we can get a better idea of the merits of a meal from the dinner guests than we can from the cook. Therefore it is often valuable to do a survey of

397

student opinion, both to help instructors know if they are effective as teachers and to give the institution some basis for evaluation of performance.

Leadership Training
The Milwaukee-Waukesha Chapter
American Red Cross

Session _____   Date _____

Your name _____   Time _____

1. What is your appraisal of the presentation which has just been given?

Not done   └────┴────┴────┴────┘   Very well
well   1   2   3   4   5   done

2. Did the instructor effectively help you learn the material he wished to teach?

Not   └────┴────┴────┴────┘   Very
effective   1   2   3   4   5   effective

3. Is the material presented necessary to those who have leadership responsibilities in the Red Cross?

Not   └────┴────┴────┴────┘   Very
necessary   1   2   3   4   5   necessary

4. To what degree is the information you have just gained valuable to you in your everyday life?

Not   └────┴────┴────┴────┘   Very
valuable   1   2   3   4   5   valuable

5. How effective is (are) the instructional methods used in this session?

Not   └────┴────┴────┴────┘   Very
effective   1   2   3   4   5   effective

6. Other reactions:

A sample evaluation sheet.

A Student course-evaluation form utilized at the University of Wisconsin-Milwaukee (see page   and   ) is made available to students on a voluntary basis and is distributed by the University Student Government to the faculty. The information is used solely by the instructor to aid in improving instruction. The evaluation sheet is reproduced here for possible use by teachers of adults. Faculty members have found this a useful method for obtaining feedback,* as no signature is required. My experience with this rating sheet is that students welcome the opportunity to criticize the insturction as well as to contribute to the improvement of that instruction.

A simple punch card has been developed at Northern Illinois University for use by students for teacher evaluation. A sample card is given on page   for possible adaptation in other colleges and universities. Another evaluation sheet was worked out with the Milwaukee-Waukesha Chapter of the American Red Cross (see page   ) to determine the extent to which the adult students in a Leadership Training class felt they had learned. Responses are given on a continuum from low effectiveness to high effectiveness in each category. Such devices have proven useful in program improvement.

UTILIZING EVALUATION IN CONFERENCE AND INSTITUTE PLANNING

The person planning a conference, or the conference planning committee, often feel at a loss to know if the objectives of the conference have been achieved. Time and effort have gone into putting together the best program possible, with the most effective speakers or leaders to be found. The question then becomes, "In the sessions planned, was the learning objective achieved, and to what extent?"

An example would be that of a high-level conference planned for "Personnel Management for Nursing Home and Sheltered Care Home Administrators and Supervisors" which attracted administrators from throughout a state. In it an attempt was made to evaluate the sessions for participants. (see pages   , , and   ). An evaluation report was distributed at the final session, and participants were asked to mark their reaction. The evaluation took no more than ten minutes and proved invaluable in future program planning.

Also shown is an open-ended program-evaluation form used by the University of Wisconsin in its Engineering Institutes, which draw engineers from all parts of the world (see page   ).

ILLINOIS NURSING HOME ASSOCIATION*

EVALUATION REPORT

Your frank and candid judgments in response to the following questions and statements will help us to program for similar workshops within the Illinois Nursing Home Association.

GENERAL EVALUATION

Please underline one phrase in each item that best describes your judgment of events.

1. Was the information available in this conference - - - -
useless / not very useful / somewhat useful / useful / very useful

COMMENT: _____

2. Was the organization of the conference - - - (scheduling, sequence of speakers, meals, breaks, etc.)
disorganized / not very organized / somewhat organized / well organized / very well organized

COMMENT: _____

3. Were the physical facilities (main conference room, sleeping facilities, restaurant arrangements, etc.) - - - - - -
most unsatisfactory / not very satisfactory / somewhat satisfactory / satisfactory / very satisfactory

COMMENT: _____

4. Were the printed materials - - - - useless / not very useful/ somewhat useful / useful / very useful

COMMENT: _____

5. Were the speakers - - - - completely ineffective / not very effective / somewhat effective / effective / very effective

COMMENT: _____

6. I prefer the - - - - one day conference
two day conference
three or more days conference

7. I profit most in a conference of this nature from - - - -
lecture / small-group discussion / demonstration / question-answer period / panel presentation

SPECIFIC EVALUATION

8. What topics should we consider as having a priority in future conference planning? (rate in 1, 2, 3 order of importance)

EVALUATION OF THE ADULT EDUCATION AGENCY

I find that a study of the agency of adult education can give clues to better understanding adult learners and their purposes for continuing their education. In sending students of adult education

	(Medical-Legal Responsibilities	_____
	(Financial Management	_____
	(Leadership	_____
	(Community Relations	_____
Group 1	(Total Care of Patients	_____
	(Medicare	_____
	(Inservice Training of Personnel	_____
	(Facilities Planning	_____
	(Utilization Review	_____
	(Purchasing	_____
	(Pharmacy Services	_____

Also rate in 1, 2, 3 order of importance:

	(Supervision Practices for Director of Nursing	_____
	(Restorative Care Practices	_____
	(Use of the Nurse Aide	_____
	(Dietetics and Cooking	_____
Group 2	(Specialized Training for Nursing Personnel	_____
	(Recreation and Activity in Nursing Homes	_____
	(Office Practice for Clerks and Secretaries	_____
	(Modern Housekeeping Practice for Custodians	_____
	(Medical Records	_____

9. If there was a 'highlight' in this conference, what was it?

COMMENT: _____

_____

10. What suggestion(s) do you have for improving this conference?

Suggestion 1: _____

Suggestion 2: _____

_____

THE SPEAKERS

Your evaluation of the speakers will be most helpful to us in the future and beneficial to the speakers themselves. Please underline one phrase in each item that best describes your judgment of events.

1. "A BETTER UNDERSTANDING OF EFFECTIVE SUPERVISION OF EMPLOYEES" Dr. LOUIS SHUSTER

Presentation by Dr. Shuster: completely ineffective / not very effective / somewhat effective / effective / very effective

Group Discussion Session _____
Name of Leader
useless / not very useful / somewhat useful / useful / very useful

2. "LITTLE LULU THEORY OF LABOR RELATIONS" DR. NOVAK

Presentation by Dr. Novak: completely ineffective / not very effective / somewhat effective / effective / very effective

Group Discussion Session _____
Name of Leader
useless / not very useful / somewhat useful / useful / very useful

3. "EFFECTIVE WAYS TO HANDLE PERSONNEL AND PERSONNEL PROBLEMS" DR. PECENKA

Presentation by Dr. Pecenka: completely ineffective / not very effective / somewhat effective / effective / very effective

4. "NEOADMINISTRATIVE PROBLEMS AND GOVERNMENT REGULATION" LYMAN McKEAN

Presentation by Lyman McKean: completely ineffective / not very effective / somewhat effective / effective / very effective

5. OPEN HOUSE – PINE ACRES RETIREMENT CENTER
not very useful / somewhat useful / useful / very useful

6. "DEVELOPMENTAL SERVICES IN REHABILITATION" DR. ALBERT R. SEIGEL

Presentation by Dr. Seigel: completely ineffective / not very effective / somewhat effective / effective / very effective

Group Discussion Session _____
Name of Leader
useless / not very useful / somewhat useful / useful / very useful

7. "INCREASING YOUR PROFIT THROUGH BETTER MANAGEMENT" MR. ROSS A. REARDON

Presentation by Ross Reardon: completely ineffective / not very effective / somewhat effective / effective / very effective

Group Discussion _____
Name of Leader
useless / not very useful / somewhat useful / useful / very useful

_____
Your position in the health care field

402

Inside of program evaluation.

THE UNIVERSITY OF WISCONSIN

ENGINEERING INSTITUTES

Program Evaluation

INSTITUTE TITLE _____ DATE _____

1. Please make a brief statement about strong and weak points of the:

    a. topics

    b. speakers

2. Other comments

3. Please list other engineering problems that you would like to hear discussed, either in an institute such as this or at a different institute.

4. Please suggest competent speakers (name, address and field of interest) for this or other institutes.

5. Please list on the reverse side the names, addresses, and fields of interest of colleagues and friends who would like to know about these programs.

Signature optional _____

Outside of program evaluation.

To:
ENGINEERING INSTITUTES
University Extension Division
The University of Wisconsin
Madison, Wisconsin 53706

NAME _____

TITLE _____

COMPANY _____

ADDRESS _____

out to study an agency, the points presented on page ____ are to be used as a guide for an interview with the administrator of the agency.

The outline can be used effectively whether the agency is a YMCA, an evening college, or a community-action agency. If the interviewer can get the administrator to state the goals and objectives of the agency, then a good deal can be known about the agency. Experience has shown that unclear objectives lead to a heterogeneous program and often the interview will sharpen up the objectives in the mind of the adult educator being interviewed.

Many agencies of adult education have not clarified their objectives in writing, and the experience of having to delineate learning objectives as a result of the interview by students of adult education has proved revealing and often helpful to the director of adult education programs, regardless of the particular agency.

EVALUATION OF MATERIALS IN ADULT EDUCATION

Often teachers of adults have questions relating to the adequacy of teaching materials for certain groups. I have found that having adult students participate in examining materials, using them, and then appraising their effectiveness is a way of finding out whether teaching materials should be rewritten, updated, or withdrawn. Every instructor of adults has an obligation to preview a film before using it is class. If he or she is not satisfied that the film will contribute to the learning objective of that teaching session, he or she may want to have a group preview the film with him. Admittedly, this is time-consuming, but to do otherwise can be educationally disastrous.

For example, in a preretirement planning course, an instructor brought a film that he had not previewed. The adult students had been hand-picked from industry for a pilot project. The film was shown to the preretirees without knowing what impact it might have upon the new students, of which there were twenty, all approaching retirement within five years. The program was voluntary, although persons were carefully "recommended" by the company. The film depicted the difficulty a man had in finding a satisfactory adjustment to his new-found leisure in retirement; he kept returning to his old work to visit his old associates and finally found his "successful retirement" in the lakes of Arkansas fixing small gas engines.

The film had more emotional impact than had been anticipated by the lecturer, and he should have known better than to show

A GUIDE FOR STUDYING AN ADULT EDUCATION AGENCY

PURPOSE—Objectives
What are the goals, purposes, and objectives of the agency?
Are they stated anywhere?
Does the administrator have other goals and objectives?
Are there short-term goals?
What are the long-term goals?
Have the purposes changed through the years? How?
Is the agency affiliated with local, state, or national associations?

ORGANIZATION AND ADMINISTRATION

Program
Who determines what shall be offered?
Is there an advisory committee?
  How large? Broad representation?
Does the director have final decisions on
  policy?
How are new programs initiated?
Where does the staff look for program ideas?
Is there a stated program philosophy? Where
  is it printed?
How often is the program printed?
How is it promoted?
How are instructors chosen? Are they certified?
  By whom?

Staffing
What is organizational structure?
Who are the supportive staff?
  (business manager, clerk, etc.)
How often are staff meetings held?
Are there planned in-service programs?
Are promotions from within?
What is the professional training of
  the staff? Professional associations?

FINANCE
Self-support? partial subsidy? complete subsidy? Foundation support? tax support?
Are fees charged? On what basis?
Can one register by mail?
Is there a charge for adult counseling and testing?
How much are instructors paid per instructional hour?
What is the refund policy?

EVALUATION
What types of evaluation are used by instructors?
What types of evaluation are made of the students? How?
Is there any type of self-evaluation made by the agency?
Have there been any institutional self-studies? What were the results?
Are consultants used for evaluating the program?
What kinds of improvements are contemplated? How are these to be implemented?

AUDIO-VISUAL EVALUATION SHEET

Student _____ Pts. _____

The classroom setting: Max. Pts. (100)

Topic _____   Class size _____

Audience type _____   Preparation of room _____ (4)

Media Used   1. _____
              2. _____
              3. _____

Introduction

1. Appropriateness of subject matter to audience   _____ (6)

2. Motivational effect of introduction   _____

3. Appropriateness of media selected   _____

4. The quality and quantity of media used   _____ (36)

Development of Topic

5. Involvement of audience (i.e. questions, assigned
   tasks, handouts, responses)   _____

6. The degree of effectness of A-V equipment and aids used _____

7. The thoroughness of explaining the topic   _____ (18)

Conclusion

8. Extent of summarization   _____

9. Degree of satisfaction or involvement in program   _____

10. Degree of structural organization   _____ (18)

Content Evaluation

11. Appropriateness of language, style, and gestures   _____

12. Degree of enthusiasm exhibited   _____ (12)

Performance Evaluation

13. Handling of equipment   _____

14. Handling of aides and continuity   _____ (12)

Follow-up Plans and Self-Improvement Program

15. Extended activities   _____

16. Method of appraising program   _____ (12)

Instructor's Comments: Time _____ min.

the film the first session; for he had not previewed the film nor had it evaluated by persons who were nearing retirement. Three of the adult students never returned to the class. Preretirees found the ideas presented too threatening. The instructor would have benefited from showing the film first to a group of knowledgeable professionals in the field of gerontology for their evaluation. The same can be done with pamphlets, film strips, text materials, and records. One of the most productive days spent by a mental-health group was the showing of six films in that single day along with extensive evaluation by those who would be using the films in their teaching and with community groups.

Often evaluation sheets can be obtained from a curriculum library or your audio-visual department. The university extension worker in your area can be of invaluable assistance in constructing evaluation instruments. [3] He or she can put you in touch with psychologists and curriculum specialists.

By having the student check an evaluation list immediately following the showing of a film, we have obtained some useful reactions for future film use. By having the viewer write reactions on the back of the card, one can obtain information that may not by included on the check list. An example is presented on page 207.

Exhibits may be useful as a medium for acquainting adults with needed information in a dramatic format. Following are questions to be asked in evaluating an exhibit:

WHAT TO LOOK FOR IN AN EXHIBIT [4]
(Or "How Not To Be 'Snowed' ")

1. Has the material been tested by an objective agency such as a University Center? What were the qualifications of the evaluators?
2. With what groups has the material been tested? How does the group compare with your potential clientele? Is there any age limitation best for children, adults, etc.?
3. Do you know any person or groups that have successfully used the exhibit material? Will the exhibitor suggest some of the limitations of the materials?
4. What are the economic factors to be considered? Can you purchase the materials as reasonably elsewhere?
5. Is the material geared to the class level of the adult group you will be working with?
6. In what ways will the materials be useful for practical-life applications? (Employment, health, family life, etc.)
7. Is the material as useful for an individual as for a group?
8. Is the art work lively, attractive, and interesting? Is the

artwork deceptive - overshadowing the content?

9. Will the material be adaptable? Can I use the material with different levels of economic achievement?
10. What supplementary materials can I develop from these exhibit materials?
11. Have you compared the exhibit material with other systems?
12. Are the exhibit materials being revised regularly? How often?
13. What background experience does the exhibitor have in this field? What are the long-range commitments of the company?

SUMMARY

We have seen that evaluation is a part of the learning process and that by finding out what has been learned and what has not been learned the adult can be motivated through the satisfaction of successful accomplishment and encouraged to do better in skills yet unlearned.

We have many methods of evaluation - tests, written testimonies, notebooks, check sheets, and verbal feedback. The adult education program can be improved through evaluation techniques designed to measure success, student reaction, the extent to which certain objectives have not been achieved, and behavioral change. We have learned that instruments of self-evaluation are preferred by adults and that adults like evaluation as long as their work is not compared with that of others or held up to ridicule. By involving members in program evaluation, the assessment can be a part of the learning process. Evaluation committees are sometimes useful, and advisory committees can be helpful both in setting objectives and in evaluation of results.

The adult instructor will be wise to utilize a self-appraisal rating sheet. Students' evaluations may be valuable to both the teacher and the adult education institution for improving instruction, and sample sheets are provided and may be adapted. A format for the analysis and evaluation of an adult education agency will be a useful tool for the novice adult educator and may act as a guide for appraising the program of an institution. Finally, we considered the evaluation of materials in adult education and gave examples of devices for evaluating a film and a questionnaire to be used in examining exhibits.

Alert and inquisitive teachers of adults will continually be developing new and ingenious ways of evaluating the progress of their students. As long as the evaluation is used as a part of the learning process to help in placement, progress appraisal, learner self-understanding, and as an aid to the teacher and the student in planning future study, the effort will be well worthwhile.

QUESTIONS:
1. Why is evaluation often one of the most difficult tasks for educators?
2. How can we use evaluation as a motivating factor in learnning?
3. Why are clear objectives so fundamental to effective evaluation?
4. How would you use evaluation as a means to program improvement?
5. What are three principles for program evaluation as given in this chapter?
6. How would you use a committee for evaluation? An advisory committee?
7. How might you use the self-evaluation instrument suggested for the instructor?
8. How would you use evaluation in conference and institute planning?
9. How would you make use of the "guide for studying an adult education agency"?
10. How might you adapt the "audio-visual evaluation sheet" to your learning situation?
11. How would you use an exhibit as a learning devise in adult education? Give examples.

Bibliography

Apple, Michael, W., Subkoviak, M.J., and Lufler, H.S., Jr., (eds). **Educational Evaluation: Analysis and Responsibilitiy,** Berkeley: McCutchan Publishing Corporation, 1974.

Caro, Francis G., (ed). **Readings in Evaluation Research.** New York: Russell Sage Foundation. 1971

Cassette Tapes on Selected Evaluation Topics. Available from American Educational Research Association, 1126 16th Street, N.W., Washington, D.C. 20036.

Furst, Edward J. **Constructing Evaluation Instruments.** New York: Longmans, 1958.

Gephart, William J. **Evaluation: Past, Present, and Future** - Occasional Paper #17. Bloomington, IN: Phi Delta Kappa.

Gottman, John M. and Clasen, R. E., Evaluation in Education: A Practitioner's Guide, Itasca, Illinois: F. E. Peacock Publishers, Inc. 1972.

Guthrie, E. R. The Evaluation of Teaching. Seattle: U. of Washington Press, 1954.

Harris, Chester, W. (ed). Problems of Measuring Change. Madison: U. of Wisconsin Press, 1963.

Isaac, Stephen and Michael, W. B. Handbook in Research and Evaluation, San Diego: Robert R. Knapp Publisher, 1972.

Jaeger, Richard, Law, Alexander, Popham, W. James, Stuffle-
beam, Daniel and Tyler, Ralph. Expanding Technology of Educational Evaluation, 9F, 1974.

Lindenberger, Alice and Verner, Coolie. A Technique for Analyzing Extension Course Participants. Adult Education, 1960.

Morris, Lynn L. and Fits - Gibbon, Carol T. (eds.) Program
Evaluation Kit. Sage Publications, Beverly Hills, CA, 1978 -
individual volumes as follows:

    Evaluators's Handbook
    How to Calculate Statistics
    How to Deal with Goals and Objectives
    How to Design a Program Evaluation
    How to Present an Evaluation Report
    How to Measure Program Implementation

Popham, W. James. An Evaluation Guide Book: A Set of Practical
Guidelines for the Educational Evaluator. Los Angeles: The
Instructional Objectives Exchange, 1971.

Popham, W. James. (ed.) Evaluation in Education: Current Applications, Berkeley: McCutchan Publishing Corp., 1974.

Rieck, Robert E. Evaluating Agriculatural Economics Extension
Teaching. Journal of Farm Economics, Vol. 47, No. 3, 1965.

Steele, Sara. Contemporary Approaches to Program Evaluation.
Implications for Evaluating Programs for Disadvantaged Adults.
Washington, D.C. Education Resources Division Capital Pub-
lication, Inc., 1973 (ERIC Clearinghouse on Adult Education,
Syracuse, N.Y.).

Tripodi, Tony, Fellin, P., and Epstein, I. **Social Program Evaluation: Guidelines for Health, Education and Welfare Administrators,** Itasca, Illinois: F. E. Peacock Publishers, Inc., 1971.

Tyler, Ralph W. Basic Principle of Curriculum and Instruction.
Chicago: U. of Chicago Press, 1950.

Tyler, Ralph W. **An Evaluation of General Extension** Work by Land
Grant Institutions. Speech, American Association of Land Grant
Colleges and Universities, 1961.

Walberg, Herbert J. (ed.). **Evaluating Educational Performance:
A Sourcebook of Methods, Instruments, and Examples.** Berkeley:
McCutchan Publishing Corp., 1974.

Wholey, Joseph S., and others, **Federal Evaluation Policy: Analyzing the Effects of Public Programs.** Washington, D.C.: The
Urban Institute, 1970.

Wick, John W., and Beggs, D. L. **Evaluation for Decision-Making
in the Schools,** Boston: Houghton Mifflin Company, 1971.

Worthen, Blaine R. and Sanders, J. R. **Educational Evaluation:
Theory and Practice,** Worthington, Ohio: Charles A. Jones
Publishing Co., 1973.

FOOTNOTES CHAPTER 21

1 Gale Jensen, A. A. Liveright, and W. Hallenbeck (eds.), **Adult Education, Outlines of an Emerging Field of University Study**, Adult Education Association, U.S.A., Washington, D.C., 1964, p. 291.

2 "Techniques for Teachers of Adults," National Association of Public School Adult Educators, February 1965.

3 Edward J. Furst, **Constructing Evaluation Instruments**, Longmans, New York, 1958.

4 First published by R. W. Axford in **The Clearing House**, Vol. 41, No. 6 (February 1967), p. 327.

Chapter XXII

RESEARCH IN
ADULT EDUCATION

Too often programs are based on tradition, guess, or
blithe assumption - rarely upon scientific study. One
major problem is the tremendous diversity of content,
methods, and agencies involved in activities labeled "adult
education."

-Burton W. Kreitlow, **Educating the Adult Educator**, Bulletin 573, University of Wisconsin,
March 1965, p. 5

RESEARCH - THE QUEST FOR KNOWLEDGE

Who of us would not like to know more about ourselves? This
is true of the educator of adults as much as it is of other individuals. We need more information about ourselves and about
our programs. The day is far past when we can program by
impulse or evaluate by emotional elation. We need to know more
about our clientele, our learning theory, our program planning,
our teaching techniques, and which are our most effective instruments for evaluation and program improvement.

"Leaders in the field of adult education for some time have
felt a need for a greater amount of penetrating information,
reliable research data, and factual knowledge relating to various
areas in adult education. Such a body of knowledge has been in
evidence to undergird future progress and planning in most fields
of education, but has been particularly lacking at the adult level."[1]
This observation was written by Robert Maaske in 1950. Many
organized contributions to needed research in adult education
have been made since, but more is needed.

As early as 1951 Ronald Lippitt, a leading researcher in adult
education identified three aspects of the research problems in
adult education:

Producing more and better research.

Producing better research workers and involving them in
adult education research.

Getting practioners to interpret and unilize the large body
of existing relevant research.[2]

METHODS OF EDUCATIONAL RESEARCH
The basic methods of educational research are 1) historical research; 2) descriptive research; and 3) experimental research. We shall consider each of these in order to appreciate which is appropriate for approaching an educational problem.

HISTORICAL RESEARCH
Historical research has as its purpose understanding an historical development as applied to a particular subject matter. It is used to ascertain the meaning and reliability of facts in the social sciences, in the natural sciences, and the law. It has as a procedure the statement of the problem, collection of data, with primary sources preferred over secondary resources, formulation of hypotheses to explain events, the drawing of conclusions and the reporting of findings. Archives are the main source of data.

Historical research is limited, as it is only as good as the amount of available material. One cannot experiment, can only make generalizations about past events, and cannot make accurate predictions about the future. Some claim that the only thing "we learn little from history". Yet it has a major value in understanding how institutions developed.

DESCRIPTIVE RESEARCH
Descriptive research is often described as what actually exists. It asks the question "what is the present status of these phenomena?" The goal of descriptive research is to gather facts, predict and identify relationships among variables. Some typical sorts of descriptive research include school surveys, job analyses, public opinion surveys, community surveys, and documentary analyses. Another type is interrelationship studies--where the investigator examines what a phenomena is, like in a natural setting and how and why it occurs. The method is limiting because one cannot control for confounding variables.

Correlational studies have as their objective -- to predict. An example of the causal comparative correlational study is the effect of typing speed in proportion to the amount of time spent glancing at the copy.

The case study has as its purpose an intensive investigation of a social unit, for example, an individual as used in a social history of patients in a hospital setting.

Development studies have as their purpose the investigation of changes that take place over time. Research studies of this type include studies which are costly. Descriptive research continues longitudinal to be a most popular research method for educators.

413

EXPERIMENTAL RESEARCH

Experimental research ascertains the how and the why a particluar event occurs. The important distinction is that it consists of the manipulation of an independent variable under highly controlled conditions. The hypothesis suggests that an independent variable is related to the occurance of another condition (dependent variable). In experimental research, control is obtained through usage of a control group and through randomized assignment procedures.

Fred F. Barnes lists ten characteristics of experimental research:[3]

1. Research ideas are restricted by the requirement that they are testable.
2. Theories and speculations are closely related to reality.
3. Simplicity in ideas and conceptualizations is ideal.
4. Research sets out to test, not to prove.
5. The concept of "failure" is an archaic interference in research activities.
6. The potential value of a research project is directly related to the cogency of the question asked.
7. The methods of research are intentionally devised to prevent the researcher's deluding himself and others.
8. Values play a legitimate and important part in research activities.
9. The methods of analysis, of logical deduction and statistical inference, should fit the limitations inherent in the problem being investigated.
10. The researcher courts recognition through the power of his tested ideas, not through the attractiveness of his rhetoric.

Barnes also explains the ways of reasoning and steps in the research process. Barnes emphasizes the "tentativeness" of the findings of the researcher:

"The competent researcher would never approach the reports of other researchers as superhuman works quite insulated from humanity. He would be more likely to regard them as tentative glimpses into another human being's way of thinking, glimpses which should be carefully criticized and challenged. Most important, he would probably recognize that the chief value of someone else's researches lies in the clues they may offer for further studies of his own. He would certainly not think of them as the final word on any subject in which he is interested."[4]

Historical, descriptive, and experimental are the three best known approaches to research. Let us now examine what is the status of adult education research in our society.

WHAT IS THE STATUS OF ADULT EDUCATION RESEARCH?

Dr. Burton W. Kreitlow, University of Wisconsin adult educator and experienced researcher has said, "Unless a body of knowledge is adult education is soon developed by rigorous research in the field, it may be concluded that there is no such field."[5] Giant strides still need to be taken in adult education research. A perusal of existing research will give evidence of important contributions, but there also appears a lack of structure and theory which could be the basis for new research and for integrating the research done to date. In a discussion of needed research, Kreitlow laments the need for integrating the research we now have in adult education.[6]

Fortunately, however, 'the field of adult education is maturing, with both the quality and the quantity of research moving progressively upward. The growing departments of adult education, both in the United States and in Canada, with emphasis upon training in research methodology, are having positive effects on the field. Instruction is now offered in quantitative and historical methods of research. Closer coordination and cooperation between educationists and other social scientists, is becoming more of a reality.

It is an important point that the need for adult education research is being recognized, and more financial support is forthcoming. Edmund deS. Brunner cites several thousand titles examined as evidence of interest, and Kreitlow lists over one hundred references in his research and development study, "Educating the Adult Educator."[7]

RESEARCH STUDY IN NON-VOCATIONAL ADULT EDUCATION - EDMUND deS. BRUNNER

A definitive study of the needs and findings of research in adult education was undertaken by the Bureau of Applied Social Research at Columbia University under the direction of Brunner and his staff.[8] The study inventoried research in nonvocational adult education and deals with the status of research and its development, particularly since the mid-1920's. The major purpose of the project was to discover whether the present research findings have produced any generalizations on which policy can be based and which could be used for guidance of those entering the field as professional adult educators.

A second purpose of the study was to point up specific problem areas and areas which would benefit from additional research by students of the field in order to strengthen programs of nonvocational adult education. Between 4,000 and 5,000 titles of books, monographs, bulletins, articles, and unpublished theses were examined, and more than 600 are cited in the report. The practitioner of adult education will do well to have this reference as a part of the library, for a review of the research is made in adult learning, motivation to learn, attitudes, adult interests and education, participants and participation, organization and administration, programs and program planning, methods and techniques, use of discussion, leaders and leadership (lay and professional), group research, the community and its institutions, and problems of evaluation research.

RESEARCHER-PRACTITIONER COOPERATION

The alert educator of adults will recognize the important interdependency which exists between the adult education practitioner and the adult education researcher. Very early the worker in the field realizes that not only does the researcher provide valuable research findings that are of use to the practitioner, but also the practitioner, the program planner in the field, is a most important source of ideas about pertinent problems concerning which the researcher can usefully conduct investigations.

Then the question may be asked, "But who needs the research findings?" Alan B. Knox, tries to answer the question.

What we need in adult education research depends to a large extent upon whom we ask, and what we mean by adult education research. Let's assume that adult education research results when adult educators or researchers in related fields such as psychology, sociology, education, administration, and economics, produce research findings that are directly and somewhat uniquely relevant to problems confronted by adult educators. This suggests an answer to the question, "Need by whom?" The answer is needed by the adult education practitioner. [9]

Who are these practitioners of the art of educating adults? They include the county extension agent in cooperative extension, the deans and program people in general university extension, librarians, directors of public school adult education, directors of training in business and industry, and directors of voluntary agencies such as YMCA's and YWCA's, church workers, media people, and the multitude working in training and recreation.

416

Practitioner of adult education.

It is this author's conviction that administrators in adult education need to take more cogniance of the important function of research in adult education. The administrator can provide field experience, pose some vital questions, and benefit from the findings of seasoned researchers. Aker and Schroeder have pointed out that the administrator plays three important roles which can lead to the improvement of the education of adults:

1. As a stimulator of needed research
2. Interpreter of research findings
3. Producer of "action" research.[10]

417

Kreitlow reminds us that no definitive study of the quantitative research output in adult education has been made, but there
is evidence "the upward spiral of completed studies each year
parallels that of the expanding graduate programs".[11]

There is need for foundation support and state and federal
support for research. Kellogg, Ford, and Carnegie have given
leadership in providing private funds to support fellowships to
underwrite graduate students who have produced some of the significant research through our departments of adult education.
There is a need for major blocks of monies to support advanced
study in our universities.

Alan B. Knox, in his book **Adult Development and Learning**
concludes his book with a wise admonition to adult educators.
He says, "Practitioners should encourage and support research
on adult development"[12] In the appendix of the book Knox gives
some helpful hints on conducting research on adult development
and learning. Any adult educator embarking on a research proposal will do well to examine the details of Knox's six broad
categories of information: 1) Purpose, 2) Rationale, 3) Procedures,
4) Resources, 5) Budget, and 6) Reporting.

RESEARCH AREAS NEEDING ATTENTION

In a Cooperative Research Project directed by Kreitlow, a
study was made of the problem of "Relating Adult Education to
Other Disciplines." Kreitlow and his team of researchers found
that there is a most pressing need for research in the following
areas: the adult as a learner; the adult's response to socio-
cultural phenomena; the adult education enterprise including
purposes and goals; understanding of adult education; the educational process; the educational program; administration of programs; counseling adults; preparation of adult educators; and
evaluation of programs.[13] The study found that chief among
the disciplines that can make substantial research contributions
are sociology and psychology. The applied fields of communications, human relationships, and social work also are useful.

In a discussion of the changing adult education agency and its
implications for the administrator, William S. Griffith points
out that there is an increasing interest in systems research, and
that a growing number of administrators of large adult education
institutions are showing more and more concern for research
directed at increasing the understanding of organizational change.

After describing a model for institutional growth and development, Griffith concludes that although his study provides some
insights into the process of institutional growth, it accentuates

418

the primitive state of existing knowledge regarding institutional growth, adaptation, and decay. We need more information on **the process**. Says Griffith:

Research is sorely needed to increase our understanding of the processes by which adult education institutions adapt or fail to react to environmental changes. How can an established organization revise and revitalize its program without losing its identity? How can an institution which has reached its desired size maintain creativity, flexibility, and self-renewal without producing accompanying changes in scale? What are the changes associated with institutional decay and what corrective action might be useful under varying conditions?[14]

Griffith laments the fact that administrators of adult education, who serve the continually changing needs of our society, find little research to help them in solving their complex problems associated with directing the process of organizational growth and adaptation to new social conditions. He urges additional human and material resources for investigation and research at once.

Clearly there are two major problems when we examine research as it relates to adult education: one is the pin-pointing of important researchable questions by those working in the multifaceted programs of adult education, and the other is the conducting and utilization of adult education research.

The professors of adult education who started meeting in 1955 have had **research needs** as one of their main points of interest. In 1957 the "Commission of the Professors of Adult Education" of the Adult Education Association, U.S.A., embarked upon a five-year series of seminar meetings with support from the Kellogg Foundation. The formulation of a theoretical framework for adult education and the identification of curriculum needs for graduate-level programs for adult educators were primary purposes for the organization of the group and the seminars.

An outgrowth of the meetings is the book, **Adult Education: Outlines of an Emerging Field of University Study**,[15] which is directed to those responsible for planning and conducting adult education programs, and to university and college officials whose job is to organize training programs for professional adult educators.

DATA-BANK NEED FOR THE GROWING BODY OF RESEARCH KNOWLEDGE

The foregoing is not meant to suggest that there is not already a body of knowledge regarding adult education. There is - but

419

it is scattered. There are no sources readily available for drawing on the research findings in the various fields. There is need in adult education for a data bank on the various aspects of adult and continuing education. A beginning has been made with the Library on Continuing Education at Syracuse University, from which many professional adult educators are drawing bibliographies and abstracts. At Syracuse University also the U.S. Office of Education has established the Educational Research Clearing House for Adult Education. A network of data-retrieval stations would prove invaluable to the field and might be implemented through the inter-university agency known as EDUCOM.

As the field of adult education expands so does the collection of information specific to that field. The body of knowledge which has been building was, at first, scattered and inconsistently catalogued, stored and disseminated. In 1964 the U.S. Office of Education established the Educational Resources Information Center (ERIC), a national information system which disseminates educational research results, research-related materials, and other resource information. Through a network of specialized centers, or clearing houses, each of which is responsible for a particular educational area, information is acquired, evaluated, abstracted, indexed, and listed in the Resources in Education (RIE) catalogue. In addition there is a vast amount of literature published in periodicals and journals which is indexed and disseminated through the Current Index To Journals in Education (CIJE). Both the RIE and the CIJE are divisions of ERIC.

ERIC consists of a coordinating staff in Washington, D.C. and 16 clearing houses located at universities or with professional organizations across the country. These Clearinghouses, each responsible for a particular educational area, are an integral part of the ERIC system. Information specific to the field of the adult education is handled at the Adult, Career and Vocational Education Clearinghouse currently housed at Ohio State University in Columbus, Ohio. Research-related materials and resources pertinent to adult education are gathered in and prepared for dissemination through the ERIC system by personnel at this Clearinghouse.

Over the nation there are other small organizations which handle adult education information either by gathering it in from contributors or disseminating it to information seekers. However, the central system for this kind of activity is ERIC. Adult educators, like all educators, can and do tap into this system as their needs dictate.

Adult education organizations and councils have been instrumental in promoting research and making results of studies available to practioners in the field. Listings of these organizations may be found in the **Encyclopedia of Associations** available in any good library. In addition there are directories of information sources available through the National Dissemination Forum.[16]

There is a question as to whether because of the diversity and heterogeneity of the field of adult education we can build a coordinated and cohesive body of research. In reporting on "Research in Adult Education," Kreitlow said we may have to borrow from other fields:

> It is possible that the diversity of the field of adult edu - cation is such that the research must always be borrowed from another field, or at least have the bulk of it come from other disciplines? This may be true until such time as there is more clarity as to what adult education actually is . . . What this final outcome might be is only conjecture at this point. Is it a foundation in the disciplines of social science with an interpretation of their implications for adult education? Is it a concentration of research by adult educators with but small concern for research in the related fields? Is it a base in the fields of sociology, psychology, communication, and political science with selective but critical descriptive, analytical, and experimental research in the "adult classroom?" Whatever it might be, within a reasonably short time research must be developed to gain the knowledge needed to improve adult education and adult learning.[17]

Kreitlow reminds those of us in adult education that we must organize and examine the various parts that constitute the field in order to make the field a stronger professional area of study. Otherwise, the educator of adults will be apt to become absorbed into the related professions. A lack of clear visibility for workers in the field now exists, and more adequate integration of research findings will benefit the profession.

SOURCES FOR RESEARCH INFORMATION ON ADULT EDUCATION
EDUCATIONAL ORGANIZATIONS

5067
ADULT EDUCATION ASSOCIATION OF THE U.S.A. (AEA)
810 18th St., N.W.   Phone: (202) 347-9574
Washington, DC 20006   Dr. Linda S. Hartsock, Exec. Dir.
Founded: 1951. **Members:** 3000. **Staff:** 5. **Regional Groups:** 12. **Local Groups:** 60. "To further the concept of education as a process continuing throughout life." Works to stimulate local, state,

and regional adult education efforts and to encourage mutual cooperation and support; to keep in touch with proposed legislation and to initiate legislative action. Sponsors Commission of Professors of Adult Education, which seeks to make adult education a defined Profession. Conducts special studies; bestows awards; provides career information and referral service. Publications: (1) Lifelong Learning The Adult Years, 10/year; (2) Adult Education, quarterly; also publishes books, manuals, and pamphlets. Absorbed: (1926) American Association for Adult* Education. Convention/Meeting: annual - 1979 Oct. 29 - Nov. 2, Boston, MA; 1980 St. Louis, MO; 1981 Anaheim, CA.

* Source: Encyclopedia of Associations p. 436.

5068
AMERICAN FOUNDATION FOR CONTINUING EDUCATION
(Adult Education)
Dissolved 1973. Copyright was taken over by Syracuse University Publications in Continuing Education.

5069
CENTER FOR THE STUDY OF LIBERAL EDUCATION FOR ADULTS
(Adult Education)
Defunct. Copyright was taken over by the Syracuse University Publications in Continuing Education.

5070
CONTINUING EDUCATION COUNCIL (Adult Education) (CEC)
Six N. Sixth St.   Phone: (804) 648-6742
Richmond, VA 23219   Homer Kempfer, Exec. Dir.
Founded: 1974. Staff: 3. National professional and trade associations, business and industrial organizations, labor unions, cultural societies, public affairs organizations and individuals. Purpose is to raise the quality of continuing education programs through accreditation, consultation and related means. Goals are: to provide a self-improvement process through evaluation, planning and consultation; to interface more closely with higher education; to justify acceptance of courses for credentials, certification, licensure and registration; to encourage worthy educational programs and discourage the inferior; to gain outside validation for programs; to improve public image; to attract students; to qualify under certain state laws and regulations; to meet requirements of business and industrial firms which approve only accredited courses for attendance, reimbursement and personnel decisions; to qualify for public or private grants or contracts. Publications: Newsletter, quarterly; also publishes list of accredited continuing education programs. Convention/ Meeting: annual Invitational Conference.

5071
COUNCIL OF NATIONAL ORGANIZATIONS FOR **ADULT EDU-**
CATION (CNO-AE)
c/o Elizabeth Olsen
American Red Cross
2025 E. St., N.W.   Phone: (202) 737-8300
Washington, DC 20006   Elizabeth Olsen, Pres.
Founded: 1952. **Members:** 25. Federation of national organizations
with a concern for and program in adult education (10); interested
individuals (15). **To provide an opporu**
individuals (15). **To provide an opportunity for national organizations to work cooperatively in research demonstrations, and
consultations in the their adult education interests.** Currently
sponsors I Can program, a self-administered "test" which lists
the competencies an individual has acquired through experiences.
**Publishes papers on community problems and social issues and
training materials on issues pertaining to adult education. Formerly:
(1960) Council of National Organizations of the Adult Education
Association. Convention/Meeting:** periodic board meetings; also
holds meetings of task forces.

5072
INSTITUTE OF LIFETIME LEARNING **(Adult Education) (ILL)**
1909 K St., N.W.   Phone: (202) 872-4800
Washington, DC 20049   Kathleen Chelsvig, Educ. Specialist
Founded: 1963. **The continuing adult education service of the
National Retired Teachers Association and the American As-
soication of Retired Persons.** "Stimulates and provides opportunities for continuing education for older persons. Works with
educational institutions, organizations, legislators and the older
population to develop meaningful programs and services. Serves
as liaison in the education community for NRTA-AARP and its
programs." The Institute is intended for older persons in all walks
of life and is adapted to the needs and capabilities of the older
person. Provides consultation to any and all educational institutions conducting or planning to conduct senior citizen learning
programs. **Disseminates information to older persons about educational opporutnities, develops educational materials and stimulates awareness of new learning options and research.** Comple-
ments existing local programs and sponsors extension institutes throughout the country.

5073
LEARNING EXCHANGE **(Adult Education)**
Box 920   Phone: (312) 273-3383
Evanston, IL 60204   Diane Reiko Kinishi, Exec. Dir.

Founded: 1971. **Members:** 8500. **Staff:** 17. Individuals who give monetary support to the service. To enable anyone in the Chicago area who wishes to teach, learn or share an interest in the topics or subjects of their choice to do so. People form own tutorial arrangements, small classes and interest groups in homes, offices, libraries, churches, community centers and restaurants. Currently offers 3000 different topics for people to teach, learn or share an interest in. Has 30,000 users who have registered over 3000 subjects. **Maintains speakers bureau. Publications: (1) Peoplephile, monthly; (2) Newlsetter, quarterly; also publishes a catalog.**

5074
NATIONAL ASSOCIATION FOR PUBLIC CONTINUING AND **ADULT** EDUCATION (NAPCAE)
1201 16th St., N.W.   Phone: (202) 833-5486
Washington, DC 20036   Dr. James R. Dorland, Exec. Dir.
Founded: 1952. **Members:** 6000, **Staff:** 6. Administrators and teachers of adult education. To stimulate and expand public continuing adult education programs throughout the country. Provides consultation services. **Publications: (1) Pulse of Public,** 8/year; **(2) Techniques,** 8/year; **(3) Swap Shop** 6/year; also **publishes Almanac and Directory of Public Continuing and Adult Education. Formerly:** (1969) National Association for Public School Adult Educators. **Convention/Meeting:** annual - 1979 November, Boston, MA.

5075
NTL INSTITUTE (Adult Education)
1501 Wilson Blvd.   Phone: (703) 527-1500
Arlington, VA 22209   Edith W. Seashore, Pres.
Founded: 1947. **Members:** 300. **Staff:** 20. Non-profit corporation offering training consultation, research and publication services. Created the laboratory method, an experience-based training process that can change outlook and behavior; the Adjunct Staff which provides the means for elaborating, testing, refining and applying the laboratory method. Programs are created and conducted by a faculty of 300 selected and trained social scientists located at over 40 universities, for individuals and teams from occupational groups and corporations, as well as for leaders in schools and colleges and for community development leaders. **Publications: (1) Journal of Applied Behavioral Science,** quarterly; **(2) Social Change** quarterly; also **publishes monographs, books, and training materials. Formerly:** (1954) National Training Laboratory in Group Development; (1959) National Training Laboratories; (1967) NTL Institute for Applied Behavioral Sciences.

5076
SCHOOL OF LIVING (Adult Education) (SOL)
P.O. Box 3233   Phone: (717) 755-1561
York, PA 17402   Jubal Lee, Dir. Of Educ.
Founded: 1936. Members: 2000. To demonstrate, organize and
promote adult education using seventeen distinguishable, major
problems of living. Centered in a philosophy of organic rather
than mechanistic aspects of life. Espouses life-styles consistent
with this philosophy, primarily the modern homestead, intentional
communities and decentralization. Promotes and organizes social,
economic and political changes which allow ready access to
land and natural resources. Promotes psychological insight into and
understanding of self and human relations. Conducts seminars,
Sells books; maintains exchange program with several colleges
and universities. Committees: Education. Publications: (1) Green
Revolution, 10/year; (2) Directory, annual; also publishes numerous pamphlets and books. Convention/Meeting: annual; also holds
weekend seminars, May through October.

5077
SYRACUSE UNIVERSITY PUBLICATIONS IN CONTINUING EDU-
    CATION (Adult Education) (SUPCE)
Syracuse University
224 Huntington Hall   Phone: (315) 423-3421
Syracuse, NY 13210   Alexander N. Charters, Editor
Founded: 1968. Staff: 2, Serves as a publishing outlet for quality
studies in the field of higher adult education. Manuscripts considered
for publication may be philosophical or theoretical in content, or
consist of reports on activities of research in continuing education.
Furnishes funds for editing, printing, and distributing manuscripts
accepted for publication. Its monograph series includes Notes and
Essays, Occasional Papers, and Landmark Series. Holds copyright to publications of former Center for the Study of Liberal
Education for Adults; American Foundation for Continuing Education; Fund for Adult Education.

5078
TAMIMENT INSTITUTE (Adult Education)
c/o Stephen C. Vladeck
1501 Broadway   Phone: (212) 354-8330
New York, NY 10036   Stephen C. Vladeck, Sec.
Founded: 1921. Staff: 2. Adult educational institution devoted to
the furthering of a better understanding of the political, social,
and economic complexities of contemporary society. By gift in
1963, the Tamiment Institute Library, comprised of extensive
collections of rare printed and manuscript materials pertaining

to labor development and to radical movements in the United States, became part of the New York University Libraries system. **Publications:** Labor History, 3/year. **Formerly:** (1973) Tamiment Institute and Library. **Convention/Meeting:** annual.

HOW SHALL PRIORITIES BE ESTABLISHED?

Because there are many areas of adult education that call for additional investigation, we must help answer the question, "What research is most needed?" Although there are many ways of establishing such a priority list, some of those most effective might be: (1) Question adult educators and find out where the utilization of research findings or the lack of such has contributed to their program success of failure. (2) Examine the literature of research to find where there are gaps and where research would benefit the field of adult education. (3) Examine what research has been supported in the past and find if more is needed or if new areas need exploration. (4) Query directors of adult education programs. (5) Question researchers and faculty persons who have been investigating areas closely related to adult education in the social sciences. One investigation, for example, may lead to the need for investigation of what program needs would most interest and benefit the retiree. (6) Sometimes excellent ideas can be obtained from field investigators who have worked on a research problem and who see the possibilities and need for more depth and scope in a given area of research. Brainstorming with research workers is most productive, and adult program people must be continually brought together with research personnel. It is one of the regrettable realities of the recently sophisticated field of adult education that so few practitioners feel comfortable with and can talk the language of the researcher. And the researcher needs to cultivate understandable language to communicate findings more intelligibly to the citizen and the program person in the field.

DISSEMINATION OF RESEARCH FINDINGS

The universities have a major responsibility not only for formulating carefully structured research designs but for seeing that the pertinent information gets into the hands of those who can put the research findings to use. For example, the Cooperative Extension Service of the U.S. Department of Agriculture has been most successful in establishing research stations, utilizing the expertise of the colleges and universities, and then disseminating the findings through bulletins, agricultural agents, demonstrations, and other media of adult education communication.

Wisconsin's one-time president, Charles R. Van Hise, reminded the state legislature and the university faculty that the knowledge stored up in the halls of learning must be put out where it will benefit the people. He made the extension divisions of the university the third leg of the "milk stool" of the land-grant institution, then derisively called a "cow college!" Teaching, research, and public service (extension) is the threefold function of a great university, proclaimed Van Hise. The outreach of the university, taking out the findings of the research laboratories, will enrich the lives of the people, improve the economy, and benefit the entire society.

The educator of adults will be research-conscious, will utilize the benefits of research, will be acquainted with the agencies of research and use them, and will keep abreast of the research needs in the community, the agency, and society. To question, to inquire, to want to know, are the prerequisites of the researcher.

Any industry that does not have a division of R & D (research and development) is asking to be left behind in the technological revolution. This is no less true of educational institutions. Had it not been for minds devoted to research and development, we might still be reading by kerosene lamp and riding a horse and buggy. Foundations must assist the agencies of adult education to learn more about adult needs, adult learning, adult motivation, agency organization, and the many facets of adult education that are growing by astronomical figures. If our resources, both financial and human, are to be well spent, we must know how to do the task best, with the most benefit for the least expenditure. Only through research and knowing "what to do" and "how to do it" will we be able to build a society in which lifelong learning is a part of the fabric of society, and learning how to learn[18] is put at the top of the priority list in our planning for the future. Peace and the full life are at the gate of the society that embraces the "research attitude," the desire to know, and the insistence that all shall have that right.

WHAT IS HANDICAPPING OUR RESEARCH EFFORT?

Fortunately, in recent years more federal money is being expended for research in education. The future for adult education is looking brighter. Some of the factors handicapping the quality and the quantity of research in our field have been identified by Sheats, Jayne, and Spence.[19]

In the past some professors of adult education have had little opportunity for training in research methodology.

Too few students planning adult education majors in graduate programs are required to develop good social science backgrounds.

Well-trained researchers in related fields have not seen adult education as a field where funds are available for developing research teams.

Many practitioners have lacked sensitivity to the need for research. Therefore a large number have not thought of making their facilities available as research settings.

The relative newness of the profession and the multitude of agencies involved in educating adults are major factors handicapping the research effort. Practitioners are often overwhelmed by demands made upon their time. Relatively few have been primarily research-oriented, many having come from other administrative posts.

Until recently the primary limitation for research capacity was lack of funds, but lack of expertise to do the job is rapidly becoming the leading drawback. Too few practitioners have acquired the research competency for really sound research.

What may be needed are regional research centers, with the capacity for assisting a number of agencies with their research needs. Since many universities have this capacity, they must be made to see it as an opportunity for training graduate students and for attracting research funds to expand their capacity for service.

The handicaps which confront the growth of an adequate research base in adult education also plague research efforts in other areas of education. But now that we have enumerated some of the major hurdles we must overcome to initiate meaningful research, our energies can more effectively be directed to overcoming the handicaps.

SUMMARY

Recognizing that curiosity is at the base of useful research, we see that adult education, like other fields, needs to know more about its clientele, its effectiveness in program planning, its learning theory, and its evaluation techniques.

We examined the three methods of research, historical, descriptive, and experimental. We listed the ten characteristics of experimental research as a guide for the novice researcher. We considered the administrator's role in research, and concluded that the researcher needs to give answers to the administrator of adult education programs, and the administrator needs to provide questions to be answered. Presented are the six broad categories of information needed for the adult educator embarking on a research proposal.

In looking at the status of the adult education research, we find that more rigorous research is needed both in quality and in quantity. Adult education is gaining more research-minded professionals as our graduate programs in the field produce persons with expertise in research methods, historical as well as quantitative methodology being included in the curriculum. Fortunately, more financial support is coming from both federal and state sources, though still it is not enough to give the practitioner the information he needs.

Edmund deS. Brunner and his staff gave us the most definitive study of the needs and findings of research in nonvocational adult education. Kreitlow pointed out that we must develop a more rigorous research in the field or it may be concluded that there is no field of adult education. Knox emphasized the need for closer cooperation between the practitioner and the researcher, and suggested the answer to "Who needs research findings?" may be the practitioner. Kreitlow examined areas needing research and enumerated the adult learner; purposes and goals of the adult education enterprise; the educational process; administration of programs; counseling; preparation of adult educators; and evaluation techniques. Griffith emphasized the need for research on problems of institutional growth and development, and recommends sorely needed research to help adult educators increase understanding of the processes by which institutions adapt or fail to react to environmental changes.

A data bank for the growing body of research information is suggested on a national or international basis, and a prototype is suggested in the ERIC at Syracuse University. In reviewing the literature on research in adult education, Kreitlow suggests we may have to borrow research information from other disciplines because of the diversity of the field, at least until we get a sharper definition of what adult education is. He delineates the critical research needs from his interviews with twenty-eight prominent professionals who responded to thirty topics, rating them from critical to immaterial. Motivation, reaching the lower social classes, the effect of social values on participants, and the client involvement in program objectives rated highest in that order. In answering the question, "What research is most needed?" it is felt that questioning adult educators as to what utilization of research findings contributed to program success or failure should have high priority.

The universities have a major responsibility for structuring research designs, training researchers, and dissemination of research findings. True adult educators will be research-conscious, avail themselves of research facilities, learn to read the findings of adult education research, and ferret out research needs in their agencies, communities, and society.

What handicaps our research efforts? We found that, while funds have been a primary hurdle and continue to be, more state and federal funds are now available for demonstration projects and research efforts. Now we need competent researchers who can assist the program planner or the agency administrator to learn more about his clientele and how he can be more effective in serving the adults in his institution. Fortunately, more institutions of higher learning are adding graduate programs for the preparation of adult educators, and experience in research techniques is being acquired.

The prospects for adult education research were never brighter, but at the same time the need was never greater. Through the various groups such as the Commission on Research of the Adult Education Association and the annual professional meetings, more and better research can be done by educators of adults. We must push for that goal.

QUESTIONS:

1. How does our economy effect what is needed for research in adult education?
2. What is the administrator's role in adult education research?
3. What should go into a good research proposal?
4. How would you describe the status of adult education research?
5. What improvements could be made in dissemination of adult education research findings?
6. How would you establish priorities for adult education research?
7. What are some factors limiting effective adult education research?
8. How would you utilize ERIC in your adult education research?
9. What are some sources for Research information from organizations working in Adult Education?

Bibliography

Boshier, Roger - "**Motivational Orientations Revisited: Life Space Motives and the Education Participation Scale,**" Adult Education Journal of Research and Theory, Vol. 27, No. 2 (Winter 1977); pp 89-115.

Boshier, Roger - "**Factor Analysts at Large; A Critical Review of the Motivational Orientation Literature,**" Adult Education Journal of Research and Theory, Vol. 27, No. 1, (Fall, 1976); pp. 24-47.

Cross, Patricia K. - **Accent on Learning,** (San Francisco: Jossey-Bass, 1976), Chap. 5, pp. 111-33

Even, Mary Jane - Lifelong Learning: The Adult Years, **"Current and Future Trends in Adult Education Research"** Nov. 1978

Gould, Roger - **"Adult Life Stages: Growth Toward Self-Tolerance,"** Psychology Today, Vol. 8, No. 9, (1975); pp. 74-78.

Kogan, Nathan - **"Educational Implications of Cognitive Styles,"** in Lesser, Gerald S. (ed) Psychology and Educational Practice (Glennview, Ill: ScottForesman, 1972).

Lumsden, Barry D. and Sherron, Ronald H. - **Experimental Studies in Adult Learning and Memory,** (Washington, DC: Hamisphere Publishing Corp., 1975).

Messick, Samuel - et al., **Individuality in Learning,** (San Francisco; Jossey-Bass, 1976).

Monette, Maurice L. - **"The Concept of Educational Need; Analysis of Selected Literature,"** Adult Education Journal of Research and Theory, Vol. 27, No. 2, (Winter 1977); pp. 116-27.

Neugarten, Bernice - **"Adaptation and the Life Cycle,"** The Counseling Psychologist, Vol. 6, No. 1, (1976) pp. 16-20.

Sperry, Roger W. - **"Left-Brain, Right-Brain,"** Science Review (August 8, 1975), pp. 30-32; Hunter, Madelin, **Right-Brained Kids in Left-Brained Schools,"** Today's Education N.E.A. Journal (Nov.- Dec. 1976), pp. 45-48; Trotter, Robert J. **"The Other Hemphere,"** Science News, Vol. 109, (April 3, 1976); pp. 218-20, 223.

Ziegler, Warren L. - **The Future of Adult Education and Learning in the United States: Final Report Under Project Grant No. oeg-0-73-5232** (Syracuse, N.Y.; Educational Policy Research Center, Syracuse Research Corp., Feb., 1977). 34 pps. SRC-TR 76-600.

1 Robert J. Maaske, "Research Needs in Adult Education," **Adult Education Bulletin,** Vol. 14, No. 4 (April 1950), p. 120.

2 Paul Sheats, Jayne Clarence, and Ralph Spence. **Adult Education: The Community Approach,** Holt, New York, 1954, p. 465.

3 Barnes, Fred P. **Research for the Practitioner in Education,** National Association of Elementary School Principles, 1801 No. Moore St. Arlington, Va. 22209, 1972 pp. 13-18.

4 Barnes, **Ibid** p. 7.

5 Burton W. Kreitlow, "Research Reports, their Significance in Building and Communicating a Body of Knowledge," **Adult Education,** Vol. 11, No. 2 (Winter 1961), p. 67.

6 Burton W. Kreitlow, "Needed Research," **Review of Educational Research,** Vol. 35, No. 3 (June 1965) p. 240.

7 Burton W. Kreitlow, "Educating the Adult Educator," Bulletin 573, University of Wisconsin, Experiment Station, College of Agriculture, March 1965.

8 Edmund deS. Brunner, et al., **An Overview of Adult Education Research**, Adult Education Association, U.S.A., Washington, D.C., 1959.

9 Alan B. Knox, "Current Needs in Adult Education Research," Adult Education Association Conference, Milwaukee, Wisconsin, November 1964 (author's files).

10 Aker, George, and Schroeder, Wayne, in Shaw's **Administration of Continuing Education**, National Assoc. for Public School Ad. Ed. Washington, D.C. 1969 p. 350.

11 Kreitlow, Burton in Smith, Aker, and Kidd, **Handbook of Adult Education**, MacMillan, 1970, p. 144.

12 Knox, Alan B., ADULT DEVELOPMENT AND LEARNING, Jossey-Bass, San Francisco, Cal. 94111, 1977 p. 578.

13 Burton W. Kreitlow, "Relating Adult Education to Other Disciplines," Cooperative Research Project, E-012, Office of Education, U.S. Department of Health Education, and Welfare, 1964, p. 50-89.

14 William S. Griffith, "The Changing Adult Education Agency - Implications for the Administrator," paper presented at the Adult Education Commission on Research Symposium, 14th National Conference, Adult Education Association, U.S.A. Milwaukee, Wis., Nov. 17, 1964. Also see his "A Growth Model of Institutions of Adult Education," unpublished PhD. dissertation, Department of Education, University of Chicago, 1963.

15 Gale Jensen, A. A. Liveright, and W. Hallenbeck, **Adult Education: Outlines of an Emerging Field of University Study**, Adult Education Association, U.S.A., Washington, D.C., 1964. (Although the make-up of the book is poor, the content is excellent.)

16 Thanks to Mary Lee Carter, AEIS Program Coordinator, Bureau of Educational Research and Services, Arizona State University for help with the above.

17 Burton W. Kreitlow, "Research in Adult Education," in Malcolm Knowles, **Handbook of Adult Education in the United States**, Adult Education Association of the U.S.A., Washington, D.C., 1960, p. 115.

18 See J. Roby Kidd, **How Adults Learn**, Association Press, New York, 1959.

19 Paul Sheats et al., **op. cit.**, pp. 466-467.

Appendix A
EVALUATIVE CRITERIA FOR PUBLIC SCHOOL ADULT EDUCATION PROGRAMS

INTRODUCTION

The following guiding principles and evaluative criteria were prepared by a committee of the National Association for Public School Adult Education. Their purpose is to bring material on adult education to the attention of the National Study of Secondary Schools for its consideration in preparing the 1970 revised edition of **Evaluative Criteria**. The preparation of the material was financed by a grant from the Ford Foundation.

I. GUIDING PRINCIPLES

The purpose of education in a democratic society is to enable the individual to adjust to and influence the changing conditions of his environment. Our elementary and secondary public school system was built upon the assumption that this preparation could be largely accomplished in childhood. This terminal concept of education is no longer tenable. Sweeping societal change now dictates a reappraisal of this earlier philosophy which placed nearly its total investment in the education of the child. The impact of automation, the accelerated obsolescence of knowledge, increasing longevity, the shrinkage of the world - all these are factors which now render the continuing education of the adult a social imperative.

A distinct and significant role of the public school in this expanded program of education is both logical and inescapable. Its responsibility for the creation and maintenance of an enlightened citizenry is unquestioned. The continuing education of the adult is in reality an extension of this responsibility. Just as the Kalamazoo decision established the role of the public schools in extending education to the twelfth-grade level, so now do the conditions of our time dictate the public school's responsibility for setting up a program of education for the individual that is coterminous with the total life experience.

In addition to historical precedent, sound judgment dictates that continuing education be a responsibility of the public schools. In every community the public schools already possess the physical facilities, the professional leadership, and the intimate knowledge of the community which are needed for the development of such a program. These resources may be used to complement and extend the program for the child, giving the community a richer return on its education investment.

In the exercise of its responsibility for providing continuing education programs for adults, the public schools should be guided by certain basic principles:

1. The educational needs of adults grow out of personal aspirations and responsibilities of individuals, with respect to such concerns as earning a livelihood, home and family living, participation in community affairs, and personal fulfillment and self-realization. These are also major concerns of secondary education.

2. Because adults, unlike children, are voluntary participants in education, programs provided for them must be:
   (a) attuned to the self-realized needs which prompt participation
   (b) offered at times and places convenient and conducive to attendance
   (c) of such quality and relevance, in terms of content, instruction, and facilities, as to assure continued participation, and
   (d) widely publicized, promoted, and interpreted to the community.

3. The inherent nature of adult education programs and their clientele dictates that the programs be administered more flexibly than programs for children and youth usually are administered.

4. Because of the greater life experience of adult students, including occupational experience, travel, self-study, social participation, and home and family living, the continuing education program should:
   (a) place greater emphasis on the measurement and evaluation of student experience in terms of education equivalency
   (b) place greater emphasis on promoting and granting credit on the basis of ability to demonstrate competence rather than completion of a prescribed number of class hours, and
   (c) make greater use of student resources in the instructional process.

5. Because adults who participate in continuing education programs are usually employed, the programs should frequently include late afternoon, evening, and weekend classes, flexible program schedules, and varied student participation patterns.

6. A continuing education program for adults can be effective only when citizens participate in its planning and operation.

7. The continuing education program can provide a neutral setting in which citizens can engage in systematic study and exploration of community problems through fact-finding, discussion,

434

objective analysis, and impartial consideration of alternatives.

8. The continuing education program for adults provides the participant a direct and immediate return on his tax-dollar investment in public education.

Following are detailed check lists of evaluative criteria for adult education programs in the areas of organization and administration, program, and school facilities.

II. ORGANIZATION AND ADMINISTRATION

Check List

The adult education program of the local school district:

( ) 1. Has an adequate written policy approved by the Board of Education defining its philosophy, role, and scope.

( ) 2. Regards the Board of Education as its responsible, policy-making body.

( ) 3. Requires its administrator to be responsible to the chief or a deputy chief school administrator.

( ) 4. Provides adequate time for administrative supervision.

( ) 5. Utilizes an advisory committee with clearly defined responsibilities for overall planning and operation.

( ) 6. Utilizes advisory committees with clearly defined responsibilities (subject evaluation, planned progression, etc.) in various subject areas of the curriculum.

( ) 7. Has conducted a comprehensive survey and utilized other appropriate means to identify educational needs of adults in the community; in performing this identification the adult education administrator:

    ( ) Allows for continuous updating of the survey.

    ( ) Utilizes an advisory committee representative of the total community.

    ( ) Reaches into all segments and levels of community life.

( ) 8. Utilizes the survey and other means to meet the identified needs of the community.

( ) 9. Has a plan for the cooperative involvement in (a) program development, (b) extension of community services (e.g., rehabilitation of students), and (c) avoidance of duplication in educational effort, of community agencies and organizations such as:

    ( ) business and industry

    ( ) labor unions

    ( ) churches

    ( ) state employment service offices

    ( ) local and state government agencies

(e.g., public welfare, police, health)
( ) Community Action Programs
( ) Headstart (parent education)
( ) libraries
( ) vocational education
( ) U.S. Census experts
( ) Research departments of local schools and universities
( ) sociology departments of universities
( ) other institutions offering adult education programs
(e.g., YMCA, League of Women Voters, junior college, evening college)
( ) young-adult groups
( ) senior citizen organizations
( ) service clubs and other voluntary associations
( ) other: —————————————————————

( ) 10. Provides for continuing evaluation of the instructional program.
( ) 11. Provides budget expenditures for:
    ( ) administrative and supervisory costs
    ( ) consultant services
    ( ) instructional aids and equipment
    ( ) instructional salaries
    ( ) counseling services
    ( ) advertising, public information, and public relations
    ( ) library materials
    ( ) maintenance and overhead
    ( ) secretarial services
    ( ) staff travel
( ) 12. Receives an appropriate portion of the total school operating budget:
    ( ) less than 1%
    ( ) 1% - 2%
    ( ) 2% - 4%
    ( ) 4% - 5%
    ( ) more than 5%
( ) 13. Is supported by (indicate percentages):
    ( ) local taxes: ——%
    ( ) state aid: ——%
    ( ) federal aid: ——%
    ( ) registration or enrollment fees: ——%
    ( ) service fees: ——%
    ( ) private contributions: ——%
    ( ) other: ——%
( ) 14. Provides a rate of compensation for teachers and administrators comparable to that paid in the day school program.

436

( ) 15. Includes coverage in the Board of Education insurance policy.
( ) 16. Requires its administrator to be properly qualified to carry out his responsibilities.
( ) 17. Keeps on file in the office of the superintendent a job description of the position of continuing education administrator, as approved by the superintendent and Board of Education.
( ) 18. Requires faculty members to be properly certified or gives appropriate consideration to their occupation background qualifications for the subject area concerned.
( ) 19. Provides systematic in-service training for teachers and staff.
( ) 20. Offers programs:
    ( ) during regular school hours (8 a. . to 3 p.m.)
    ( ) during other than regular school hours
    ( ) during the summer months
    ( ) on weekends
( ) 21. Has defined optimal class size for different subject areas (e.g., 50 for history, 20 for clothing, 10-15 for basic education, etc.)
( ) 22. Provides guidance and counseling services by professionally prepared personnel.
( ) 23. Is part of a program of systematic and regular referral of dropouts from the day school to the adult program.
( ) 24. Has a public relations program which includes:
    ( ) an open house
    ( ) radio and television coverage
    ( ) publications (program announcements, annual report, etc.)
    ( ) promotional materials
    ( ) news releases
( ) 25. Provides police protection for staff and students in parking areas and on school grounds.

Supplementary Data

1. Describe briefly the growth of the enrollment in the continuing education program for adults over the past five years.
2. Describe briefly the public interest (news coverage, community group interest, etc.) in the adult program over the past five years.
3. Indicate the percentage of the total adult population of the community:
    ( ) less than 5%
    ( ) 5% - 10%

( ) 10% - 15%
( ) 15% - 20%
( ) more than 20%
4. Does this figure include duplicate enrollments? Yes——No——
5. Indicate the number of staff members who devote all or part of their time to the continuing education program for adults for the current year, 19— - 19—.

Staff	Number of Staff Members		Total Full Time Equivalent of all Members
	Full Time	Part Time	
Administrator (s)			
Classroom teachers			
Guidance counselors			
Instructional materials center personnel			
Specialists and consultants			
Secretaries and clerks			
Custodial and maintenance personnel			
Others			
Total			

6. Indicate the total student enrollment for the last complete academic year, 19— 19——: ——————————.

Evaluation

1. Is the number of the instruction and administrative personnel adequate?
2. Is the instructional and administrative staff adequately qualified and prepared?
3. To what extent is the organization and administration of the program consistent with the philosophy and guiding principles?

III. PROGRAM

Check List

The adult education program of the local school district:
( ) 1. Has an adult basic education program.
( ) 2. Has a high school completion program (leading to a high school diploma) through:

438

( ) credit courses
( ) credit by examination
( ) equivalency examination
( ) work experience
( ) 3. Has a vocational-occupational training program for:
    ( ) job-entry
    ( ) upgrading
( ) 4. Has a program for the foreign-born:
    ( ) leading to U.S. citizenship
    ( ) other: ——————— ——————————
( ) 5. Has a program designed to prepare adults for worthy use of leisure time and life enrichment through courses in:
    ( ) music
    ( ) art
    ( ) leadership training
    ( ) other: ————————————
( ) 6. Has a home and family life education program:
    ( ) for parents of mentally retarded children
    ( ) other: ——————————————
( ) 7. Has a consumer education program.
( ) 8. Has a health education program:
    ( ) for senior citizens
    ( ) in lip reading
    ( ) other: ————————————
( ) 9. Has a public affairs program (e.g., forums) designed to develop an informed electorate through study and discussion of:
    ( ) current political issues
    ( ) current social problems
    ( ) international issues
( ) 10. Provides:
    ( ) free textbooks
    ( ) a textbook sales office in the school
    ( ) programmed learning materials
    ( ) audio-visual equipment
    ( ) educational television (when available to other parts of the school system)
    ( ) language laboratories
    ( ) library services
    ( ) medical and health services (e.g., eye examination for adult basic education students)
    ( ) guidance and counseling
    ( ) diagnostic and achievement testing
    ( ) placement and referral services
( ) 11. Has made provision for the utilization of the various

439

community resources for program enrichment.

Evaluation

1. How adequately do the variety and quality of adult education offerings meet individual and societal needs?
2. How adequate is the plan for continuous study and evaluation?
3. To what extent is the content of the program consistent with the philosophy and guiding principles?

IV. SCHOOL FACILITIES

In many communities existing school buildings originally designed for the education of youth provide facilities reasonably well suited for a continuing education program for adults. The furnishings and equipment already available can often provide most of what is needed for such a program. Forward-looking communities are now planning secondary school facilities in cooperation with the director of continuing adult education and locating them with a recognition that the building and site may provide extended service as a community center, and a gradually growing number of communities are providing facilities for the exclusive use of the adult program.

Regardless of how the facilities have originated, for the purposes of this section they should be evaluated in relation to the needs of the continuing education program. A separate checklist should be made for each facility used by adult students.

Check List

( ) 1. The facility is located in an area convenient to the adults being served.

( ) 2. The dual use of buildings and equipment is an administrative responsibility shared by the day and evening school administrators.

( ) 3. Planning for building alterations, as well as new construction, is shared by day and evening school administrators.

( ) 4. There is adequate administrative space.

( ) 5. The administrative space is used exclusively by the adult education administrator and his staff.

( ) 6. The classroom furniture is appropriate in type and size for adult use.

( ) 7. The instructional aids and equipment adequately meet instructional needs.

( ) 8. Separate and adequate storage space is available for the

materials of the continuing education staff.
( ) 9. Adequate storage space is available for individual student projects.
( ) 10. The faculty lounge is available for use by adult school teachers.
( ) 11. A lounge is provided for the use of the adult students.
( ) 12. Provision is made for coffee breaks or smoking periods for the adult students.
( ) 13. Space is available for informal social activities.
( ) 14. Adequate space is provided for counseling services.
( ) 15. Adequate library facilities are provided for the adult program.
( ) 16. Adequate bulletin board and display areas are provided for the adult school teachers and students.
( ) 17. The facilities for parking are adequate and well lighted.
( ) 18. Appropriate safety precautions and other considerations (e.g., available toilets, ramps on stairs, etc.) are made for senior citizens and the physically handicapped.
( ) 19. Clear directions are posted for:
    ( ) fire emergency
    ( ) air-raid emergency
    ( ) first aid

Evaluation
1. To what extent is the school identifying problems regarding facilities and working toward their solutions?
2. To what extent does the school recognize the facilities needed for the continuing education program for adults in its plans for the future?
3. To what extent are the facilities consistent with the philosophy and guiding principles?

V. SPECIAL CHARACTERISTICS OF THE CONTINUING EDUCATION PROGRAM

1. In what respects is the continuing education program for adults most satisfactory and commendable?
    a.
    b.
    c.
    d.
2. In what respects is there greatest need for improving the continuing education program for adults?
    a.
    b.
    c.
    d.

VI. GENERAL EVALUATION OF THE CONTINUING EDUCATION PROGRAM FOR ADULTS

To what extent does the continuing education program for adults meet the needs of the students and the community?

Appendix B
CONTINUING EDUCATION RESIDENTIAL CENTERS

CONTINUING EDUCATION RESIDENTIAL CENTERS	Spaces	
University of Alabama Continuing Education Center	68	University, Al 35486
Appalachian State University Center for Continuing Education	168	Boone, NC 28607
Arizona State University Conference Center at Castle Hot Springs	100	Tempe, AZ 85281
University of Arkansas Continuing Education Center	300	Fayetteville, AR 72701
Ball State University Kitselman Conference Center	40	Muncie, IN 47306
University of California Conference Center	110	Lake Arrowhead, CA 92352
California State Polytechnic University, Pomona: Kellogg West Center for Continuing Education	102	Pomona, CA 91768
University of Chicago Center for Continuing Education	230	1307 E. 60th St., Chicago, IL 60637
University of Colorado College Inn Conference Center	200	970 Aurora, Room 217 Boulder, CO 80302
University of Northern Colorado University Center	4	Greeley, CO 80639
Colorado State University Pingree Park	80	Fort Collins, CO 80523
Colorado State University: Rockwell Hall-Residential Conference Center	86	Fort Collins, CO 80523
University of Connecticut Bishop Conference Center	300	Box U-56, Storrs, CT 06268
University of Delaware John M. Clayton Hall	750	Newark, DE 19711
Dominican College Meadowlands Continuing Education Center	54	San Rafael, CA 94901
University of Georgia Center for Continuing Education	260	Athens, GA 30602
University of Houston Continuing Education Center	0	4800 Calhoun, Houston, TX 77004
Humboldt State University Jolly Giant Conference Center	1209	Arcata, CA 95521
Indiana University at Bloomington: Indiana University Conference Bureau	306	Conference Bureau, Indiana Memorial Union L-9, Bloomington, IN 47401
University of Illinois, Urbana-Champaign: Allerton House Hott Memorial Center	100	120 Illini Hall, Champaign, Champaign, IL 61820
Northern Illinois University Adult Education Division Conference Office	200	Williston Hall #320 Dekalb, IL 60137
University of Iowa Center for Conferences and Institutes	190	Iowa City, IA 52242
University of of Kentucky Carnahan House Conference Center	0	Lexington, KY 40506
Western Kentucky University Continuing Education Center	164	Bowling Green, KY 42101
Louisiana State University Continuing Education Conference Center	140	Pleasant Hall, LSU, Baton Rouge, LA 70803
University of Maryland College Center of Adult Education	212	University Blvd. at Adelphi Rd., College Park, MD 20742
University of Massachusetts Murray D. Lincoln Campus Center	350(hotel) 10.000(dorm)	920 Campus Center Amherst, MA 01002
Memphis State University Richardson Towers Conference Center	244	Memphis, TN 38152
University of Michigan: Michigan League	48	227 S. Ingalls Ann Arbor, MI 48109
University of Michigan Towsley Center for Continuing Medical Education	0	1107 Towsley Center Ann Arbor, MI 48109

(2) Continuing Education Residential Centers   Spaces

University of Michigan: Michigan Union	144	530 S. State St., Ann Arbor, MI 48109
University of Michigan Graduate School of Business Administration Kalmbach Management Center	35	291 Business Administration, Ann Arbor, MI 48109
Eastern Michigan University Hoyt Conference Center	400	850 W. Cross Street Ypsilanti, MI 48197
Northern Michigan University Don H. Bottum University Center	800(summer) 4(school year)	Marquette, MI 49855
Michigan State University Kellogg Center for Continuing Education	368	East Lansing, MI 488824
University of Mississippi E. F. Yerby Center for Continuing Education	180	University, MS 38677
University of Southern Mississippi Gulf Park Conference Facility	150	Hattiesburg, MS 39401
University of Nebraska Center for Continuing Education	196	33rd & Holdrege Streets Lincoln, NB 68583
University of Nevada Stead Conference Center	300	Reno, NV 89557
University of New Hampshire (fiscal agent) and the Universities of Maine, Connecticut, Massachusetts, Rhode Island and Vermone: New England Center for Continuing Education	80	15 Garrison Avenue Durham, NH 03824
University of New Hampshire New England Center for Continuing Education	82	15 Garrison Ave. Durham, NH 03824
Eastern New Mexico University Conference Center	200	Portales, NM 88130
New York State School of Industrial and Labor Relations, Cornell University ILR Conference Center	0	Ithaca, NY 14853
University of North Carolina at Chapel Hill: Carolina Inn	200	209 Abernathy Hall, 002-A Chapel Hill, NC 27514
University of Notre Dame Center for Continuing Education	80	Box 72 Notre Dame, IN 46556
Oakland University Meadow Brook Hall	38	Meadow Brook Hall Rochester, MI 48063
Ohio State University Fawcett Center for Tomorrow	186	2400 Olentangy River Rd. Columbus, OH 43210
University of Oklahoma Center for Continuing Education	500	1700 Asp Avenue Norman, OK 73037
Oklahoma State University: O.S.U. Educational Conference Center	85	Suite 101 Union Hotel Plaza, Stillwater, OK 74074
Purdue University	5,500(summer) 508(acad.yr)	116 Stewart Center West Lafayette, IN 47907
University of Rhode Island Whispering Pines Conference Center	36	Victory Highway West Greenwich, RI 02816
Rutgers - The State University: Continuing Education Center	72	Clifton Avenue, Douglas Campus, New Brunswick, NJ 08903
Saint Louis University: Fordyce House Conference and Retreat Center	61	316 Grimsley Station Road St. Louis, MO 63129
University of South Carolina Capstone Conference Center	1,074	Columbia, SC 29208
Syracuse University Washington Arms Conference Center	60	610 East Fayette Street Syracuse, NY 13202

Syracuse University Minnowbrook Conference Center	64	610 E. Fayette Street Syracuse, NY 13202
Texas A & M University J. Earl Rudder Center	50	College Station, TX 77843
Tufts University Conference Bureau	1000	Medford, MA 02155
U. S. Civil Service Commission - Bureau of Training: Berkeley Executive Seminar Center	40	2449 Bancroft Way Berkeley, CA 94704
U. S. Civil Service Commission - Bureau of Training: Kings Point Executive Seminar Center	·36	Kings Point Long Island, NY 11024
U. S. Civil Service Commission - Bureau of Training: Oak Ridge Executive Seminar Center	35-40	Broadway and Kentucky Aves Oak Ridge, TN 37830
U. S. Civil Service Commission - Bureau of Training: Wilmington Executive Seminar Center	37	2600 Pennsylvania Avenue Wilmington, DE 19806
U. S. Civil Service Commission: Federal Executive Institute	67	Route 29 North Charlottesville, VA 22903
West Virginia University Towers Conference Center	1800	Morgantown, WV 26506
Virginia Polytechnic Institute and State University: Donaldson Brown Center for Continuing Education	246	Blacksburg, VA 24061
University of Wisconsin - Extension: University Bay Center for Continuing Education	147	702 Langdon Street Madison, WI 53706
University of Wisconsin - Extension: Wisconsin Center Guest House	147	702 Langdon Street Madison, WI 53706
University of Wyoming Trail Lake Ranch	100	Laramie, WY 82071

NONRESIDENTIAL CENTERS:

University of Alabama: Ann Jordan Lodge

University of Arkansas at Little Rock: Conference Center

Armstrong State College: Division of Community Services

Central Michigan University, University Center

Cleveland State University, University Center

University of Delaware, Division of Continuing Education: Goodstay Center

University of Delaware, Division of Continuing Education: Wilcastle Center

Drake University: Olmsted Center

Florida State University: Center for Professional Development and Public Service

Georgia Southern: Rosenwald Georgia Southern

Indiana University at South Bend: Center for Lifelong Learning

University of Northern Iowa: Office of Extension and Continuing Education

Iowa State University: Scheman Continuing Education Building

Upper Iowa University: Mason City Center

Lamar University: The Brown Center

University of Michigan: Chrysler Center for Continuing Engineering Education

University of Michigan - Dearborn: Fair Lane Conference Center

University of Minnesota: Earle Brown Center for Continuing Education

University of Minnesota: Nolte Center for Continuing Education

University of Missouri - Columbia: Office of Conferences and Short Counseling
University of Missouri - St. Louis: Continuing Education - Extension
University of Nebraska Medical Center: Center for Continuing Education
University of Nebraska at Omaha: Eppley Conference Center
New York Institute of Technology: deSeversky Conference Center
New York State School of Industrial and Labor Relations, Cornell University: Western District Conference Center
State University of New York at Oswego: Continuing Education - Hewitt Center
New York State School of Industrial and Labor Relations, Cornell University: Metropolitan District Conference Center
North Carolina State University, Raleigh: Jane S. McKimmon Center for Extension and Continuing Education
Pennsylvania State University: J. Orvis Keller Conference Center
Purdue University Calumet Campus: Student Faculty Library Center
Saginaw Valley State College: Doan Center
San Diego State University: Aztec Conference Center
South Dakota State University: Pugsley Center for Continuing Education
University of South Dakota: Center for Continuing Education
University of Southern California: Davidson Conference Center for Continuing Education
Southern Illinois University at Edwardsville: John M. Olin Conferences and Institutes
Wayne State University: McGregor Memorial Conference Center
University of Wisconsin - Extension: The Wisconsin Center
University of Wyoming: Knight Hall Conference

The Danish Folk High School is an important adult education agency, each with a special emphasis.

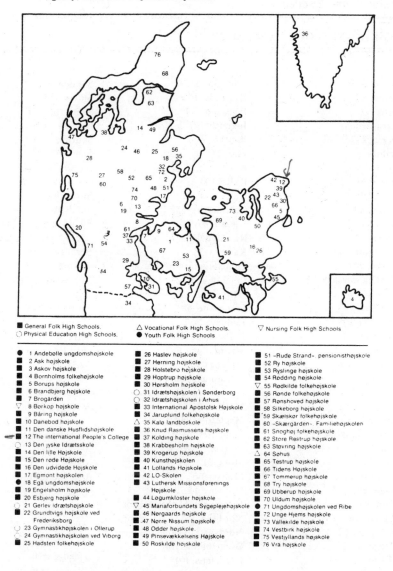

■ General Folk High Schools.   △ Vocational Folk High Schools.   ▽ Nursing Folk High Schools
◯ Physical Education High Schools.   ● Youth Folk High Schools

● 1 Andebølle ungdomshøjskole
■ 2 Ask højskole
■ 3 Askov højskole
■ 4 Bornholms folkehøjskole
■ 5 Borups højskole
■ 6 Brandbjerg højskole
■ 7 Brogården
▽ 8 Børkop højskole
■ 9 Bâring højskole
■ 10 Danebod højskole
■ 11 Den danske Husflidshøjskole
◀■ 12 The international People's College
◯ 13 Den jyske Idrætsskole
■ 14 Den lille Højskole
■ 15 Den røde Højskole
■ 16 Den udvidede Højskole
■ 17 Egmont højskolen
● 18 Egå ungdomshøjskole
■ 19 Engelsholm højskole
■ 20 Esbjerg højskole
◯ 21 Gerlev idrætshøjskole
■ 22 Grundtvigs højskole ved
   Frederiksborg
◯ 23 Gymnastikhøjskolen i Ollerup
◯ 24 Gymnastikhøjskolen ved Viborg
■ 25 Hadsten folkehøjskole

■ 26 Haslev højskole
■ 27 Herning højskole
■ 28 Holstebro højskole
■ 29 Hoptrup højskole
■ 30 Hørsholm højskole
◯ 31 Idrætshøjskolen i Sønderborg
◯ 32 Idrætshøjskolen i Århus
■ 33 International Apostolsk Højskole
■ 34 Jaruplund folkehøjskole
△ 35 Kalø landboskole
■ 36 Knud Rasmussens højskole
■ 37 Kolding højskole
■ 38 Krabbesholm højskole
■ 39 Krogerup højskole
■ 40 Kunsthøjskolen
■ 41 Lollands Højskole
■ 42 LO-Skolen
■ 43 Luthersk Missionsforenings
   Højskole
■ 44 Løgumkloster højskole
▽ 45 Mariaforbundets Sygeplejehøjskole
■ 46 Nørgaards højskole
■ 47 Nørre Nissum højskole
■ 48 Odder højskole
■ 49 Pinsevækkelsens Højskole
■ 50 Roskilde højskole

■ 51 »Rude Strand«, pensionisthøjskole
■ 52 Ry højskole
■ 53 Ryslinge højskole
■ 54 Rødding højskole
▽ 55 Rødkilde folkehøjskole
■ 56 Rønde folkehøjskole
■ 57 Rønshoved højskole
■ 58 Silkeborg højskole
■ 59 Skælskør folkehøjskole
■ 60 »Skærgården« Familiehøjskolen
■ 61 Snoghøj folkehøjskole
■ 62 Store Restrup højskole
■ 63 Støvring højskole
△ 64 Søhus
■ 65 Testrup højskole
■ 66 Tidens Højskole
■ 67 Tommerup højskole
■ 68 Try højskole
■ 69 Ubberup højskole
■ 70 Uldum højskole
● 71 Ungdomshøjskolen ved Ribe
■ 72 Unge Hjems højskole
■ 73 Vallekilde højskole
■ 74 Vestbirk højskole
■ 75 Vestjyllands højskole
■ 76 Vrå højskole

See Also: The Danish Folk High School, Himmelstrup, Per, Denmark
Sydjysk Universitetscenter, 18 pp.

Folkhögskolor i Sverige 1978

Axevalla 64
Billströmska 55
Birka 93
Birkagårdens 1
Blekinge läns 40
Bollnäs 85
Bosöns 109
Brunnsviks 80
Bäckedals 94
Dalarö 13
Edelviks 97
Eslövs 50
Fellingsbro 75
Finska 108
Folkliga musiksk 72
Fornby 79
Forsa 86
Framnäs 106
Fridhems 48
Fristads 59
Färgelanda 60
Gamleby 35
Geijerskolan 73
Glimåkra 42
Gotlands 39
Grebbestads 54
Grimslövs 31
Gripsholms 18
Göteborgs 111
Hagabergs 12
Hampnäs 90
Hantverkets 84
Hellidens 67
Helsjöns 62
Hjälmareds 61
Hola 89
Hvilans 47
Hållands 95

Härnösands 92
Högalids 37
Ingesunds 71
Jakobsbergs 7
Jämshögs 41
Jära 25
Kaggeholms 10
Kalix 104
Karlskoga 76
Katrinebergs 52
Kjesäters 19
Klarälvdalens 70
Kävesta 74
Landsorganisationens 4
Liljeholmens 24
Lillsveds 8
Ljungskile 58
Lunnevads 21
Löftadalens 53
Malmfältens 107
Malungs 82
Mariannelunds 112
Marieborgs 22
Markaryds 33
Medlefors 98
Mellansels 91
Molkoms 69
Mora 81
Mullsjö 66
Nordens 15
Nordens folkl akademi 56
Nordiska 56
Nordvästra Skånes 45
Oskarshamns 34
Pitedalens 101
Samernas 102
S:t Eriks 2
S:t Sigfrids 32

Sigtuna 6
Sjöviks 83
Skara stifts 68
Skinnskattebergs 78
Skurups 49
Stensunds 17
Storumans 100
Strömbäcks 99
Sunderby 103
Sundsgårdens 46
Sydöstra Skånes 44
Södra Vätterbygdens 28
Sörängens 26
Tollare 9
Tornedalens 105
Tärna 77
Vadstena 23
Valla 20
Vara 65
Wendelsbergs 57
Wiks 14
Vimmerby 36
Vindelns 96
Visingsö 29
Viskadalens 63
Vårdinge 11
Väddö 3
Värnamo 27
Västanviks 110
Västerbergs 87
Västerhaninge 5
Ålsta 88
Åsa 16
Ädelfors 30
Ölands 38
Önnestads 43
Östra Grevie 51

448

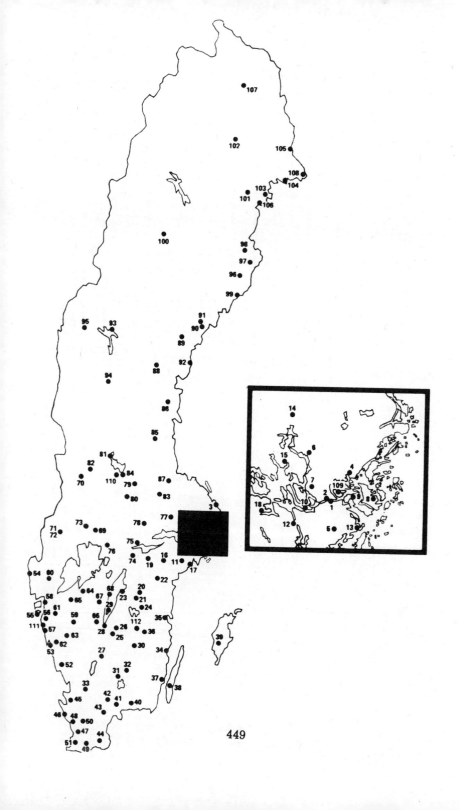

449

List of Folk High Schools in Sweden

Almost all the schools have general courses, but the fields that are stressed have been noted below:

Birkagårdens folkhögskola Sveavägen 41, 111 34 Stockholm
Music.
Third year: social sciences

St. Eriks folkhögskola vid Borgarskolan, Kungstensg. 4,
114 25 Stockholm
Second and third-year course: Social sciences

Väddö folkhögskola, 760 40 Väddö
Third-year course: social sciences

Landsorganisationens folkhögskola, 180 20 Åkers-Runö
Social sciences

Västerhaninge folkhögskola, 137 00 Västerhaninge
Third-year course: social sciences

Sigtuna folkhögskola, 190 30 Sigtuna
Third-year course: social sciences
Youth counselor course being planned

Jakobsbergs folkhögskola, 175 00 Jakobsberg
Third-year course: social sciences

Lillsveds gymnastikfolkhögskola, 130 31 Norra Värmdö
Physical education and youth counselorship

Bosöns filialfolkhögskola, 181 90 Lidingö
Sports and youth counselorship

Tollare folkhögskola, 130 21 Klinten
Youth counselorship.
Third-year course: social sciences

Kaggeholms folkhögskola, 170 10 Ekerö
Third-year course: the developing countries
Christianity

Number of Pupils at Folk High Schools

Number of pupils

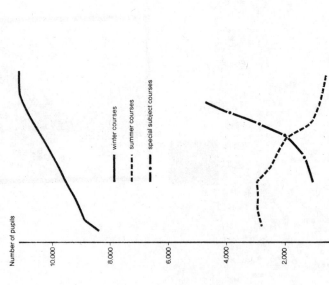

winter courses

summer courses

special subject courses

10,000

8,000

6,000

4,000

2,000

56/57   59/60   66/67   Fiscal year

Vårdingeskolan, 150 21 Mölnbo
Pupils between 16 and 18 years old

Hagabergs folkhögskola, 151 31 Södertälje
Youth counvelorship

Dalarö folkhögskola, 130 54 Dalarö
Third-year course: international affairs

Uppsala läns folkhögskola, Wik, 755 90 Uppsala

Nordens folkhögskola, Biskops-Arnö 190 60 Bålsta
Scandinavian and international affairs.
Communication and mass media

Asa folkhögskola, 640 24 Sköldinge
Third-year course: social sciences

Stensunds folkhögskola, 150 14 Vagnhärad
Youth counselorship

Valla filialfolkhögskola, 585 90 Linköping
Developing countries

Gripsholms folkhögskola, 150 30 Mariefred
The arts

Gripsholms filialfolkhögskola, 632 20 Eskilstuna
Subject courses for housewives and jobless persons

Kjesäters folkhögskola, 643 00 Vingåker
The arts

Lunnevads folkhögskola, Sjögestad, 590 50 Vikingstad
Music

Marieborgs folkhögskola, 602 23 Norrköping
Drama.
Third-year course: social sciences

Vadstena folkhögskola, 592 00 Vadstena
Youth counselorship.
Third-year course: the developing countries

Liljeholms folkhögskola, 590 41 Rimforsa
Third-year-course: social sciences and stress on the developing countries

Jära folkhögskola, 570 21 Malmbäck
Third-year course: social sciences

Sörängens folkhögskola, 571 00 Nässjö
Third year course: social sciences

Värnamo folkhögskola, 331-01 Värnamo

Södra Vätterbygdens folkhögskola, 552 66 Jönköping
Home economics

Visingsö folkhögskola-Braheskolan, 560 34 Visingsö
Second-year course: social sciences

Ädelfors folkhögskola, 570 15 Holsbybrunn

Grimslövs folkhögskola, 340 32 Grimslöv
Youth counselorship
Home economics

Grimslövs filialfolkhögskola, 360 51 Hovmantorp
Pupils between 15 and 17 years old

S:t Sigfrid folkhögskola, 355 90 Växjö

Markaryds folkhögskola, 285 00 Markaryd

Oskarshamns folkhögskola, 572 00 Oskarshamn
Music
Drama (church)

Gamleby folkhögskola, 594 00 Gamleby

Vimmerby folkhögskola, 598 00 Vimmerby
Third-year course: social sciences

Kalmar läns södra landstings folkhögskola, Högalid, 380 26 Smedby
Home economics
Textile art

Kalmar läns södra landstings folkhögskola i Ölands Skogsby, 380 61 Ölands Skogsby
Home economics

Gotlands folkhögskola, 620 12 Hemse
  Home economics
Blekinge läns folkhögskola, 370 10 Bräke-Hoby
  Third-year course: social sciences
Jämshögs folkhögskola, 290 63 Jämshög
  Youth counselorship
Önnestads folkhögskola, 290 28 Önnestad
  Third-year course: social sciences
Sydöstra Skånes folkhögskola, 273 00 Tomelilla
  Developing countries
Nordvästra Skånes folkhögskola, 260 80 Munkaljungby
Sundsgårdens folkhögskola, 266 01 Råå
  Third-year course and additional course: social sciences
Sundsgårdens filialfolkhögskola, 280 64 Glimåkra
Folkhögskolan Hvilan, 230 47 Åkarp
Fridhems folkhögskola, 268 00 Svalöv
  Home economics
  Special courses for applicants to the graduate schools of
  social work and public administration
Vemmenhögs m fl häraders folkhögskola i Skurup,
274 00 Skurup
  Journalism and public relations
  Home economics
Eslövs folkhögskola, 241 00 Eslöv
  International course (Swedish for foreigners),
  Third-year course and additional course: social sciences
Östra Grevie folkhögskola, 230 17 Östra Grevie
  The arts
Katrinebergs folkhögskola, 310 58 Vessigebro
  Third-year course: social sciences
Löftadalens folkhögskola, 430 31 Åsa station

Göteborgs och Bohus läns folkhögskola, 450 81 Grebbestad
Billströmska folkhögskolan, 440 60 Skärhamn
  Navigation
Nordiska folkhögskolan i Kungälv, 442 00 Kungälv
  Nordic and international affairs.
  Third-year course: social sciences
Wendelsbergs folkhögskola, 435 00 Mölnlycke
  Third-year course: youth counselorship
Västkustens ungdomsskolas folkhögskola, 450 10 Ljungskile
  Music.
  Home economics.
  Social educational
Älvsborgs läns folkhögskola i Fristad, 510 47 Fristad
  Home economics
Stockslycke filialfolkhögskola, 441 00 Alingsås
Älvsborgs läns folkhögskola i Färgelanda, 450 60 Färgelanda
  Third-year course: social sciences
Hjälmareds folkhögskola, 441 00 Alingsås
Helsjöns folkhögskola, 510 10 Horred
Viskadalens folkhögskola, 510 34 Seglora
  Third-year course: social sciences
Axevalla folkhögskola, 530 50 Axvall
  Third-year course: social sciences
Vara folkhögskola, 534 00 Vara
  Home economics
Mullsjö folkhögskola, 560 41 Mullsjö
  Third-year course: social sciences
Hellidens folkhögskola, 522 00 Tidaholm
  Youth counselorship
  The arts
Skara stifts folkhögskola, 544 00 Hjo
  Third-year course: youth counselorship

Värmlands läns folkhögskola, 660 60 Molkom
Klarälvdalens folkhögskola, 680 51 Stöllet
Ingesunds folkhögskola, 671 00 Arvika
  Third-year course: social sciences
Folkliga musikskolan, 671 00 Arvika
  Three-year course for music teachers
Geijerskolan, 684 00 Munkfors
  Third-year course: church music
Kävesta folkhögskola, 690 72 Sköllersta
  Third-year course: social sciences
Kävesta filialfolkhögskola, 703 62 Örebro
  Third-year course: social sciences
Fellingsbro folkhögskola, 710 41 Fellingsbro
  Youth counselorship
Karlskoga folkhögskola, 691 00 Karlskoga
  Journalism
  Three-year counselorship courses
Västmanlands läns folkhögskola i Tärna, 730 74 Tärna
  Third-year: social sciences
Skinnskattebergs folkhögskola, 770 30 Skinnskatteberg
  Social sciences
  Special courses in the arts
Fornby folkhögskola, 681 00 Borlänge
  Special sciences
Brunnsviks folkhögskola, 771 04 Ludvika
  Third-year course: social sciences
  Special courses for trade-union leaders
Mora folkhögskola, 792 00 Mora
  Third-year course: social sciences
Malungs folkhögskola, 782 00 Malung
  Third-year course: social sciences

Sjöviks folkhögskola, 775 00 Krylbo
  Youth counselorship
Folkhögskolan i Leksand, 793 00 Leksand
  Business administration
  The arts and handicrafts
Gävleborgs läns folkhögskola i Bollnäs, 821 00 Bollnäs
  Music
Forsa folkhögskola, 820 65 Forsa
  Textiles
  Special course for disabled pupils
Gästriklands folkhögskola i Västerberg, 812 00 Storvik
  Third-year course: social sciences
  Two-year art course
Gästriklands folkhögskola, filialskola, 802 22 Gävle
Medelpads folkhögskola i Ålsta, Fränstavägen, 840 12 Fränsta
Hola folkhögskola, 870 54 Prästmon
Nora Ångermanlands folkhögskola å Hampnäs, 890 24 Själevad
  Librarian course
Folkhögskolan i Mellansel, 890 42 Mellansel
  Third-year course: social sciences
Anundsjöbygdens ungdomsskola i Bredbyn, 890 40 Bredbyn
  Music
  Pupils between 15 and 17 years old
Härnösands folkhögskola, 871 00 Härnösand
  Youth counselorship
Birka folkhögskola, 830 43 Äs
  Music
Bäckedals folkhögskola, 829 00 Sveg
Hallands folkhögskola, 830 11 Halland
  Third-year course: social sciences

Västerbottens läns folkhögskola, 920 10 Vindeln
Third-year course: social sciences

Edelviks folkhögskola, 930 20 Burträsk

Medlefors folkhögskola, 931 03 Skellefteå
Third year course: social sciences

Strömbacks folkhögskola, 910 25 Stockeby
Third-year course: social sciences

Storumans folkhögskola, 920 60 Storuman
Youth counsellorship

Pitdalens folkhögskola, 942 00 Älvsbyn
Third year course: social

Samernas folkhögskola, 960 40 Jokkmokk
Lapp civilization

Sunderby folkhögskola, 950 17 Södra Sunderbyn
Three-year artistic education

Folkhögskolan i Kalix, 952 02 Kalix
Social educational
The developing countries: Mass media

Folkhögskolan i Kalix, 952 02 Kalix
Pupils between 16 and 18 years

Tornedalens folkhögskola i Matarengi, 950 94 Övertorneå
Third year course: social sciences

Framnäs folkhögskola, 940 20 Öjebyn
Three-year music course

Framnäs filialfolkhögskola, Kapellsbergs musikskola, 871 01 Härnösand
Music
Younger pupils

Malmfältens folkhögskola, 981 03 Kiruna
Youth counsellorship

Addresses in Finnish adult education

Ministry of Education,
Rauhank. 4, 00170 Helsinki 17. Tel. 90-171 636

The National Board of General Education,
Hakaniemenk. 2, 00530 Helsinki 53. Tel. 90-7061

The National Board for Vocational Education,
Hakaniemenk. 2, 00530 Helsinki 53. Tel. 90-7061

Institute of Adult Education, Tampere University,
Kalevankatu 4, Tampere. Tel. 931-156 111

The Society for Popular Culture (Kansanvalistusseura),
Museokatu 18 A 2, 00100 Helsinki 10. Tel. 90-406 925

The Finnish Association of Adult Education Organizations
Hietalahdenkatu 8, 00180 Helsinki 18. Tel. 90-608 093

The People's Educational Association (Folkets Bildningsförbund),
Jarrumiehenk. 2, 00520 Helsinki 52. Tel. 90-142 758

The People's Educational Association (Kansan Sivistystyön Liitto),
Jarrumiehenk. 2, 00520 Helsinki 52. Tel. 90-141 311

The Union for Rural Education,
Pursimiehenkatu 15, 00150 Helsinki 15. Tel. 90-170 311

The Central League for Study Circle Activity,
Pohj. Rautatiekatu 23 B, 00100 Helsinki 10. Tel. 90-406 633

The Finnish Folk High School Association,
Pohj. Rautatiekatu 15 B 12, 00100 Helsinki 10. Tel. 90-444 090

The Finnish Library Association,
Museokatu 18 A 4, 00100 Helsinki 10. Tel. 90-492 632

Association for Free Cultural Activities,
Simonkatu 12 B, 00100 Helsinki 10. Tel. 90-642 011

The Friends of Swedish Primary Schools,
Annankatu 12, 00120 Helsinki 12. Tel. 90-174 688

The Swedish League for Study Circle Activity,
Uudenmaankatu 17 B, 00120 Helsinki 12. Tel. 90-174 066

The Union of Civic and Workers' Institutes,
Cygnaeuksenkatu 4 B 10, 00100 Helsinki 10. Tel. 90-493 246

The Workers' Educational Association,
Paasivuorenkatu 5 B, 00530 Helsinki 53. Tel. 90-718 766

Appendix C
RESIDENTIAL ADULT EDUCATION IN BRITAIN

I. LONG-COURSE COLLEGES

Courses of not less than a year. "Colleges of the second chance" for working men and women (usually between 20 and 40 years of age) who want opportunity to prove themselves in academic training for posts of leadership work with a social content, or for further academic education for the professions.

Ruskin (Oxford, 1899) Grew out of Labor Movement and drive for Social Reform. (Adoption by Labor Party in 1903 of program by parliamentary reform. Need for education of party leaders and electorate.)

Fircroft (Birmingham, 1909) Established by George Cadbury, Quaker chocolate king, who was impressed by Danish Folk High Schools' achievements in social and moral fields.

Woodbrooke (Birmingham) Also established by Cadbury and prepares men and women for service in accordance with Quaker principles.

Coleg Harlech (Harlech, N. Wales) A Welsh counterpart to Ruskin with something of the passionate belief in education of a minority nation.

Plater College (Oxford) Studies similar to Ruskin with implications of Roman Catholic beliefs.

Hillcroft (Surrey) College for women also on Ruskin principles, but with additional infusion of drive from women's emancipation movement.

Cooperative College (Manchester, then Loughborough) For the training of (a) staff, and (b) members in principles of cooperative movement. Recently has concentrated on problems of modern, competitive management.

Newbattle Abbey (Dalkeith, Scotland) A "provision" by Scottish educational bodies, rather than response to a demand from below. No obvious "Scottish" flavor. Has English director.

II. SHORT-COURSE COLLEGES

All of these conduct, for at least part of the time, a program of short public courses, varying in length between a weekend and one or two weeks, in nonvocational liberal studies. There will be at least one full-time academic person on the staff.

455

RESIDENTIAL ADULT EDUCATION

Long-course Colleges shown - Ru/. All other colleges shown conduct short courses. Centers used only for housing conferences not shown. Shading indicates land above approximately 500 feet.

Management

Private	Local Education Authority	University
As *Ashridge	AH Alston Hall (Preston)	HR *Holly Royde
AP *Attingham Park†	BB *Battle of Britain House	(Manchester)
Av *Avoncroft	(Hounslow)	RH Rewley House
BP Braziers Park	BH *Belstead House	(Oxford and
De *Denman	(E. Sussex)	Kellogg
Ki *Kingsgate†	BM *Burton Manor	Foundation)
MP Moor Park†	(6 Merseyside L.E.A.'s)	
Pe *Pendley†	DH Debden House (Newham)	
RP Roffey Park	Da Dartington (Devon)	
WM *Wedgwood Memorial†	Di *Dillington (Somerset)	
We *Westham†	GH *Grantley Hall	
WT William Temple	(W. Riding of Yorkshire)	
	TH The Hill (Monmouth, Autumn 1967)	
	KH *Knuston Hall (Northamptonshire)	
	LC Lambton Castle (Durham)	
	Ma Maryland (Bedfordshire, Autumn 1967)	
	MA *Missenden Abbey (Buckinghamshire)	
	PH Pendrell Hall (Staffs.)	
	UM *Urchfont Manor (Wiltshire)	
	Wa *Wansfell (Essex)	
	WH Wrea Head (N. Riding of Yorks)	

* These colleges were established by 1955.

†These private foundations are financially supported by one or more local education authorities.

Initials as marked on accompanying map.

III. CONFERENCE AND SHORT-COURSE CENTERS

These centers accommodate conferences and courses of the local education authority or of outside organizations, but have no public courses and no full-time academic staff. It is difficult to find how many of these centers exist, as they have no programs to advertise, but some are listed in the Yearbook of the National Institute of Adult Education:

Cowley Manor (Gloucestershire)

Buxton (Derbyshire)

Ferryside (Carmarthenshire)
Pilgrim College (Lincolnshire)
Lodge Hill (W. Sussex)
Burwell House (Cambridgeshire)
Bramby Grange (W. Riding of Yorkshire)
Glynllifon (Caernarvonshire)

ORIGINS OF THE SHORT-TERM COLLEGES OF ADULT EDUCATION

1. Education for Working Classes - University Extension - Summer Schools.
2. Education for Christian Service and Citizenship - Adult School Movement - Guest Houses of the Adult Schools.
3. Wartime Forces Education Scheme - Colleges and Courses.
4. Danish Folk High School - Recommendations of Richard Livingstone.

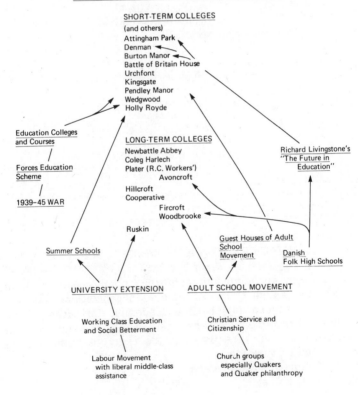

ORIGINS OF RESIDENTIAL ADULT EDUCATION IN BRITAIN

POINTS FOR DISCUSSION

1. If non vocational liberal courses and conferences can occupy only part of the time of an adult education college what should be done with the rest of the year?
   (a) Courses for vocational groups
   (b) Renting of premises by outside organizations
   (c) Nonresident activities, e.g., public lectures etc., catering engagements, nonresident courses
2. How can we persuade more men and women, and their employers, of the importance of liberal and social education?
3. Where should a residential center be situated - university campus, suburban, rural and isolated? What are the implications for staffing?
4. Should a center have a "mixed" program - its own courses and conferences, **and** "similar" events conducted by organizations renting the premises?
5. What standard of accommodation, catering, etc., should be provided? If it is to be of the highest standard, how are conferences financed so as not to exclude anybody interested?
6. What academic staff should a center have? What is the role role of the conference coordinator?
7. What are the special skills of the residential adult educator?
8. Is it an advantage to try to create and maintain a liberal educational atmosphere, even if the conferences or courses are vocational in purpose?
9. How should a residential course be structured?
10. What publicity should there be for a residential center?
11. How can residential adult education be evaluated?
12. Do we know that "living and learning together" is an effective means of adult education? Is it better than evening classes? or day classes?
13. How can experiment and research be incorporated into the program?
14. How should the residential adult educator be trained? or is he always the "inspired amateur"?
15. What organizations should conduct residential centers?
16. How should finance be provided for (a) the center itself, and (b) individual courses and conferences?

ADULT EDUCATION IN PUERTO RICO

A Case Study of Social and Industrial Development

Operation Bootstraps, independence, even statehood, are dependent upon a literate and an educated electorate. And social and industrial development depend upon an educated people.

The two universities most involved in the uplift of the populace in Puerto Rico are the University of Puerto Rico Piedras and Inter-American University in San German.

The island is only 100 miles long, and 35 miles wide. Remote areas in the mountains of the island are neglected, and educational needs are often ignored due to other institutional priorities, and the high illiteracy rate on the island.

Since the Governorship of Munoz Marin, education has had a high priority on the island. Part of the attractiveness of operation bootstraps for many factories being brought to the island has been the willingness of Fomento to provide training, vocational advisement, buildings and land, plus the tax break of no federal taxes for from 10 to 17 years. This has attracted over 800 companies from the United States to this island. Such pharmaceutical firms as Johnson and Johnson, Lilly, and Smith, Kline, and French have all taken advantage of the cheap labor available and the tax breaks for corporations willing to do business on "la isla del encanto" (the island of enchantment).

As a consultant for Inter-American University this author visited 24 factories in the Mayaguez industrial area and found a ready reception for the extension offerings of this burgeoning University. Inter-American has taken the initiative to establish extension centers throughout the island. Leadership was given to Inter-American when Dr. Roland Bauer was the president of the University. He had the wisdom to fill the vacuum of adult education needs during the 1960's and took over a chicken coop at Barranquitis in the center of the island, building the Extension Center enrollment to 300 students in a short period of time.

Visiting the directors of training and the directors of personnel pointed up the crying need for two major areas. "English for Spanish Speaking Secretaries", and "Management Training" for front-line supervisors was at the top of the list for the factories in the Mayaguez industrial area.

Electronic firms, factories manufacturing bluejeans, and pharmaceutical firms response with potential students. Computer programming was also one of the major needs for the industrial area of the island.

The University of Puerto Rico, Rio Piedras has come to be known on the island as "an elitist" institution ever since the leadership of Dr. Jaime Benitez, a follower of the late Dr. Robert Hutchins, for many years Chancellor of the University of Chicago. The Inter-American outreach filled the gap, and established service centers, extension outreach at Ramey Air Force Base, Ponce, Aguadilla, and at the front door of the University of Puerto Rico, Bayamon.

Another exciting aspect of Adult Education in Puerto Rico has been the leadership of Fred Wale for many years the Director of the Division of Social Education. Social Education means community development. Fred Wale, a former agricultural worker under the Franklin Roosevelt administration has made a major impact with his more than 60 community workers, whose education range from 8th grade education through college trained. Fred Wale is a Quaker who uses concensus in his development of program in the community.

If the community worker finds that what is desired is a new bridge, that is given highest priority. The problem is attacked by a community council made up of the indiginous citizens. His approach is four-fold. A colorful silk-screen poster is made to attract people in the community to the meeting to discuss the problems. Often a film is made of the problem (El Puente, a prize winning film of the need for a bridge, for example), a booklet describing the community problem, and an organized set of meetings to set the timetable for attacking the problem - action of the Fred Wale procedure based on consensus. His approach has been most effective in literacy training, and in solving some of the community problems at the grassroots level.

One of the problems of attracting students in Puerto Rico to higher education has been financial support. A leader in getting funding for the students enrolling in adult education has been the efforts of Mrs. Dafne Javier, Director of Financial Aid. She has attracted millions of dollars of student aid money, by working with HEW, and with the Regional Office of the U.S. Office of Education out of New York, which includes the island of Puerto Rico. With unemployment running as high as 40 per cent on the "island" there is a crying need for vocational education, and giving students a chance to develop skills which can be used both on the island and in the United States.

Migration has been a chief outlet for the overpopulation of the island. But the citizens going to the United States are a burden on the economy and to themselves if they do not have skills to offer. The universities of the Island of Puerto Rico can provide the training which will offer saleable skills to business and industry.

Many of the campuses are developing Adult Learning Centers

to fill the gap of poorly trained students, or the semi-literate. English is a fundamental skill which is highly prized in the management circles of the factories. The bi-lingual secretary and the bi-lingual manager are at a premium in the industrial scene. Although there is high unemployment, there is a ready market for well trained managers, such as in the tuna canning factories in the Mayaguez industrial area.

Adult Education has had the leadership of Dr. Felix Guzman who has headed the Adult Education Division of the Department of Education. He has utilized the Montclair State College Materials Center to train his staff, and this author found a dedicated and industrious group of teachers eager for additional information, modules, and training.

Literacy, bi-lingual education, management training, and vocational skills are in demand in Puerto Rico. We have an opportunity for life-long learning on this "Isla del Encanto," "island of enchantment." Social and industrial development of the island now depend heavily upon effective adult education.

Appendix D
CONDUCTING A
NEEDS ASSESSMENT *

Introduction

Conducting a needs assessment within your community is a major and necessary function. It should be undertaken as soon as possible after the Adult Education Director is hired.

The Advisory Council should select a needs assessment task force who will be responsible for planning, conducting and compiling the survey.

The steps to be taken and suggestions that are offered on the following pages are:-

1. General Information
   a. Why conduct a survey?
   b. Specific information you are seeking.
2. Developing a survey instrument.
3. Organization for conducting the survey.
4. Compiling information
5. Setting priorities.
6. Selecting realistic first endeavors.
7. Implementing programs and activities.

The entire section on conducting a needs assessment should be read and discussed prior to beginning the planning.

Conducting a Needs Assessment
General considerations

1. Needs Assessment to determine:
   a. Demographic data
      Much of this may be obtained through the Center for Community Education.
   b. Social problems, juvenile and adult
   c. Family problems, needs, wants
   d. Educational and Vocational needs and wants
   e. Community-wide and individual problems
   f. Cultural problems
   g. Economic problems
   h. Facility requirements
   i. Senior citizens
   j. Volunteerism
   k. Interest areas

    l. Health needs

    m. Recreation and leisure

    n. Ideas and suggestions

    o. Other

2. Evaluation and feedback
   a. To allow community to evaluate selected topics
   b. To identify effective and ineffective communication techniques
   c. For purposes of program evaluation
3. Clients and staff
   a. Identification of staff
   b. Identification of leaders
   c. Identification of those with specific needs
   d. Pinpoint resource people, volunteers
4. Public relations
   a. To identify ways of disseminating information to community
   b. To expand PR opportunities
   c. To advertise existing services
   d. To let community know we are concerned
   e. To stimulate interest in the Community Education concept
   f. To provide a means for community involvement (surveyors, respondents)
   g. To bring into the fold alienated adults who find nothing good in the community but who eventually can be turned on to work for the community
5. Awareness
   a. To determine community's awareness of the program
   b. To determine what community knows and what it would like to know about the schools, agencies, or the community.
6. Attitudes
   a. About school
   b. About community
   c. About accountability
   d. About feelings toward schools and the community
7. Clients - Identification of persons who would like to participate in various classes.
8. Identify resources - To develop a list of resource people, teachers and volunteers.
9. Drop-out problems - Why do individuals drop out of school?
10. Identification of ways to involve the total community in community affairs.
11. Other

Developing a Survey Instrument

Each community will have specific questions they will want to ask. Generally, these fall into three categories.

    1. **Needs:** Those things an individual deems as essential to

his/her well being or the well being of other individuals. Some examples may be: employment, legal counseling, health care, well baby clinic, juvenile problems, senior citizens involvement, vandalism, drug abuse, parent effectiveness, volunteer programs, political clout, etc.

2. **Wants:** Those things an individual deems as enriching to him/her self or other individuals. Some examples may be recreational activities, family oriented experiences, enrichment class, teen clubs, food co-ops, summer (intersession) programs, etc.

3. **Problems:** Those things that are immediately apparent to the community that hinder the growth of the community and the individuals within it. The prominent "ills" of the community.

Using the brainstorming method, determine the categories of questions you want answered. In writing the survey items, consider your audience. Don't turn people off with long complicated items.

Should the survey be in Spanish (or other language) as well as English? Should it be the paper and pencil type or one which an interviewer is used? We suggest the **interview** method.

Questions/items should be designed so that they answer the question you intend. For example, asking a person to check classes they would be **interested** in is not as effective as asking what activities they would **attend**.

Be aware of the possibility that the interviewees response could be an appraisal of others needs. Ascertain as clearly as possible the wants and needs of that individual while avoiding any threat to that person.

Consider how the gathered information will be compiled. Open-ended questions may be necessary in some cases, but they require many hours and many people to compile. Questions that require a yes/no or a check mark are much easier to compile and a necessity if you plan to use data processing. On the other hand, a simple check may not be enough to determine what is needed.

Is a random sample appropriate? In a word, No. Statistically a random sample is sound, but Community Education is **people**. By starting the process from the beginning, as people oriented, you will be on the right track. Striving for a 100% sample tells people you are interested in what **they** have to say. Don't take the easy way out by using a random sample. The block organization plan is discussed later to assist in a total needs assessment.

During this stage, unless the council has a person experienced in survey procedures, it is wise to request outside help. The Center for Community Education will be happy to assist you.

SUMMARY CHECKLIST FOR CONDUCTING A NEEDS ASSESSMENT

Have you considered these items?
1. **HYPOTHESIZING** - WHAT DO YOU WANT TO STUDY
2. **DESIGNING** - PROCEDURES AND METHODS
3. **PLANNING** - MATERIALS AND PERSONNEL REQUIRED
4. **FINANCING** - SUPPORT FOR THE STUDY
5. **SAMPLING** - WHO AND HOW MANY
6. **DRAFTING** - FRAMING QUESTIONS
7. **CONSTRUCTING** - FIRST DRAFT OF QUESTIONNAIRE
8. **PRE-TESTING** - VALIDITY OF QUESTIONS
9. **TRAINING** - TEACHING INTERVIEWERS
10. **BRIEFING** - INSTRUCTING INTERVIEWERS
11. **INTERVIEWING** - SECURING DATA
12. **CONTROLLING** - SEEING THAT INTERVIEWS ARE COMPLETED
13. **VERIFYING** - CHECKING DATA ACCURACY
14. **CODING** - PREPARING DATA FOR ANAYLSIS
15. **PROCESSING** - ORGANIZING DATA FOR ANALYSIS
16. **ANALYZING** - INTERPRETING THE DATA
17. **REPORTING** - SHARING THE INFORMATION

Organization for Conducting the Survey

The Community Education concept is **people**; therefore, the best survey is the one that attempts to reach every person in the community. By doing this, we tell every person in the community that we are interested in what YOU have to say.

There are two basic types of surveys discussed here:
1. **Paper and Pencil**: This type is one which the person receiving the survey sits down and fills out the information requested. If this type is used, it should be distributed by an organized group (such as, the **block** organization plan) and picked up by the same person at a designated time. Obviously, sending surveys home with school children defeats the purpose. First, it doesn't reach the **total** community, and, second, experience has shown that a high percentage of the surveys never get home.
2. **Interview survey**: Although more time consuming, this method is more personal and therefore more valuable as a Community Education tool. This type of survey should use the **block** organization plan also. (discussed on page 35.)

The following pages give suggestions for using the interview technique.

INTERVIEW SURVEY PROCEDURES

This survey is being taken to help determine the problems, needs, and wants of the people of the community. We hope these needs and desires may be partially met through Community Education. Each interviewer should have: letters of introduction
copies of questionnaire
list of names and addresses of persons to be interviewed
questionnaire envelopes

Interview Steps
1. Determine names and addresses of persons to be interviewed.
2. Receive interview materials and be briefed on interviewing procedures.
3. Contact people on the list.

Procedure for Interviewing
1. Introduction: "Good day (or evening). I'm ——————— representing the Community Education Committee. We are in the process of finding out the needs and desires of the people of this community. This letter will explain our study." (At this time, present the letter of introduction.)
2. At this time, if you have not previously arranged the time of the interview, ask if it would be convenient to complete the interview now or at a time in the near future. If it is not convenient then, set a definite time within the next two days.
3. If you are refused entry or the person is very negative, thank him and go on to the next person on your list.

Before completing the Questionnaire
1. Restate that your purpose is only to find out information and opinions. You are not selling anything or representing any company.
2. State that the questionnaire is completely confidential. It has no name or identifying marks. You may wish to have separate sheet for names and addresses of those who wish to volunteer or be contacted for a specific purpose.
3. Allow the person a choice of a) filling out the questionnaire himself or b) having you ask the questions and record the answers. Either a) or b) is acceptable, but a) is preferred.
4. State that the answers to the questionnaire will be used only to determine how Community Education may serve the people of ———————.
5. Answer any questions the interviewee may have. Be as forthright as possible. Do not be afraid to state you do not know if a question is asked to which you do not have the

answer. Invite them to call the Community School Director or Principal to find the answer to questions you can not answer. Their phone numbers should be on the letter of introduction.

6. If the person does not wish to respond to the questionnaire, thank him and leave courteously.
7. If the interviewee is agreeable, complete the questionnaire.
8. After completing the questionnaire, have the interviewee place the questionnaire in the envelope and seal it.
9. Thank the interviewee and go on to the next name on the list.

Some Interview Tips

1. Be courteous at all times. If the interviewee becomes negative, argumentative or abusive, simply leave as quietly as possible. Attempt to show the person the importance and non-obligation of the questionnaire, but do not argue or "talk back" to the interviewee.
2. Do not leave the questionnaire to be mailed or picked up later. State that the questions will take only a few minutes to answer and you would prefer either to wait or to return at a later time to have the interviewee respond to the questionnaire.
3. Tell the interviewee that he/she and all of his/her neighbors are being asked the same questions. By compiling all of the responses, a "picture" of the needs, wants and problems of the community will be obtained.
4. Interview as many people within the household as possible.
5. Make the respondent feel his answers to the questionnaire are important to the study. Some of the questions may seem unimportant, but they have been carefully selected to help determine the needs and desires of the community.
6. If a respondent objects to anwering or is unable to answer any specific question, simply allow **him** to skip that item and complete the rest of the questionnaire.
7. Try to conduct the interview in a quiet place. Suggest a room where the TV is not on, etc.

Block Organization Plan

The **Block Organization Plan** is one used by many communities as a very successful delivery system for surveys as well as future programming and dissemination. The method is simple in organizing but often difficult in acquiring needed support. To organize a Block system, you

1. Outline the geographic area of your Community School.
2. Within **each** block of the community, acquire a volunteer who lives within the block to be "block leader." This does take time but will be well worth the effort. Their assistance will be extremely valuable for the survey effort

and in future endeavors. If there are blocks for which you cannot find a volunteer, either find one from another block or go ahead with the survey in other blocks and find additional volunteers as you go along. As a last resort, you can always cover "non-leader" blocks yourself.

3. Block leaders should be trained as to the purpose and procedure of the survey.

4. They should become the nucleus of your dissemination system.

For further information on how block leaders can be used, contact the Center for Community Education.

Compiling Information

Once the surveys are returned to the Community School Director (with a predetermined deadline), they are ready to be compiled.

A "Compilation Committee" should have been organized and ready to go to work at this point in time.

If the survey was designed with open-ended questions, the committee should design a method of compiling all responses to each question.

The committee should have ample space to work without interruptions.

If surveys were designed for data processing, the surveys may need to be coded and arrangements should have been made for:

1. Key punching
2. Computer time
3. Out-put date

Assistance in making these arrangements can be obtained through the Center for Community Education.

SAMPLE I - FEASIBILITY ASSESSMENT
COMMUNITY EDUCATION PROGRAM QUESTIONNAIRE

The following series of questions are designed to poll your opinions and attitudes concerning whether or not ——————— School should adopt community education concept.

The community school's concept embraces the idea that a school should be available to the public in general for the purpose of providing leisure time, recreational, cultural activities, community services, and supplemental educational programs.

Would you please answer the questions below so that we will be able to determine if ——————— School should incorporate the community education concept.

Statistical Information:
1. Sex:——— Male or ———Female

2. Age:――― 26-35, ――36-45, ――56 and over
3. Years living in the community: ――0-1, ――2-3, ――4-5,
   ――6-10, ――11 or more

Read each of the questions below carefully and answer them by
checking whether you agree, disagree or are undecided about the
answer.

A - Agree   D - Disagree   U - Undecided

A   D   U
                1. The schools in my community are being
                   adequately used for the tax dollars being
                   spent on them.
A   D   U
                2. Schools in general should be used as centers
                   for leisure time, recreational, and cultural
                   activities.
A   D   U
                3. Schools in general should be used as centers
                   for community services such as: child coun-
                   seling; probation and juvenile services; family
                   counseling; community health; etc.
A   D   U
                4. Schools in general should provide evening sup-
                   plemental education programs to help people
                   complete their education or to give them
                   additional educational opportunities.
A   D   U
                5. The community education program should be
                   free of charge to the participants.
A   D   U
                6. ――――――― School should provide a com-
                   munity education program.

*** If you **disagree** with question #6, there is no need for you to
continue the questionnaire.

Read each of the questions below carefully and answer them by
checking the statement or statements under each question which
you **agree** with.

7. The community education program should include:
   ――a. Leisure time and recreational activities
   ――b. Community services (child counseling, health services,
        etc.)
   ――c. Supplemental Education programs
   ――d. Other: explain ――――――――――――――――――
8. The community education programs and services should be

470

available to:

——a. Parent/Student teams. (A parent could attend only if they were accompanied by their child or vice-versa.)

——b. Only those people who live in the community surrounding —————— School.

——c. The general public.

——d. Other: explain ——————————————————

9. The hours for the community education programs and services should be:

——a. After school until 10:00 pm.

——b. During school hours, 8:00 am - 4:00 pm (Assuming it doesn't interrupt classes)

——c. Weekends

——d. Other: explain ——————————————————

10. The Community Education program should be financed by:

——a. The district's general fund budget.

——b. A special tax override.

——c. Tuition and/or class fees.

——d. Private gifts or contributions from individuals or service groups such as the PTA

——e. Other: explain ——————————————————

11. The community education program should be developed by:

——a. The regular school administration and staff.

——b. A parent group composed of parents of —————— School students.

——c. A joint group composed of parents, school staff, and students.

——d. An independent group of community representatives.

——e. Other: explain ——————————————————

12. The community education program should be operated by:

——a. The regular school administration and staff.

——b. A parent group composed of parents of —————— School students.

——c. A joint group composed of parents, school staff, and students.

——d. An independent group of community representatives.

——e. Other: explain ——————————————————

13. If a community education program were established, I would be willing to attend its programs.

——a. At least once or twice a week.

——b. At least one or twice a month.

——c. Daily.

——d. Other: explain ——————————————————

14. If a community education program were established, I would use the community services, (i.e., child counseling, day care, community health, etc.)

471

————a. Frequently
————b. Occasionally
————c. Never
————d. Other: explain ————————————————
15. If a community education program were established, please check which activities you would like to participate in:
————Swimming
————Metal Shop
————Needle Work
————Wood Shop
————Languages
————Sports
————Other ————————————————————

————Parent Effectiveness
————Physical Fitness
————Plants and Gardens
————Consumer Law
————Real Estate
————Art
————Upholstering
————Business Skill
————Folk Dancing
————Self Defense
————Crafts
————Sewing

16. If a community education program were established at ————
School which of the following community services might you use:

————Child Counseling   ————Consumer Help
————Probation Officer   ————Day Care
————Welfare   ————Rooms available for meetings by
————Family Counseling   private non-profit organizations
————Community Health   or clubs
————Other: explain ————————————————

17. If ———————— School incorporates the community school concept, would you be willing to share any of your skills or talents by creating and teaching a class or giving a demonstration, etc.?
a. ————Yes   b. ————No   c. ————Undecided
18. If you answered yes to question 18, list on the back of this page any skill or talent you would be willing to share.
Reprinted by Permission - Leo Tuck, Emerald Junior High

SAMPLE II - NEEDS ASSESSMENT
FLORENCE COMMUNITY SCHOOL SURVEY

What is a community school?

It is a school available to everybody, not just to school age children during class hours. That is the idea behind "Community Education." Whenever space is available, why not use the facilities at Florence for games, crafts, adult classes, recreation or service to the community? If the need is for activities at other locations in our area, the community school program will arrange off site activities in the Hillcrest area.

Florence Elementary School has been chosen by the San Diego Unified School District to be one of San Diego's six "community schools." A director and clerical help will be provided by the school district. However, volunteers with both general and specific skills are vital to its success. Do you have time or talent to volunteer? Do you know of a neighbor who has a skill or talent in a specific area? If so, as we ask questions in specific areas, please indicate if you or an acquaintance might help.

This questionnaire is designed to find out what you, as a Hillcrest citizen, would like to see included in the program.

NAME —————————————————————————

ADDRESS ——————————————— PHONE —————

1. There are ——— people in our household.
2. They are between ——— years of age. List number in each category and star your own age group.
    Under 12 ———
    12-15 ———
    16-21———
    22-25 ———
    26-35 ———
    36-45 ———
    46-55 ———
    56 and over ———

PLEASE CIRCLE THE APPROPRIATE ANSWERS

3. Will you need child care services to attend activities? YES NO
    If yes, what time of day or evening? —————————————
4. Will you need transportation to attend activities? YES NO
5. Would you be willing to form a car pool to attend activities? YES NO
6. What area of Hillcrest would be best for you to attend classes,

activities, etc.? ————————————————————

7. What day(s) would be best for you to attend activities?
   Sunday Monday Tuesday Wednesday Thursday Friday Saturday

8. What time of day would be best for you to attend activities?
   9-12 pm   12-2 pm   2-4 pm   4-6 pm   6-8 pm   8-9 pm
   OTHER ————————————

9. Some recreational activities are listed below. Indicate in
   Column 1 if you are interested in any of the activities listed
   and in column 2 if you or anyone you know has special skills
   or talents in this field.

	Yes, Interested	Resource Person Who Might Help
Backpacking		
Basketball		
Exercise		
Football		
Gymnastics		
Handball		
Self-Defense		
Soccer		
Softball		
Swimming		
Tennis		
Track		
Racquetball		
Yoga		
Other 1.		
2.		
3.		
4.		

10. Would you be interested in these classes for   ADULTS   TEENS   CHILDREN ?
    (circle your choice)

11. Do you know of existing classes or activities in these areas already being
    offered in or near Hillcrest? _____ If so, please list below.
    1. _____
    2. _____
    3. _____
    4. _____

12. Some educational activities are listed below. Indicate in column 1 if you
    are interested in any of the listed activities and in column 2 if you or any-
    one you know has special skills or talents in this field.

	Yes, Interested	Resource person who might help
Government		
Local		
National		
State		
Other 1.		
2.		
History		
American		
Californian		
San Diegan		
Other 1.		
2.		

	Yes, interested	Resource Person who might help

Science
    Earth Science _____ | _____
    Life Science _____ | _____
    Other 1._____ | _____
          2._____ | _____

Mathematics
    Algebra _____ | _____
    General _____ | _____
    Geometry _____ | _____
    Other 1._____ | _____
          2._____ | _____

Foreign Language
    Conversational French _____ | _____
    Conversational Italian _____ | _____
    Conversational German _____ | _____
    Conversational Spanish _____ | _____
    Other 1._____ | _____
          2._____ | _____

Business Practices
    Bookkeeping _____ | _____
    Shorthand _____ | _____
    Typing _____ | _____
    Other 1._____ | _____
          2._____ | _____

Consumer Survival
    Insurance _____ | _____
    Purchasing _____ | _____
    Saving _____ | _____
    Other 1._____ | _____
          2._____ | _____

GED (high school equivalency)
    English _____ | _____
    Math _____ | _____
    Reading _____ | _____
    Science _____ | _____

English
    Creative Writing _____ | _____
    Journalism _____ | _____
    Other 1._____ | _____
          2._____ | _____

Child-parent-school-related subjects
    Doing volunteer tutoring at school ___ | _____
    Understanding your child's math program ___ | _____
    Understanding your child's reading program ___ | _____
    Understanding your child's science program ___ | _____
    Other 1._____ | _____
          2._____ | _____

Would you be interested in these classes or activities for ADULTS TEENS CHILDREN.
(circle your choice)

Do you know of existing classes or activities in these areas already being
offered? In or near Hillcrest? _____ If so, please list below.

_____
_____
_____

Some art/craft and general skills subjects are listed below. Indicate in
Column 1 if you are interested in classes or activities in this area, and in
Column 2 if you or any one you know has special skills or talents in this
field.

	Yes, interested	Resource person who might help
Arts and Crafts		
Art appreciation		
Candlemaking		
Ceramics		
Decoupage		
Drawing		
Flower arranging		
Graphic Arts		
Jewelry making		
Lapidary		
Macrame		
Needlepoint		
Painting		
Photogaaphy		
Rug making		
Sculpture		
Stained glass		
Stitchery		
Weaving		
Other 1.		
2.		
General Skills		
Auto Mechanics		
Bike repair		
Cooking		
Crochet		
Dressmaking		
First aid		
Gardening		
General Household repairs		
Interior Decoration		
Knitting		
Metal Shop		
Pet care		
Radio (ham, C.B.)		
Sewing		
Upholstery		
Woodworking		
Other 1.		
2.		

16. Would you be interested in these classes or activities for ADULTS   TEENS
    CHILDREN   (circle your choice)

17. Do you know of existing classes and activities in these areas already being
    offered in or near Hillcrest? _____ If so, please list below.
    _____
    _____
    _____

18. Some music and dance subjects are listed below. Indicate in Column 1 if you
    are interested in classes or activities in this area and in Column 2 if you,
    or someone you know, has special skills or talents in this field.

	Yes, interested	Resource person who might help
Music		
Group instrumental		
What instrument		
What kind of instrument		
Classical		
Folk		
Jazz		
Pop		
Rock		
Group Singing		
History of music		
Instrumental music		
Music appreciation		
Voice		
What kind of voice?		
Classical		
Folk		
Jazz		
Pop		
Rock		
Other 1.		
2.		
Dance		
Ballet		
Ballroom Dancing		
Belly Dancing		
Creative Dance		
Folk Dance		
Modern Dance		
Rock		
Sufi		
Tai chi		
Other 1.		
2.		

19. Would you be interested in these classes or activities for ADULTS TEENS
    CHILDREN (circle your choice)

477

20. Do you know of existing classes and activities in these areas already being offered in or near Hillcrest? _____ If so, please list below.

_____
_____
_____

21. Some theater arts subjects are suggested below. Indicate in Column 1 if you are interested in classes or activities in this area and in Column 2 if you, or someone that you know, has special skills or talents in this field.

	Yes interested	Resource Person who might help
Acting		
Backstage		
Clowning		
Pantomime		
Plays		
Skits of readings		
Speech		
Other 1.		
2.		

22. Would you be interested in these classes or activities for ADULTS   TEENS   CHILDREN   (circle your choice)

23. Do you know of existing classes or activities in these areas already being offered in or near Hillcrest? _____ If so, please list below.

_____
_____
_____

24. Some possible health subjects are listed below. Indicate in Column 1 if you are interested in 1 or 2 hour classes in this area and in Colmmn 2 if you or someone you know has special skills or talents in this field.

	Yes, interested	Resource Person who might help
How to select and use:		
Clinics		
Doctors		
Health care societies		
(American Cancer Society, Visiting)		
Nurse Association, Arthritis Foundation, etc.		
Hospitals		
Mental Health Facilities		
Everything you always wanted to know		
about a health care facility but were		
afraid to ask		
Family Planning		
Health care for children		
Health care for men		
Health care for women		
Heart Disease		
Medicare		
Nutrition		

478

The cost of medical care - What is involved _____
Other 1._____ | _____
       2._____ | _____

25. List all human relations activities such as parent effectiveness training, dealing with stress, transcendental meditation, etc. that you would be interested in.
    1._____
    2._____
    3._____
    4._____

26. Do you know of existing classes and activities in these areas already being offered in or near Hillcrest? _____ If so, please list below.
    _____
    _____
    _____

27. List all health care services you are aware of in the Hillcrest area.
    1._____
    2._____
    3._____
    4._____

28. Some community service subjects are listed below. Indicate in Column 1 if you are interested in classes or activities in this area and in Column 2 if you, or anyone you know has special skills or talents in this field.

	Yes, interested	Resource Person who might help
How to get around San Diego		
Facilities (parks, pools, museums, etc. available in San Diego)		
How San Diego (city) government works		
Study of city departments and their functions		
Study of city, state and federal services		
Free community services		
Other 1.		
2.		

29. List all the community services you can think of in the Hillcrest area.
    1._____
    2._____
    3._____
    4._____

30. Do you know of existing classes or activities in these areas already being offered in the Hillcrest area? _____ If so, please list below.
    _____
    _____
    _____

479

31. Identify those persons in your community who you feel represent positions of leadership.
   1._____
   2._____
   3._____
   4._____

32. List the planning groups and neighborhood associations who meet in your area.

	Are you a member?	Would you like to be a member?
1.		
2.		
3.		
4.		

33. Do you have any other special community concerns?
   _____
   _____
   _____
   _____

Reprinted by Permission
Florence Community School Advisory Council
Danny Walker, Community Services Specialist

APPENDIX I

SAMPLE III - NEEDS ASSESSMENT, YOUTH SURVEY

FLORENCE COMMUNITY SCHOOL

Teacher_____ Room_____ School_____

Name_____ Age___ Boy___ Girl_____

Address_____ Phone_____ Grade_____

Names and ages of brothers and sisters living at home.
1._____Age_____ In school? yes or no _____
2._____ _____ _____
3._____ _____ _____
4._____ _____ _____
5._____ _____ _____

Would you attend after school activities if we have them here at Florence?
_____Yes _____No

If you attend after school activities, what time would be best for you?
2:30_____ 3:30_____ 4:30_____ 5:30_____ 6:30_____ 7:30_____

Would you like activities at Florence on Saturday? _____Yes _____No
If answer is yes, would you prefer morning_____ or afternoon_____?

480

MASTER BIBLIOGRAPHY

GENERAL REFERENCE

Anderson, Darrell. ADULT EDUCATION AND THE DISADVAN-TAGED ADULT. Bethesda, Maryland: ERIC Clearinghouse on Adult Education, 1969.

Bergevin, Paul E. PARTICIPATION IN TRAINING FOR ADULT EDUCATION. St. Louis: Beechway Press, 1965.

Brunner, Edmund de Schweinitz. AN OVERVIEW OF ADULT EDUCATION RESEARCH. Chicago: Adult Education Association of USA, 1959. LC5219.B73

Clark, Burton R. ADULT EDUCATION: A STUDY OF INSTITU-TIONAL INSECURITY. Berkeley: University of California Press, 1956. HM1C25xVI:2

Clark, Burton R. THE MARGINALITY OF ADULT EDUCATION. Berkeley: Center for the Study of Liberal Education for Adults, 1953. LC6251C4 No. 20

Corbett, Edward A. WE HAVE WITH US TONIGHT. Toronto: Ryerson Press, 1957.

Fund for Adult Education. ABLE PEOPLE WELL PREPARED. White Plains, NY: Fund for Adult Education, 1961. LC5219.F78

Grattan, Clinton H. AMERICAN IDEAS ABOUT ADULT EDUCATION, 1710-1951. New York: Bureau of Publication, Teachers College, Columbia University, 1962. LC5251.G68

Green, Ernest. ADULT EDUCATION: WHY THE APATHY? London: Allen and Unwin, 1953. LC5216.G74

Houle, Cyril O. CONTINUING YOUR EDUCATION. New York: McGraw Hill, 1964. LC5215.H68

Jensen, Glenn and et al. ADULT EDUCATION: OUTLINE OF AN EMERGING FIELD OF UNIVERSITY STUDY. Washington: AEA of USA, 1964.

Kreitlow, Burton W. RELATING ADULT EDUCATION TO OTHER DISCIPLINES. Madison: University of Wisconsin, 1964. LC5251.K7

Linderman, Edward C. THE MEANING OF ADULT EDUCATION. Montreal: Harvest House, 1961.

Liveright, Alexander A. A STUDY OF ADULT EDUCATION - THE UNITED STATES. Brookline, Mass: Center for the Study of Liberal Education, 1968.

McGhee, Paul A. A SCHOOL FOR OPTIMISTS. Chicago: Center for the Study of Liberal Education for Adults, 1953. LC6251C4 No. 6

New York Adult Education Council. ADULT EDUCATION FOR EVERYBODY. New York: Adult Education Council, 1954.

Powell, John W. ADULT EDUCATION: ISSUES IN DISPUTE. Chicago: AEA/USA, Social Philosophy Co., 1960. LC5215P68

Sheats, Paul and et al. ADULT EDUCATION. New York: Dryden Press, 1953.

Smith, Robert M., Aker, George F., and Kidd, J.R., eds. HANDBOOK OF ADULT EDUCATION. New York: The MacMillan Co., 1970.

Ulrich, Mary E. PATTERNS OF ADULT EDUCATION. New York: McGraw Hill, 1965.

Verner, Coolie. ADULT EDUCATION. Washington: Center for Applied Research in Education, 1964. LC5215V4

PHILOSOPHY AND HISTORICAL BACKGROUND (Most references prior to 1950 are included)

Adams, James Truslow. FRONTIERS OF AMERICAN CULTURE. New York: Charles Scribner and Sons, 1944. LC5251.A63

American Association for Adult Education. HANDBOOK OF ADULT EDUCATION 1934. New York: American Association for Adult Education, 1934. LC5251.H3

Axford, Roger. ADULT EDUCATION: THE OPEN DOOR. Scranton, PA: International Book Co., 1969. LC5215.A9

Beak, Ralph Albert. THE LITERATURE OF ADULT EDUCATION. New York: American Association of Adult Education, 1941.

Bergerin, Paul E. A PHILOSOPHY OF ADULT EDUCATION. New York: Seabury Press, 1967.

Blakely, Robert J. ADULT EDUCATION IN A FREE SOCIETY. Toronto: Guardian Bird Publications, 1958.

Blakely, Robert J. TOWARD A HOMEODYNAMIC SOCIETY. Brookline, Mass.: Center for the Study of Liberal Education for Adults, 1965. LC6251.C4 No. 49

Brameld, Theodore Burghard Hurt. PHILOSOPHIES OF EDUCATION IN CULTURAL PERSPECTIVE. New York: Holt, Rinehart, and Winston, Inc., 1966. LB875.B723

Brems, Robert W. SOCIOLOGICAL BACKGROUND OF ADULT EDUCATION. Chicago: Center for the Study of Liberal Education, 1964.

Bryson, Lyman, ADULT EDUCATION. New York: Cincinnati American Book Co., 1936. LC5215.B7

Bryson, Lyman. THE DRIVE TOWARD REASON, IN THE SERVICE OF A FREE PEOPLE. New York: Harper, 1954. E169.1 B895

Cartwright, Morse Adams. TEN YEARS OF ADULT EDUCATION. New York: The MacMillan Co., 1935. LC5251.C3

Coady, Mose M. MASTERS OF THEIR OWN DESTINY. New

York: Harper & Brothers, 1939. HD345ON6C57

Columbia University. SUGGESTED STUDIES FOR ADULT EDU-CATION. New York: Teachers College Institute of Adult Education, 1942.

Cotton, A.C. A HISTORICAL EXAMINATION OF THE SUPPORTING LITERATURE OF ADULT EDUCATION. Chicago: University of Chicago Press, 1968.

Debaten, Frank M. ADMINISTRATION OF ADULT EDUCATION. New York: American Book Co., 1938. LC5215.D4

Dewey, John. EXPERIENCE AND EDUCATION. New York: The MacMillan Co., 1938. LB875.D3943

Ely, Mary L. ADULT EDUCATION IN ACTION. New York: American Association for Adult Education, 1936. LC5215E5

Ely, Mary L. HANDBOOK OF ADULT EDUCATION IN THE UNITED STATES. New York: Teachers College, Columbia University, 1948.

Flesch, Rudolf F. MARKS OF A READABLE STYLE: A STUDY IN ADULT EDUCATION. New York: Teachers College, Columbia University, 1943. LB5C8, No. 897

Grattan, Clinton H. IN QUESTION OF KNOWLEDGE: A HISTORIAL PERSPECTIVE ON ADULT EDUCATION. New York: Association Press, 1955. LA21G7

Harrison, John F. LEARNING AND LIVING 1790-1960. Toronto: University of Toronto Press, 1961. LC5256G7H3

Hawkins, Gayrell. EDUCATION FOR SOCIAL UNDERSTANDING. New York: American Association for Adult Education, 1940 HV40H35

Houle, Cyril O. THE DESIGN OF EDUCATION. San Francisco: Jossey-Bass, 1972. LC5215.H69

Hutchinson, Dorothy Carleton (Hewitt). ADULT EDUCATION: A DYNAMIC FOR DEMOCRACY. New York: Appleton Century Co., 1937.

Ingham, Roy John. INSTITUTIONAL BACKGROUNDS OF ADULT EDUCATION: DYNAMICS OF CHANGE IN THE MODERN UNIVERSITY. Brookline, Mass.: Center for the Study of Liberal Education for Adults, 1966. LC6251.C4 No. 50

Jessup, Frank. ADULT EDUCATION TOWARDS SOCIAL AND POLITICAL RESPONSIBILITY. Hamburg, Germany: UNESCO, 1953.

Kallen, Horace M. PHILOSOPHICAL ISSUES FOR ADULT EDUCATION. Springfield, Illinois: Thomas, 1962. LC5215.K25

Kaplan, Abraham Abbott. SOCIO-ECONOMIC CIRCUMSTANCES AND ADULT PARTICIPATION IN CERTAIN CULTURAL AND ADULT EDUCATIONAL ACTIVITIES. New York: Teachers College, Columbia University, 1943. LB5C8, No. 889

Keppel, Frederick Paul. EDUCATION FOR ADULTS AND OTHER

ESSAYS. New York: Columbia University, 1926. LC5215K4

Knowles, Malcolm. THE ADULT EDUCATION MOVEMENT IN THE U.S. New York: Holt, Rinehart, and Winston, 1962. LC-5251K55

Kotinsky, Ruth. ADULT EDUCATION COUNCILS. New York: American Association for Adult Education, 1940.

London, Jack. ADULT EDUCATION AND SOCIAL CLASS. Berkeley: University of Calif., 1963. LC5219L65

Mann, George C. DEVELOPMENT OF ADULT EDUCATION IN CALIFORNIA. Sacramento, Calif.: State Department of Education, 1957. LI24B62 v.26:13

Morris, Van Cleve. PHILOSOPHY AND THE AMERICAN SCHOOL. Boston: Houghton Mifflin Co., 2d ed. 1976. LB885M47

Nelson, Thomas H. ADULT EDUCATION FOR SOCIAL NEEDS. New York: American Press, 1933.

New York State University. ADMINISTRATION AND ORGANIZATION OF EMMIGRANT EDUCATION FOR NEW YORK. Albany: The University of the State of New York Press, 1922.

Overstreet, Harry A. LEADERS FOR ADULT EDUCATION. New York: American Association for Adult Education, 1941. LC5251.08

Reeves, Floyd W. ADULT EDUCATION. New York: McGraw-Hill, 1938.

Rowden, Dorothy. HANDBOOK OF ADULT EDUCATION IN THE UNITED STATES. New York: American Association for Adult Education, 1936.

Stacy, William H. INTEGRATION OF ADULT EDUCATION, A SOCIOLOGICAL STUDY. New York: Teachers College, Columbia University, 1935. LB5C8 No. 646

Studebaker, John W. ADULT EDUCATION: A BULWARK OF A FREE SOCIETY. Chicago: American School, 1952.

Studebaker, John W. SOCIAL CHANGE AND EDUCATION. Washington, D.C.: The Dept. of Superintendence of NEA/USA, 1935. L13.A363

Thorndike, Edward L. ADULT EDUCATIONAL INTERESTS. New York: The MacMillan Co., 1935. LC5219.T55

Titus, Harold. LEARNING FOR ADULTS: ADULT EDUCATION IN MICHIGAN. Ann Arbor: State Board of Control, 1945.

Titus, Harold. TRAINING FOR ADULTS: ADULT EDUCATION IN MICHIGAN. Ann Arbor: State Board of Control, 1945.

Verner, Coolie. POLE'S HISTORY OF ADULT SCHOOLS. Washington: AEA/USA, 1967. LC5256.G7P55

ADULT PSYCHOLOGY AND LEARNING

Aker, George. AN EPITOME ON RESEARCH AND READINGS IN ADULT LEARNING. Tallahassee: Florida State University,

1969.

Atkinson, John W. and Feather, Norman T., eds. A THEORY OF ACHIEVEMENT MOTIVATION. New York: R.E. Krieger Publishing Co., 1974. (Reprint of the ed. published by Wiley, New York). BF 683.A88

Bischof, Ledford J. ADULT PSYCHOLOGY. New York: Harper & Row, 2d ed., 1976. BF724.5 B57

Center for the Study of Liberal Education for Adults. PSYCHO-LOGICAL BACKGROUNDS OF ADULT EDUCATION. Chicago: CSLEA, 1963.

Fund for Adult Education. THE CHALLENGE OF LIFETIME LEARNING. Pasedena, Calif.: Fund for Adult Education, 1953.

Houle, Cyril O. THE INQUIRING MIND. Madison: University of Wisconsin Press, 1961. LC5219.H6

Kazemias, Andreas. TRADITIONS AND CHANGE IN EDUCATION, A COMPARATIVE STUDY. Prentice Hall, 1965.

Kidd, James R. HOW ADULTS LEARN. New York: Association Press, 1973. LC5219.K5

Knowles, Malcolm J. THE ADULT LEARNER: A NEGLECTED SPECIES. Houston: Gulf Publishing Co., 1973. LC5215.K59x

Knowles, Malcolm J. SELF DIRECTED LEARNING. New York: Association Press, 1975.

Kublen, Raymond G. PSYCHOLOGICAL BACKGROUNDS OF ADULT EDUCATION. Chicago: Center for the Study of Liberal Education for Adults, 1963.

Lorge, Irving and et al. ADULT LEARNING. Washington, D.C.: AEA/USA, 1965.

Maslow, Abraham H. MOTIVATION AND PERSONALITY. New York: Harper & Row, 2d ed., 1970. BF683.M37

Miller, Harry L. TEACHING AND LEARNING IN ADULT EDU-CATION. New York: The MacMillan Co., 1964. LC5219M52

National Conference on Architecture for Adult Education. CREAT-ING A CLIMATE FOR LEARNING. Washington, D.C.: AEA USA, 1959.

Powell, John Walker. LEARNING COMES OF AGE. New York: AEA/USA, 1956. LC5215.P6

Roueche, John and et al. A MODEST PROPOSAL: STUDENTS CAN LEARN. San Francisco: Jossey-Bass, Inc., 1972. LB-2331.R66

Sheets, R. Wayne. FOR ADULTS ONLY: A LIFETIME OF LEARN-ING. Salt Lake City: Deseret Book Co., 1968.

Sjogren, Douglas. THE INFLUENCE OF SPEED AND PRIOR KNOWLEDGE AND EXPERIENCE ON ADULT LEARNING. Lin-coln, Nebraska: University of Nebraska, 1965. LC5251.S56x

Snyder, Robert E. THE INTERNAL AND EXTERNAL VALIDATION OF CONCEPT INVOLVEMENT. 1969

Solomon, Daniel. TEACHING STYLES AND LEARNING. Chicago: Center for the Study of Liberal Education for Adults, 1963. LC5219.S6

Solomon, Daniel, ed. THE CONTINUING LEARNER. Chicago: Center for the Study of Liberal Education for Adults, 1964. LC5219.S58

Stern, Bernard H. HOW MUCH DOES ADULT EDUCATION COUNT? Chicago: Center for the Study of Liberal Education for Adults, 1955. LB2360.S8

Symour, Percival M. FROM ADOLESCENT TO ADULT. New York: Columbia University Press, 1961.

Tough, Alan. THE ADULTS LEARNING PROJECTS. Toronto: The Ontario Institute for Studies in Education, 1971. LC5219.T58

Verner, Coolie and Davison, Catherine. PSYCHOLOGICAL FACTORS IN ADULT LEARNING AND EDUCATION. Tallahassee: Florida State University, 1971. LC5215.V47x

Verner, Coolie and Davison, Catherine. PSYCHOLOGICAL FACTORS IN ADULT LEARNING AND INSTRUCTION. Tallahassee: Florida State University, 1971.

Whipple, James E. and et al. ESPECIALLY FOR ADULTS. Chicago: Center for the Study of Liberal Education for Adults, 1957. LC6251C4 No. 19

Wientge, King M. FACTORS ASSOCIATED WITH THE ACHIEVEMENTS OF ADULT STUDENTS. St. Louis: Washington University Press, 1964. LC5251.W48

ADULT COUNSELING

American Association of University Women. COUNSELING TECHNIQUES FOR MATURE WOMEN. Washington: AAUW, 1966. HD6056A48x

Bennett, Margaret, ed. GUIDANCE AND COUNSELING IN GROUPS. New York: McGraw Hill, 2d ed., 1963. BF637C6B35

Curran, Charles. COUNSELING - LEARNING: A WHOLE PERSON MODEL FOR EDUCATION. New York: Grune and Stratton, 1972. LB1027.C93

DeGabriele, Eugene M. GUIDANCE SERVICES FOR ADULTS. Sacramento: California State Department of Education Bulletin, 1961. L124E62v30:7

Dickinson, William J. COUNSELING IN AN ORGANIZATION. Boston, Harvard University, 1966.

Dolan, Eleanor, ed. COUNSELING TECHNIQUES FOR MATURE WOMEN. Washington: American Association of University Women, 1966. HD6056A48x

Fisher, Joseph A. EDUCATIONAL COUNSELING FOR ADULTS. Drake University, 1969.

Fourre, Pierre. ADULT EDUCATION TECHNIQUES IN DEVELOP-
ING COUNSELORS: A GREEK CASE STUDY. Paris: Organization for Economic Cooperation and Development, 1965. LC-
5341F6

Heston, Joseph and Frick, Willard B., ed. SYMPOSIUM ON
COUNSELING FOR THE LIBERAL ART CAMPUS. Yellow Springs:
The Antioch Press, 1968. LB2343S9

Klein, Paul E. COUNSELING TECHNIQUES IN ADULT EDUCATION.
New York: McGraw Hill, 1946. LC 5219.K55

Knowles, Malcolm S. INTRODUCTION TO GROUP DYNAMICS.
New York: Association Press, 1959. HM131K62

Miller, Harry L. UNDERSTANDING GROUP BEHAVIOR: A DIS-
CUSSION GUIDE. Chicago: Center for the Study of Liberal
Education for Adults, 1953. BF 199M5

Moser, Leslie and Moser, Ruth Small. COUNSELING AND GUI-
DANCE: AN EXPLORATION. Englewood Cliffs: Prentice Hall,
1963. LB1027.5M66

Muthard, John E. ed. CONFERENCE ON COUNSELING THE
OLDER DISABLED WORKER. Iowa City: Institute of Gerontology, State University of Iowa, 1961. HD6256U6C6

Tollefson, Nona. COUNSELING CASE MANAGEMENT. Boston:
Houghton Mifflin Co., 1968. LB1027.5 T63

Van Hoose, William and Pietrafesa, John J., eds. COUNSELING
AND GUIDANCE IN THE TWENTIETH CENTURY: REFLEC-
TIONS AND REFORMULATIONS. Boston: Houghton Mifflin
Co., 1970. LB1027.5V2925

ADULT BASIC EDUCATION

Barnes, Robert F. A REVIEW AND APPRAISAL OF ADULT
LITERACY MATERIALS AND PROGRAMS. Columbus: Ohio
State University Research Foundation, 1965. LC149.B27

Brooke, W. Michael, ed. ADULT BASIC EDUCATION: RESOURCE
BOOK OF READINGS. Ontario: General Publishing Co., 1972.

Cass, Angelica W. ADULT ELEMENTARY EDUCATION. New
York: Noble and Noble Co., 1956. LC5215.C3

Finocchiaro, Mary. ENGLISH AS A SECOND LANGUAGE. New
York: Regents Publishing Co., 1965. PE1128A2F5

Florida State University. RESEARCH AND PRACTICE SERIES.
Tallahassee: Research Information Processing Center, Florida
State University, 1971. (A series of 10 booklets designed for
ABE personnel).

International Bureau of Education. LITERACY AND EDUCATION
FOR ADULTS. Geneva, Switzerland: 27th International Conference on Public Education, 1964. LC5212.15x

Lanning, Frank W. BASIC EDUCATION FOR THE DISADVAN-
TAGED ADULT: THEORY AND PRACTICE. Boston, Houghton
Mifflin Co., 1966. LC151L3

Leibert, Robert E. THE DEVELOPMENT OF INFORMAL TESTS
OF READING PERFORMANCE OF ADULTS ATTENDING BASIC
EDUCATION CLASSES. 1967.

Mezerow, Jack and et al. LAST GAMBLE ON EDUCATION.
Washington, D.C.: Adult Education Association, 1975.

Michigan State Board of Education. ADULT EDUCATION AND
COMMUNITY SERVICE: BIBLIOGRAPHY OF MATERIALS IN
ADULT BASIC EDUCATION. Lansing: State Board of Edu-
cation, 1967.

Miller, James. THE LEARNING LABORATORY IN ADULT BASIC
EDUCATION. Ohio State Department of Education, 1969.

Mocker, Donald. A REPORT ON THE IDENTIFICATION, CLASS-
IFICATION, AND RANKING OF COMPETENCIES APPROPRIATE
FOR ADULT BASIC EDUCATION TEACHERS. Kansas City,
MO: Center for Resource Development and Adult Education,
University of Missouri, 1974.

Mocker, Donald, ed. WHY TEACH THE HUMANITIES TO ADULT
BASIC EDUCATION STUDENTS? Kansas City, MO: Center for
Resource Development and Adult Education, University of Mis-
souri, 1975.

New York State Bureau of Adult Education. AMERICANIZATION
AND ADULT ELEMENTARY EDUCATION BIBLIOGRAPHY.
Albany: New York State Bureau of Adult Education, 1960.
Z5814A24N7, Ref.

Northern Arizona University. THE ARIZONA ADULT BASIC
EDUCATION DATA PROCESSING SYSTEM. 1969.

O'Donnel, Michael. TEACHING READING TO THE UNTAUGHT.
New York: Multimedia Education, Inc. 1972.

Otto, Wayne and Ford, David. TEACHING ADULTS TO READ.
Boston: Houghton Mifflin, 1967. LB1050.508

Rossman, Mark H. AN EVALUATION OF ADULT BASIC EDU-
CATION PROGRAMS IN MASSACHUSETTS. Amherst: School
of Education, University of Massachusetts, 1970.

Rossman, Mark H. A MODEL TO RECRUIT ADULTS TO ADULT
BASIC EDUCATION PROGRAMS. Amherst: School of Education,
University of Massachusetts, 1971.

Seaman, Don F. and et al. BEHAVIORAL SKILLS FOR ADULT
BASIC EDUCATION: A RESOURCE DOCUMENT AND INSTITUTE
REPORT. Mississippi State University, 1969.

Sullivan Associates. PROGRAMMED READING FOR ADULTS.
New York: McGraw Hill, 1966-1967. LC5225R4S8x   Book 1,
2, 3, 5, 6, and 8.

University of Hawaii. EDUCATION FOR ADULTS IN CORRECT-

IONAL INSTITUTIONS: A BOOK OF READINGS, Volume 1 and
11. Honolulu: Education Research and Development Center, 1975.

Vonderhaas, Kathleen and et al. TESTS FOR ADULT BASIC
EDUCATION TEACHERS. Kansas City: Center for Resource
Development in Adult Education, School of Education, Uni-
versity of Missouri, 1975.

Waldon, Bobbie. RECRUITMENT AND RETENTION OF THE
ADULT LEARNER. Montgomery: Alabama State Department
of Education, 1975.

Walton, T. M. A SELECTED BIBLIOGRAPHY OF INSTRUC-
TIONAL MATERIALS FOR ADULT BASIC EDUCATION.
Phoenix: State Department of Public Instruction, 1966.

ADMINISTRATION

Argyris, Chris. INTEGRATING THE INDIVIDUAL AND THE
ORGANIZATION. New York: Wiley, 1964. HF5549A8968

Bell, Wendell. PUBLIC LEADERSHIP. San Francisco: Chandler
Publishing Co., 1961. HM141B38

Bergerin, Paul. ADULT EDUCATION PROCEDURES. Seabury
Press, Inc. 1966.

Blanchard, Kenneth and et al. MANAGEMENT OF ORGANIZA-
TIONAL BEHAVIOR. Englewood Cliff: Prentice Hall, 1972.

California Association of Adult Education Administration. PRO-
FESSIONAL STANDARDS FOR ADULT EDUCATOR ADMINIS-
TRATION. Sacramento: Bulletin of the Calif. State Dept. of
Education, 1955. L124B62V.24:16

Drucker, Peter. MANAGING FOR RESULTS: Economic Tasks and
Risk-Taking Decisions. New York: Harper & Row, 1964. HD38D7

Essert, Paul L. CREATIVE LEADERSHIP IN ADULT EDUCATION.
New York: Prentice Hall, 1951. LC5219.E8

Hartley, Harry J. EDUCATIONAL PLANNING AND PROGRAM
BUDGETING. Englewood Cliffs: Prentice Hall, 1968. LB2806N36

Herzberg, Frederick. WORK AND THE NATURE OF MAN. New
York: World Publishing Co., 1966. HF5549.5J63H43

Houle, Cyril O. THE EFFECTIVE BOARD. New York: Association Press, 1960. AS6H65

Kidd, James R. FINANCING CONTINUING EDUCATION. New
York: Scarecrow Press, 1962. LC5251.K5

Knowles, Malcolm S. INFORMAL ADULT EDUCATION: A GUIDE
FOR ADMINISTRATION, LEADERS AND TEACHERS. New York:
Association Press, 1950. LC5215.K6

Liveright, Alexander A. STRATEGIES OF LEADERSHIP IN CON-
DUCTING ADULT EDUCATION PROGRAMS. New York: Harper
& Row, 1959. LC5219.L54

McGregor, Douglas. THE HUMAN SIDE OF ENTERPRISE. New

York: McGraw Hill, 1960. HF5549.M27

Pfiffner, John McDonald and Presthus, Robert Vance. PUBLIC ADMINISTRATION, 6th ed. New York: Ronald Press Co., 1975. JK421.P65

Shaw, Nathan C., ed. ADMINISTRATION OF CONTINUING EDUCATION: A GUIDE FOR ADMINISTRATORS. Washington: NAPSAE, 1969. LC5219.A28

Tarcher, Martin. LEADERSHIP AND THE POWER OF IDEAS. New York: Harper & Row, 1966. BF637L4T3

Verner, Coolie. A CONCEPTUAL SCHEME FOR THE IDENTIFICATION AND CLASSIFICATION OF PROCESSES FOR ADULT EDUCATION. Chicago: AEA/USA, 1962.

TEACHING, PROGRAMS, METHODS, ETC.

Alford, Harold J. CONTINUING EDUCATION IN ACTION. New York: John Wiley & Sons, Inc., 1968. LC5251.A73

Chester, Mark and Fox, Robert S. ROLE PLAYING METHODS IN THE CLASSROOM. Chicago: Science Research Associates, 1966.

Crabtree, Arthur P. CIVIC EDUCATION: PROGRAM D FOR ADULTS. Washington, D.C.: NAPSAE, 1956.

Dees, Norman, ed. APPROACHES TO ADULT TEACHING. New York: Pergamon Press, 1965. LC5215.D44

Hill, Richard J. A COMPARATIVE STUDY OF LECTURE AND DISCUSSION METHODS. White Plains: The Fund for Adult Education, 1960. LC5219.H5

Houle, Cyril O. THE DESIGN OF EDUCATION. San Francisco: Jossey Bass, 1972. LC5215.H69

Houle, Cyril O. THE EXTERNAL DEGREE. San Francisco: Jossey Bass, 1973. LB2381.H68

Houle, Cyril O. PROFESSIONAL PREPARATION OF ADULT EDUCATORS: A SYMPOSIUM. Chicago: Center for the Study of Liberal Education for Adults, 1956. LC6251C4 No. 15

Klevins, Chester. MATERIALS AND METHODS IN ADULT EDUCATION. New York: Klevins Publication, 1972. Lc5215.K58

Knowles, Malcolm S. and Knowles, Hulda F. INTRODUCTION TO GROUP DYNAMICS. New York: Association Press, 1959. HM131K62

Knowles, Malcolm S. THE MODERN PRACTICE OF ADULT EDUCATION: ANDRAGOGY VS PEDAGOGY. New York: Association Press, 1970. LC5215.K62

Knowles, Malcolm S. SELF DIRECTED LEARNING. New York: Association Press, 1975.

Leonard, Henry L. ADULT TEACHERS AND THEIR STUDENTS. New York: New School of Social Research, 1962.

Lowry, Louis, ADULT EDUCATION AND GROUP WORK. New York: Whiteside Inc., 1955.

MacKenzie, Assian. CORESPONDENCE INSTRUCTION IN THE UNITED STATES. New York: McGraw Hill, 1968.

Miller, Harry L. EVALUATING LIBERAL ADULT EDUCATION. Chicago: Center for the Study of Liberal Education for Adults, 1961. LC5219.M5

Miller, Marilyn V. ON TEACHING ADULTS: AN ANTHOLOGY. Chicago: Center for the Study of Liberal Education for Adults, 1960. Lc6251.C4 No. 32

Morgan, Barton. METHODS IN ADULT EDUCATION. Danville: Interstate Printers and Publishers, 1963. LC5219.M6

Mueller, Alfred Don. PRINCIPLES AND METHODS IN ADULT EDUCATION. New York: Prentice Hall, 1937.

NAPSAE. IN-SERVICE TRAINING FOR TEACHERS OF ADULTS. Washington, D.C.: NAPSAE, 1961.

NAPSAE. IT CAN BE DONE: SUGGESTIONS FOR BUILDING AN ADULT EDUCATION PROGRAM THAT HAS IMPACT. Washington, D.C.: NAPSAE, 1964.

NAPSAE. TECHNIQUES FOR TEACHERS OF ADULTS. Washingtion, D.C.: NAPSAE, 1964. LC5219.T4

NAPSAE. WHEN YOU'RE TEACHING ADULTS. Washington, D.C.: NAPSAE, 1961.

Neal, Kenneth. TEACHING METHODS IN FURTHER EDUCATION: A GUIDE TO THE LITERATURE. Manchester: College of Commerce (Dept. of Libriarianship), 1968. Z5814A24N4, Educ.

Otto, Wayne and McMenemy, Richard A. CORRECTIVE AND REMEDIAL TEACHING, PRINCIPLES AND PRACTICES. Boston: Houghton Mifflin Co., 1966. LB1029R408

Pugni, J. L. ed. ADULT EDUCATION THROUGH HOME STUDY. New York: Arco Press, 1965. LC5219.P8

Rossman, Mark H. A SERIES OF NINE SELF-CONTAINED INSTRUCTIONAL MODULES FOR TEACHERS OF ADULTS. Amherst: Division of Continuing Education, University of Massachusetts, 1974.

Rossman, Mark H. TEACHING ADULTS: A HANDBOOK FOR INSTRUCTORS. Ontario: New Press, 1973.

Staton, Thomas F. HOW TO INSTRUCT SUCCESSFULLY: MODERN METHODS IN ADULT EDUCATION. New York: McGraw Hill, 1960. LC5219. S68

Symouk, Percra. SYMPOSIUM ON THE EDUCATIONAL IMPLICATION OF AUTOMATION. Washington, D.C.: National Education Association, 1962.

Tough, Allen M. THE ADULTS LEARNING PROJECTS. Toronto: The Ontario Institute for Studies in Education, 1971. LC5219.T58

Watson, Goodwin B. NO ROOM AT THE BOTTOM: AUTOMATION

AND THE RELUCTANT LEARNER. Washington, D.C.: National Education Association, 1963. LB1065W37

Thanks for the assistance of Dr. Mark Rossman with this bibliography.

*Used by permission of Dr. Wayne Robbins, San Diego Center for Community Education.

INDEX

By Author and Subject